S0-BWX-231

The Comprehensive School

Guidelines for the Reorganization of Secondary Education

The Comprehensive School

Guidelines for the Reorganization of Secondary Education

by

ELIZABETH HALSALL

Department of Educational Studies, University of Hull

PERGAMON PRESS

OXFORD · NEW YORK · TORONTO
SYDNEY · BRAUNSCHWEIG

Pergamon Press Ltd., Headington Hill Hall, Oxford
Pergamon Press Inc., Maxwell House, Fairview Park, Elmsford, New York 10523
Pergamon of Canada Ltd., 207 Queen's Quay West, Toronto 1
Pergamon Press (Aust.) Pty. Ltd., 19a Boundary Street, Rushcutters Bay, N.S.W. 2011, Australia
Vieweg & Sohn GmbH, Burgplatz 1, Braunschweig

First edition 1973

Library of Congress Cataloging in Publication Data

Halsall, Elizabeth.
The comprehensive school.
(The Commonwealth and international library. Education and educational research division)
Bibliography. p.
1. High schools—Great Britain—Administration.
I. Title.
LB2901.H34 373.2′5′0942 72–10107
ISBN 0–08–017068–4

Printed in Great Britain by A. Wheaton & Co., Exeter

To

My Father

Contents

Foreword

THIS book has been written from the conviction that, although there have now been published a number of books and a considerable number of articles on various aspects of secondary reorganization, no one has yet really attempted to relate the practical problems and issues, as they are encountered inside the schools in the course of administration and policy-making, to the research available on at least some of these problems and issues.[1] To do this has required a great amount of reading, occasionally in areas where the writer had only general rather than specific expertise, and even more reflection, in order to piece together material from different areas of research and see the significance of the whole, into which the interlocking parts of the material had been combined, for a specific problem of organization or policy. This difficult task was made easier by the writer's experience of teaching in and organizing a comprehensive school on the one hand and in research on the other. It was therefore possible to arrive at a synoptic view, but no claim is made that the conclusions reached are without error, only that an honest attempt has been made, from a position of vantage, to weigh up the relevance of the material to the problems facing the schools.

[1] This is not to decry such work as that of Benn and Simon in *Half Way There*, indeed much of it was most relevant to some of the problems discussed, but the point of view is different. In their book, necessarily, the issues are viewed from outside rather than inside the schools.

CHAPTER 1

The Comprehensive Movement

THE movement towards comprehensivization in British schools during the early and middle sixties has recently shown signs of losing momentum, especially since the withdrawal of Circular 10/65; and the variety of types of reorganized schools set up has led some to question the need for, and the value of, the whole reform. This book is in some places critical of the policies followed in England and Wales; but at no point is the desirability of the reform questioned. This is because a study of comparative education, viewed both historically and contemporaneously, leads to the conclusion that in education, as in other aspects of political and social life, there are general movements which affect large areas of the world and which it is pointless to oppose, since they are powered by deep motivations of great force. These deep desires produce decisions of policy often taken outside education, sometimes inside it; either way they affect it right down to classroom level, and result in persistent common trends in educational systems which, individually, are unique. Opposition to such deep and powerful forces is futile. We get better results by tapping them.

If we look for a moment at other periods than our own, periods in which we ourselves are not emotionally involved, we have a chance of generating more light than heat and we are all the better prepared to look at our own times with the measure of detachment that is needed if we are to make sense of what is happening now.

There are several clearly distinct periods in secondary education in Western Europe, each of them linked to distinct social situations and reflecting their needs, both in school organization and in curriculum: the medieval period, the Renaissance and post-Renaissance period, the period of the first Industrial Revolution and of the political revolution, and the first half of the twentieth century. In every country of Western Europe in turn we see the same phenomena recurring within a particular period. In the small space available it is possible only to stress the main lines of development, without the qualifications that a more detailed analysis would demand, but, as our purpose is insight and understanding of our own period, this should be enough.

Although others attended it, especially in the later period, the medieval academic school was essentially a pre-vocational school for clerics, and its curriculum, as exemplified in the trivium and quadrivium, by covering the main areas of the domain of knowledge, prepared its pupils for the higher studies of philosophy and theology. The knight and the artisan mainly got their training for adult life outside this school.

With the advent of gunpowder, the rise of nation states and the creation of mercenary armies—indeed the nationalization of the army—the medieval knight found himself if not unemployed, at least underemployed. His solution to the problem of increased leisure in more settled local conditions was to go to school and study classical literature. This was sufficiently like the medieval literature of vernacular lays and epics to which he was accustomed, to please him better than the more science-based trivium and quadrivium of the medieval school. Hence a change in the nature and aims of education in the Renaissance and post-Renaissance period and, to a considerable extent, in its curriculum. Since the knight had turned gentleman, and so too had the scholar, and the wealthy merchants and professional men who aped both, education was geared to the production of gentlemen of leisure. Hence the typical continental academic school of the Renaissance and post-Renaissance period, whether northern European Latin school or southern European Jesuit college, was a product of vast economic and social changes involving the redundancy of the knight and the rise of the middle class.

The restricted character of the curriculum of the academic school ensured that the poorer members of the middle class would look elsewhere for their education, to the French school of the Continent or the eighteenth-century dissenting academy of England; these schools served practical needs for such subjects as geography, mathematics and French, the language of international trade, as pre-vocational studies for commerce. Even the nobility, who were replacing churchmen as administrators, had to found courtly academies with broader-based studies. As the range of knowledge and skills needed increased, so did the range of the curriculum. Again a general European sociological situation had produced a general European educational development, coloured by local variations in timing and organization.

The French Revolution and the Industrial Revolution are in some senses watersheds in both the social and educational history of the West. The growing complexity of social and commercial tasks in a technologically developing society made it increasingly imprudent to use status by birth as an index of capacity for a function, or patronage as a means by which a post could be obtained. Such a change in practice could only be brought about in an atmosphere which stressed the worth of men as individuals, as individuals with rights as well as duties. Democratization was probably the inevitable corollary of industrialization. It is no coincidence that public secondary examination systems began to be set up in Western Europe from the late eighteenth century onwards. They provided that evidence of capacity that birth was unable to furnish. England was a late starter in this new development, but this fact does not invalidate the argument. In any common development countries proceed at their own pace and for their own reasons.

In the same way secondary academic schools organized and supported by the state or the public authorities also began to be set up, and a drive began, to establish the new modern subjects as equivalent in prestige to the older classical subjects. These two movements dominate secondary education in the nineteenth century, and approximately by the end of it have found expression in every industrializing Western European country. We can set alongside them the movement for mass literacy, and with it the foundation of the elementary school, and subsequently of the advanced elementary school for the further education of artisans. All of them are responses to the expansion of knowledge and technology, the increasing complexity of industrial and social life and the beginnings of democratization.

The advanced elementary schools are of particular interest. Even their names significantly echo the fact that they are responses to a situation common to all countries, though with features peculiar to each. In Germany, Sweden, Denmark and Belgium, we have the *mittelschüle*, the *mellemskole* and the *école moyenne* or *middelbare school*, in Holland the *ULO school* (extended lower education school), in France the *école primaire superieure*, in England the higher-grade school. All survived, except the last, until the mid-twentieth century. They often combined general and prevocational training in a sub-academic type course and led to intermediate posts in commerce, industry or agriculture or to a higher specialized vocational training. Their fees were cheap enough for parents who could not afford secondary education for their children and their curriculum was often peculiarly responsive to local or national economic and social needs.

Their existence underlined the fact that there were two separate and parallel systems of education for different social classes. Even for the older age-groups there was no sharing of facilities, teachers or students. An industrialized civilization could not manage without literate workers, including some of quite considerable knowledge, but the prejudice against the kind of knowledge required by the working class and the vast gulf that separated the social classes at the time ensured that the middle and the working classes would be educated in different school systems all over Europe. The school system reflected the social system and the state of technology, and it did so everywhere.

The retention of separate educational systems for different classes is perhaps only possible while the community remains moderately static. An industrialized society is of necessity more mobile than a peasant economy and it manifests an increasing need for the well educated, not to be found in sufficient numbers in the middle class alone. Western Europe reached this stage in the early years of the twentieth century, when the idea of equality of educational opportunity, or at least of *la carrière ouverte aux talents* began to be preached, and arrangements began to be made for training the intellectually gifted children of the lower middle and working classes, by means of scholarships and free places at secondary schools. These became available as technological growth provided the money, and idealism and enlightened self-interest provided the will, to pay for them. Hence in the early part of the twentieth century there is a moderate intellectualization of the academic secondary school, as ability to profit, as well as ability to pay, became a criterion of entry. As bright children moved from the elementary into the secondary school, almost inevitably there was a gradual change from the idea that the elementary system and the secondary system are parallel systems of education based on social class to the view that they are stages of education end on to each other.

As a result types of school hitherto considered part of the elementary school system began to move into the secondary system, and the same types of course to occur in two different kinds of secondary school. Thus the French *école primaire superieure* was brought into the secondary system as the *collège moderne*, and the Belgian *moderne* course was to be found in the traditional academic school, the *athénée*, and in the advanced elementary school, the *école moyenne*. The first movement produces a secondary system with several types of school, the second a reason for amalgamating them. Indeed the Swedish movement towards comprehensivization was prompted by the need to reduce the number of types of school and to avoid duplication of courses as much as by the wish not to make too early distinctions between children. In England the killing off of the higher-grade school and the general anti-vocationalism of English education prevented the development of a large number of types of secondary school. Otherwise England was left with the same problem as all the other Western European countries, namely, that the schools newly introduced into the secondary system did not have the prestige of the traditional academic school. The latter, in a period of increasing affluence and increasing aspiration after the Second World War, therefore became the focus of increasing competition as pupils strove to get into it.

At the time further expansion of the curriculum made it more and more difficult for one-stream academic schools to survive and so the setting up of common schools in many rural areas became inevitable.

The Common School

Meanwhile the U.S.A. and the U.S.S.R. had already moved on to the common school. The Latin school had never had the same hold in the United States as elsewhere, because of the need to deal appropriately with the ever-expanding and novel needs of an ever-expanding and shifting community, in a country where there was a continual influx of immigrants from different ethnic groups and cultures. Hence by 1850 the principal type of secondary school was the academy, fee-paying and private, but very flexible in its curriculum. The high school in turn replaced the academy, after the Kalamazoo case of 1874, where the underlying issue was much the same as that in the Cockerton judgement in England. The judgement given, however, was actually the reverse and led to a massive expansion of free publicly supported high schools, with very varied curricula and for children of all social classes. Hence by 1930 half the 15–18-year-olds were receiving full-time education.

Russia developed the common school after 1917 as a matter of political principle and as a result of political revolution. The school was created in conditions of low technological development. As a result the Russian approach to common schooling was different from that of the U.S.A. As economic conditions improved the U.S.S.R. delayed longer and longer the age at which children were divided up and sent off into specialized schools. By 1940 the 7-year common school was found nearly everywhere, but qualifying examinations determined progress up the educational ladder. Now there is a 10-year common school.

The Western European movement towards the common school began significantly in Sweden, a country not impeded economically by world wars and one in which social stratification is less intense than in some other countries. After a period of well-planned experimentation during the 1950s, accompanied by scientific evaluation, the common school for pupils aged 7 to 16 was made compulsory by the Education Act of 1962. In the last 3 years of the course, optional subjects were to be gradually introduced and in the last year the course was divided up into nine different sections. The 1968 Education Act has subsequently reduced the amount of differentiation and has also decreed the setting up of a unified school for the 16–19-year-olds for 1971. Similar, though less extensive, developments have also taken place in the other Scandinavian countries.

Most other Western European countries, having greater social, academic or administrative divisions, have been moving with greater difficulty towards the common school. France produced notable reports and plans for reform, but, owing to political instability, structural stratification in the Ministry of Education and conflicts between church and state and between the bourgeoisie and the workers, no serious changes took place until the return of de Gaulle to power. The Berthoin reform of 1959 was, however, soon replaced by the Plan Fouchet of the middle 1960s, as the absence of real unification became apparent. In 1963, twenty-three junior secondary multilateral schools (*collèges d'enseignement secondaire*) were set up experimentally. Their 4-year courses involved observation and guidance of pupils. By 1967, 1200 of these schools had been established, with 1975 as the date for the completion of the reform. The C.E.S. is followed by differential upper secondary education, in which the traditional lycée is evolving from an 11–18 school to a 3-year school on sixth-form college lines.

In Italy, Holland and Federal Germany moves towards educational change have been made. Italy established a common middle school by the Law 1854 of 1962. Holland passed the Mammoth Law in 1963 and began to implement it in 1968. It allows for a common curriculum[1] for 12-year-olds, but in three types of schools; some comprehensive schools are, however, already being developed. Germany published the Rahmenplan in 1959 and the report of the Federal Educational Council in 1970, the latter recommending the unification of secondary education; but the decentralization of power to the various Länder since the war has prevented any overall reform; so far change has occurred only locally. Both Germany and Holland have been hindered by the diversified character of their second-level education. The tendency to think that in a common school the interests of the able child cannot be protected without the creation of very large schools, an erroneous line of thinking common over a long period in England, has faced Holland with an as yet unsolved dilemma; owing to the arrangements for municipal, Protestant and Catholic school systems, she has a large number of small schools.

This group of countries is not moving easily towards the common school and, it would appear, is moving towards a junior secondary school which is multilateral rather than comprehensive. It is not yet clear whether for them this is a final or interim stage. If previous educational evolutions are anything to go by, this stage is an interim one, though the present continental tendency to set up options for whole courses, rather than for separate subjects, strengthens the multilateral approach.

To sum up the trends in school organization at the secondary level in the years 1900–70, it is clear that as a result of increased industrialization, social mobility and democratization, the barriers between the elementary and secondary systems of education were gradually broken down. The concept of secondary education as a stage following the elementary or primary stage replaced that of secondary education as a different kind of education suited for a different social class of pupil from those educated in the elementary system. In a particular country the process usually takes several stages:[2]

1. the acceptance of the idea that all children should have a common primary school so as to give all an equal chance of the first phase of secondary education;
2. progressive raising of the school-leaving age to give all children a chance of the first phase of secondary education;
3. abolition of fees in secondary schools and provision of maintenance grants;
4. intellectualization of the academic secondary school, as elaborate systems of selection for different types of school are developed in countries with different types of post-primary education; the intellectually selective grammar school is thus a stage in the evolution from parallel elementary and secondary systems for different social classes to primary and secondary systems end on to each other and for a wider social spectrum;
5. the tendency to put off until later and later both the choice of vocation and the introduction of highly specialized vocational teaching;
6. at the junior stage of secondary education the adoption of a common curriculum, and of an orientation and guidance period, by different types of school;
7. the amalgamation of different types of schooling and the development of comprehensive or multilateral junior, and sometimes senior, high schools, where rigorous

[1] Provision of a common curriculum is sometimes the first sign that a more radical organizational reform is in the offing.

[2] Not every country goes through every stage.

selection is replaced by student guidance in the choice of an appropriate course or group of subjects at the senior stage.

As a result education is increasingly catering, not for a number of different social classes in different schools, but for a wide range of occupational and personal requirements in a single school, with a common curriculum at the bottom and a measure of increasing specialization at the top, reflecting the wide variations in types of jobs currently available in an industrialized society. This evolution has taken place in a general context of lessened social division, increased social aspiration and increased economic wealth, such as was experienced in the U.S.A. soon after the century opened.

The development of the British comprehensive school from small beginnings in London, Coventry and some rural areas in the early post-war years, with increasing momentum in the 1960s, can now be seen against the background of a similar evolution in Western Europe. It has taken place in the same atmosphere of political and academic controversy common elsewhere and has had its own peculiar handicaps. The lack of a sense of direction in the central authority and a period of economic stringency, produced Circular 10/65—rather than a government bill—with its suggestions of several varieties of comprehensive school, as already set up by innovating local authorities. Other handicaps would appear to be the earlier lack of an upper elementary school, easily transformable into a junior comprehensive school—a common development elsewhere—and the fact that the first public examinations take place a year later in the secondary course than is true of some continental countries. Hence a 5 year + 2 year arrangement of stages of secondary schooling rather than the 4 + 3 or 3 + 4 found elsewhere. These latter structures produce separately viable schools of easily manageable size. The English 5 + 2 structure leads to the "all through" comprehensive school, which tends to be large, or arrangements involving a change in the middle of a course, or the hiving off of the short upper 2-year course into the sixth-form college, which will only be a really satisfactory educational institution when the course is lengthened to 3 or 4 years.

One may conclude perhaps with the following reflection. Comparative historical studies demonstrate at particular periods the existence of common educational trends. These may proceed at varying speeds in different countries according to the quirks of local and national circumstances, but everywhere the particular evolution eventually reaches completion. There is no reason to suppose that the present evolution towards a common school is any exception to this persistent pattern.

A comparative study of the present educational scene thus shows that, although the research on the effects of selection, carried out in this country by Vernon and others in the 1950s, was valuable in alerting educationists to the inefficiency of the most efficient selection process in existence, the result of these investigations merely added fuel to flames that were already burning. As has been demonstrated by comparative educationists,[3] other countries in Western Europe, where research in educational psychology was less plentiful or non-existent, were also moving towards a common school under the influence of strong and persistent social and economic pressures. Even if the psychologists' results had been to confirm the efficiency of the selection process,[4] these forces would not have been denied.

[3] For example, in *World Survey of Education*, Vol. III. *Secondary Education*, Unesco, 1961, pp. 85–110.

[4] In fact, the evidence on the effects of selection, though sparse, all points in the same direction. Attempts to segregate produce erroneous decisions and unselective systems obtain at least as high levels of attainment as selective systems, perhaps higher. (Yates, A., *The Organization of Schooling*, Students Library of Education, Routledge & Kegan Paul, 1971, p. 53.)

Once industrialization takes place, once every man has the vote, once examination certificates become the initial passports to power, the education system can evolve, in the long term, only in the direction of greater communality. Whatever the educational problems this evolution produces, it is wiser, and also more effective, for all concerned with education to cooperate with the inevitable.

Relevance of Research

Granted that Western Europe in general, and Britain in particular, is moving towards the common school, such a massive revolution must of its nature bring in its train many problems. Some of these can perhaps only be solved by a nice observation of the process of the evolution as it takes place; certainly the details of any solution as it affects a particular school, with particular buildings and particular staff, can only be worked out by those on the spot. At the same time research can sometimes offer insights which will prevent the committing of serious errors. It therefore seemed worth while to review the results of research with regard to certain main issues basic to the reform and to see if enough sense could be made of them to be of service to heads and staffs engaged in implementing the necessary changes. The writer, who has had practical experience in comprehensive schools and a background in research, approached this task with some trepidation, for various reasons. The results of any piece of research in the educational field are rarely clear cut, because of the complexity of the factors that have to be evaluated. Hence reputable research workers tend to be diffident in stating their conclusions and to hedge their bets. Moreover, some investigations get publicity beyond their worth because their results fit a trend of opinion that is becoming fashionable at a particular time. In addition, on some issues a good number of studies have to be undertaken before all or most of the factors bearing on them emerge. On such issues the early investigations give very contradictory answers because some of the factors have not been identified and their masked influence is affecting the results of different studies in contradictory ways. As a result the science master who would cheerfully accept the fact that a large number of researches was required to elucidate a knotty problem in chemistry will sometimes pour scorn on educational research because two investigations produce contradictory results. Such an attitude is not scientific. It would be more profitable to consider why the results are contradictory. At the same time it must be admitted that the quality of much early educational research was not very high. Given the conditions under which it was done, by comparison with the money and facilities available for research in almost every other subject, this is not surprising, though regrettable. However, since the late 1950s more attention has been given in Britain to the funding of educational research and consequently better based investigations have been undertaken. At the same time the volume of earlier research, often undertaken as training exercises by teachers working part-time for higher degrees, is such that shrewd guesses can often be made as to the factors that underlie important issues in education. Even though such studies do not always stand up to the most stringent criteria of research, it is worth while to use them provisionally, rather than to rely solely on the hunches that come to us from the more circumscribed experiences of our own personal working lives. To use them provisionally as a starting-off point for the decisions that have to be taken in the implementation of a reform is a better approach than that of total commitment to a prepared position, taken up on the basis of very inadequate evidence, or no evidence at all. We are then committed to nothing but the search for wise decisions and can change without loss of face a course of action that proves fruitless.

In the present reform there appear to be four issues which, in one way or another, underlie every other. One of them, pertinent in any move to introduce comprehensive schools, but especially so at a time when the leaving age has been raised, is the problem of the less able and the culturally disadvantaged children, who do not particularly want to stay on at school and who have to be motivated to do so with a good grace in an economy which, by and large, no longer needs the services of 15-year-olds.[5] In so far as education has succeeded in its objectives, it has succeeded with the academically able child and, though much could be said to show that this success has been relative, the point of real failure has been with those who leave as early as they can. Hence this issue has been concentrated on; the research on the subject has been described, and the curricular and other implications explored, in the context of a society where the education of adults will become endemic.

Another problem reviewed is that of the streaming/non-streaming controversy, on which findings that have appeared in the 1960s come near to settling the issue.

A third topic discussed is that of counselling. It has become increasingly clear that the task of the school is no longer purely educational in the restricted sense, that the school acts as a channeller to jobs and that by its decisions pupils' future lives are often decided without either they or their parents being aware of it. It is also clear that the school is often the only institution with which the child now has a link, other than with his family. Where the family is failing in its task, as the nucleate family may more often than the old extended family, the school has often to undertake a counselling function, if the child's development is to be safeguarded. Linked to both the vocational and the personal counselling functions, there is the function of educational guidance and counselling which has always been the peculiar prerogative of the school, but which has been made more complex both by the increase of knowledge about it and by its link with the other two.

Connected with the above topics, but also having a standing in their own right, are the questions of the curriculum and of general school policy in the light of the school's aims and its function in society. A chapter is, therefore, devoted to this central issue also.

In addition, the problem of size of school is discussed, which has obvious connections with the range of curricular offerings. Many of the schemes of reorganized schooling have been decided on in the light of ideas about the "right" size of school but on the basis of very inadequate evidence. Findings on the effects of size of school on academic results, curricular offerings, school climate, participation by pupils, truancy and staying-on rates and teachers' work, are presented and some conclusions are reached about the "ideal" size of school. Since heads and staffs often do not work in schools of this size, suggestions are offered, on the basis of research evidence, where available, as to ways in which schools of larger or smaller size can offset their respective deficiencies.

Finally, since ideas about size of school have considerably affected the type of reorganization chosen in some areas, a chapter has been devoted to a survey and to a discussion of such evidence as there is on the relative advantages and disadvantages of different types of reorganized school.

Effects of Comprehensivization

Before we proceed to discuss the above topics, a very brief review of the effects of reorganization on academic standards is pertinent, since this issue has been one of the chief points of

[5] It is not proposed in this book to consider the de-schooling controversy, which is a much wider issue and merits more consideration than can be given here.

controversy in all countries. The evidence is sparse and some of the comparisons over simple, in that results of individual comprehensive schools have been compared with national averages for the rest of the system, without taking into account the effect of varying socio-economic factors and possible differences in IQ. However, the data available all points in the same direction. Unselective systems produce as high levels of attainment as selective systems, and perhaps higher.[6] The International Project for the Evaluation of Educational Achievement (Mathematics) confirmed that in comprehensive schools the standards of the ablest children were not affected and the total yield from all pupils was significantly increased, and, though this study has some weaknesses, there is no reason to suppose that this result masks undetected variables.

The effect of comprehensive schooling on attitudes to school and staying-on rates, on which academic standards depend, was studied first by Miller[7] and later by Alice Griffin.[8] Both were found to be better in comprehensive schools than in grammar or secondary modern schools.

Holly's[9] investigation suggests that middle-class pupils get more scholastic and social benefit from comprehensive schools than do the children of the less skilled manual workers, so that one must infer that a comprehensive school does not provide the whole answer to the problem of the disadvantaged.

Staying-on rates are also better in comprehensive schools than in the grammar and secondary schools combined.[10]

In short, the evidence, generally, points one way, to the greater stimulating power of the comprehensive school.

[6] Postlethwaite, Neville, *School Organization and Student Achievement*, Almqvist & Wiksell, Stockholm, 1967, pp. 11–22, 128–31.

[7] Miller, T. W. G., *Values in the Comprehensive School*, Oliver & Boyd, 1961, pp. 89–94.

[8] Griffin, A., Selective and non-selective secondary schools, their relative effects on ability, attainment and attitudes, *Research in Education*, no. 1, 1969, pp. 15–19.

[9] Holly, D. N., Profiting from a comprehensive school: class, sex and ability, *Brit. J. Sociology*, vol. XVI, no. 2, June 1965, pp. 150–8.

[10] See p. 32, footnote 61.

CHAPTER 2

Streaming and Non-streaming in the Comprehensive School

THE controversy over the comprehensive issue in Britain has been followed by the controversy over the streaming issue. The two are clearly interrelated at the philosophical and political level. A rigidly stratified society where social position is determined solely by birth is not likely to develop a system of comprehensive schools or to unstream its classes, nor would a country imbued with egalitarianism set up such an institution as the English public school. Similarly, economic trends can affect both inter-school and intra-school aims. A society where an educated minority is sufficient to provide leadership and a working population needs only the three Rs in order to achieve the society's economic goals will not go in for the same educational practices as a country that needs a highly trained labour force of great flexibility and adaptability. Hence at classroom level, as much as at organizational level, the needs of the society are likely to affect teaching practices.[1]

The social elitism so characteristic of English nineteenth-century education began to be replaced by intellectual elitism at the turn of the century. The Education Act of 1902 and subsequent measures set up a revivified grammar school which gave a proportion of free places to bright working-class youngsters. The consequent pressure on the primary schools caused them to promote their bright children early so that they might adequately prepare them for the free place examination. Hence in the same class at the top end of the primary school there would be bright young children alongside rather older children of average and below average ability. This situation was felt to be undesirable,[2] and, as primary schools grew in size, promotion through the standards based on attainment was abandoned and year groups were divided into classes based on common age and homogeneous ability. This practice also appeared in the grammar school itself, for the latter had in view university places for able youngsters. Hence the practice of streaming became general in the 1930s and remained so until the 1960s.

Yet, throughout the period when British schools were developing streaming, continental schools, in systems which were just as socially elitist and almost as intellectually elitist, continued with the old grade or standard promotion system. Under this system in the first years of secondary schooling, for example, there would be in every class of the early years of

[1] How far-reaching this can be was first realized by the writer in an investigation which showed that in Belgium teaching methods for French had been radically affected in the 1930s by political legislation, that apparently had nothing whatsoever to do with teaching methods.

[2] Yet research has shown that social acceptance by other children of pupils older or younger than themselves is more related to mental age than to chronological age. Taylor, E. A., Some factors relating to social acceptace in eighth grade classes, *J. Educ. Psychol.*, vol. XLIII, no. 5, 1952, pp. 257–272.

the academic school[3] children with IQs varying from 90 approximately to 140+.[4] However, class teaching was the rule, and about a quarter of the children who could not reach the expected standard by the end of the school year were kept down. This procedure acted as a substitute for streaming in a context of class teaching, but the fact remains that continental teachers have experience of teaching a wider range of ability than the typical British "streamed" teacher has. Even by the third or fourth year the bottom level of IQ in the academic school would be about 90, though there would be very few pupils left in the class with this low level of intelligence and they would have been kept down at least once.[5]

The educational practices of an elitist society were in fact also reinforced by the early findings of the psychologists. They concluded that intelligence was not only largely innate, but also constant and not subject to change and development, and that it could be accurately measured for all time by means of verbal intelligence tests. The concept of intelligence itself had also been insufficiently explored. Hence the view that children needed separating into different classes and even into different schools according to their capacity tended to be supported by the psychologists.

A. Research on Streaming and Non-streaming

Although value orientations and economic need condition the educational system and practices of a society, educationists and teachers, amongst others, would be failing in their duty if they did not explore the effects of particular schemes of organization in a school system or in a school upon the children themselves. Hence over the last 40 years there have been many investigations into methods of grouping inside schools, just as, for example, there have been many on linguistic aptitude. Curiously enough, they follow rather a similar pattern, with a long period of conflicting results, until researchers became aware of the many complex factors affecting apparently simple issues in educational research, and made allowance for them in their research designs.

The problem about much of the research about streaming and non-streaming, in the context of the present British secondary school reform, is that much of it is American and not necessarily of immediate relevance, and that much of it refers to the primary or elementary level of schooling and that less is directly known, especially in the British context, of the effects of different types of grouping at the secondary level. This point having been made, what evidence is there on this question to guide heads and staffs of comprehensive schools in their policy-making?

The evidence up to the middle sixties has been well reviewed in the extensive and scholarly survey in *Grouping in Education* edited by Yates.[6] It covers a long period and comes from a diversity of countries, Denmark, Sweden, Israel and the U.S.A. amongst others. It has to be remembered, therefore, that much of it has been carried out in classes which, for example, included children who were repeating classes as well as children who had been promoted, and which did not contain merely a single age group as in Great Britain.

[3] One Belgian headmaster said to the writer in the late 1950s that neither he nor his staff could conceive of how to teach a class without at least one bright child to act as a pacemaker or a source of ideas for the others and the methods used in one subject, the teaching of which the writer observed over a long period, were based on this assumption.

[4] See Halsall, Elizabeth, Intelligence, school and social context: some European comparisons, *Comparative Education*, vol. 2, no. 3, 1966, p. 185.

[5] *Ibid.*, p. 190.

[6] Yates, A. (ed.), *Grouping in Education*, Almqvist & Wiksell, Uppsala, 1966.

In the studies reviewed in Yates's book there are wide variations in (a) the size of the samples studied, which range from 50 to 70,000, and the size of groups within the sample; (b) the duration of the investigations, ranging from very short periods to up to 5 years, with possible complication of change of teacher in the longer studies; (c) methods of assessing control groups; (d) teaching content and method; (e) use of teachers in the experiment;[7] (f) techniques of evaluating results of the tests, which varied in number from one single test to a large battery of tests.

1. *Academic Effects of Streaming and Non-streaming*

Of the early research between 1917 and 1928, mainly in America,[8] reviewed by Billett and quoted by Passow,[9] 108 studies were uncontrolled, two partly controlled and four controlled. The evidence the former produced is therefore very unreliable; eighty-eight of the uncontrolled studies produced results which favoured streaming, ten studies gave doubtful results and four did not favour it. In the controlled or partly controlled studies three favoured streaming, two were doubtful and one against it. Billett's review tended on the whole to suggest that streaming favoured the slow and the average child but that a stage arrived when the bright children tailed off under conditions of streaming and did less well.

In Ekstrom's later review of over thirty investigations carried out between 1923 and 1958, thirteen studies favoured streaming, fifteen reported no differences or found streaming detrimental, five studies gave mixed results. Results tended to favour streaming where teaching methods and materials were differentiated to meet the needs of different levels of ability. Making due allowance for the greater unreliability of the earlier results reviewed by Billett, one may perhaps infer that the decline in the proportion of studies favouring streaming may conceivably be related to improved teaching methods in unstreamed classes, which make heavier demands on teachers' techniques than do streamed classes. But that inference, at best, could only be tentative.

During the 1950s there were renewed efforts to settle the question of the academic effects of streamed and unstreamed classes, and an interest in exploring their social and emotional effects.

In the U.S.A. Justman in 1952 compared eighty-eight pupils of high IQ in normal (i.e. in the American context unstreamed) classes and in special progress (i.e. streamed) classes and found that the differences favoured the high flyers who were in the special progress classes. French's study of 1959 showed no significant relationship between achievement and the degree of homogeneity in the classes investigated and Borg's study of 1964 was also inconclusive, although it did suggest that perhaps streaming might motivate the bright child and also give minor advantages to the less able.

Since the beginning of the Swedish school reform in the late 1940s and the early 1950s a good deal of evidence has been gathered in Sweden on the effect of streaming and non-streaming, but it cannot be properly evaluated without some understanding of its educational context. Sweden, like other continental countries, has no tradition of streaming inside

[7] In some experiments the same teacher taught both the control group and the experimental group, with consequent bias arising from the teacher's own attitudes to streaming and non-streaming; in others, different teachers were used, with bias arising from different styles of teaching.

[8] Where teaching took place mainly in unstreamed classes.

[9] In Yates, *op. cit.*, pp. 161–9. Much of this survey is taken from Passow and the abstracts that follow his chapter.

schools as the British understand it. But her division of secondary education into several different types of schools, suited in the main for different levels of ability, accustomed her teachers to teaching moderately, though not very, homogeneous groups.[10] When the experimental period of her reorganization began, as is well known, it was decided that Stockholm itself should be divided into two sections, one to continue the old selective schools system, the other to develop comprehensive schools which would contain the full range of ability and which would be unstreamed, since there was no streaming tradition, as far as the inside of schools was concerned, in the Swedish system. Although in other respects the Swedish reform was very well planned, little or nothing was done until quite recently to retrain the teachers to cope with this new, really unstreamed, situation.

The Stockholm experiment was carefully monitored. Husen and Svensson[11] found that IQ scores of lower-social class pupils in "plus-select" classes (streamed pupils of higher ability) were better than those in undifferentiated classes and those in undifferentiated classes better than those in "minus select classes" (streamed pupils of lower ability). Those in the upper social strata showed about the same gain whether they were in "plus-select" or undifferentiated groups. In attainments children of manual workers profited more from the "plus-select" milieu, middle and upper class children relatively little. The "plus-select" classes had graduate teachers, the others not. The study showed that the effects of streaming were negligible by the age of 15 and there was some evidence that less able pupils scored better in unstreamed groups. When the evidence was reviewed by Dahloff he found that Svensson's tests had not a high enough ceiling and that his results, though a fair reflection of what was learned in common by both streamed and non-streamed classes, did not reflect any extra learning done in either of them. Whereas unstreamed classes took 73·2 lessons to cover the syllabus, academic streams took only 32·8 lessons and then went on to other unexamined topics; thus in unstreamed classes bright children went on to over-learning, not new learning. Reappraising Svensson's Stockholm study and evaluating work done by Carlson in Växgo and Borg in Utah, Dahloff[12] found that very often there are differences of no statistical significance (i.e. very small differences) but a constant trend; able pupils in streamed classes do better in mathematics than those in unstreamed, but less able pupils do equally well in either situation. It should perhaps be pointed out that Swedish teachers in the main had not reorientated their teaching methods to cater for an unstreamed situation. One can only speculate on (a) what the results of the Stockholm experiment would have been if they had, (b) how far any evaluation of different methods is valid if one group of teachers is less expert on the method they are expected to follow than another group with which they are being compared, and (c) to what extent similar situations have occurred in other investigations.

British research in the field of streaming gathered momentum in the 1950s. Daniels[13] gave an early report in the *Times Educational Supplement* of 29 July 1955 of his findings that

[10] Say half the total ability range.

[11] Husén, T. and Svensson, N. E., Pedagogic milieu and development of intellectual skills, *School Rev.*, vol. LXVIII, 1960, pp. 36–51. Svensson, N. E., *Ability Grouping and Scholastic Achievement*, Almqvist & Wiksell, Uppsala, 1962, pp. 182–3.

[12] Dahlöff, U., *Ability Grouping, Content Validity, and Curriculum Process Analysis*, Univ. of Gotheborg, 1969.

[13] Abstracts of these researches, with references, are to be found in Yates. A more recent investigation by Rouse (Rouse, S., The effect upon attainment levels in mathematics and English of unstreaming. *Univ. of Manchester School of Educ. Gazette*, vol. **13,** 1969, pp. 12–14) found that after 4 years of non-streamed teaching the slower children had benefited, and the brighter ones had not been held back.

streaming tended to differentiate children increasingly in terms of IQ. His study also showed that in unstreamed classes the average IQ of all children increased in level, as did their scores in English and arithmetic. The range of their scores was also smaller.

In 1958 Blandford, however, in his study of the performance of 1700 pupils from twenty-six primary schools on six tests found no support for the suggestion that streaming tended to preserve differences between pupils' rates of progress and levels of attainment or that streaming widened the gap between the able and the less able. His correlations did not reach significance level. In the same year Rudd found no significant differences between the performance of streamed and unstreamed classes of 11-year-olds in a London central school.

Conversely, Douglas came to the conclusion that streaming had self-fulfilling aspects and that the more able and the less able drew further away from each other in attainment in succeeding years.

Important evidence was to come in the early 1960s from a large international study undertaken by the Unesco Institute of Education in Hamburg, the International Evaluation of Achievement study, in which the 13-year-olds of twelve countries were tested for their scores on internationally standardized tests of mathematics, reading, geography, science and nonverbal aptitude. Although the investigation's results were rendered somewhat less reliable than was desirable by international sampling errors, one clear conclusion was that countries which went in for streaming practices achieved lower average scores and a wider dispersal or range of scores than countries which did not stream their children inside the schools but operated on a grade placement system. This conclusion was substantiated by the later I.E.A. investigation of mathematics.[14]

More recently still, the N.F.E.R.[15] investigation in primary schools has found no differences in the average academic performance of pupils of comparable ability and class, though "divergent thinking" test scores were higher for pupils in unstreamed schools taught by a typically child-centred non-streaming teacher. Nor was there any evidence in the N.F.E.R. survey that children of different social classes did academically better or worse in either a streamed or an unstreamed school. In general children of lower social class deteriorated in reading performance relative to children of higher social class. The survey also showed that school organization had most effect on children of average and below average ability.

To what conclusions can the inconsistencies of many of these reported investigations lead, other than to the view that research workers are gluttons for punishment? They must lead to the belief that until recently at least there were factors operating in the streamed–unstreamed controversy which had not been properly studied and which were preventing the emergence of clear-cut data, because they had not been disentangled from already known factors. Similar inconsistencies were found over many years in studies of linguistic aptitude and only much clearer analysis of possible elements in it led to more conclusive results in later investigations.

2. *Teacher Effects in Streamed and Non-Streamed Classes*

With regard to streaming and non-streaming researchers have become much more aware

[14] Husén, T. (ed.), *International Study of Achievement in Mathematics*, Wiley, 1967.

[15] A notable investigation; 2000 schools took part, and 5500 children were tested at 7 years old, in 1964, and then annually until 1967. The test battery covered nine different areas: attainment in reading, English and mathematics; verbal and non-verbal reasoning; "creativity" or "divergent thinking", interests; attitudes about school; personality; sociometric status; participation in school activities; occupational aspirations. Reported by Lunn, J. C. Barker, *Streaming in the Primary School*, N.F.E.R., 1970, pp. 57–70.

that teachers' attitudes to this particular question and their teaching techniques might have a bearing on the issue, since it has been shown in other contexts that teachers' attitudes make a difference to children's performance and behaviour. Different teachers may react differently to the streamed situation (and to the unstreamed). When their results are averaged, the average may mask differences of reaction by different teachers to the same teaching situation, differences due, say, to some teachers accepting the new situation and adapting their methods to it, others accepting the situation but presuming their old methods were equally applicable to this new form of organization, and others again neither accepting it nor adapting to it. Failure by research workers to consider these points has at times been due to the naïveté of some researchers in education; it has also been due to the inability of some teachers to accept, without feeling threatened, investigation of their educational practices and the results of them—even in the absence of any reliable data on the basis of which teachers themselves could make an informed choice of technique.

Already by 1960 Rudd and Daniels had done something towards investigating the effects of teachers on children and of children on teachers in the context of streaming or unstreaming. Rudd had looked at teachers' estimates of personality and found no significant difference in their estimates as between children in streamed and unstreamed classes. At the same time Daniels' work showed that most teachers in the schools at the time were in favour of streaming as emotionally sound and good for all children, but especially the less able child. He also showed that streaming streamed teachers just as it streamed pupils.

It was, however, the N.F.E.R. survey which concentrated to a greater extent than any other previous investigation on the effects of teacher variables in the streaming–non-streaming context. Notably its finding with regard to the development of divergent thinking well demonstrates the influence of teachers on children. A child-centred approach and the freer atmosphere it engenders would appear to make divergent thinking more likely and the non-streamed situation make a child-centred approach more necessary.

According to the N.F.E.R. survey also, just as the type of school organization had more effect on children of average and below average ability than it had on more able children, so too with the type of teacher. The best attitudes in average and below average children were produced by teachers working in unstreamed schools who were committed to non-streaming. The poorest attitudes were formed amongst pupils in unstreamed schools who were taught by teachers who were "typical streamers". The organization and the teacher have to match.

Hence, one result of the N.F.E.R. study was to show that any effect associated with streaming or non-streaming was unlikely to be the result solely of the form of organization chosen. Mrs. Barker Lunn has commented; "Teaching method, the ideas which underline disciplinary systems, the views teachers hold about their children, in short the whole climate of relationships built up by what teachers say and do and what they appear to their pupils to imply may well be the critical factor."[16]

One other finding of the N.F.E.R. survey with regard to teachers is also worthy of mention and comment, namely that teachers in streamed schools were found to be more united in their beliefs and in their teaching methods. Teachers in non-streamed schools showed a wide divergence of opinion. This result is only to be expected in view of the newness of unstreaming in the context of the British school. Similarly in some unpublished work on teaching

[16] Incidentally, the N.F.E.R. survey showed that teachers tend to overestimate the ability of higher-social-class children and to underestimate the ability of lower-class children, confirming earlier evidence in this regard.

methods in continental schools the writer found the greatest divergence in opinion, practice and degree of efficiency amongst teachers who were using new methods, the greatest unity and uniformity in all three amongst those using well-established methods, a result that was only what one would have expected. This factor too may well have affected results in many investigations.

3. *Wrong Placements in Streamed Classes*

Before we leave the academic issue to consider the social effects of streaming and non-streaming, another set of results of the N.F.E.R. survey with regard to organizational aspects merits mention. The findings of the 1950s with regard to wrong placement of children in different types of schools after the 11+ are interestingly paralleled by N.F.E.R. findings of wrong placings in different streams of the same primary school. The survey showed that 15 per cent were known to be wrongly placed but only 6 per cent were transferred. The number of children transferred also decreased as pupils progressed up the school, probably because differentiation of syllabuses between streams made pupil transfer increasingly difficult and only to be undertaken in the most obvious cases. Children remaining in too high a stream tended to improve, those in too low a stream to slip back. Similarly again, promoted children tended to make progress, demoted children to deteriorate, the streamed class thus mediating teacher expectation and demands on children.

4. *Social and Personal Effects of Streaming and Non-streaming*

There would appear on the whole to be more consistency in the results with regard to the social effects of streaming and non-streaming than there is with regard to their academic effects.

As early as 1960 Pape noted the tendency for A streams to have an undue proportion of girls and autumn-born children and for lower streams to have an undue proportion of boys and summer-born children. This data on the interaction between date of birth and streaming was to be confirmed by the N.F.E.R. survey, and is well documented by Pidgeon.[17]

With regard to social class effects both Khan (1956) and Douglas (1964) showed that early streaming reflected social class structures more than real ability and reinforced the process of social selection. A contribution by Luchins in the 1940s had already indicated that streaming led to the development of something like a caste system. The N.F.E.R. study likewise found an undue proportion of working-class children in the lower streams of streamed schools. Mutual friendships tended to be from the same social class and range of ability in both streamed and unstreamed classes, but there was a greater number of mixed ability friendships in unstreamed schools. Cone (1970) found that in unstreamed classes the choice of friends from a different social class was more frequent.

Evidence as to the effect on personal development is less clear cut though trends on the whole favour the non-streamed class. Luttrell found that streaming reduced the incidence of boastfulness and bossiness and work by Kubovi and Flum in Israel showed that E.S.N. children taught in special classes were better socially.[18] Rudd, however, found that pupils,

[17] Pape, A. V., The duds of summer, *Education*, vol. 116, 18 Nov. 1960, pp. 952–3. Pidgeon, D. A., Date of birth and scholastic performance, *Educ. Res.*, vol. 8, no. 1, 1965–6, pp. 3–7.

[18] This result needs to be seen in its context. Israeli children have been demonstrated to have a very high level of aspiration, compared with those of other countries, a factor which could conceivably affect their reactions to the streamed and unstreamed class, so that they might be rather different from those of E.S.N. children of other countries with their lower social aspirations.

estimates of themselves indicated emotional stress after transfer in a streamed school and high individual responses to regrouping. None the less, he found no permanent effects. He also found evidence of more aggressive behaviour and less attention to work in streamed classes. Willig found less anxiety about tests and less neuroticism in unstreamed classes than in streamed and, according to Cone, there was a greater sense of security and no evidence of lower ability children in unstreamed classes being affected in motivation by the presence of their higher ability peers. Pearce carried out a sociometric study which showed that a pupil's status tended to correspond to a composite score reflecting his abilities in all subjects. In a class where streaming or anything else produced a sense of failure or a reputation of inferiority, a decline in morale, effort and attainment occurred.

The effect of terminal promotions in streamed classes was also studied by Pearce. He found that they took away from lower streams the children best in attitudes and effort and caused some of the really slow to be "unwanted" in every subject. Chetcuti came to similar conclusions.[19]

The N.F.E.R. survey also found that the emotional and social development of children of average and below average ability was strongly affected by streaming or non-streaming.

Evidence as to social interaction favours the unstreamed school. Rudd demonstrated that children in streamed groups made fewer social contributions to lessons. Work by Willig confirmed this; he noted that social interaction, adjustment, and attitudes were better in unstreamed classes. The N.F.E.R. survey found that more children in non-streamed schools participated in school activities. In both streamed and unstreamed schools the bright children and those of higher social class were more active in this respect, but the trend was much more pronounced in streamed schools.

5. *Conclusions*

1. Much of the research on streaming and non-streaming has not taken cognizance of all the factors, because for a long while it was insufficiently realized just how many there were. Both teachers turned research workers and educational psychologists have made this mistake.

2. With regard to the intellectual effects of streaming and non-streaming the verdict must still be not proven either way, but the importance of the teacher's attitude and methods in either situation has now been demonstrated. Such differences as there are in regard to effectiveness of teaching, even when statistically significant, are often not practically important.

3. Streaming produces errors of allocation, just as selection for different types of school does.

4. On the whole, the social effects of non-streaming are better than those of streaming, in relation to the accepted values of present-day society.

The sense the hard-bitten headmaster, anxious to do the best he can for his school, can make of these results must depend partly on the school's circumstances. If his staff wish to unstream this will be a good reason for doing so, if not his policy will be less self-evident. In a society where the different social classes see less of each other than formerly, because better transport has made it easier for them to live in different areas, there are good reasons for pursuing a policy of non-streaming, especially in a school with a mixed catchment area. Ultimately, too, with the advent of various technological aids and of programmed learning there is likely to be, over time, a general move towards unstreamed classes. The stimulation that most results show is given to the less able child in the unstreamed class would also be a

[19] Most of these references are abstracted in Yates.

good reason for unstreaming in a society where increasing education is likely to widen the intellectual gap between the most and the least able. So, for all these reasons, cautious steps should probably be taken towards unstreaming, but they should be accompanied by measures towards the retraining of the teachers in the school concerned in the methods that this form of classroom grouping requires.[20]

5. For the hard-bitten administrator grappling with the task of adapting buildings constructed for a selective system for use in a non-selective one, there is one main lesson from the research on streaming. If the only point at issue in a decision were what range of ability can be taught within one class—and such a situation would be unlikely—then even a one-stream comprehensive school would be viable.

B. The Approach to Unstreaming

If a school decides to start unstreaming it faces many problems.

First of all, it is unlikely that all members of staff will feel favourably inclined towards unstreaming, especially where it has become a tradition that certain teachers always, or mostly, take the 'A' stream. The prestige which gradually attaches itself to both the 'A' stream and the 'A' stream teacher is immediately at stake. Unstreaming may be seen by such teachers as threatening their status, just as comprehensivization itself is so viewed by many grammar-school teachers. Other teachers may find unstreaming difficult to cope with because of teaching habits which have become ingrained over the years. Because they lack experience outside their own classroom, they have no immediate source of other ideas which would suggest new ways of orienting their teaching and which they are certain are practical. Others again find unnerving the prospect of both interesting and keeping in good order children of such a wide range of intellectual ability. Hence unstreaming is not lightly to be undertaken or, for that matter, likely to be undertaken successfully, if the conditions are not right or if they cannot be made so.

Clearly, if a new school is being started, a head can gather together staff who already have experience of unstreamed classes or who are willing to try their hand at non-streaming. If a school is obviously failing, and the staff recognize that this is so, there is every incentive to try something new; the new cannot be worse than the old. However, if a school is not obviously failing, and perhaps not obviously succeeding either—or if at least inclination plus a reading of the evidence suggests that unstreaming will enable it to do better—then many decisions have to be taken, and taken rightly, if a successful evolution is to be achieved.

Reading accounts of how, and for what reasons, individual schools[21] have unstreamed, visiting a number of schools which have unstreamed, and having taken part in a partial unstreaming have led the writer to certain conclusions with regard to the best methods of unstreaming. Various approaches are possible. Thus the approach used by Thompson of Woodlands, which involved demonstrating the degree of overlap between IQs in different forms, was likely to produce in the staff the conviction that ultimately non-streaming would be more efficient as well as more humane. Barnes' approach at Ruffwood[22] started not from the intellectual angle but from the social and the organizational. His school, purpose-built

[20] It is noteworthy that Swedish teachers eventually had to insist on having several days of retraining per year in the new methods needed.

[21] See, for example, Unstreaming: two viewpoints, two strategies, by Barnes, A. R. and Thompson, D. respectively in Halsall, Elizabeth (ed.), *Becoming Comprehensive: Case Histories*, Pergamon Press, 1970.

[22] *Ibid.*, pp. 238–45.

for a house system, found itself with a teaching organization, based on streamed forms, split from the social organization, based on houses. This split reduced the impact of the pastoral care provided at the house level. In another area this might not have been a serious problem; in Ruffwood's context it was serious, because of the many social difficulties in the locality, and it was seen by the staff to be serious. Hence, since the buildings were house-based and could not be altered, there occurred a gradual evolution towards a system of unstreamed classes based on houses, in which the teaching and the pastoral care groups coincided.

Another approach to the question of unstreaming is to start from the unreliability of data coming from the primary schools. In view of the known differences of practice in the primary schools with regard to coaching for standardized tests,[23] if used, or the known inability of teachers to rate their pupils' performances with regard to pupils from other schools —though they are very capable of ranking their own pupils with reference to each other—in view of all this, a secondary school head is entitled to look at the results presented to him with some degree of scepticism, especially if they come from a large number of primary schools. All these factors, plus the fact that all test results are at best an approximation[24] to the pupils "true" scores, entitle a school to decide to allocate pupils to forms alphabetically on entry for, say, a month or a term. Such has been the practice in many schools for a long time. A move towards unstreaming can be started from it, with the term extended to a year. Teachers who have grappled successfully with the problems of mixed ability teaching for a term can contemplate with some confidence the extension of the period to a year.

Another approach, which the writer knows from personal experience to be a successful one, is to start by unstreaming non-academic subjects. Allocation of pupils to streamed classes is normally carried out by using information on pupils' attainment in mathematics and English and their IQ score; that is to say, the measures used are such as are thought to be related to future achievement in academic subjects. Their predictive power with regard to such subjects as needlework and domestic science, arts and crafts and P.E. is much less certain. Therefore the teachers of these subjects already have experience of teaching classes which, as far as their subjects are concerned, are not really homogeneously grouped. Moreover, methods for teaching these subjects already tend to aim at the individual rather than the class. Hence teachers of these subjects have had some measure of experience with less homogeneous groups and more individual teaching techniques. As a result they seem both more willing to try unstreamed classes and more confident in their ability to teach them.

Another group of comprehensive school teachers, other than those taking non-academic subjects, who have often had some experience of teaching mixed ability classes, are the teachers of what one may call the "fringe" subjects of the fourth- or fifth-year timetable, namely those subjects which tend, in a particular year, for one reason or another, to get few takers. Staffing-wise it is not possible to allocate two teachers to such a small class of pupils. Yet its members may vary quite widely in ability, especially if the school pursues a policy of allowing parent and child a considerable say in the final choice of subject. In these circumstances the teachers concerned have to develop methods more suited to mixed ability groups than are the traditional class methods. From these teachers also there develops a group with both the expertise and the confidence to undertake teaching the larger unstreamed classes of the lower school.

[23] Watts, A. F., Pidgeon, D. A. and Yates, A., *Secondary School Entrance Examinations*, N.F.E.R., 1952, p. 15.

[24] Hence the 10 per cent error in selection for grammar schools.

CHAPTER 3

Cultural Deprivation and the Comprehensive School

THE comprehensivization of the secondary school in Britain and the recent raising of the school-leaving age have combined to raise again as a matter of urgency an issue which has been with us since 1944, namely, how do you educate at the secondary level children who are less able or/and are culturally deprived, to use the contemporary jargon, and who in many cases are dying to leave school? Not that the problem of educating such children had been unknown before 1944.

There were plenty of 13-year-old under-achievers from humble backgrounds tagging along in standard V or VI of the elementary school and never reaching the top standard, in the period between the wars. In the effort to get bright children through the scholarship examination they were sometimes neglected. In general the main aim was to make them literate, if possible; there was also provided not much more than "capes and bays" geography and "kings and queens" history, with singing and drawing, and some craft work at a centre.

A. The Achievements and Failures of the Secondary Modern School

The passing of the 1944 Act, the hiving off of all pupils of 11 and over into secondary schools and the raising of the school-leaving age gave the opportunity for a considerable rethinking of the curriculum of these children, and indeed of average children, and in many places, though by no means in all, the opportunity was seized. The lack of prestige that dogged the secondary modern school from its inception, because it competed with the well-established and socially superior traditional grammar school and because at first it could not put its pupils in for examinations, should not blind us to the considerable achievement of many secondary modern school teachers in loosening up the curriculum, introducing new subjects, using new methods of teaching and assessment and in generally introducing new ideas. Whilst grammar school teachers moved very little over a period of 15 years with regard to either curriculum or method, circumstances obliged their colleagues in the secondary modern school to start more or less from scratch, and to be much more conscious of the need to interest their pupils, many of whom were at first very resentful about the extra year of school attendance. Hence the gradual introduction into the curriculum of general science,[1] of locally oriented history, geography and biology, of drama, of a more widely conceived physical education, not limited to traditional team games; hence the use of the

[1] More successful in the secondary modern school than in the grammar school where examination pressures caused it to disintegrate into its component subjects.

discovery method, of projects, of centres of interest, of concrete material, of visual aids, and also the introduction of new methods of assessment. Not every experiment was successful, but, when one looks back on the period, it is surprising how many were. But because the secondary modern school got the grammar school rejects and could not at first send out pupils armed with certificates, it was therefore a less prestigious school. Its teachers never received the full credit that they should have done for some notable achievements. Another reason for the lack of credit with the public was the low level of attainment that some pupils had reached on leaving school, the reasons for which were then not clearly understood, quite apart from the apparent decline of attainment due to the more able pupils going off in larger numbers to grammar school.

The factors which tended to depress learning in the secondary modern school in the 1950s were of two kinds, one which concerned a general lack of incentive that affected all children in the school, the other which concerned and still concerns the development of intelligence and academic skills in working-class children specifically.

First, the lack of any material incentive in the shape of a public external examination or even a local certificate depressed motivation and achievement in a group of children, namely working-class children, whose lives, mores and parental and social influences taught them to look for material incentives in education rather than intellectual ones. Of all social groups, this group was the least likely to respond to the challenge of learning for its own sake. There is some evidence, for example, that working-class students in higher education tent to opt for more practically career-oriented courses and to go to institutions that provide them. Yet the working-class child in the secondary modern school was asked to learn for learning's sake, when his brother in the grammar school or his middle-class contemporary in the same school were, by the nature of the case, provided with material incentives in the shape of public examinations and certificates.[2]

Secondly, genetic factors apart, the factor of cultural deprivation in working-class children, especially in the children of the unskilled worker, diminished their capacity to cope with a school and a curriculum which assumed the possession of verbal and social skills these children did not possess and which were in fact by and large middle-class orientated. In the 1950s and the 1960s elements in this cultural deprivation were disentangled and its effects elucidated in Britain and in several other countries. Without a review of these findings we cannot really hope to discover precisely what policies and what curricula and teaching methods are needed to deal with cultural deprivation.

B. The Nature of the Problem

The Social Class Factor in Relation to the Culturally Deprived Child

Everywhere in Western Europe where the matter has been studied it has become clear that working-class children have less chance of getting into an academic school or into a university, for the same level of measured intelligence, than middle-class children, that in the non-academic school itself the lower a child is in the social scale the more he is likely to under-achieve, in relation to his ability, and to leave early. The position of girls is even

[2] See Halsall, Elizabeth, A comparative study of attainments in French, *Int. Rev. Educ.*, vol. 9, no. 3, pp. 41–57 for a comparison of attainments of Dutch and Flemish children with those of English children of the same IQ in a subject where in the long run the former were, materially, much better motivated than the latter.

worse than that of boys and that of children from larger families worse than that of children from small families.[3]

The IQ scores of culturally deprived pupils become lower relative to those of middle-class pupils as they get older. Such pupils tend to have a lower level of self-esteem and a low level of aspiration, and this is even more true of boys than of girls. They feel themselves more controlled by external forces of circumstance and of luck and less capable of controlling what will happen to them than do middle-class pupils.[4] Because of crowded living conditions, lower-class children play out more often in the street away from parental supervision, whereas middle-class children tend to play in the garden under their mother's eye. The result is that low-income parents yield much of the influence they might have on their children during their formative years to the children's peer group.[5]

Other conclusions reached on differences between middle-class and working-class styles of upbringing[6] are that

(a) the psychologically orientated discipline characteristic of the middle-class, by words rather than by concrete and physical rewards and punishments, also helps to develop a verbal style of thinking;
(b) the working-class child is more orientated to the present, less time and sequence conscious,[7] less supervised, less trained to put off present satisfaction in favour of future satisfaction through effort and achievement;
(c) the amount of noise in culturally deprived homes leads to a loss of auditory discrimination.
(d) low intellectual home background correlates with high commitment to the teenage role and high involvement in the youth culture correlates with low commitment to school goals.[8]

Mothers of working-class pupils who stay on at school are more likely to have encouraged their children's schooling and to have known families where children stayed on. Working-class children in primary schools containing a number of middle-class children do better than those in one social class schools, the middle-class children acting as pacemakers.[9]

[3] Halsey, A. H. (ed.), *Ability and Educational Opportunity*, O.E.C.D., Paris, 1961, pp. 26–37; Little, A. and Westergaard, J., The trend of class differentials in educational opportunity in England and Wales, *Brit. J. Sociology*, vol. XV, no. 4, pp. 301–6; Rupp, J. C. C., *Helping the Child to Cope with the School: a study of the importance of parent–child relationships with regard to primary school success.* [Opvoeding tot schoolweerbaarheid.] Wolters-Noordhoff, Groningen, 1969.

[4] Coleman found this sense of control over the environment second only to family background in its effects on school achievement, and very strong in its effect on school achievement regardless of economic level. (Coleman, J. S. *et al.*, *Equality of Educational Opportunity*, U.S. Dept. of Health, Education and Welfare, Office of Education, 1966, pp. 288–9, 320–5.)

[5] Strom, R. D., *Teaching in the Slum School*, Merrill, Columbus, Ohio, 1965, p. 40.

[6] N.B. Findings over many years in the U.S.A. suggest that very few child-rearing practices are *consistently* middle class or *consistently* working class. Zigler has disputed the extent to which the differences in child-rearing practices could make such differences in school performance. (Zigler, E., Social class and the socialization process, *Rev. Educ. Res.* vol. 40, no. 1, Feb. 1970, p. 88.)

[7] N.B. His father is paid by the week, not by the month, and in the very poorest families one wonders whether it would not be psychologically disabling to be future-orientated. The troubles of the present week are enough. Reduction in poverty would make it psychologically more possible to look to the future. Incidentally, the rise in IQ and in achievement levels over the last 30 years found in several national surveys should probably be linked to a rise in economic levels. See p. 43.

[8] Sugerman, B. N., Social class and values as related to achievement and conduct in school, *Sociological Rev.*, vol. 14, no. 3, 1966, pp. 287–301, and: Involvement in youth culture, academic achievement and conformity in school, *Brit. J. Sociology*, vol. XVIII, no. 2, 1967, pp. 151–64.

[9] Jackson, B. and Marsden, D., *Education and the Working Class*, Routledge & Kegan Paul, 1962.

Working-class parents may often express the wish that their children shall stay on at school, middle-class parents expect it.

Variation within the culturally deprived school population and its several sub-groups has been reported in a number of studies. Miller[10] found that some pupils were inadequate in the school situation, others were hostile to school and rejected it, others again found it irrelevant. Hunt[11] also found much variation amongst lower-class children.

The list of researches in the 1950s and 1960s on the effects of social class is almost endless. These researches set the boundaries of the problem and they sometimes give help to the administrator.[12] They give no help to the head of a school in search of a policy or to the teacher in his search for a stimulating curriculum, subject matter and teaching methods.

Language Factors

One of the first signs of change was to come with the publication of Bernstein's work, although even his investigations are not of direct and immediate assistance to the teacher. Still, his work helped in that it studied the reasons why working-class children as a whole did less well academically than middle-class children. It showed that the language development of working-class children tends to be rather different from that of middle-class children. Their language is not so well organized syntactically,[13] however expressive, not to say colourful, it may be. The ability to formulate questions tends not to mature as questions are so rarely answered.[14]

Hess and Shipman's study of maternal teaching styles[15] supported Bernstein's thesis. They found that lower-class mothers, in attempting to teach their children a game, gave very cryptic, rather uncommunicative instructions. One further clue about children's language development was obtained in a study by Olim and others.[16] The tendency of a mother to use abstract language was found to be a better predictor of the child's ability with abstract concepts than either the verbal IQ of the mother or the child's own IQ.

There are also differences of perception and conceptualization between working- and middle-class children. When one researcher asked for definitions of words, the latter tended to produce more abstract and fewer concrete definitions than the former. The relevance of this fact to the Piagetian theory of mental development is clear. Working-class children tend to stay more frequently at the level of concrete operations and not to reach that of formal operational thinking so often as middle-class children.

Daniels showed that the difference between the two groups of children is not so great for non-verbal as for verbal ability, which is what one would expect in view of the slant of working-class occupations.

[10] Miller, David R. and Swanson, Guy E., *Inner Conflict and Defense*, Henry Holt, New York, 1960.

[11] Hunt, J. McV., *Intelligence and Experience*, Ronald, New York, 1961.

[12] For example, any administrator keen to improve working-class children's performance would consider the research on the effect of the presence of middle-class children in primary schools when arranging catchment areas.

[13] Modifications of the Bernstein thesis have since been suggested by Coulthard.

[14] Some of the answers require more knowledge and education than the parents have.

[15] Hess, R. D. and Shipman, V. C., Early experience and the socialization of cognitive modes in children, *Child Development*, vol. 36, no. 4, Dec. 1965, pp. 869–86.

[16] Olim, E. G., Hess, R. D. and Shipman, V. C., *Relationship Between Mothers' Language Style and Cognitive Styles of Urban Pre-school Children*. Urban Child Study Center, Chicago, 1965.

Bernstein[17] has concluded: "Social class factors have been shown to affect not only the level of educational attainment but also the very structure of ability itself",[18] and another writer has well summed up the position: "The most important deficit of the culturally deprived is their difficulty in interpersonal communication."[19]

The school is geared very largely to the verbal, to the theoretical and to the abstract. It is probably more geared to the verbal than society as a whole. Long-standing traditions, reaching perhaps as far back in Western society as the development of the alphabet, still give prestige to the highly literate man and in any case assume that everyone shall be literate. They do not assume that everyone shall be mechanically minded, although many, perhaps most, people will now drive a car or operate a domestic electrical appliance,[20] as often, perhaps more often, than they will read a book or a newspaper. Yet no one is ashamed if they cannot put a washer on a tap; this affects no one's prestige. People have been known to boast of it. But who will confess he cannot read? In past societies non-readers would have gone to the scribe in the way we now send for the plumber.

The school still stands in the shadow of an over-verbalized tradition. Unlike the Greek school, which began with music, it assumes that its first and immediate job is to teach children to read, whether or not they are as yet sufficiently sensitized to language as to be capable of assimilating the abstract symbols of the written language. Indeed, until recently, no one has ever really questioned that children might be insufficiently sensitized to language. Hence the conflict between the school's unconscious assumptions and the lower-class child's capacities must inevitably lead to failure. It has always been supposed that it is the child's failure. Recent evidence suggests the failure lies just as much with the school, in making unwarranted assumptions, in failing to recognize the real problem, and in tackling the child first at his weakest point, and at a level above his current capacity.

The Home Environment, its Influence and its Interaction with School

Although the social-class concept has been of real service in helping us to understand the problem of the disadvantaged, many teachers were aware, either because of their teaching experience or from their own personal experience of growing up in the working class, that as a measure of cultural deprivation it was crude.

Research workers began therefore to try and sort out the factors in the working class which made for deprivation. Carter,[21] for example, distinguished three groups of working class families: (a) home-centred traditional families with the father in a steady, responsible job, interested in long-term goals and with some, if only modest, ambitions; (b) families taking life as it comes, not too interested in school and taking the view that one job is as good as another, provided the wages are satisfactory; (c) the "rough" families, living for the moment, that do not accept the values of the school and want to get children into jobs as

[17] Bernstein, B., Language and social class, *Brit. J. Sociology*, vol. XI, no. 3, 1960, pp. 271–6, gives a fair summary of the Bernstein position.

[18] Very recent research suggests that most middle-class mothers tend to talk far more to their children in the second year of life and afterwards than do working-class mothers, and that a concurrent greater rise in IQ takes place in middle-class children than in the IQ of working-class children.

[19] Wall, W. D., *Adolescents in School and Society*, N.F.E.R. Occasional Publication No. 17, 1968.

[20] On the other hand, they will not need to know a great deal about its workings from day to day and will only be troubled by their lack of electrical and mechanical knowledge and aptitude on the day it breaks down.

[21] Carter, M. P., *Home, School and Work*, Pergamon Press, 1962, p. 7, pp. 30–67, and *Into Work*, Pergamon Press, 1966, pp. 50–59.

soon as possible. The researches listed in the I.E.A. Mathematics Study[22] demonstrate +0·8 correlations between the variables in the home environment and children's achievements, higher than those between the socio-economic standing of the parents and the children's attainments. The Plowden surveys[23] also show that more of the variation in children's school achievement is accounted for by variation in parental attitudes than by variations in parents' material circumstances or by variations in schools and that the relative importance of parental attitudes increases as children grow older. Only about a quarter[24] of the variation in parental attitudes is conditioned by variation in circumstances. "Home" variables have nearly twice the weight of "neighbourhood" and "school" variables put together,[25] though the "neighbourhood" factor is more important than the social class of the parents.[26] Of the home factors influencing attainment measures of maternal care are the most important. Dirt and crime are more important than poverty. Cultural deprivation prevents the flowering of latent abilities and the higher the potential the more catastrophic the result is likely to be. The proportion of bright children in the schools is reduced by the adverse effects of home, neighbourhood and school conditions. Cultural deprivation does not merely affect the lower ability ranges. Adverse effects are cumulative and most damage is done before children start school.

The factors[27] inside the home which prevent the development of ability have to do with the literacy of the home[28] and the attitude of parents towards books and school.[29] Hence the existence of many homes in the working class favourable to children's educational development, and of many unfavourable homes in the middle class, in spite of genuine social class differences. The interest of the child's parents in his progress at school influences his attainments, maternal support tending to permit better progress by backward children and paternal interest being most effective with the able. The role of the mother in protecting and supporting the weak child and of the father in stimulating and encouraging the strong came out very clearly in the analysis.[30] Where children are short of such support and encouragement, their intellectual, linguistic and social growth is sapped and failure at school is almost inevitable, with serious consequences for their own view of themselves and for their own self-respect.

The failure at school that results from poor linguistic and social skills produces a negative self-image, often rebellion against defeating school experiences, a search for status outside school and often membership of an in-group of delinquents or semi-delinquents which protects a youngster from isolation. Hence children and adolescents of lower social class are in trouble with the law seven times as often as middle-class children according to Douglas.

[22] Husén, T. (ed.), *International Study of Achievement in Mathematics*, Wiley, 1967, pp. 200–1.

[23] Department of Education and Science, *Children and their Primary Schools*, H.M.S.O., 1967, vol. 2, appendix 4, pp. 181–2.

[24] *Ibid.*, pp. 188–9.

[25] *Ibid.*, pp. 188–9.

[26] Robson, T. B., *Urban Analysis. A Study of City Structure*, Cambridge Univ. Press, 1969, pp. 244, 248.

[27] D.E.S. *op. cit.*, vol. 2, appendix 9, p. 372. (Plowden Report.)

[28] As shown by, for example, the number of books in the home, parents' membership of the public library, paretns' reading, etc.

[29] These findings have been confirmed by a Dutch study. See Rupp, J. C., *Helping the Child to Cope with the School: a study of the importance of parent–child relationships with regard to school success* [Opvoeding tot schoolweerbaarheid], Wolters–Noordhoff, Groningen, 1969.

[30] There are guidelines in this finding for headmasters and housemasters as to which parent to appeal to particularly, if both parents are equally co-operative and capable.

Those few who are successful in school have group pressures against identifying with school values; success means danger to them.[31]

In practice, of course, the schools to some extent may delude the children as to their abilities, though not, of course, intentionally. As traditionally conceived, they concentrate almost entirely on scholastic achievement and in addition they mark pupils competitively with reference to each other. In so doing they probably diminish the motivation of those whose incentives need to be increased and increase that of pupils who are already well motivated. Some pupils therefore leave with the idea that they are exceptionally capable, which is true with regard to academic work, but dangerous to them if they imagine that scholastic capacity necessarily always infers other capacities. Other pupils leave school with the idea that they are in every way incapable, by the school's standards, and this may be equally false outside the scholastic context. For example, the writer remembers one 12-year-old with an IQ of about 80 and scholastic attainments to match who was an excellent little organizer, but then she was the eldest of eight children and had had plenty of practice in management! Similarly a group of children from one particular area had an average IQ and English scores at 11+ which were only 95 or 94, but their wit and humour were a delight, when they were not used as a device for getting out of work—and sometimes when they were. Temperamentally they were born actors and comics and the area has indeed produced an above average proportion of the nation's comedians. It would be interesting to measure the creativity and histrionic gifts of children in this area.

The point I am trying to make is that the school, as at present constituted, is to some extent an inefficient developer of talent for a world that needs many kinds of talent, yet it has been given the job of talent-developer in chief in modern society. By tradition it concentrates on scholastic and academic talent, and, as increasingly certificates become passports to jobs, those with other talents than academic will find it more and more difficult to get a foothold in society. We cannot turn back the pages of history. Because of the desire to have objective measures of talent in a democratic society, the school will probably long continue to be the chief assessor of talent in the young. Therefore, at some point, the school will have to reconsider how far its traditional curricula and teaching and assessing policies offer a youngster a true insight into himself, and whether the educational system as we know it can be allowed to go on, unwittingly, to some extent falsifying youngsters' pictures of themselves and issuing to pupils certificates that in some cases tell only half the story to a prospective employer and to society. How this is to be done is not completely clear to the writer but that it needs doing is a matter of conviction.

Differences in Intelligence and in Rate of Growth of Intelligence

The studies on home and language factors in the development of ability, to which reference has been made, have relevance to the tasks of all teachers. Their implications for the tasks of secondary school teachers will be clearer if we add to them other evidence on the relative power of genetic and environmental factors in the development of ability and on differences in rates of mental growth at various ages.

[31] An extreme example of this situation was encountered by one of the writer's students, who had worked as an art master in an approved school. He found that whenever he praised any of the boys' work in front of his class, the boy himself immediately ruined it, presumably for fear the other boys would rate him as identifying with the values of the masters. The teacher learnt that the work would only survive intact if he praised the boy in private.

The nature–nurture controversy was revived after Jensen argued in 1969 that the compensatory education movement in the U.S.A. had failed for reasons extrinsic to the programmes themselves. The latter were based on the premise that differences in intelligence are a consequence of environmental variations rather than genetic factors, and that in fact the reverse is true. Although the controversy is in many ways a sterile one, teachers have to face their jobs with realism. What is the true position? Can we in fact state what the true position is?

Evidence summarized by Vernon[32] suggests that genetic factors are the most important in the development of intelligence. They probably account, according to this school of thought, for 70 per cent or above of the total development. Large reported changes in measured IQ usually refer to children below puberty, mentally subnormal and deprived children or the severely disturbed emotionally. With regard to the approximate 30 per cent of intelligence developed by environmental factors Bloom[33] suggests that the effect of a deprived environment may be such as to produce a difference of 20 IQ points compared with a productive and encouraging environment.

Supporters of Jensen's views quote studies showing a greater degree of correlation between the IQs of identical twins than between the IQs of non-identical twins, and between IQs of foster children and those of their natural mothers than between IQs of the same children and those of their foster mothers. Supporters of the view that environment has a more important role than it has been given credit for by those who stress heredity point to these very same studies. They use, however, not the indices of correlation, but the *actual* difference of average IQs between twins raised in different environments and stress the fact that the *actual* IQs of foster children are generally more similar to those of the foster parents than they are to those of the natural mothers. Shulman[34] comments that both conclusions are tenable. Heredity makes a major contribution to the relative rank ordering of intelligence scores, with environment held constant, but it is the degree of abundance or deprivation of the environment which seems to contribute most to the actual attained IQ status of individuals. Also data on IQ are of primarily theoretical interest, whereas school achievement data are of great practical significance. All studies show a significant lower heredity factor in school achievement. It also stabilizes later than IQ, remaining sensitive to environmental change for a longer period.

Even if we take the somewhat pessimistic view of Bloom,[35] where a less able working-class child would score 70 points on an IQ test, the less able middle-class child would score 90 and the corresponding more able children 110 and 130 points respectively. The educational consequences of these differences are considerable.

None the less there may possibly be social-class differences in intelligence. Tests[36] which are "culture reduced" as between middle and lower-class children but not "culture-free" have still produced performances significantly related to social class. The results still correlated with social status, about +0·22 to +0·24 compared with +0·33 to +0·44 for IQ tests.

On the basis of an exhaustive analysis of data gathered over many years, including the results of longitudinal studies, it has also been argued by Bloom that "in terms of intelligence

[32] Vernon, P. E., A new look at intelligence testing, *Educ. Res.* vol. 1, No. 1, 1958, pp. 5–6.

[33] Bloom, B. S., *Stability and Change in Human Characteristics*, Wiley, New York, 1964, pp. 88–9.

[34] *Rev. Educ. Res.*, vol. 40, no. 1, Feb. 1970, p. 382.

[35] Both Ausubel and Cattell express more optimistic opinions.

[36] McArthur, R. and Elley, W. B., The reduction of socio-economic bias in intelligence testing, *Brit. J. Educ. Psychol.*, vol. 33, no. 2, June 1963, pp. 107–19.

measured at age 17, about 50 per cent of the development takes place between conception and age 4, about 30 per cent between ages 4 and 8, and about 20 per cent between ages 8 and 17". Zigler,[37] also, believes that the basic cognitive processes are stable in character and increasingly lose their plasticity after about the third year of life. In addition he uses his data on changes in the quality of mental functioning to support the view that they are often based on changes in affective states (e.g. motivation, task involvement) and that affective processes are more malleable than cognitive ones. Hence changes in the affective areas as well as concerted attention to the conative aspect (development of skills, etc.) can result in limited shifts in cognitive achievement.

Another problem with the culturally deprived is that their mild mental retardation is infrequently recognized in early childhood, probably due to the lack of demands made on such children by their familial tasks and to the fact that so far their ability is not yet so clearly and obviously impaired by the effects of an adverse environment for it to be evident to everyone. Mild mental retardation, affecting both IQ and attainment, reaches its peak in adolescence, when educational demands are also at a peak[38] and when adolescent alienation and hostility are also at their height. The hostility and the retardation may be connected. It has been suggested that the bias against intellectual achievement common in adolescent peer groups, especially amongst the culturally deprived, has a deterrent effect on cognitive development in adolescence.[39]

Mild mental retardation is rare in families of high social class and common in the lower. The discrepancy is so great as "to indicate that mental retardation without detectable lesions is virtually specific to the lowest social classes and their cultural setting".[40] Thus the epidemiological evidence supports the rest.

That such retardation is not necessarily completely irreversible has been shown by various studies. It has been demonstrated that in mentally retarded infants a change of environment can have striking effects, due partly to receiving affection, but also partly to the amount of interaction with other human beings. The removal of infants from an impersonally run institution to an institution where they received personal mothering from mentally retarded young women stimulated their intellectual development to the point where they became fit for adoption. The gains proved to be permanent.[41] However, this finding refers to infants, not adolescents, and, as has already been said, it is likely that only 20 per cent of the total intellectual growth up to age 17 occurs in the adolescent and pre-adolescent period (age 8–17).

As far as adolescents are concerned they too, none the less, can make some recovery from retardation. Clarke and Clarke[42] found that the young adults whom they studied made some gains in IQ up to their late twenties. Their results are indirectly confirmed by Susser.[43] He found that the numbers of mentally retarded decline sharply in early adulthood, presumably because they make the gains noted by Clarke and Clarke.

[37] Zigler, E., *op. cit.*, p. 110.

[38] Susser, M., *Community Psychiatry: Epidemiology and Social Themes*, Random House, New York, 1968; quoted in *Rev. Educ. Res.*, vol. 40, no. 1, Feb. 1970, p. 59.

[39] Braham, M., Peer group deterrents in intellectual development during adolescence, *Educational Theory* vol. 34, Winter, 1964, pp. 3–21.

[40] Stein, Z. A. and Susser, M., Mild mental subnormality: social and epidemiological studies, *Social Psychiatry*, Baltimore, 1969, also quoted in the same volume of the *Rev. Educ. Res.*, p. 59.

[41] *Rev. Educ. Res.* vol. 40, no. 1, Feb. 1970, p. 43.

[42] Clarke, A. M. and Clarke, A. D. B., Recovery from the effects of deprivation, *J. of Midland Mental Deficiency Socy.*, vol. 4, 1957, pp. 58–62.

[43] Wall, W. D., *op. cit.*, p. 113.

However, Bloom's findings suggest that the recovery from cultural deprivation that can be made during and after adolescence is much less than that which can be achieved earlier. A survey of all the material must lead to agreement with Wall who took a cautious view. He thought it grossly unrealistic to ignore the fact that, in general, only extremely limited results with regard to purely cognitive development *per se* were attainable for the Newsom children even by the best schemes at the secondary stage. He thought that the best hope of effecting academic improvement at the secondary stage *lay in stimulating motivation.* None the less he also expressed the view that even a limited gain might be of real significance if it took a pupil across one of Piaget's maturational thresholds, such as that between concrete operational thinking and formal operational thinking. It would make a real difference if the increment in development, however small in itself, took a pupil from the level of ability to reason from or about the concrete to the stage of abstract thinking. Also, as has already been said,[44] it is amongst E.S.N. children, the deprived and the emotionally disturbed, that the greatest gains have been reported. Hence realism does not suggest inaction; it should lead to greater efforts, and especially with regard to stimulating motivation.

C. Motivation and the Deprived Child

One of the dilemmas that confront schools in making policy decisions with regard to the less able and the culturally deprived is that, although their greatest cognitive need is for further instruction in the basic skills, those subjects which children find most interesting are not the "skill" subjects such as mathematics or learning to read but the "content" subjects, such as history or geography.[45] If we are to tap motivation to undertake further study of basic skills in the "early leaver" groups, for example, we have got to find some very powerful incentives and some effective ways of changing attitudes.

As has been well said by Wall, "what an individual can learn will, to a large extent (but with considerable flexibility) be determined by intelligence; what he *will* learn will be determined by his motivations to learn, by opportunity and by the way the experience intended to provoke learning is presented to him".[46]

What evidence is there as to the kind of motivational forces which will induce an apathetic or hostile teenager of rather low ability to take an interest in his lessons?

We will look first of all at motivation which is extrinsic to the curriculum.

The Sense of Control of the Environment

One clue as to the motivation of adolescents is provided by Coleman's finding[47] that a

[44] See p. 27. The writer recall from personal experience one boy who began his secondary education in the remedial class of a comprehensive school, having been placed there on the results of IQ, English, arithmetic and non-verbal standardized tests, and who left it to enter university. Even allowing for illness or error in the earlier results, this constitutes a massive improvement. Other such improvements have been reported in the literature.

[45] See work by Pritchard, R. A. (*Brit. J. Educ. Psychol.* vol. 5, 1935, pp. 157–79 and 229–41), Lambert, C. M. (unpublished M.A. thesis Univ. of Lond. 1945), Lewis, F. (*Durham Res Rev.* vol. 14, 1963, pp. 95–105) and Stevens, M. (*The Living Tradition*, Hutchinson, 1961, p. 291).

[46] Research into attainment with regard to modern language learning, for example, shows that approximately one third of the attainment results from the amount of linguistic aptitude, one third from the degree of motivation and one third from other, including teaching, factors. (Pimsleur, P., Mosberg, L. and Morrison, A. L., Student factors in foreign language learning: a review of the literature, *Modern Language J.*, vol. XXVI, no. 4, Apr. 1962, p. 169).

[47] See p. 22, footnote 4.

sense of control over the environment is second only to family background in its effect on school achievement, and very strong in its effect on achievement regardless of economic level. Whether a pupil believes his fate in life is going to be decided by luck and circumstance or that it is in his own hands has a powerful influence on effort. Mayeske's results[48] confirmed that of the Coleman study. He also found that a student's sense of ability to control and influence his environment had a greater influence on his test scores than either his concept of himself with regard to learning and success in school or his interest in school and persistence in reading outside school. If it is relevant to our culture this result is encouraging, because it means that it is possible to get over, or at least to mitigate, the effects of a pupil's distrust of himself in respect of success at school, if one can convince him that he has a measure of control over his environment. In the British context of free secondary and higher education, as regards objective availability of opportunity, the lower working-class boy has as much control of his environment as the middle-class boy. Money-wise he has, of course, less, since his family needs his wage-earning power more. But, basically, what he is lacking in mainly is motivation, and to some extent ability, to take advantage of his opportunities.

We may perhaps link these results with another finding which seems to be indirectly connected with motivation. Early leaving[49] has been shown to be related to the level of expansion of the economy and particularly to the increase in the number of white-collar jobs. The greater the increase, the fewer the leavers. Presumably the youngsters reckon their best chances of getting jobs lie in the fields where there is a shortage of candidates and perceive the worthwhileness of further study, since it can lead to those jobs. This finding with regard to early leaving may, of course, not be applicable to the United Kingdom.[50] If it is, for those areas with excessive proportions of early leavers and poor economic conditions, there is most hope of improving staying-on rates if economic expansion[51] takes place and takes place in white-collar jobs. Conceivably also, a school in such an area which made great efforts to impress on its pupils the white-collar job opportunities at the national level would provide a powerful incentive to stay on for those children who could be induced to look beyond their own locality. It looks as if one should link this research finding to the motivation of the adolescent to stay on at school, a motivation which is likely to increase in a world where general trends in job opportunities over the years have been towards a decline in agricultural and blue-collar jobs and an increase in white-collar ones.[52]

Although studies of attitudes and motivation have shown that adolescents from lower social classes are more anti-school than those from middle-class backgrounds,[53] Riessman takes the view that they and their parents have a basically positive attitude to

[48] Mayeske, George W. *Educational Achievement among Mexican Indians. A Special Report from the Educational Opportunities Survey*, U.S. Department of Health, Education and Welfare, Office of Education, Technological Note No. 22, Washington D.C. Reported in *Rev. Educ. Res.*, vol. 40, no. 1, Feb. 1970, p. 74.

[49] Dentler, R. A. and Warshauer, M. E., *Big City Dropouts and Illiterates*, Special Studies in U.S. Economic and Social Development, Praeger, 1968, pp. 54–5.

[50] Indirect confirmatory evidence would seem to come from the Midlands, where there is a high rate of early leaving and yet till recently a good level in the economy. But it is in the area of blue-collar jobs, many of them unskilled and requiring low levels of education, that expansion has taken place, not in white-collar jobs.

[51] There is a fair amount of evidence accumulating round the world that educational expansion owes more to economic expansion than economic expansion owes to educational.

[52] Presumably the present recession will prove only temporary.

[53] e.g. Hieronymous, A. N., A study of social class motivation relationship between anxiety for education and certain socio-economic and intellectual variables, *J. Educ. Psychol.* vol. 42, no. 4, Apr. 1951, pp. 193–205.

education or at least to its possible benefits, with regard to future jobs and the ability to cope with bureaucratic red tape, though a negative attitude to schools and teachers.[54] They have to be convinced that the school itself is on their side, i.e. indirectly that they themselves have greater control of their environment because of this. Yet, owing to their linguistic, educational and social deficits, this is not too easy for the school to make clear. Here the comprehensive school has certain advantages over grammar and secondary modern schools, because of the many complexities of its educational and administrative arrangements. These produce higher staying-on rates and it may well be that they do so because they produce in the children a greater sense of control over their environment. The present writer's experience of work in a socially very deprived area may suggest clues as to why this is. In the four comprehensive schools of the area it was administratively as well as educationally essential for the content of the curriculum of the fourth and fifth year, the subject choices and the vocational choices they would lead to, to be more than usually well demonstrated to both parents and children. As a result 40–50 per cent staying-on rates were being achieved in the early 1960s, when national rates were much lower, and in schools where the mean IQ was only around 94. The effort expended to make parents and pupils really understand what was possible presumably convinced many that the schools were on their side and that there was hope for them for the future.[55] Both feelings would increase pupils' sense of control over their environment.

Parental Involvement

Further clues on motivation come from some American studies, which plot the degree of influence of parental involvement in school on children's achievement.

Brookover and others[56] compared the development of three randomly assigned groups of low-achieving junior school pupils, one of which received weekly counselling sessions, the second having regular contacts with particular subject specialists and the third group's parents having weekly meetings with members of the school staff about their children's development. At the end of the year the first two groups had shown no greater achievement as a result of their special treatment, whereas the third group showed a heightened self-concept of their ability and had made significant progress.[57]

Rosenthal and Jacobson[58] demonstrated that children who profited from positive changes in teachers' expectations of their ability all had parents who were known by the teachers to be involved to some degree in their child's development.

Another study found that parents of all social classes who were involved in school were likely to believe school and education could actually effect change for their children.[59]

[54] Riessman, F., *The Culturally Deprived Child*, Harper, New York, 1962, pp. 10–15.

[55] Most comprehensive schools have experienced higher staying-on rates than the national average. The explanation of this general phenomenon may lie here also. Certainly there is room for research on this point. Miller's work, which indicated greater pupil satisfaction in comprehensive schools, might well provide the link in the chain of causation.

[56] Brookover, W. B. *et al.*, *Self-concept of Ability and School Ahievement*, East Lansing Bureau of Educational Research Services, Michigan State University, 1965.

[57] See, however, p. 34 for different results on the effect of counselling. More studies are clearly required on its effects.

[58] Rosenthal, R. and Jacobson, L., *Pygmalion in the Classroom*, Holt, Rinehart & Winston, New York, 1968.

[59] Clowood, R. A. and Jones, J. A., Social class: educational attitudes and participation in education, In: Passow, A. H., *Education*(ed.) *in Depressed Areas*, Teachers' College, Columbia, New York, 1963, pp. 190–216.

Since a child's sense of control over his environment is an important factor in success, and lower-class children tend to lack such a sense of control, there is a pointer here as to the link between parental involvement, parental belief in the school's capacity to improve their children's future prospects, and their children's achievements.

An investigation by McDill and others[60] also has relevance to the present theme. In a large-scale study of schools, it suggests that a chief source of variation in the "climate" effects of schools on the achievement of pupils is the extent of parental and community involvement in the school. The greater the involvement, the greater the pupils' achievement.

It follows from these findings that schools ought to stress, as major policy objectives in tapping motivation, the goals of seeking to enhance their pupils' sense of control of their future and to involve parents more in the work of the school. It seems at least possible that the intensive efforts made by comprehensive schools to place their varied wares before their pupils at the third-year course meetings and interviews have already resulted in tapping motivation, since staying-on rates have been higher in comprehensive schools than in the rest of the system.[61] It would seem important that now the school leaving age has been raised similar efforts should be made in the fifth form, both for the sake of pupils' personal and vocational development and in order to take them willingly off a labour market which will no longer want juveniles.[62]

It is easy enough for the school to present its wares to the children, and to the parents if they will come, by all the paraphernalia of careers conferences, course choice meetings, interviews and so on, whether in the third or the fifth year, but to get parents in socially very deprived areas really to be involved in their children's education is very much more difficult. Although there are many happy exceptions, many of the parents in this group do not come to school easily, except in anger. At this point their inhibitions and sense of inferiority are overcome by rage. They are, of course, by middle-class standards, easily provoked to rage, but middle-class teachers do not always, sometimes cannot always, make enough allowance for the predicaments of lower working-class life.[63]

The school needs to think out ways of involving these parents. A more relaxed attitude on the part of the authorities to the sorts of jobs a working-class father might help with around the school at the week-end, in the construction of badly needed, but unable to be afforded, extra facilities might be of some help. A correspondingly relaxed attitude would also be required on the part of the unions. In some schools there has been reported the happy effects of getting mothers to help with the binding of books, thus giving them also the opportunity to see what their children would be learning. Lectures on the new mathematics are less likely to appeal to this group of parents, though they are not impeded by overmuch know-

[60] McDill, E. L., Rigsby, L. C. and Meyers, E. D., Educational climates of high schools: their effects and sources, *Amer. J. Sociology*, vol. 74, 1969, pp. 567–86.

[61] Percentages at age 15, 16 and 17 are now about the same (54, 24–23, 14–15) for comprehensive schools as for all other schools put together. Since most comprehensive schools get a lower average IQ at intake their performance in promoting staying-on rates is still therefore superior. (Calculations from figures in *Statistics of Education. England and Wales*, vol. I, 1970, H.M.S.O., pp. 18–19.)

[62] Until society finds some better way of occupying unemployed juveniles school is a better place for them to develop than the street.

[63] Hence the writer was sometimes met by requests from such mothers to give their children the cane rather than keep them in for detention after 4 o'clock. The children concerned were needed—in large families particularly—for going errands, often done daily by these families, in the effort to spin the money and the food out till the next pay-day. Moreover, the word "detention" itself smacked of the dangerous concept "prison" to some of these families, whereas caning was no more important to them than the "battering" the parents gave their children themselves.

ledge about the old, but chicken suppers on a house or year basis have been tried in some schools, with or without an educational talk afterwards. Elsewhere we hear of Christmas Fairs, Harvest Homes and the like, with the parents helping out. In other places baby-sitters for parents with young children are provided from the sixth form so that parents can attend meetings. Some schools, as it were, take the school to the parents and hold local "surgeries".

It is also in the context of parental involvement that the teacher–social worker has an important role to play, by trying to get on easy, relaxed terms with parents as a preliminary to informal help and advice that will further their children's progress at school. He can, in addition, try to discover what problems the child and the family face and how they might be considered or even catered for at the school end.

But what if the chicken suppers cannot be afforded, the fathers and mothers "don't like" coming to school to help out, or treat the teacher–social worker as hostilely as some treat the welfare or attendance officer and accuse him of unwarranted interference? What if all the efforts to entice certain parents into school go off like damp squibs? We are still left with a few who do not come to school and apparently cannot be lured there, except in bad temper or if their child is in serious trouble.

It is the writer's conviction[64] that, to impress all parents with the importance of their taking a serious interest in their children's education and of consulting the school regularly, and to have some lever on this group of parents particularly, some administrative measure should be introduced, whether by a local by-law or by the school with the support of the local authority, to compel parents to come to school at least once a year to discuss the school's report on the child. The parents of some children do not receive the school report even if it is posted to them, their offspring taking good care to see they do not get it. If such a measure were introduced, some parents who are both too poor and too shy to come to school now would be convinced of the seriousness of the need to consult the school. Others who do not come or who are hostile and belligerent—and they are relatively few—might perhaps be induced to come or at least to adopt a more co-operative attitude, if they got a really warm welcome on arrival at the school.[65] But "first catch your hare . . .".

A final comment. We compel parents to see that their children attend school and fine them if they do not. There is no logical reason why we should not also compel them to consult the school and so help to ensure their children take advantage of their schooling. Certainly, a point at which serious efforts should be made towards setting up arrangements for regular consultation with parents would be in cases of truancy or poor literacy. In the latter case steps could be taken to show parents how to supplement the school's efforts. Many parents would welcome simple tuition from the remedial department that would enable them to improve their children's reading performance. Such classes have been arranged in some

[64] This conviction is based on relevant experience. An attendance of forty parents at a parents' meeting, from a school of 700, was turned into a 96 per cent attendance at a third-year course choice meeting by a change of policy. Three different days and times were provided for the meetings. It was also intimated that the school *could* not and would not take the responsibility for promoting pupils into the fourth year unless the parents saw the school staff to help with the discussions on fourth-year course choices. Children, not wishing to be separated from their friends, put pressure on parents and parents attended the meetings. The 4 per cent that did not were going to have to be seen anyway, and were. The school's parents' meetings were always well attended subsequently, the ice having been broken, and the parents convinced that we were doing our level best for their children. None the less, the school had had qualms at taking such drastic measures and had stuck to the hope that, if the move got adverse publicity in the local newspaper, even this could, with a little editorial help, be turned to good account. In the event we got none.

[65] I know of one headmaster who regularly offers such parents a lift home in his car if it can be conveniently arranged. This works wonders for relationships.

places If parents are not literate themselves, this would provide an opportunity for giving them the chance to become so, a chance many adults might welcome in view of the stigma that illiteracy confers and the inconvenience it causes.

Other Ways of Influencing Motivation

1. *Counselling.* The effects of counselling, both group and individual, on motivation have also been studied by research workers. Two investigations[66] showed that 10-minute individual counselling interviews twice a week produced a significant improvement in academic performance and attendance at school, compared with the results for a control group. Another study[67] found improvement occurred in reading and use of English and in levels of aspiration and vocational development. There is also evidence of reduction in levels of anxiety amongst youngsters in the transition from school to work as a result of small group counselling.[68]

2. *Work experience.* In the last few years, in the effort to make the curriculum more relevant to the needs and aspirations of teenagers, a movement towards introducing work experience has developed in a number of countries. Soviet Russia was the first to start such a movement.[69] Her first attempt failed and was abandoned, her most recent experiment has been modified. Sweden and the United States have also experimented along these lines, amongst others. A review of American work study programmes has highlighted nine projects as of particular value. The Mott Foundation programme in Flint, Michigan,[70] for example, involved pupils in going to school in the morning and attending work in the afternoon. School attendance increased, work skills were acquired and there were fewer dropouts. In their review of research on compensatory education, Bloom *et al.*[71] were led to recommend work-study projects as well as emphasis on language and reading. Another study[72] showed that work experience significantly and favourably modified academic performance and school attendance. But such programmes need to be very well thought out,[73] and to be thoroughly accepted by employers.

Thus Professor Barlow, chief architect of the American Vocational Education Act of 1968, set up a project involving occupations in the area of health, which urgently needs trained workers. Of the 100 pupils partaking, 15 per cent were able, 60 per cent average and 25 per cent low achievers. Each pupil was assigned to follow a member of the hospital staff

[66] McGowan, R. J., The effect of brief contact interviews with low ability, low achieving students, *The School Counselor*, vol. 15, 1968, pp. 386–9. Benson, R. C. and Blocker, D. H., Evaluation of developmental counseling with groups of low achievers in a high school setting, *ibid.*, vol. 14, 1967, pp. 215–20.

[67] Gilliland, B. E., Small group counseling with Negro adolescents in a public high school, *J. Counseling Psychol.*, vol. 15, 1968, pp. 147–52.

[68] Clements, B. E., Transitional adolescent anxiety and group counseling, *Personnel and Guidance J.*, vol. 45, 1966, pp. 67–71.

[69] See p. 74.

[70] Burchill, G. W., *Work Study Programs for Alienated Youth: a Casebook*, Science Research Abstracts, Chicago, 1962.

[71] Bloom, S. B., Davies, A. and Hess, R., *Compensatory Education for the Culturally Deprived*, Holt, Rinehart & Winston, New York, 1965, p. 38. N.B. In developing countries it has been found helpful to tie in literacy programmes for adults with job opportunities. Basically, this is the same problem, at a different level.

[72] Bunda, R. and Mazzan, J., The effects of a work experience program on the performance of potential dropouts, *The School Counselor*, vol. 15, 1968, pp. 272–4.

[73] For an account of a British example, see Day, Alison, Work experience, *Times Educ. Suppl.*, 8 Oct. 1971, p. 34.

around regularly and to question him about his job. Results so far suggest much improved attendance and motivation for school, as pupils realize the educational implications of particular jobs. They also suggest the value of a prevocational slant to learning provided the vocational areas being prepared for are those where vacancies really exist.

3. *Miscellaneous.* The importance of motivation in improving attainment can also be seen from the results of the Chicago Literacy Programme for high-school dropouts. Over 60 per cent of those taking part made on average 2 years' progress in less than 5 months' full-time instruction. A spell of unemployment on leaving school had convinced them of the need for literacy.[74] Our problem is to convince some pupils of the need for education and of the willingness of the school to help them to it before the end of compulsory schooling.

The difficulty of maintaining motivation that has been artificially induced in school is illustrated by a study in which achievement motivation training was given to under-achieving high-school boys.[75] The immediate effect was to improve the motivation of both high and low social-class boys. When the training effect was measured 6 months later, the increase had been retained by the high social-class pupils but lost by the lower. The latter were in an environment not supporting or rewarding induced achievement motivation. With them, for the training to be ultimately effective, it would have had to be continued.

The Role of the Teacher in Improving Motivation

1. *The personality of the teacher.* However good the curriculum, the educational process for the under-achievers, as for all children, is strongly affected by personal interaction with their teachers. Few teachers seem to be effective with all types of pupils, all seem to be effective with some. At the same time a number of studies suggest that teachers with a warm personality,[76] other things being equal, are the most effective of all in promoting better motivation and achievement. Such teachers reduce anxiety levels and are more likely to be seen by their pupils as models. Certain behavioural characteristics of teachers are thought to have positive effects on pupils' views of themselves, which in turn affect learning positively. What these characteristics are is not, however, known in detail. Moreover, since identification of self with another is an important motivation inducer, success or failure in improving achievement levels in deprived children may depend not only on the teacher's warmth, but also on the extent to which they see him as trying to promote their own best goals,[77] and therefore the extent to which they can identify with him.

The need for "warmth" in counsellors has also been demonstrated. Low achievers were found to respond best to a "warm" attitude on the part of counsellors. Accurate empathy, non-possessive warmth and genuineness in the counsellor produced significant improvements

[74] Encouraging results have also been achieved in British army courses for illiterate recruits.

[75] *Rev. Educ. Res.*, vol. 35, no. 5, Dec. 1965.

[76] McDill *et al.*, *op. cit.*, p. 12.

[77] Gottlieb's research on the role of the teacher showed that important factors in teacher–pupil relationships were that the pupil must see that his goals are the same as those of his teacher and that the teacher has the ability and the desire to help him attain them. He also found that lower-class youngsters were less likely to perceive the teacher as wanting to help them reach their goals. Perhaps this finding accounts for the practice of some heads in placing with culturally deprived classes teachers "who can speak to them in their own language", or teachers whose own origins are in the working class. (Research reported in *Rev. Educ. Res.*, *op. cit.*)

in academic performance, so that 71 per cent of thus counselled pupils moved from "probationary" to "passing" status, compared with only 46 per cent of the control group.[78]

Clearly a question that heads should consider in appointing a counsellor or in allocating teachers to classes where there are many low achievers is whether the personalities of these members of staff are such as to make identification of the pupils with them likely.

2. *The teacher's approach.* There are various aspects of the teacher's approach which have relevance for levels of attainment. A more stable level of performance is better maintained in a democratically oriented classroom than in either an authoritarian or a *laissez faire* classroom. Even when the teacher is out of class the output is higher.[79] Teachers also need to consider the pupil's past emotional conditioning in conducting classroom activity.[80] If they are to operate effectively they have to be aware of the way in which their pupils' behaviour in class is related to, and conditioned by, socio-cultural differences in pupils' background and the way in which the culture clash between teacher and taught affects the latter's behaviour.

At the same time, the tendency amongst teachers to accept lower standards of output from socially deprived children tends to reinforce these children's low criteria of work and provides the best predictor of continual performance at that level.[81] On the other hand, unrealistic expectations are likely to increase anxiety levels, which in turn promote lower achievement.[82] Teachers of these children are for ever on a tightrope.

What, it would appear, teachers of low-achieving adolescents have to do is first to arrange for success at the activity to be learnt and to recondition pupils long made apathetic by failure to a history of success with material at their immediate level.[83] Experiments with teaching reading found that emphasizing daily success was very effective.[84] In other words, attitudes have to be altered, through the teaching process, before skills can be learnt. Programmed texts in some subjects are relevant in this context. There is some evidence that their use by-passes the hostility to the teacher in the low achieving and the disturbed. More informal step-by-step structuring of the material would also be relevant. Belief in the children, willing acceptance of them and continual praise are also necessary if the children are to fight their way back from apathy and hostility. All learning psychologists emphasize that rewards[85] promote learning; extrinsic rewards are useful and should be used, but the best reinforcer is the feeling of success. Only when children have re-established their self-confidence can material that is a little harder be placed in front of them, but the ultimate goal has always to be kept in view. All this is very much easier to tell of than to accomplish. It requires a high degree of skill in the teacher. Joyce's analysis of the job of the teacher of

[78] Dickinson, W. A. and Truax, C. B., Group counseling with college underachievers, *Personnel and Guidance J.* vol. 45, 1966, pp. 245–7.

[79] Lewin, K., Lippitt, R. and White, R. K., Patterns of aggressive behaviour in experimentally created social climates, *J. Social Psychol.*, vol. 10, 1939, pp. 271–99. Anderson, H. H. and Brewer, J. E., Studies of teachers' classroom personalities. *Applied Psychology Monographs*, 1946, no. 6, pp. 106–8, pp. 145–9. Wall, W. D., The wish to learn, *Educ. Res.*, vol. 1, no. 1, 1958, pp. 23–37.

[80] White, W. F., *Psychosocial Principles Applied to Classroom Teaching*, McGraw-Hill, 1969, p. 88. At the individual level, this can be a counsel of perfection, in the classroom context.

[81] *Ibid.*, p. 87.

[82] Sarason, G. *et al.*, The effect of differential instructions on anxiety and learning, *J. Abnormal and Social Psychol.*, vol. 47, 1952, pp. 561–5.

[83] White, *op. cit.*, p. 7.

[84] *Ibid.*, p. 91.

[85] *Ibid.*, p. 20–1.

the culturally deprived showed their need for a wide variety of skills and a capacity to use them under different conditions. Such a high degree and versatility of skill demand the rate for the job. It also demands a high degree of training, including experience in deprived areas during training.[86]

One might assume that if warmth in a teacher is a significant factor in pupils' achievements, similarly warmth in the overall school climate would also be so. The measures of "intimacy", i.e. warmth of interaction, between teachers and headmaster, on the OCDQ school climate[87] scale do show that there is some relationship, but it is a small one, amounting to only 3 per cent of the total achievement of pupils. In many ways this is not surprising, since this "warmth" operates at one remove from the pupil and there are many other factors which operate on him more strongly and from nearer to him.[88] The influence of the teacher is more important than the influence of the school.[89]

In spite of the research done it is clear that we do not yet know all that we need to know about the influence of the teacher on the pupil, especially those in disadvantaged areas, and the factors that affect their influence. The Plowden recommendation that experienced teachers should be sent on training courses so that they might act as teacher–social workers is relevant in this regard. Their further experience in the field would throw up data that would provide hypotheses for research. Tested hypotheses are the most fruitful source of increased knowledge of a really sure kind, surer than the anecdotal,[90] that will help us to promote the full development of a deprived child's potential.

The Growth Tasks of Adolescence

So far the main studies on motivation and attitudes we have reviewed have produced a number of ideas that could be implemented by schools, but few of them are of a kind that can be directly implemented in the curriculum. We have to turn to the known growth tasks of adolescence before curricular implications are strongly visible.

Wall[91] suggests that there are in adolescence four main growth tasks, social, sexual, vocational and philosophic.

> Between say 13 and 25, the growing boy or girl has to develop a social self, oriented to others, aware of a place in society, of duties as well as privileges, and in general emancipated from egocentric dependence on parents or indeed on others. A sexual self too must be shaped, capable of a range of feeling from friendly indifference to deep involvement with a member of the opposite sex, adequate adjustment in marriage and the ability to found and care for a family. For the boy, and increasingly for the girl, vocational adjustment, a working self, is also essential, not only to economic independence but as a basis of self-respect and self-knowledge. This aspect is complex and consists of both a certain satisfaction derived from work and of a sense of being needed, and of being something more than a replaceable unit. Finally, however simple it may be, most of us need an interpretation of life, philosophic, religious, political, vaguely or clearly formulated, something by reference to which major decisions can be taken and the behaviour and attitudes of others understood.

---

[86] *Ibid.*

[87] See p. 86.

[88] Andrews, J. H., School organizational climate: some validity studies, *Can. Educ. Res. Dig.*, vol. 5, 1965, pp. 317–34.

[89] N.B. It is also clear that schools in disadvantaged areas have shown less "openness" in overall school climate, on the complete OCDQ scale, which measures along a continuum from very "open" to very "closed" climates. See p. 89.

[90] Not that the anecdotal is to be despised. If there are enough anecdotes pointing in the same direction, a research worker has a useful hypothesis to start from.

[91] Wall, W. D., *op. cit.*, 1968, p. 13.

The growth tasks of adolescence include verbal and intellectual components, it is true, but if, as Wall says, we compare the goals in detail with the content and manner of the education provided for teenagers, there is a large discrepancy between the two. The present curriculum of subject disciplines,[92] unsupported by anything else and with little effort made to indicate the relevance they may have for a pupil's present or his future, do not provide the material or the motivation for the accomplishment of the growth tasks of adolescence, especially in the case of the less able child, whose curiosity about academic disciplines has been blunted by repeated failure. We will return to this issue at a later stage.

Conclusion. It would appear that there are various initiatives, apart from curricular decisions, which a school can take to improve motivation in the disadvantaged child.

First, it can try to strengthen pupils' sense of control of their environment and it has been suggested that one important way of doing this would be to make certain that they really grasped what the comprehensive school can offer them in the way of different course options and the sorts of jobs these can lead to. Moreover, it seems likely that the raising of the school-leaving age to 16, which would enable almost all, perhaps all, pupils to sit for a public examination in at least one subject will enhance this sense of control and hence their motivation, because hard work rather than luck is the key to control. For many children there has never been any opportunity of sitting for a public examination, as long as the end of compulsory schooling was at age 15. They have had no real incentive for working hard in the early and middle teens, except to please teachers, a motive not calculated to appeal to adolescent boys especially, or out of curiosity or for sheer pleasure of learning; both of these last have been damped down by repeated failure.

Secondly, really determined efforts will have to be made to involve parents of deprived children with the school and with its aims for their children. In some cases what we really have to do is to educate the parents themselves. We shall not learn how this may be done if we do not get them to the school. Schools in deprived areas are going to need extra staff if the massive sort of operation they need is to be mounted. Since deprived children are probably functioning in many cases at as much as 20 IQ points below their true capacity by comparison with middle-class children, every effort needs making to improve their performance so as to reduce this gap for the next generation.

Thirdly, counselling would appear to be of some use in improving attainment, by stimulating better motivation and a more realistic assessment of job possibilities in relation to educational potential.

Fourthly, we ought further to develop more and better work experience programmes so that pupils can better assess the job situation and be more gently eased from school into work.

Lastly, we can train and retrain our teachers better, so that they are more aware of (a) the effects of their attitudes to deprived children, on the development of the latter's self-respect, and (b) the effects of cultural deprivation on children's learning capacity.

Of all the above courses of action it is difficult to establish, from research, an order of priorities. Indeed much educational research has concentrated on deciding which of two alternatives is better when, for policy-making in a school, one often requires to establish a series of priorities as regards several courses of action. Hence the need for "systems analysis" techniques to be applied in educational research.

[92] For discussion on this point, see pp. 69–71.

However, the evidence presented does suggest, for example, that if we have to choose between allotting effort and expense to getting parents involved in their children's schooling and allotting the same effort and expense to counselling of children without reference to parents, the first is likely to produce greater results.[93]

D. Purely Cognitive Development

Given that our main aim must be to improve motivation in deprived children at the secondary stage, because the cognitive development is likely to be small, we must still investigate what leads there are as to how to achieve purely cognitive improvement, as opposed to cognitive improvement induced by better motivation. It is not, of course, very easy to separate the two.

From the spate of programmes of compensatory education begun by the American "Head Start" we can gain a few clues, though most of the programmes were developed without any attempt to evaluate them scientifically. Indeed it has been well said that compensatory education is being undertaken in the absence of knowledge of whether, for example, there are right points at which to start a particular programme, because of the stage of development a child has reached; of whether the results achieved are due to programme or maturational effects; of whether there are delayed effects requiring long-term evaluation; of whether the "fade-out" so often encountered in the pre-school programmes, when a child starts school and soon loses his advantage, is due, for example, to the child with pre-school experience taking his cue as to standards from the other children or to a rapid spurt occurring in the others when they start school, a phenomenon known to occur from other sources.

Given this welter of ignorance, what clues are there that would be of service to a secondary school teacher? Two papers[94] describe the results of programmes that were properly evaluated, the one reporting the results of 100 programmes, the other fifteen. Most of them were not conducted at the secondary level, but at primary and pre-school level. However, in the paucity of evidence we must look for leads where we can.

Successful projects were found in both investigations to be characterized by

(a) careful planning and a clear statement of academic objectives;
(b) systematic procedures and time schedules for the implementation of plans;
(c) small groups, e.g. of five pupils, and a high degree of individualization of instruction;
(d) instruction and materials that were relevant and closely linked to the objectives of the programme;
(e) high intensity of treatment;
(f) teacher training in the methods of the programme.

In the second paper Posner also urged that funds should be allocated at all maturational levels, pre-school, primary and secondary, in spite of Bloom's finding that most intellectual development takes place in the pre-school years, and that they should not be concentrated

[93] See p. 31.

[94] Hawkridge, D. G., Tallmadge, G. R. and Larsen, J. K., *Foundations for Success in Educating Disadvantaged Children*, U.S. Office of Education final report, project 107143, 1968, and Posner, J., *Evaluation of "Successful" Projects in Compensatory Education*, U.S. Office of Education, Office of Planning and Evaluation, Occasional paper no. 8, 1968, quoted by McDill, E. L., McDill, M. S. and Sprehe, J. T., *Strategies for Success in Compensatory Education*, Johns Hopkins, Baltimore, 1969, pp. 55–7.

on pre-school programmes to the extent of strangling efforts in the schools. He found that some of the more successful pay-offs relative to cost had been achieved with students who were more mature chronologically. The Homework Helpers programme in New York City, for example, had shown gains in reading skills for both the culturally deprived adolescent tutors and their young primary-school pupils, an excellent example of positive results at low cost.

There have been two outstanding programmes in the U.S.A., the Bereiter–Engelmann Academic Pre-School Program and the Early Training Project at Peabody College, Nashville, Tennessee.[95]

The former taught language, reading and arithmetic skills, using a very structured approach. Specific learning objectives were stated and teaching methods to achieve them developed, involving specification of well-defined concepts and procedures for each subject, with a heavy emphasis on constructions and intensive drills in predetermined sequences. Classes were conducted, with groups of five children in each class, for 2 hours daily 5 days a week for a whole academic year. The children concerned were extremely deprived. They were told what they were to learn, what the criteria of learning were and what the usefulness of the material would be in the larger social world. Cognitive, not socio-emotional, development was the main objective. Teachers were suitably trained and parents involved. This programme consistently achieved measurable, sustained results, with no "fade-out" in the following years. It was scientifically shown[96] to achieve better cognitive results than other less highly structured programmes, or programmes "emphasizing social objectives and the broadening of experience with the world". Not perhaps surprising with children under 5, in the latter case. One difficulty of applying these findings at the secondary level would be that the 14- or 15-year-old semi-literate pupil's thirst for knowledge has largely been exhausted. He would not put up with 2 hours of intensive language drill except under army orders, though he might put up with a lesser amount if the prize were literacy.

The Early Training Project[97] had both a cognitive and an affective aspect. Perceptual development (perception of similarities and differences), concept formation (classifying, reclassifying and generalizing) and language development were stressed in the cognitive programme. On the affective side, steps were taken to establish confidence and promote striving and valuation of achievement, by exposing pupils to situations in which they could compete successfully; increasing small, but personally advantageous, delays in seeking gratification were also induced. Interest in activities related to school and identification with suitable role models, especially through contact with males for children without fathers, were stimulated. Mothers were given instruction over an extensive period on how to help their children. Attempts to measure motivational aspects of the programme were unsuccessful, due to the lack of appropriate measuring tools, but testing of cognitive development showed permanent improvement relative to control groups.

Although there is little research material of real worth on compensatory education at the secondary level, what there is seems to confirm the value of the Bereiter–Engelmann

[95] Bereiter, C. and Engelmann, S., *Teaching Disadvantaged Children in the Pre-School Environment*, Prentice Hall, Englewood Cliffs, N.J., 1966. The programmewas evaluated by Rusk (quoted by McDill, *op. cit.*, p. 59.)

[96] Karnes, M. B., A research programme to determine the effects of various pre-school intervention programs in the development of disadvantaged children and the strategic age for such intervention. Paper presented at A.E.R.A. meeting, Chicago, 1968, and quoted by McDill *et al.* (1969), p. 60. The results were confirmed in another paper by Rusk presented at the A.E.R.A. meeting, Los Angeles, 1969.

[97] Quoted by McDill, pp. 62–5.

approach, namely the use of very structured material. A study by Woolman describes a secondary-school programme in which the use of specially constructed materials, designed to allow each student to proceed at his own rate, directed to the interests and values of the children, and providing step-by-step procedures, which were adaptable to any setting and required the minimum of participation by teachers, produced average gains of 1·28 years among culturally deprived youth after only 40 hours of instruction. Another study employed very effective teachers, using material already available and an intensive remedial and developmental approach, and produced 1·5 years' average gain of reading score for thirty-five youths aged 14 to 17.[98] Another attempt at improving reading skills also produced significant results. The programme provided extensive reading materials in special reading rooms, with aides to assist in routine duties and in programmed exercises carried out 1 day a week. Failure rates fell and students read and wrote more.[99]

The drift of all these researches is clear. For children requiring remedial instruction, a structured and intensive approach, with carefully specified objectives, step-by-step procedures and carefully worked-out techniques to meet the objectives, is the most successful in eliminating disabilities in skills. Part of the success of these procedures would seem, incidentally, to derive from the fact that they arrange for success at the activity to be learnt, by the clarity, specificity and step-by-step character of the teaching style. As has already been indicated,[100] it is known that anxiety, unless of a mild kind, correlates with failure, that success has to be arranged for, and that these pupils who, by their long linguistic, social and educational history, have been conditioned to failure, have to be reconditioned in their attitudes by success. Step-by-step procedures, which take a little at a time and enable a child to experience success and to consolidate his gains, have therefore motivational as well as cognitive advantages, provided that at other times the pupil's educational diet is varied and attractive. Success in the secondary school depends more on attitude and motivation than on any other school factor.[101]

Variability amongst Deprived Children

The studies reported on pp. 23–4 indicated variability in attitudes to school and in learning styles amongst deprived children. The implication is that different groups of them need different approaches. This means an expansion of our repertoires of teaching techniques, since several investigations have shown that different curricula and methods have different effects on different children. However, all that this implies in respect of curricular planning is by no means clear. It does seem likely that it will be more profitable for a teacher to ask for "many good answers" rather than for one unique solution, in all those subjects where such an approach is appropriate, for example, in subjects where the main emphasis is on content.

E. Some Final Comments

Extent of the Problem

How large is the group of children who are culturally deprived? This question is somewhat

[98] Both studies reported in *Rev. Educ. Res.*, vol. 35, no. 5, Dec. 1965, p. 88.
[99] Reported in *Rev. Educ. Res.*, vol. 36, no. 4, Oct. 1966, p. 418.
[100] See p. 36.
[101] Wiseman, S., *Education and Environment*, Manchester Univ. Press, 1964, p. 161.

difficult to answer in terms of IQ or reading disabilities, since many children who are culturally deprived do not rank as E.S.N. or near it or have reading disabilities.[102] They are none the less functioning at a lower level than their potential. Moreover, even if one could name a national average, this would be singularly unhelpful to the head and staff of a particular school, that is unless by chance the proportions of such children in it were large enough to enable the school to qualify for more extra money than is envisaged by the present Educational Priority Areas scheme. Also, speaking practically from the teaching point of view, there are two points at which cultural deprivation really hits the school. The first and least obvious as the effect of cultural deprivation is the cut-off point between Piagetian concrete operational and formal operational thinking. When children do not attain the capacity for abstract thought, some of the objectives of the secondary school curriculum cannot be achieved and lower cognitive objectives have to be accepted, if stimulus measures prove ineffective. The second and most serious level at which cultural deprivation hits the school, especially the unstreamed school, is at the literacy threshold. If a child cannot read reasonably easily by the time he reaches secondary school, his plight is desperate. In an unstreamed school he cannot read the worksheets or write the answers.

Wall[103] suggests that about one pupil in five, *on average*, has a serious reading handicap. On sheer ability levels one would expect the figure to be one, in ten only. The group of pupils with reading disabilities which they should not have in terms of measured IQ will include the maladjusted,[104] since it is known that few maladjusted children do well at school,[105] some of the delinquents, especially the truants,[106] and those who have experienced poor primary school preparation.

The measures taken to deal with poor reading ability not mainly due to low IQ will of course vary according to the predisposing cause. Where maladjustment is the culprit, the help of the form teacher, the school counsellor[107] and, in the worst cases, the child-guidance clinic have in their turn to be invoked in the effort to free the child from the emotional distortions which are affecting his school performance. Where truancy is the cause and it is due more to the forces of the sub-culture rather than to individual maladjustment, a well-thought-out scheme of prevention is at least part of the answer.[108] As long as a child is not in school he cannot take in what the school has to offer.

Effects of Stimulating Cognitive Growth on Emotional and Behaviour Problems

It seems possible that successful attempts to prevent or remedy mild mental retardation that is culturally induced would lessen the incidence of behaviour problems in the secondary school. Douglas, as has been noted, found lower-class children seven times as likely to appear before the courts as middle-class children. There is other evidence of long

[102] See p. 25.

[103] *Op. cit.*, p. 114.

[104] Estimates from eight investigations in the U.S.A., New Zealand, Britain and France suggest 4–12 per cent of children have *serious* maladjustment (Wall, *op. cit.*, p. 111).

[105] Chazan, M., The relationships between maladjustment and backwardness, *Educ. Rev.*, vol. 15, 1962, pp. 54–61. Backward readers often show some symptoms of maladjustment, as many as 60–80 per cent.

[106] The writer noted a consistent relationship between school failure and the typical truancy pattern of odd days off, over a period of 5 years in a school in a difficult area.

[107] See p. 62 for the report by Kennedy on the successful treatment of fifty cases of school phobia by school counselling.

[108] One Liverpool school has taken measures which have reduced the incidence of truancy considerably.

standing of a relationship between low literacy levels and behaviour and delinquency problems. Many teachers must have noticed that it is the very same children who find most difficulty in grasping abstract concepts who are most often in trouble, are least amenable to appeals to their moral sense, however simply the appeal is expressed, and find the greatest difficulty in giving reasons for their behaviour, of whatever kind it may be.[109] There is some evidence that increasing cognitive growth is accompanied by increasing capacity to experience guilt.[110] Inability to understand, for example, grammatical structures is therefore likely to be accompanied by inability to appreciate moral issues and by the tendency to hit out rather than to take thought in a difficulty. These children do not make the step from Piaget's concrete operational stage to his formal operational stage in any of the aspects of their lives, and their handicap is therefore as serious at the moral as at the mental level.[111] Anything that can help them to make this step seems likely also to reduce the incidence of behaviour problems.

Society's Role in Respect of Deprivation

Whatever may be done by the educational system to improve the abilities and achievements of deprived children should not blind us to the responsibilities of society as a whole. Evidence gathered in the United States with regard to the education of negroes has shown that since money was at last poured into the schools for negroes in the southern states, in the attempt to avoid desegregation, their educational level has gone up considerably. Also, Sherif[112] reported that an increase in the socio-economic level of an area was followed by a rise in occupational, educational and financial goals. Evidence is building up round the world of a link between economic and educational levels.

There exists a highly suspicious relationship between poor health, poor nutrition, difficult pregnancy and birth histories and low school achievement, even if we do not know precisely what the elements in that relationship are. That such a relationship exists is shown in a general way by several surveys in the United Kingdom and in America,[113] and is confirmed by the evidence about the rise of reading levels in Britain since the war during a period of increasing economic growth. In each of the surveys mentioned improved economic and social environments for whole populations have been accompanied by a rise in IQ levels and a decline in the frequency of mental retardation. We are not likely to get rid of mild mental retardation that has been culturally induced without programmes of economic and social advance as well as educational programmes. Although the abandonment of selection is improving staying-on rates and perhaps educational performance there are limits to the progress which the comprehensive school movement can achieve in reducing cultural deprivation.

The conclusion come to by Stein and Susser in the *Review of Educational Research*[114] is that there is good evidence in both individuals and populations of systematic changes in IQ

[109] The ubiquitous answers "I don't know, miss" or "I don't know, sir", so often given by less able children.
[110] Katz, P. and Zigler, E., Self-image disparity: a developmental approach, *J. Personality and Social Psychol.*, vol. 5, 1967, pp. 186–95.
[111] Hence probably, at least to some extent, the reason why they appear in court more often than middle-class children, who more often reach the formal operational stage. Hence also the fact that they are less influenced by symbolic rewards than middle-class children.
[112] Sherif, M. and Sherif, C. W., *Reference Groups*, Harper & Row, New York, 1964, p. 259.
[113] England (Leicester) 1930 and 1949, Scotland 1933 and 1947, U.S.A. 1930 and 1940.
[114] Vol. 40, no. 1, Feb. 1970, pp. 63–4.

being brought about by other changes. With regard to individuals the greatest improvement, and the greatest deterioration, is produced by a total exposure to a new favourable, or a new unfavourable, environment. The degree of change in the IQ depends partly on the age of the individual and partly on the degree of exposure to the new situation. In whole populations the changes of IQ are related to improvements in the social environment of disadvantaged groups. The greatest progress will come, as it has in the past, from a concerted attack on poverty, unemployment, poor housing and a poor and inappropriate education. Society is not entitled to rely on the school for everything in the attempt to improve the lot of the culturally deprived, but it must be able to rely on the school to be effective within its own province, limited though that is.

CHAPTER 4

Reorganization and the Guidance and Counselling Movement

IT WOULD appear to be more than a mere coincidence that, just as in the U.S.A. school counsellors began to be appointed to high schools in small numbers after the schools had developed into common high schools taking in pupils of all levels of ability, so in Great Britain the establishment of comprehensive schools has also been followed, at least in a few of the larger ones, by the appointment of counsellors. It seems as if, when schools begin to take in all ranges of ability, they are obliged to undertake a more formal appraisal of a role which has already been theirs but of which they have been perhaps to some extent unaware. Probably within the next few years the school counsellor will become an integral part of a British comprehensive-school staff.

At the same time it is clear that it is not merely a broadening of the intellectual intake inside the schools which has led to the introduction of counsellors. In past centuries and in many regions of the world schools have taught children of a very wide range of ability. Yet they felt no need to introduce counsellors. Why not?

The evidence would seem to suggest that, in past centuries and in other societies, firstly, guidance was undertaken by other institutions than the school and that, secondly, the avenues along which the young were to be guided were far fewer. Perhaps the clearest examples of societal guidance systems are the caste system of India and the feudal system of Europe. In the former and to a large extent in the latter everyone's future was mapped out from birth to death, by the very accident of birth. Any guidance system within the schools of these societies would have been completely superfluous.

At the same time we should distinguish between guidance systems in schools and guidance functions of schools. It is possible for a school to have a guidance function even though it employs no guidance specialists, and nowhere more than in a society based on, or moving towards, a social class system or in an educational system characterized by selection. Thus the medieval Latin school delimited, advantageously, the student's future, as did the eighteenth-century academy or the nineteenth or twentieth-century academic grammar school, by the kind of curriculum and pre-vocational preparation it offered him. How important the vocational guidance function of the grammar school has been can be seen from the pressure to gain entry to it. That function was, however, able to be performed for a very long time without the services of any specialist in guidance. This was because the purpose of the school was to prepare students for a rather narrow range of future positions, within the compass of every schoolmaster's capacity to advise. It was also because the whole range of careers in past times was rather restricted and because in a socially rather immobile society only a few people moved outside their own native social orbit. Hence the academic grammar school's traditional tendency to provide little or no vocational guidance until the end of the school course, which survives even now. Admission to grammar school already constitutes guidance and it was traditionally assumed also that all parents with children at grammar school would be knowledgeable enough, along with the form master, to map out a suitable career for them.

Secondary schools for all pupils, however, have a much more complex task of vocational guidance than the academically slanted grammar school, simply because they take in all children. Democratization of education transforms pupil guidance because it transforms the role of the school in society. The guidance function of the school, within the school, becomes much more obvious in consequence and the need for a more formal appraisal of the task more evident.

A. Vocational Guidance

The Impact of Technological Development on the Guidance Process

The traditional practice of the grammar school no longer fits the needs of modern industrial societies. Technological development, especially since 1900, has transformed the occupational structure, increasing the number, variety and specialization of jobs, has produced a growing demand for qualified and highly qualified labour[1] and has necessitated for all a more advanced kind of general and vocational education.

With the advent of a bewildering variety of occupations parents have been unable to fulfil their age-old function of offering their children advice on their future vocational roles. It is not that there is no information available to parents and their children. There is a welter of information if only they knew where to find it and could make sense of it all when they had found it, in terms of the standard and type of educational qualification required for admittance to particular occupations. Such research as is available in this country[2] shows that usually neither parents nor children know enough about the range of jobs in their locality, and do not know enough about what particular jobs entail. Hence a reasoned choice between occupations is not possible.[3] Jahoda[4] found that less than half of the fathers and only one-third of the mothers of secondary modern school pupils advised their children on jobs in the early 1950s and more recently the Government Social Survey found that a third of the parents of 15-year-old leavers still did not advise their children on this subject.[5] Even well-informed middle-class parents can often no longer cope with the task of advising their children on their vocational prospects and the type of secondary school course that a particular career demands. Moreover, the Government Social Survey also showed that 66 per cent of 15-year-olds wanted help from the school or the Youth Employment Officer in finding a job and 56 per cent wanted advice on what work they were best suited for.[6]

[1] The present recession appears likely to be only temporary.

[2] Carter, M. P., *Home, School and Work*, Pergamon Press, 1962, pp. 88–9.

[3] Self-recruitment is high amongst sons of unskilled workers and also amongst those of professional people. See: *Occupational Choice. Science Policy Studies* No. 2, Department of Education and Science, 1968, p. 9.

[4] Jahoda, L., Job attitudes and job choice among secondary school leavers. *Occupational Psychology* vol. 26, 1952, pp. 206–24.

[5] Schools Council Enquiry No. 1. *Young School Leavers*, H.M.S.O., 1968, p. 126. N.B. The reasons given suggest parents' diffidence in the face of headstrong youth or the wish to teach their offspring independence, but one wonders whether the real reasons do not go deeper and include unacknowledged diffidence in the face of a bewildering variety of jobs and a lack of access to information.

[6] *Ibid.*, p. 103.

The lack of readily available knowledge and advice from the school is known to result in some frustration of interests already developed by some pupils,[7] even in America, where guidance and counselling are much more common than they are in Britain. This may be particularly serious in the case of above-average working-class pupils, because of the rather strong influence of fathers and friends on their vocational choices, on which there is a fair amount of evidence. Wilson[8] also found that secondary modern school pupils' knowledge of jobs was not strongly related to level of intelligence. Some of the more intelligent will therefore go into jobs below their capacity.

One remedy for parental and pupil incapacity to sort out vocational prospects and their educational implications is for the school and the community to reappraise their own functions in this regard. The school in particular, as the agency nearest the children, has to widen its overt role to include more than the purely pedagogic. The new role in guidance and counselling is, however, a very complex one. In the end, therefore, the task has to be given to the paid professional, and to the specialist within the professional field at that, for even the form master now often finds himself out of his depth in this area.

British Attempts at Vocational Guidance

The first reaction to this changed situation in the British context came with the setting up of Apprenticeship and Skilled Employment committees in many cities by 1900, the undertaking of some vocational guidance work by Care committees and the passing of the Education (Choice of Employment) Act of 1910. This Act empowered L.E.A.s to help pupils in their choice of jobs. A standard school-leaving card was gradually introduced and between the wars the youth employment service began to develop.[9] After the passing of the Employment and Training Act of 1948 it emerged in its present form. Typically, the Careers Officer (formerly the Youth Employment Officer) now gives one group talk and one interview to every school leaver, and his services have more recently been extended to the grammar school.

Meanwhile the grammar school was responding to the pressure of this problem by appointing careers masters, and this practice gradually spread to other types of school also, so that, according to the Government Social Survey, most schools now give advice on jobs and careers. Typically the task of careers guidance was, and still is, allotted to a teacher mainly occupied with the teaching of a specialist subject or group of subjects who has not been specifically trained for careers work[10] and who may not have a clear idea of his role.[11] If the teacher is lucky, he may have a careers room, but more frequently he has to make do with a display shelf or two and a couple of racks inside or outside the library, devoted to books and pamphlets on careers.[12] He will be luckier still if he is allotted half a dozen periods for careers work with individual pupils and there is unlikely to be any provision on the school timetable for teaching whole classes or smaller groups about careers prospects.

[7] Powell, M. and Bloom, V., *The American Teenager*, Bobbs–Merrill, New York, 1958.

[8] Wilson, M. D., The vocational preferences of secondary modern school children, *Brit. J. Educ. Psychol.*, vol. XXIII nos. 2 and 3, 1953, pp. 97–113 and 163–79.

[9] Daws, P. P., *A Good Start in Life*, C.R.A.C., 1968, p. 6.

[10] *Schools Council Enquiry* No. 1, p. 121.

[11] Carter found that some careers teachers saw themselves as providing a counselling service, others as suppliers of information, others as including job placement in their work.

[12] The wide variations in provision have been documented in: Science Policy Studies No. 2, *Occupational Choice*. Department of Education and Science, 1968, p. 14.

Moreover, if there is, such periods will probably be timetabled too late in the school course for some children, who will already have made unfortunate subject choices. One consequence of this absence of thoroughgoing vocational guidance in the hands of someone whose special job it is to watch over pupils' vocational interests is that, when subject choices have to be made by a pupil, they tend to be made on the sole basis of his performance and interest in particular subjects and without reference to the career he has in view—if he has one—except in the case of high fliers aiming at higher education. Yet both interest and performance are likely to improve if a subject is seen by a pupil to have vocational relevance.

Another consequence is that when subject choices are made they are often made from the vocational point of view too early. The decision as to when a particular subject choice is made tends to be viewed only from the teaching point of view, that is to say, how long it will take the pupils concerned to reach a given—and unquestioned—standard within the framework of the current curricular arrangements,[13] and not from the point of view of how many pupils it is going to force into a curricular choice they will later regret. Yet in making curricular decisions, the educational system as a whole could, if it so desired, lay as much emphasis on future vocational aspects as on teaching aspects of these decisions.

Equally when, owing to an increase in numbers, additional staff are appointed to a school, they are likely to be used to put additional subjects on the timetable, once arrangements have been made to teach the additional numbers of children, rather than to advise pupils on the vocational implications of their curricular choices. Nor are L.E.A.s very keen in many instances on allowing any extra provision of staff for this purpose and, indeed, with the quota operating, they may not be able to. The school is thus viewed almost solely as a teaching institution, teaching as it were in a social and economic vacuum. Moreover, the power structure of the British school system enhances the probability that decisions will be taken on the basis of unquestioned teaching requirements. Although there are forces that bear on the school from the outside the real power structure within the school itself consists of the head and staff only. Parents exercise little influence on school policy. Yet they are the people likely to welcome vocationally based educational guidance for their children. Indeed one study has shown that 15-year-old school-leavers and their parents view the job of the school as largely to help them to get the knowledge and skills necessary to obtain the best jobs available, whereas teachers think their main job lies elsewhere, in the development of mind and personality.[14]

Yet the school has already been for over half a century the main channeller to jobs and, by the decisions entered into within the school, it has more often than not determined how many people and of what quality will be available to fill particular jobs 10 years after the decisions were taken.[15] Until they are sufficiently seized of their vocational role the schools

[13] Often, of course, the school has no option but to follow current curricular arrangements, because of university pressures.

[14] *Schools Council Enquiry* No. 1, p. 45.

[15] Currently, the British school has been, for example, engaged in committing academic suicide, as the numbers for the arts side of sixth forms were allowed to increase and those for the science side to decline. For years headmasters have wrung their hands because they cannot get suitably qualified science staff but have taken no steps whatsoever in their schools to ensure that the universities get at least approximately equal numbers of almost equally able candidates for the two sides. They have traditionally insisted on a minimum of four 'O' levels for entry into the sixth but have done nothing to produce incentives for pupils to go into the science sixth. Yet they have only to close the arts sixth list at a given number of pupils to induce some of the waverers between Arts and Science, who are intent on higher education in whatever faculty they can get into, to change their allegiance. And all this, without waiting for the implementation of any of the series of reports on the sixth form that have been issued by various bodies in the last 10 years. The schools are insufficiently

are not likely to take serious enough steps to study the future vocational problems of the children in their care.

It would seem that one of the effects of the rather poor careers guidance available in the British educational system is to increase the influence of family and friends on job choice to a greater degree than is warranted in an industrialized society that depends on social mobility for the throwing up of talent. Where family and friends are the source of job information, the range of jobs open to the student is thereby limited to the same sorts of jobs these contacts themselves occupy or know of.

Another effect, as has already been said, is to increase the incidence of wrong choices of subjects by pupils unaware of the vocational implications of these choices. Hence in many cases, home, peer group and school effects interact to ensure wastage of talent. Careers guidance, which in practice does not recognize the length of time during which occupational choice and selection are in fact being made, can do little to counteract this. Careers guidance has to be developmental.

Hence the rather poor guidance services provided by the British school and the Central Youth Employment Executive have only a small influence on the process of choosing a job. Few of the young know what a particular job entails and what its prospects are.[16] Jahoda found that the effectiveness of the Youth Employment Service as it was then called was limited and that it served only to confirm choices already made by the young.[17] She similarly found the influence of secondary modern teachers on boys' job choices small, as did Carter[18] later. In 1968 only 5 per cent of school-leavers said they would consult teachers, including careers teachers, about a job.[19] With regard to grammar schools the evidence is conflicting, Chown[20] and Hill obtaining contradictory results: Hill's study, the larger of the two, found the students in his sample did not receive very valuable advice.[21] Maizels, on the other hand, noted that boys who had got into skilled trades they wanted to enter had more often had teachers' advice than those that had not.

The help of the Youth Employment Officers (as they were then called) was found more helpful than that of career teachers by most early leavers, perhaps because of the placement help, as distinct from vocational counselling, offered by the Service with regard to the rather low level jobs many of them enter. The Careers Officer has, however, little time available for real vocational counselling at an earlier stage.

It may be, of course, that even if the vocational guidance service were very effective, its impact on the young would still be less than that of family and friends. However, until we have one that is, we cannot know. Meanwhile, the problem of finding the right job for the right child grows more complex every year, and as Wall has well said "the choice of and adjustment to work is crucial to adolescent and adult mental health, and anxieties and misadjustments arising in the years preceding and following school-leaving can in many

---

seized of the fact of their vocational role and therefore do not take steps to meet its demands, even to provide themselves with enough teachers to man the schools in the future, much less, say, to provide engineers who will earn the money needed by the educational system. Were it not for increased entry into higher education in the 1960s the schools would now be in an impossible position.

[16] Maizels, J., *Adolescent Needs and the Transition from School to Work*, Univ. of London Press, 1970, p. 308.

[17] Jahoda, L. (1952), *op. cit.*

[18] Carter, *op. cit.*, p. 43.

[19] *Schools Council Enquiry* No. 1, p. 129.

[20] Chown, S. M., The foundation of occupational choice amongst grammar school pupils, *Occupational Psychology*, vol. 32, no. 3, 1958, pp. 171–82.

[21] Hill, G. B., Choice of career by grammar school boys, *Occupational Psychology*, vol. 39, no. 4, 1965, pp. 279.

cases be traced to disturbances in the vocational field".[22] He also adds: "the problem is a complex one, not confined to the establishment of employment services but concerned with the much broader ones of personal, educational and vocational guidance in the setting of the whole transition period from full-time schooling to full-time gainful employment, involving close co-operation between the schools and factories or offices and between education, psychological, medical and industrial staff over at least the last two years of school and the first two years of work." Such a task cannot be undertaken from the school side by one careers teacher with half a dozen periods per week allotted for careers work. Yet this is still the position of vocational guidance in many British schools. Inevitably then, the guidance task of the school, which it has whether it likes the job or not, is done rather badly.

The Tools of Vocational Guidance

The necessity of a more sophisticated approach to vocational guidance than we have been used to is evident. What techniques, tools and information are at our disposal, and are they good enough to be of use?

In undertaking vocational guidance we are assuming that the young have different basic capacities, which we must discover, and that individual happiness and social efficiency and harmony depend on fitting each person as far as possible into his right niche. The basis of modern guidance is therefore conceived of in terms of discovering (a) the aptitudes and capacities of each individual and (b) the needs of society and the economy, and of trying to match the two. Vocational guidance therefore, if properly conducted, is heavily dependent on a knowledge of the date of appearance of specific aptitudes and interests, as well as on a knowledge of the nature of intelligence. It is also dependent on information as to job opportunities available at the time of counselling and likely to be available in the future.

Already by 1939 Rodger[23] had evolved a seven-point plan to analyse the causes of occupational success and failure, which, though comprehensive, was never thought of by its author as complete. Still, it was a worthy contribution to the elucidation of what vocational guidance really consists of. He listed as aspects to be considered: physical make-up, attainment, general intelligence, special aptitudes, interests, disposition and domestic circumstances. Some of these are susceptible of scientific investigation and a fair body of knowledge now exists about them.

Ability and Aptitude

Already in the 1920s and the 1930s a scientific approach to the task of elucidating abilities and aptitudes was becoming apparent in some quarters. There was, for example, the work by Burt (1926) in the field of psychometric tests. Factor analysis was eventually to produce some evidence, not entirely consistent, on the nature of intelligence and aptitudes. Two main schools of thought emerged, the American (Thurstone, Guilford) and the English (Burt, Vernon). As is now well known, some common general features are found, first of all a 'g' factor, denoting a general ability, and then certain group factors differentiating individuals

[22] Wall, W. D., *Adolescents in School and Society*, N.F.E.R. Occasional Publications No. 17, 1968, pp. 96–7.

[23] Daws, P. P., *op. cit.*, p. 27.

with the same degree of general ability. The English school has emphasized the former, the American the latter, on the whole. The best established group factors are the verbal, the numerical and the spatial, but the evidence is mostly tentative about their stability over the years. Differentiation has already begun by the age of 6,[24] but full differentiation is not reached till the teens.

Although the spatial factor is measurable in the early teens various studies (e.g., Peel[25]) provide inconclusive evidence as to the age at which "technical" aptitude emerges. Bernyer found that at age 15 four separate factors of technical aptitude existed and that by 18, after apprenticeship training, a more hierarchical pattern and more organized arrangement of the factors had emerged. The English analyses appeared to dismiss the possibility of the psychologically founded allocation of pupils to technical education before the age of 14 at the earliest; Bernyer's study suggested structuralization of factors between the ages of 15 and 18 through the impact of technical training and thus perhaps the development of aptitude in part through experience, in line with other research on aptitude.[26]

Vernon's summary[27] stresses, however, that there are not two really distinct types of pupil, the academic and the technical, because general ability is a major factor in the performance of both groups. At the same time evidence suggests that results of spatial ability tests and non-verbal tests are related to mathematical and scientific, as well as to technical, abilities.

Research in France on the development of literary and scientific aptitudes[28] showed that from about 14, that is from the third year of the lycée course, literary and scientific aptitudes began to show themselves. By the fifth year of the course the divergence between the two was at its most marked, and did not develop any further in the last year of the course. These results are rather broadly in agreement with the work on technical aptitude.

There is also some evidence of the existence of musical and general aesthetic factors and also of general psycho-motor and physical-athletic factors.

Swedish research[29] on a large scale into the development of children aged 12–15 supports the idea of gradual differentiation during these years. It shows the increasing importance of verbal and mathematical factors.

The American study Project-Talent[30] demonstrated that there were different growth rates for different abilities: perceptual, spatial and reasoning abilities develop before numerical abilities and verbal abilities develop more slowly still.

Thurstone found that 80 per cent of the adult standard was achieved in perceptual speed

[24] Meyers, C. E. *et al.*, *Primary Abilities at Mental Age 6*, Monograph Soc. for Res. Child Devel. no. 82, 1962.

[25] Peel, E. A., Evidence of a practical factor at age 11, *Brit. J. Educ. Psychol.* vol. XIX, no. 1, 1949, pp. 1–15.

[26] The implications, for example, of 30 years or more of research on linguistic aptitude are that particular, types of linguistic experience are factors helping to determine the particular slant of linguistic aptitude.

[27] Vernon, P. E., *The Structure of Human Abilities*, Methuen, 1961, p. 64. N.B. Vernon tends to take up the general position that there is relatively little differentiation of abilities in adolescence, by comparison with Burt's position that there is.

[28] Langier, H. and Weinberg, D., *Recherches sur la solidarité et l'indépendance des aptitudes intellectuelles d'après les examens écrits du Baccalauréat*, Imprimerie Chantenay, Paris, 1938, and Bonnandel, R., Évolution des liaisons entre les réussites et les diverses matières scolaires, *Journal de Psychologie Normale et Pathologique*, vol. 44, 1951, pp. 438–71.

[29] Ljung, B. O., *The Adolescent Spurt in Mental Growth*, Stockholm Studies in Educational Psychology No. 8, Almqvist & Wiksell, Stockholm, 1965.

[30] Flanagan, J. C. *et al.*, *Project Talent. The American High School Student*, Pittsburgh: Project Talent Office, University of Pittsburgh, 1964.

by age 12, in space and reasoning by 14, in number and memory by 16, in verbal comprehension by 18, in verbal fluency by 20.[31]

In short, evidence is accumulating that ability becomes more differentiated with increasing age and that differential aptitude tests have greater predictive value than measures of general intelligence.[32]

It has been suggested[33] that aptitude develops on the basis of interaction between intelligence and interests that have become stable in the individual. As yet there is no completely demonstrated proof of this theory, and early teens' interests are notoriously unstable, but it does provide a working hypothesis. Interest determines choice of activities, at, say, age 11 and by 15 continual choice of these activities, because of a stabilized interest, results in the acquirement of an aptitude. Whether particular interests remain static or change between 11 and 15 would have a crucial effect on the development or non-development of an aptitude in an individual.

However this may be, it seems likely that by the age of about 14 or 15 many pupils are showing enough evidence of particular aptitudes on the basis of scientifically standardized tests for a counsellor to be able to advise them with some measure of confidence about the general direction their future careers should take, other things being equal.

Interests

Vocational guidance is likely to take into account not only abilities and aptitudes but also the direction of pupils' interests and their motivation.

Although the development of psychometric tests for the measurement of affective aspects of personality lags behind that of cognitive tests, there is broad agreement in practice on the usefulness of interest questionnaires, whatever theoretical problems they raise. The American E. K. Strong, who has specialized in this field, has stated: "Whatever it is that the interest questionnaire measures, whether tastes, preferences, values or aims, it certainly measures something fundamental that is an important factor in the choice of a profession."

An investigation[34] of the interests of boys aged 10–12 in France revealed seven coherent groups of activities or interest areas: intellectual and cultural, technical, sporting, rural, social, trade, handicrafts and arts.

Several studies by Strong have shown that interest scores tend to fluctuate below the age of 16 to 17, as has also a study by Mallinson and Crumbine.[35] After this age they become stable.[36] The use of expressed interests or hobbies of pupils as a guide to vocational choice has therefore only a limited value if the pupils are below 16, since the interests may be only temporary.

With regard to the development of vocational interest itself Jahoda[37] showed that it increases as pupils move into the senior classes, that patterns of motivation become more

[31] Thurstone, L. L., *The Differential Growth Rate of Mental Abilities*, Paper No. 14, Psychometric Laboratory, Univ. of North Carolina, 1955, pp. 1–8.

[32] *Review of Educational Research*, vol. 36, no. 4, Oct. 1966, p. 412.

[33] Husén, T. and Henrysson, S., *Differentiation and Guidance in the Comprehensive School*, Almqvist & Wiksell, Stockholm, 1958, p. 132.

[34] Husén, T. and Henrysson, S. (1958), *op. cit.*, p. 132.

[35] Mallinson, G. G. and Crumbine, W., An investigation of the stability of interests in high school students, *J. Educ. Res.*, vol. 45, Jan. 1952, pp. 369–83.

[36] Bloom, *op. cit.*, pp. 166–7.

[37] Jahoda, G. (1952), *loc. cit.*

definite and ideas about future jobs more realistic. By this time a pupil's social experience has begun to influence not only his own personality and abilities but also his perception of the occupational implications of his own characteristics.[38] In other words, a climate of opinion begins to establish itself within a student which makes vocational counselling both possible and fruitful. Moreover, Gribbons and Lohnes[39] found that scores obtained at about age 14 on a test of readiness for vocational planning predicted criteria of vocational competence when a student was 2 years out of high school. If this American research is relevant in the British situation, certain types of intervention in career decision-making may have long-range as well as short-range effects.

Needs and Values

Rodger, in setting out his Seven-point Plan, omitted to consider the impact on a young person's attitude to his job of his own needs and values. These are important in that they are bound to affect his satisfaction with his job. At the moment, however, we cannot match the needs and values of the young to job satisfaction, because we lack information on the different kinds of satisfaction produced by different jobs.[40]

To sum up, there are now enough tools and enough information about the emergence of aptitudes and stable interests for serious vocational counselling to be undertaken from about age 14. One implication of this fact is that it is unwise to oblige pupils before this age to take decisions about subject choices, since this means that vocational decisions have *ipso facto* been taken.

Job Information and its Background

Information for the careers specialist about the individual pupil, derived from psychometric tests, school marks and assessments, record cards, medical examination, teacher's comments, and interviews with parents and child constitute only one half of the information that is needed in vocational counselling. The other half, especially vital for the pupil, as has been seen from the work done for the Schools Council by the Government Social Survey, is information about available jobs and courses. The careers specialist can perform a most useful function by acting as a mediator between the vast quantities of information available and the children and their parents. He needs to create channels of communication for them. He can take steps to increase their knowledge by arranging lectures or film shows, by providing them with pamphlets, by being available at careers conferences and the course-choice meetings which are arranged by the comprehensive school, by arranging individual interviews. Neither the form master nor the head has time to collect and digest the vast range of information needed nor to disseminate it properly, if informed choices are to be made. But neither can the careers specialist do this without adequate time.

One problem which arises for the counsellor stems from the difficulty of predicting the future demands of the economy for particular types of skills. It has been said that vocational counselling which does not include an estimate of future possibilities and prospects in particular fields is hardly worthy of the name. The careers specialist's job is therefore likely to be

[38] Morrison, A. and McIntyre, D., *Schools and Socialization*, Penguin Books, 1971, p. 177.
[39] Gribbons, W. D. and Lohnes, P. R., *Emerging Careers*, Teachers' College, Columbia, New York, 1968.
[40] Daws, P. P. (1968), *op. cit.*, p. 13.

easier in a country like France, where some attempt has been made to relate present educational planning to economic planning for the future, or in the U.S.A., where local surveys of vocational needs may help the careers specialist to advise his clients.[41] Follow-up studies in the latter country also help to improve guidance procedures by assessing how far the school's courses are still relevant and whether changes in course content are required. The information gathered by the Government Social Survey on behalf of the Schools Council[42] about the relative stability in apprenticeships would also give the careers specialist clues as to probable trends in this area of employment in the near future.

It may be that democratization of the school, in the long run, implies careful planning of the economy. The problem here is a double one, as far as guidance is concerned. It is a question of knowing whether to advise students to take up courses solely in the light of their own abilities and motivation or whether merely to take account of the openings available now and likely to be available in the future, or which of these two aspects to give most weight to. It is not in the best ultimate interests of students to direct their attention to sectors of the economy which are unable to accommodate them, any more than it is to ignore their natural bents. Hence guidance requires at a strategic level a proper appreciation of the immediate and the distant economic outlook, as well as expertise in the study of individuals. It may be that the former is more difficult to acquire than the latter.

Conclusion

The need for better vocational guidance than we provide at present is clear. We have some tools of a fair degree of sophistication with which to undertake it. So far Britain has not yet made really effective use of them.

B. Personal and Educational Counselling

In relation to the need, if not by comparison with some other countries, Britain has done rather badly with regard to vocational guidance. Her record in the field of personal guidance, at least at the informal level, is much superior to that of most.

Unlike continental schools, British schools have since the days of Arnold always aimed at something more than the inculcation of academic knowledge, have aimed at pastoral care, for example, and character training as an important if subsidiary function. Hence the proviso that all teachers shall remain on the school premises throughout school hours; whereas in some continental countries they do not have to be on the premises when they are not teaching, and custodial duties are allotted to younger teachers with inferior qualifications, less experience and maturity, and, incidentally, already heavier timetables. On the Continent in many countries pastoral care—if one can dignify the care given by that name—is a duty a young teacher aims to work himself out of; whereas in a British school to be

[41] For example, an occupational survey at Elko, Nevada, by the Division of Vocational Education of the State Department of Education, working through an advisory committee that included members of the Chamber of Commerce, the employment service, and the citizens' committee, had as its object to determine the number of workers employed locally in various job classifications, what qualifications were needed and how far the schools were meeting the need both as regards qualifications and the number of students with them. The survey discovered that the Elko schools had trained only 23 per cent of the surveyed employees; this result emphasized both the need for better local preparation and the need to recognize the increasing mobility of labour, both of which had implications, including curricular implications, for the schools.

[42] *Schools Council Enquiry* No. 1, p. 141.

asked to be a form master signifies to a young teacher that he is well thought of by his headmaster, and possibly ripe for a little promotion. This difference of emphasis and of practice has led to acceptance by the form master of such duties as supervision of the progress and behaviour of the pupils in his form, consultation with subject teachers teaching them, responsibility for supervising the preparation of their reports and record cards, contact with parents on matters of academic progress and general welfare, an interest in pupils' extra-curricular activities, and a kindly concern about their personal problems, all this in addition to minutiae of general administration affecting his class. To have any of these jobs taken away from him, though it might be personally convenient to him, would leave the average British form teacher with a sense of loss of status and function. If his headmaster omits to pass on to him personal information concerning a pupil in his form he is quite likely to interpret the omission as indicating a loss of trust in his capacity for discretion. Hence the British school system provides pupils with a good amount of broad educational and personal guidance of a more or less informal kind, imitated originally from the public-school system by the grammar school and then passed on to the secondary modern and the comprehensive school. The question is: Is this really enough, especially in the context of the latter two schools? And if it is not, how does the old concept of the form teacher or tutor, or the new concept of the housemaster and year mistress, with more time for the job but still basically the same amateur approach, fit in with the idea of the professional counsellor in the comprehensive school?

There was evidence quite early that the traditional personal guidance provided by the form master in the grammar school and the class teacher in the elementary school was insufficient. As early as 1907 the Education (Administrative Provisions) Act was passed, requiring L.E.A.s to attend to the physical health of children. As a result, apart from the many school clinics set up, here and there between the wars, a number of child guidance clinics were started, and with the passing of the 1944 Act a full child-guidance service was provided, to care for children with serious behaviour and personality problems beyond the wit or knowledge of the form or class teacher.

At the same time there accumulated enough evidence of a scientific kind, as well as plenty of practical teacher experience, to show that the less intelligent and the less achieving a child is the more likely it is that he will have serious personal, social, emotional or behavioural problems. Consequently in the lower ability streams of streamed secondary modern and more recently of comprehensive schools and in all streams of unstreamed schools there is likely to be found a greater number of children in need of serious personal help than is found in the grammar school or the public school. Yet we have merely passed on to the secondary modern and comprehensive schools the pastoral institutions suited to the smaller number of serious problems found in the other two schools. It is, more often than not, a revelation to teachers and heads of grammar schools that become comprehensive to discover the tragic character of the situations to which some of their pupils are reacting. Through no fault of their own they are often poorly equipped by experience to deal with either the situation[43] or the child. Some of the cases are beyond even an experienced secondary modern school head, who may not have the time required even if he has the capacity, nor may they be suitable for reference to an already overburdened child guidance clinic. It is these children

[43] That is not to say there are no children with serious problems in grammar schools or public schools, but there are far fewer of them and in the case of the latter school the fact of boarding may insulate such children from their problems to some extent.

particularly for whom the appointment of a school counsellor is most vital, especially in the large school where it is so easy for the personal touch to be lost. A school counsellor in a large school in a difficult area can easily be occupied full time with the prevention of the need for "crisis counselling", without ever touching vocational guidance. Thus Albert Rowe, for example, sees the counsellor as visiting primary schools, identifying problem and disadvantaged children, consulting colleagues, especially those in the remedial department, contacting outside agencies, and visiting homes. In his experience this approach to counselling reduces the amount of crisis counselling needed and the number of children who present problems. This concentration of the work of the specialist on the hard cases is possible because, in the British tradition, the form teachers, tutors and housemasters continue to deal with the more normal aspects of educational and personal guidance and counselling. The school counsellor does not supplant them, he supplements their efforts at the point at which he can be most effective.

One should not, of course, assume that counselling needs starting only in large schools in difficult areas. As middle-class parents, both fathers and mothers, are more frequently divorced and are increasingly preoccupied with their jobs, as schooling extends and the period of economic dependence lengthens, whilst maturation takes place earlier, personal problems and conflicts arise also for the middle-class teenager. Indeed the social and cultural impact of the two Industrial Revolutions and of the introduction of the scientific method has been to throw the traditional beliefs, habits and customs of society into the melting pot for everyone. The family structure has weakened, the authority of parents and of social institutions counts for less, there have been changes in ideology, both political and spiritual, and in moral standards. The result has been a pluralist society, with many conflicting values, amongst which the young have to make their choices in great uncertainty and without the security of the old stable society. Such conditions generate both conflict and error and make the provision of personal guidance services necessary for the middle-class teenager also. This being said, it is still true that on the whole personal problems and conflicts occur for him less frequently and usually with less severity than they do for the teenager of lower working-class origin, where personal inadequacy of parents over a broad range of activities is much more common.

Why a Trained Counsellor?

It may be felt by some that any sympathetic, firm and experienced teacher with a little "nous" and plenty of time could fill the role of a personal counsellor without further training. One would not wish to deny the value of long contact with children. Unfortunately this contact is largely structured by the classroom situation, which, as well as a teaching situation, is also a judgemental one. It is asking too much of a teacher to divest himself of the judgemental attitudes partly necessary for his job—since he is continually and of necessity evaluating work and behaviour—without further training. Yet for the group of children that require serious personal counselling a judgemental attitude in the helper is largely counter-productive or at least unproductive. Judgement of them has to be kept down to an irreducible minimum.[44] The experience of caseworkers in the social field is very relevant in this regard.

Counselling began in the nineteenth century in connection with work by such charities as

[44] N.B. There is an irreducible minimum.

the Family Welfare Association. The attempt to organize relief for the poor soon brought the realization that for a number of them their problems were not strictly material but rather due to a shortage of human capacity to deal with problems that arose. The initial reaction to this discovery, namely to dub such people undeserving and to give only to the deserving poor, leaving the charity organization in a "holier than thou" posture, was found to be as inadequate as the inadequate themselves by as early as 1900. It had to be abandoned. Counselling in casework thenceforth over the years gathered insights from workers in various fields. The work of depth psychologists enabled social case workers to see how people's earlier experiences had structured for good or ill their capacity to deal with their later ones. The social case worker attempted not to judge the person in need, not to seek to dictate a solution to his problems, not even necessarily to offer direct advice, but rather to meet him with respect in a person-to-person encounter and to help him to find his own best solution to his dilemmas.[45] This on the whole non-directive approach to counselling has become standard in case work, since it enables the client most easily to understand and to cope with himself. It is not an easy approach for a teacher untrained in this kind of work. It goes against the grain, not necessarily of all his previous experience as a teacher, for every teacher comes across children that excite both sympathy and empathy, but of most of his previous activities and some of his ingrained habits of mind.

The counsellor has to help the children referred to him to some understanding of their own emotional needs and of the goals that they could make for themselves, goals which would make life worthwhile and significant for them. He has to do this, however rudimentary the level at which they can operate mentally. The counsellor has also to make sense of the extent to which the pupil's problems are tied up with the social environment in which he lives. Here the experience of teaching in difficult areas stands a teacher who wishes to take up counselling in good stead, since past experience is likely to have made him sensitive to the impact of the environment on children's school work. This and the fact that school counselling must be done in the school context makes it inadvisable to bring people in from outside the profession as school counsellors, since they will not have enough background and experience of schooling to gauge the effect of their actions on the school and, perhaps even more important, on their non-counselling colleagues. Sensitivity to both is vital for the counsellor. Sometimes the advice of educational psychologists with regard to children they have tested or interviewed has been ignored because that advice has been given in ignorance of what was possible in the school context. We ought not to make the same mistake with regard to school counsellors. But we should not make the mistake, either, of presuming that teachers can undertake counselling without further training.

The Role of the Counsellor

In the present state of tentative efforts to discover the counsellor's role in British schools there is great variability in tasks undertaken. Thus the Reading survey found its former students severally involved in careers guidance and vocational preparation, including interviews: psychometric services, systematic testing programmes and the administration of certain tests to individuals; counselling for personal problems; maintenance of cumulative records; liaison with outside bodies, such as the welfare and probation service, child-guidance clinics and the school psychological service; guidance activities in groups; participation in

[45] Rogers, C., *On Becoming a Person*, Sentry Edition, Houghton Mifflin, 1970.

curricular planning; interviews with parents; help to colleagues, when requested by them.[46] All of these activities are appropriate ones for a counsellor and the full-time courses that have been set up tend to provide training in each and every one of them. Which of them would take up most time in a particular school would depend on its clientèle. At the same time the headmaster who did not put high on the list of priorities for the counsellor personal counselling for children with emotional or behavioural problems would be unfair both to the disturbed children themselves and those they so often disturb in the classroom. He would also be very unwise.

This leads on to the question of whether it is really possible and effective to be both a teacher and a counsellor, assuming there is enough time to be both, as there might well be, for example, in the small school, or whether the roles are mutually exclusive.

In Britain various training institutions are taking different attitudes on this issue, as well as on the degree of professionalization of the counsellor. Thus Keele University, for example, runs a full-time one-year course for counsellors, and subscribes to the idea of both full professionalization of counsellors and to the mutually exclusive roles of teachers and counsellors. Manchester University Department of Social Administration has investigated the possibilities of the dual role of teacher–social worker, in which as social worker the teacher would undertake a number of the jobs appropriate to the counsellor.

The present position appears to be that, though now quite a number of people have been trained as full professional counsellors, on full one- or two-year courses, relatively few of them are being employed full-time in this way. Thus a follow-up of eighteen Reading students who had taken the Diploma of Educational Guidance course found only four employed as full-time counsellors.[47]

The reasons for this state of affairs are not too easy to distinguish, nor is it particularly wise to judge from a rather small number of cases. No doubt, sheer accident plays its part, in so far as teachers from relatively small schools in socially "good" areas with few problems get seconded for training, or having been trained, move to such schools. Policy, or sheer force of circumstance, may account for other cases, since a headmaster may wish to maximize the number of subjects offered on the timetable and gives this higher priority than counselling. Or he may be short of staff and use some of the counsellor's time to make up for this lack. But it seems unlikely in view of the traditions of the British school that any professional in the school will always be relieved of the necessity to do some teaching. The headmaster prides himself, as a rule, on keeping contact with what is going on at grass-roots level, and with his staff's difficulties, by doing some teaching himself. He is likely to take the view therefore that the school counsellor should do some teaching also, if only to keep in touch with the classroom situation and its effect on how teachers will view a particular child with a particular problem. The same will be true of the staff, and they are likely to pay less attention to the counsellor and to his task if he does not teach.[48] He will lose credibility with the staff and that he cannot afford to do. The dilemma then is that in some cases he may risk losing credibility with particular problem children. Either way he risks losing credibility with

[46] Schools Council Working Paper No. 15, *Counselling in Schools*, H.M.S.O., 1967, p. 28.

[47] Several of those replying reported difficulty in reconciling their roles as teacher and counsellor. Fuller, J. B., School counselling: a first enquiry, *Educ. Res.*, vol. 9, no. 2, Feb. 1967, pp. 135–6.

[48] Schools Council Working Paper No. 15, p. 23, concludes that in the British educational context "school counsellors would seem to find it politic to participate in some class teaching in the first instance even when they doubt that this is the most efficient contribution they can make".

someone, and perhaps it is better for him not to lose credibility with the staff. Otherwise some children who need help will not be referred to him.

We are now faced with the question of the role of a counsellor with respect to both head and staff. His position must inevitably be a delicate one, as he moves into a school with an array of tests and an air of mystique. In some respects his position will be more delicate in the British school than in the Continental. The staff of a continental school where pastoral care has not been thought of as necessary may view the introduction of a counsellor as a piece of modern nonsense, but they are unlikely to have vested interests that may be threatened to the extent that those of the British form master may be. They tend not to think it is any part of their job to be interested in anything but purely academic progress; the British form master does, and may resent an inquiry by the counsellor as an interference with his job as form master. Tension is always greatest at boundaries, and the no-man's land between the work of the form master and that of the counsellor a good deal narrower than that between the work of the continental academic subject teacher and the counsellor.[49] Their spheres of interest are much closer, and they are much more likely, inadvertently or deliberately, to poach on each other's territory. Clear delimitation of spheres of interest, precise delineation of boundary lines, is necessary to prevent friction, as well as plenty of goodwill on both sides in the early stages of finding out where the boundaries should lie.

Another aspect of the counsellor's role that makes for friction is its secrecy and confidentiality with regard to acute personal problems. The form master will "expect to be told" and the counsellor will sometimes not be able to tell him; or, for that matter, he may not even be able to tell the head, if a pupil discloses a particular matter only on this condition. Since in some circumstances a counsellor cannot help a pupil unless the latter does make a particular disclosure, confidentiality is essential. This implies an uncomfortable shift of position for both headmaster and form master, each of whom is used to being kept fully informed. Uncomfortable though it is to make this change—even though the situation will arise only rarely—it needs making and the result will be an improvement on the present position. At least someone in school will know of the acute personal problem or situation, instead of no-one knowing.

It seems probable also that the introduction of the post of counsellor will cause feelings amongst members of staff of being threatened as to status. The ordinary class teacher will, in many ways justifiably, feel that as usual promotion is given not for excellence as a teacher but for some capacity to do something else. This issue is part of a much wider one, the solution to which will be found only if teachers are willing to accept evaluation of their work, either by organizers or inspectors or by a panel of their peers or by some other method. Until and unless they do, promotion other than to head of department level will always tend to be given for other things than excellence in the classroom, and that which has most impact on most children will be on the whole under-valued. But only teachers have it within their power to change this situation, and as long as it continues, counsellors and others will get superior status to that of brilliant teachers.

At the same time the appointment of counsellors seems to offer an avenue of promotion to a group of teachers whose prospects are, in the long run, endangered by reorganization,

[49] Even so, Swiss teachers have been reported as having difficulties in their relationships with vocational counsellors. (*Report on a conference of European Ministers of Education on the School Population Explosion*, Strasbourg, Sept. 1967, p. 9.)

namely the non-graduate.[50] At the moment their prospects of promotion within a comprehensive school are good, because they have more experience than graduates of children with disturbed or inadequate personalities. The relevance of such experience for "year" or "house" posts, without further training, is obvious. But as graduates get such experience in comprehensive schools, the power of their additional qualifications will tell and non-graduates will stand less chance of obtaining any posts that do not require further training. With posts that do require further training, such as posts as counsellors, they will be better placed than graduates, since local education authorities look more favourably on the secondment of non-graduates for further training than is the case for graduates, for the reason that their initial training has been shorter.

C. Practice in Other Countries in Counselling

No country has longer experience of the counselling and guidance process than the U.S.A. because she reached a high level of economic development and job variability earlier than Europe, and because, concomitantly, the increasing aspirations of her people led to the evolution of the high school as a school for all. By 1964 she employed 19,000 counsellors, most of them with master's degrees and well versed in the most sophisticated techniques. Vocational guidance is viewed as a part of educational guidance and it is part of the counsellor's job to make it clear to the pupil that certain educational choices imply certain vocational choices. Hence the two are rather well integrated as a rule.

For the types of procedures used in American guidance the reader is referred to Appendix I. Two other comments appear relevant to future developments in Britain. There is an increasing tendency in the U.S.A. to make use of group guidance in vocational counselling, partly because it is more economic, partly because more is now known of the effects of group work. For example, fifteen periods are allotted in Rochester, New York, at 14, 15 and 16 years of age for this purpose. The intention of group guidance is to permit the pupil to survey the main areas of employment and to assess realistically his own capacities and interest in relation to them.

The second comment refers to the relative functions of the counsellor and other teachers. Some Americans would seem to be coming round to the view that other teachers than the counsellors also have their part to play in the counselling function, thus perhaps validating the present British approach.

Perhaps, however, the experience of European countries is more relevant to the British situation than that of America, since they are roughly at the same stage of educational and economic development and broadly influenced by many of the same traditions.

Other European countries than Britain have been engaged on thinking out procedures for vocational guidance. Notably Sweden during its early reorganization of secondary education experimented in this field.[51] All the staff of a school take part in some measure in guidance, but the main work falls to a specialist in careers work, who also brings in people from outside school as needed. There is both group and individual counselling, as well as practical vocational orientation. Pupils are taught about the labour market, working conditions,

[50] In Sweden, for example, a similar trend can be seen. Most vocational guidance specialists have come from this group.

[51] The National Swedish Board of Education. Fack S–104 22 Stockholm 22 Informatsionssektionen. *Svmmary of PM Worked out in the Board of Education re Study and Vocationel Orientation* (U. Stencil 1970: 16), p. 3.

systems of training and trade unions and they have periods of work-study.[52] There are radio and TV broadcasts, informative literature is distributed, interest and aptitude tests are administered, teachers', parents' and employers' comments are noted and individual interviews are given. The importance of the pupil understanding the connection between choice of studies and choice of career is also stressed,[53] as is the link with "lifelong education".

Practical vocational orientation was also experimented with in the early comprehensive school and became compulsory from 1962.[54] Its content was revised in 1967. Three study visits are made in grade 8, at about age 15, linked to the phases of social science studies that relate to major sections of the economy. The first visit is intended to show how a place of work functions, the second mainly to study individual employees at work and the third visit is linked to a general survey of the occupational world. The pupils, with help from the guidance specialist, search out all the relevant information before these extended visits. In grade 9 there is a fortnight of practical orientation with a firm. The counsellor may not have charge of more than 690 pupils, in the school grades 6–9.[55] It is felt that a specialist is required because there are so many and so different aspects to his work, which includes ability and personality orientation and individual guidance as well as pedagogic and administrative work.

D. The Effects of Counselling

The research on the effects of counselling, in common with many other aspects of research in the social sciences and especially in education, is somewhat lacking in sophistication.[56] There are descriptive studies, helped out with calculations of correlations, less frequently there are rather superficial experimental studies, carried out before there is enough relevant data available to generate worth-while hypotheses. Instead of the fragmentedness and unrelatedness of much work in this field, there is a need for an approach that combines cross-sectional and longitudinal investigations. Only then will the whole process of counselling be examined, with all its interacting factors. Until such a "systems approach" is available, we have to make what we can of the research already done. Some of the results from the more technically sophisticated studies do furnish worth-while clues.

The effects of counselling, both group and individual, at secondary-school level are reported in various American studies. An investigation by McGowan[57] showed, for example, that individual counselling interviews twice a week produced a significant improvement in academic performance and attendance at school compared with the results for the pupils in a control group, who received no counselling. Weekly group counselling improved similar aspects of school performance in experiments carried out by Benson and Blocker[58]

[52] *Ibid.*, p. 4.

[53] The National Swedish Board of Education. Fack S–104 22 Stockholm 22 Informatsionssektionen. *Aims, tasks and theoretical principles of professional guidance*, p. 3.

[54] National Swedish Board of Education, Fack S–104 22 Stockholm 22 Informationssektionen. *The New Practical Vocational Orientation* ("*PRYO*"), 1969.

[55] *Aims, tasks and theoretical principles*, p. 5. In America it has been suggested that a full-time vocational counsellor should not serve more than 500 pupils maximum.

[56] *Rev. Educ. Res.*, vol. 39, no. 2, Apr., 1969, pp. 273–6.

[57] McGowan, R. J., The effect of brief contact interviews with low ability, low achieving students, *The School Counselor*, vol. 15, 1968, pp. 386–9.

[58] Benson, R. C. and Blocker, D. H., Evaluation of developmental counseling with groups of low achievers in a high school setting, *The School Counselor*, vol. 14, 1967, pp. 215–20.

and also by Gilliland.[59] The latter found improvement occurred in reading and use of English, in levels of aspiration and in vocational development. A less relevant study at higher education level by Dickenson and Truax[60] showed that 71 per cent of under-achieving students who received counselling achieved passing grades by comparison with 46 per cent of a control group which did not receive counselling.

On the personal counselling side Kennedy,[61] in a study extending over a period of 8 years, found that fifty cases of school phobia responded to treatment. The phobia was eliminated by quick referral, forced school attendance, structured interviews with the parents and with the child, and specific instruction to both parents and school staff on management of the children concerned.

On the purely vocational side, the effect of giving detailed information to boys leaving school about various openings provided under the general system of French apprenticeships is shown in a study by Leon[62] and others. An experimental group received plenty of information through pamphlets, lectures and films and a control group received none. Hence the former naturally had a good deal more knowledge about jobs than the latter. More surprisingly, they were also less attracted to glamorous occupations, less ready to reject others. Their views were also more definite and logical and there were fewer boys in the experimental group who were uninterested or still undecided. Their reactions were not confined to specific jobs they had information on, but affected their attitudes to all jobs and the whole question of employment, thus making the work of the careers adviser much easier.

One feature of the research done on counselling is that individuals differ markedly in the extent to which they benefit from it; we need to know why. This is one area in which research is badly needed.

The conclusion one must draw from this research as a whole is that by and large counselling is probably effective in improving attainments and attitudes, even if much more research is needed on the whole question. In particular we need to know how its effects are achieved, and we need research into the specific problems implied in the question that most counsellors now feel needs answering, namely: "What treatment, by whom, is most effective for this individual with that specific problem?"

E. General Trends in Guidance and Consulting

The following general trends in guidance can be discerned. First, instead of fragmented aspects of the child, for example his vocation, being studied, there is a trend to consider his whole developing personality. Hence, there is emphasis on developmental guidance. Secondly, the "client-centred" or non-directive counselling advocated by Rogers has been found more successful than directive counselling and is increasingly used. Thirdly, there is increasing emphasis on group guidance, for example in the vocational field, through timetabled lessons or talks given to groups, and even to some extent in the personal field. Since

[59] Gilliland, B. C., Small group counseling with negro adolescents in a public high school, *J. Counseling Psychol.*, vol. 15, 1968, pp. 147–52.

[60] Dickenson, W. A. and Truax, C. B., Group counseling with college under-achievers, *Personnel and Guidance J.* vol. 45, 1966, pp. 243–7. Reported in the *Rev. Educ. Res.*, vol. 39, no. 2, April 1969, pp. 191–2, p. 270.

[61] Kennedy, W. A., School phobia: rapid treatment of 50 cases, *J. of Abnormal Psychology*, vol. 70, 1965, pp. 285–9. Reported in *Rev. Educ. Res.*, vol. 39, no. 2, Apr. 1969, p. 240.

[62] Husén, T. and Henrysson, S. (1958), *op. cit.*, pp. 137–9.

pupils live less as isolated individuals than as members of groups, a great deal of work can often best be done in the group situation. It is often easier to change the attitudes of whole groups than those of individuals. Fourthly, now that the main procedures for collecting and analysing information on both the individual pupil and the types of work available to him have been set up, there is more emphasis on developing techniques for acting on the knowledge available. Fifthly, there is increased concern for behaviour change outside the interview and its relationship to treatment, increased concern for the specificity of behaviour to be changed, and use of differential and specific treatment. Lastly, without denying the real need for professional training and expertise in the field of counselling, it is generally recognized that in the last analysis much depends on the personality, breadth of experience and depth of humanity of the counsellor.

It also seems likely that we shall bring the computer to our aid in the area of counselling. Recently attempts have been made to use a computer, especially in vocational counselling. The S.D.C. Vocational Counselling[63] System is a typical example of this trend. A computer stores information about individual students and also about the world of work at local and national level and about higher education institutions. The information about students includes marks for school work, standardized test scores, teachers' comments and other data from their school records. Similar information is also banked in the computer with regard to former students, along with a follow-up of their subsequent careers. The computer is programmed to provide answers to specific questions put to it by the student. He requests the information he requires by using a teletype keyboard. To provide the answers the computer relates stored data on the student to stored data on the jobs and courses available. Evaluation of the efficiency of the computer showed that it produced the same answers as two school counsellors in three-quarters of the cases. Both the computer and the counsellors identified the under-achievers and the over-ambitious equally well. The computer predicted significantly higher average marks and more potential dropouts than the counsellors. It also encouraged students to explore a wider range of academic subjects. The students thought the computer did better with regard to information on college requirements. Half the students thought it did not give enough consideration to personal interests and personality characteristics. Their final conclusion was that they nearly all wanted access to a computer, but in conjunction with a counsellor. Perhaps they felt the need of a little "warmth".

There can be little doubt that within a few years we shall see much greater development in the application of computers to vocational guidance. Cost-wise, it might eventually be well worthwhile for local education authorities to allow schools to use their computers at slack times for this purpose.

Perhaps long American experience to date with regard to the limits of the functions of the counsellor can be gauged from the conclusions of Gelatt,[64] conclusions which he reached on the basis of experience in school counselling and a survey of the literature on it. He came to the opinion that other people in a school besides counsellors have a very necessary part to play in guidance and counselling and that many jobs in it can be done by a variety of people with different levels of skill and training. Since American schools have leaned heavily on the work of the professional counsellor to the exclusion of the more amateurish efforts of the teacher, there may be a pointer here that, when we do introduce counsellors generally into schools, we should not abolish the role of the form master or house tutor in this field.

[63] Guidance and counselling, *Rev. Educ. Res.*, vol. 39, no. 2, Apr. 1969, p. 254.
[64] Gelatt, H. B., Research on school guidance programs, *Rev. Educ. Res.*, vol. 39, no. 2, Apr. 1969, p. 149.

Perhaps he is the counselling "general practitioner" to the counsellor's "consultant specialist".

F. The Future of Counselling in Britain

One other issue remains to be discussed. Is the school counsellor really likely to become a common figure in British schools when there is no declared intention to increase the pupil-staffing ratio to allow for his employment? Will heads of schools really feel able to sacrifice teaching time to this end? The answer to this question would seem to depend on two factors. First of all, the degree of motivation for a head to sacrifice a subject in his curriculum in order to provide a school counsellor will depend partly on the size of his school, partly on the number of social and behaviour problems in it and in the surrounding locality. Large schools are more likely to appoint counsellors than small ones, because staff-wise they have more room for manoeuvre and because size tends to generate behaviour problems.[65] Schools in socially difficult areas are more likely to appoint counsellors than those in socially favoured ones, because socially difficult areas also generate behaviour problems. The other factor is the factor of fashion, which seems to play a bigger part in educational thinking than perhaps it should. Quite a number of smallish schools have begun to appoint year tutors, although the year system is a device invented to help break down large schools into more manageable units. Time, teaching time, as well as allowances often go with these posts. Presumably, if some heads make these appointments, others for similar reasons of fashion, but with more real justification, will appoint counsellors, if only part-time ones.

The style of counselling done is likely to be affected by the lack of money to finance the counselling movement. It has been calculated that for really satisfactory and thorough counselling, one full-time counsellor is needed for about every 400 pupils. We are unlikely to reach that happy position for a good many years. Hence professional counselling is likely to be restricted to the most urgent or the most intractable of personal problems and to some kind of group and individual vocational counselling. The counsellor is less likely to do much work in the field of educational guidance, except at crucial points, such as the time when options choices are made, and the major part of this task will continue to be carried out in an informal kind of way by the form teachers. The existence of the form teacher thus makes easier the introduction of counselling in conditions of financial stringency.

Hence, perhaps even in poor economic conditions, once the proper apportioning of tasks as between form master and school counsellor has been achieved, the British school would appear to be far better placed than any other so far, perhaps even than the American school, to fulfil the new function of explicit guidance thrust on the school by new economic, new social and new educational developments.

However, whether the addition to the British comprehensive school staff of a new figure, the school counsellor, or the training of teacher–social workers on a larger scale, proves to be the most happy solution to these relatively new problems, with regard to the whole subject of counselling and its systematic organization within the comprehensive school one can do no better than repeat the words of Benn and Simon on this point: "A search for the most efficient and effective method within each school situation is now the urgent task of those running comprehensive schools." It is to be hoped that their efforts will be met with sympathetic consideration from the authorities.

[65] See pp. 89, 94, 99 for direct and indirect evidence.

CHAPTER 5

The Secondary School Curriculum

EMBEDDED in every school timetable is some view of what the curriculum is and what its objectives are. Sometimes the assumptions implicit in the timetable have been well pondered upon, sometimes not, but, whichever is the case, every curriculum reveals some basic assumptions, both by what it includes and by what it leaves out, how it arranges sequences and so on. In the comprehensive school timetable the issues at stake are even more complex than those of the timetable of either the grammar or the secondary modern school and the task of welding it together so as to fit complex requirements and make of it one coherent whole is even more difficult than for the other schools.

A. The Nature and Scope of the Curriculum: an Historical Survey

Views as to the nature and scope of the curriculum tend to depend on views as to the aims of education. As far back as Aristotle there seems to have been divergence of view as to whether studies should aim more to improve intellect or to improve character and whether pupils "should practise pursuits that are practically useful or morally edifying or higher accomplishments". However, the history of education, perhaps especially in recent centuries, would suggest that mainly, wherever there was a clash between the needs of the intellect and that of the character, between pure knowledge on the one hand or the aesthetic or the practically useful on the other, the intellect and pure knowledge tended to be served first and were always accorded the greater esteem. This was true, even though an underlying, undeclared aim of those undertaking purely disinterested study was to secure a socially reputable job, i.e. the aim was ultimately practical and vocational. On the whole only when social or moral conditions in school or outside it have made it imperative, as in the case of Arnold's reforms at Rugby, has the intellect tended to take second place. Hence, traditionally, as knowledge expanded and was divided into smaller compartments, the curriculum has been thought of in terms of pure knowledge, as a list of subject disciplines, often taught in an abstract and theoretical way. Only in the twentieth century has a really serious attempt been made to extend the school's responsibility so as to include the individual psychological and social development of children.[1] As a result the school curriculum has increasingly been defined in terms of all the experiences that pupils undergo under the influence of the school, and therefore it has been thought of as wider than the timetable itself.

[1] Though moral education, based on religious belief, was always considered to be an aim.

At the same time from Greek education to the present day there has been a distinction between the education suited to the "free man" of abundant leisure and the "bond man" tied to servile work. Aristotle would include in education "only such knowledge as does not make the learner mechanical". Hence right through history there has been a cleavage between education for culture and training for a specific trade or manual occupation, or indeed for manual and technical skills in general, which is still distorting the curriculum we provide.

This education for culture consisted only of the classics, because of their great prestige, until severe pressure caused by the expansion of commerce and industry forced the entry of modern languages, geography, history, science and mathematics into the secondary-school curriculum. The rate at which these subjects entered the curriculum varied from country to country according to the extent of commercial and industrial development and the spread of secondary education to the lower classes. These new subjects were taught in much the same way as the classics, that is in an abstract and theoretical way. Hence the secondary school still continued to adhere to the traditional concept of the nature and purpose of secondary education, that of a humane and liberal kind, encyclopaedic in its range of subjects, but narrow in its exclusive emphasis on the intellectual life of man, a life that could be developed only by those freed from the bondage of manual labour. The intellectually exclusive was also on the whole socially exclusive and vice versa. The academic school thus concentrated still on the general intellectual development of the human being but widened its frame of reference, knowledge-wise, as new disciplines were erected and found their way haphazardly into the curriculum. Since the latter became increasingly overloaded, by 1900 a measure of differentiation into "classical" and "modern" or scientific sides was common in many countries in the later stages of the secondary school course. Nowhere was the degree of specialization for older pupils eventually to be greater than it became in British schools. At the same time fewer and fewer people in the upper and middle classes had private incomes, more and more had to look for jobs. It was therefore reasonable for them to pay increasing attention to the vocational aspect of their education, at least in the sense of considering how good a job their school course would lead to.

Whilst these developments took place as the response of the academic secondary school to the scientific and industrial advances of the nineteenth century, other changes took place in the education or training of the "rude mechanicals". The increasing need in industry for people with specialized or semi-specialized skills at a lower level brought problems. Literacy became essential and with it mass education. Some of the vocational training earlier provided by the guilds was shifted into the schools, with in many countries a great proliferation of types of school, whether trade school, technical school, commercial school, continental middle school or upper elementary school, each with its curriculum to suit. In Britain, however, the higher grade school was largely killed off by the combined effects of the Cockerton judgement and Morant's influence in the Board of Education, and trade and technical education with its appropriate curricula was stunted in its growth.

None of the pupils educated in the elementary educational systems of Europe, including Great Britain, was thought to have much need of general education beyond the three Rs and their education was often so short that it would have been difficult to give them any. It was not till the twentieth century, with its increasing egalitarianism and new industrial demands, that changes in the education of the working classes in this direction began to take place.

The Second Industrial Revolution, with its built-in rapidity of change, has both decreased the proportion of the people in industry and agriculture and increased the need for better educated, highly flexible workers in many areas of employment, workers who understand general industrial processes, without having a long training in a particular trade skill, who are highly responsible and who can adapt themselves to changing circumstances. Technological advance has also decreased the need for so many workers. Hence a general tendency to raise the school-leaving age, to lengthen courses for pupils who would previously have left school, and to develop a broad general curriculum for them, incorporating the values and subjects of the traditional academic course, even if somewhat watered down. Another result of modern technology, alongside a fundamental revaluing of the human being, is a changed view of what an appropriate education is, and controversy as to how it can be given.

It is not surprising that from the later stages of the first Industrial Revolution and the earlier stages of the second there emerges the idea of secondary education for all, at first in separate schools but increasingly in unified schools, drawing in its curricular aspects on the "cultural" concept of general education traditional in the middle class and the "vocational" concept of specific training traditional in the working class. This new idea of the curriculum owes more, however, to the ethos of the old academic school and the middle class than it does to the old elementary or technical school and the working class. It has tended to be academic in spirit, even when only watered-down academic. Notably, though it has introduced the working-class child to academic work and values, it has done little until recently to make middle class children understand the value and creativity of technology or to teach them that intensely practical but also almost aesthetic feel for the properties of materials and structures characteristic of the artisan. The aesthetic education of both groups has always tended to be defective, though they have been better served in the last 20 years than previously.

The results of using such watered-down academic curricula in the American high school and in many British secondary modern schools, highlighted their weaknesses and their poor holding-power for children of a social class now receiving the benefits of a more extended education for the first time. The academic diet of separated disciplines, each with its own intellectual rationale, appeared not to cater for the needs and abilities of many such pupils in mid-adolescence, did not provide them with a mental training really appropriate to them and did not help pupils in their efforts to make sense of themselves and the world around them. Moreover, these children were much less motivated by learning for its own sake, than by utilitarian learning. In the U.S.A. the response was to widen the curriculum and in some places to introduce new methods of teaching. More subjects and courses were introduced and they included those aiming at specific vocational training for industry and commerce as well as those helping with the real problems of adjustment of immigrant and other children. This was the first time it was thought necessary for education to help, through the curriculum, with personal development and personal problems. The aim was to meet both the local industrial needs of society and the personal needs of pupils, and it assumed that it was possible to do both through the curriculum. The consequent proliferation of subjects and courses reinforced what was already a developing pattern of the curriculum in the U.S.A. It increasingly tended to provide for general education a compulsory group of subjects taken by all, at least in the early stages of secondary education, and, later in the course, a common core of compulsory subjects plus a group of electives, optional subjects or courses, whether traditional or of some integrated type, geared to the education and vocational needs of particular pupils and with great freedom of choice. Although the reappraisal of American education that has taken place since Sputnik has led to a more closely knit grouping of subjects, these basic premises of the American curriculum remain.

In European continental countries, however, the trends in the development of the curriculum have been rather different. Emphasis on the now outdated faculty theory of learning helped to perpetuate a curriculum common to all in a particular type of school or course, as being good for mental training, and with relatively little provision for individual interests and aptitudes. Hence a tendency to allot pupils to courses from the first year of the secondary school and at a later stage to differentiate somewhat within courses. At first sight this practice appears to generate far more specialization than is the case in Anglo-Saxon countries. In fact, differences in the time allotted to various subjects in the different courses are slight, even in the upper part of the school, and all or almost all subjects are studied by all pupils in some degree right to the end of the course. Conceivably entry into the Common Market and the start of the European movement towards equivalence of degrees and certificates could cause the British educational system serious difficulties, if it became necessary to align our practice with theirs. It has already been said by the head of one of the international schools that serve the needs of children of Common Market workers, working outside their own country for some Common Market institution, that he does not see how the British curriculum could fit into the curriculum of his school. Yet ways have been found of fitting the curriculum of the schools of each of the Six to the curriculum of the international schools.[2] Because their curricula tend all to be built on the same fundamental principles this has not been too difficult. Our problems might be more serious.

However, we can take some comfort from what appears to be a developing international trend for countries with highly differentiated and specialized courses to reduce the amount of specialization and for countries with a high general education component to introduce more options. Another international feature is to increase the length of general education, as school-leaving ages are raised, and the amount of communality in the curriculum when a common school system is introduced.[3]

The appearance, in the American secondary school since 1900 and the British secondary school since World War II, of pupils whose parents had not received secondary education and who themselves often resented staying on longer at school has forced certain fundamental questions on everyone; they are specially pertinent to the state of British secondary education at present, with the increasing comprehensivization of schools and the raising of the school-leaving age.

1. What are the aims of secondary education today and by what means can we implement them?
2. How do we fit the curriculum to the life and needs of the present day?
3. What is the nature of general education for everyone?
4. How do we provide broader cultural experiences for working-class children than was necessary for pupils coming from cultured homes without sickening them of school and without patronizing them?
5. How do we make middle-class children understand the cultural values of craftsmanship and technology?
6. Is education a purely intellectual process?

[2] Necessary because each child must take the exams of his own country to acquire his own country's qualifications, yet he has to study at the international school. Hence collation of syllabuses is necessary.

[3] *World Survey of Education*, vol. III, *Secondary Education*. Unesco, 1961, p. 144.

7. How do we combine the cultural and the vocational in the same course?
8. To what extent must we offer differentiated subjects and courses to suit different aptitudes and interests?
9. With so many demands on it, how do we organize the curriculum?

It will hardly be possible within the confines of the present chapter to discuss all these issues, but some attempt will be made to discuss the main ones.

B. The Pupils

It is hardly possible to answer any of these questions without considering first the pupils who are to be educated. This is true as regards aims of education, since it is no use to set targets that neither we nor they can reach, or targets that are below their or our capacity. It is equally true of content and methods.

Although it is dangerous to separate whole age populations into different groups in practice, at the level of theory there is something to be said for considering the characteristics and needs of pupils at either end of the IQ continuum separately, since in some respects they are different. Moreover, it makes it easier for us to appreciate the issues. We will therefore look in turn at that group which provides what we have become used to calling the early leavers and then at the more able group. The first group will get most of our attention because they are the pupils with whom, so far, we have failed.

1. *The ROSLA Pupils*

Several points are pertinent to the aims of education as far as these pupils are concerned.

First, with modern technical advance it is inevitable that pupils will be obliged to stay on at school longer and longer, that is, unless we decide to take people off the labour market by having an earlier statutory age of retirement. This alternative merits discussion, but as we are commited to ROSLA, and probably rightly so, we will try to see the relevance of this fact to curricular objectives. As a result of ROSLA we have in the schools in the older age groups, alongside the traditional academically oriented pupils, considerable numbers of children whose interests are not basically academic and within that group large numbers of children for whom learning does not come easy and who have a long experience of failure. If we do not provide material which *they* think relevant to their needs and which interests *them* they will not absorb what we do provide. This will be worse than a sheer waste of time. In an institution where attendance is compulsory, it will be counter-productive, in that engendering boredom, it will also engender idleness and hostility, in other words personal problems for the pupils and social and pastoral problems for the school and its teachers. Moreover, it will do so at the very point when the hostility feelings natural to the adolescent, as he hacks his way to independence from parents and other grown-ups, are at their height. With many adolescents it is not so much a question of what we should teach and of what they should learn, but rather of what we can teach them and of what they are willing to learn. Hence one aim of the curriculum must be the development of self-motivation in the less able pupil through study of material that interests him and through the satisfaction that comes from grappling successfully with tasks that stretch him, but not anywhere near to the point of failure.

Secondly, as we have already shown,[4] we are unlikely to stimulate much further mental

[4] See pp. 27–8.

growth in most of the pupils in this group beyond what they have already. If by chance we do so, it is a bonus. Our best chance of getting them to learn more is likely to come from improving their motivation. How large is the component of motivation in intellectual development is illustrated by, for example, a study by Pimsleur.[5] The really bright child is, of course, lucky in that he is easily motivated, is in fact self-motivated by intellectual curiosity and the success that comes with ability. But with the less able child for the reasons already stated the task will not be easy. All the more reason then, as far as the curriculum is concerned, for latching on to their own basic interests and drives of adolescence, as outlined by Wall,[6] and providing material pertinent to their growth tasks. With this group of children there are no other options that can be seriously pursued, if we wish to get the best out of them that they can give.

The growth tasks which Wall suggests making use of as motivating forces are four in number: social, sexual, vocational and philosophic. We could also have added a creative and aesthetic task.

With regard to the social, sexual and philosophic selves there is much more communality amongst all children, even if they function at different intellectual levels, than is the case in respect of the vocational self. It is in its attempts to provide for the many varied vocations of the modern world that the curriculum uses up most teaching power in all countries, particularly as regards the demands of high level university studies organized mainly on a subject-discipline basis. The result is that up to now the early leavers group have suffered a degree of neglect, partly because their vocational needs are not too clear, partly because their parents are less interested in education than other parents and do not vote with their feet.

Thirdly, since in the future everyone must consider the possibility that they will have to be retrained at a later date and since this new feature of vocational life may well affect the ROSLA group of children more than any other, it is more vital that they leave school with a favourable attitude to learning than that they leave in possession of a great number of facts. These children must want to come back to learning later. They rarely do so now.[7] This must be counted an important *aim* of education. It is as important as that they learn the basic skill of reading. The objective of inducing a favourable attitude to learning amongst children whose previous learning experiences have been unhappy must stand very high amongst the objectives of the curriculum for 14- to 16-year-olds. It demands close observation of what these children actually enjoy, appreciate and aspire to. We have also to consider why their earlier experiences were unfortunate and what can be done to prevent such situations in future.

Fourthly, it does these children no service, or any other children for that matter, if no attempt is made to relate their enjoyment and their aspirations to the real demands that society will make on them. Perhaps we could illustrate this point by a simple example. It is well known by heads and staffs that one effective way of stimulating a higher staying-on rate amongst girls has been to provide a commercial course. Even if not every one of them seriously dreams of marrying her boss, shorthand and typing have a certain glamour for many girls as being immediately related to the working world in what they view as a socially acceptable way. Shorthand, however, is beginning to be a dying art amongst many typists actually at work, having been replaced by audio-typing. It would be unfair, now, to provide

[5] See p. 29, footnote 46.

[6] Wall, W. D., *Adolescents in School and Society*, N.F.E.R. Occasional Publications, No. 17, 1968, p. 13. See p. 37 of this volume.

[7] Few of them study as grown-ups at evening school, W.E.A. courses or at the Open University.

commercial courses in which the need for this new skill was not pointed out and opportunities not given for its practice.

Fifthly, the dovetailing into each other of curricular approaches which take account of these two points is no easy matter. It demands a high level of timetabling and teaching skill.

Sixthly, it is an open question whether many of the jobs that some of these pupils will eventually get require any training at all, beyond what can be given in a couple of hours. Hutchins[8] quotes the example of illiterate Spanish women in Germany who control the operation of baking ovens by cycling up and down in front of them and watching certain lights. Yet these pupils will still need some understanding of, for example, industrial processes as they move as adults from job to job. But in a society where vocational aspirations strongly influence incentives to accept schooling, the relation between the world of work and education received is minimal for these children and by and large they know it.[9] Consequently motivating this group to take advantage of schooling is the hardest job in teaching. It requires a major share of the resources devoted to the age groups concerned, whereas in fact our too early specialization in the sixth form ensures that the major part goes to providing enough options for future sixth formers to ensure that they can take whatever subjects they please or need later. The price paid for too early specialization in the sixth form is a poor curriculum for the less able and the less motivated earlier on.

Lastly, both curricular recommendations and theoretical discussion of the issues, which are not backed up by personal experience of teaching such children, all too often appear academic in the worst sense to those engaged in serving them. They lack the feel of the problem. At the same time the teachers concerned often lack insights that would come to them if they had a better grounding in theory, given at a time when they already have some substantial experience of the problem, i.e. later than the initial training stage. This group of children need teachers who have both practical experience and are well versed in theory, who are thus in a true sense specialists along their own line and who are therefore given the rate for the job.

2. *The More Able Pupils*

If we may conclude that for many of our pupils in the fourth and fifth year our main aim in the curriculum for this generation must be to tap motivation to learn, there are many others whose requirements include also prevocational training of a high order, the word prevocational being understood here in a very broad sense, to include really academic studies. Pupils being educated at a high level in academic disciplines are receiving prevocational training just as much as those on a catering or technical course. Such training will one day ensure that they can earn their daily bread. Two factors are tending to heighten the level of competence demanded from these pupils, for example, by the universities, namely the ever-expanding horizons of knowledge and the increased competition to enter these institutions. Happily this group of pupils is highly motivated towards study, since they have always been successful at it, or the pressures on them would be unbearable. How far we can accept the steadily increasing level of specialized knowledge and competence imposed on them, particularly in arts subjects, by the forces of the academic market is another question.

[8] Hutchins, R. M. *The Learning Society*, Pall Mall Press, 1968, p. 82.

[9] They also know that they are not likely to find much pleasure or satisfaction in their jobs. See Carter, M. P., *Home, School and Work*, Pergamon Press, 1962, p. 213. This fact may also account in part for their earlier marriage rates. They have got to find some satisfaction and point in life in some direction.

Research on these children, the more gifted, has shown that the one outstanding characteristic that they almost all share is their sense of independence. This independence affects both their work habits and their attitudes to both their teachers and their peers. They are much more capable of withstanding pressures from either group than are the rest of their contemporaries, much more capable of doing independent work and of working on their own, more independent of the school environment in developing self-esteem, more able to obtain reinforcement from their own accomplishments.[10] A large body of research also supports the hypothesis that gifted children can skip classes without academic or social deficit, as long as this does not happen more than once or twice.[11] They are also in general more stable in their personalities and are more likely to conduct their future lives successfully in terms, for example, of job advancement.[12] Mentally, and on the whole morally and emotionally, they are born with silver spoons in their mouths.

From these children much is demanded in the way of prevocational competence, of high level of academic study, when they leave school. In Britain, as indeed elsewhere, their curriculum is largely geared to these demands, especially in the later years of school life. The very concept of "minority time studies", those studies which are often not in the examination calendar and which are not part of the prevocational course that is examined, betrays how little importance we attach in fact to preparation for anything except the world of work. Preparation for social and civic life, for marriage[13] and for leisure ranks as fit only for minor attention in our society, as essentially dilettante. The excessive specialization of the English sixth-form curriculum exacerbates the situation. Moreover, minority time studies get less consideration as to what they should consist of and what aims they should serve than the main course. They consist merely in many cases of "left-overs", of what can be put on in the timetable for a teacher with a few spare periods. One could nearly say that they are not an integral part of the timetable.

This conflict between prevocational and non-vocational pressures produces a number of dilemmas. To what point should vocational pressures, especially as exemplified in those very considerable demands coming from the universities, be allowed strongly to influence the curriculum of gifted children up to 'O' level, and hence that of all children? What place should be given to material enhancing their development as human beings in other ways or providing them with knowledge and skills for their roles as citizens and members of families? How far does purely academic study promote personal and moral development? These questions furnish the curriculum planner with one of his basic dilemmas, that of how to provide both a good general education and a high level of competence in studies that are basically prevocational.

[10] Smith, D. C., *Personal and Social Adjustment of Gifted Children*, Council on Exceptional Children Research Monograph No. 4. National Education Association, Washington D.C., 1962. Lucito, L. J., Independence–conformity behaviour as a function of intellect: bright and dull children, *Exceptional Children*, no. 31, 1964, p. 5013. Sears, P. S., *The Effect of Classroom Conditions on the Strength of Achievement Motive and Work Output of Elementary School Children*. U.S. Department of Health, Education and Welfare, Office, of Education Cooperative Research Project No. 873, California Univ. Press., Stanford, 1963.

[11] Klausmeier, H. J., Effect of accelerating bright older elementary pupils: a follow-up, *J. Educ. Psychol.*, vol. 54, 1963, pp. 165–71. Gallagher, J. J., *Teaching the Gifted Child*, Alleyn & Bacon, Englewood Cliffs N.J., 1964. This fact is of particular relevance to small comprehensive schools.

[12] Terman, Lewis M. and Oden, M. H., *The Gifted Group at Mid-Life*, Stanford Univ. Press, 1959, p. 143.

[13] The last two generations have been less well prepared for the demands of family life than previous generations who, as members of large families, got informal and incidental preparation for looking after children by looking after their own brothers and sisters under supervision. There is a yawning gap in the curriculum here.

To add further complication to the curriculum, there is also an intermediate group of pupils between the two groups already mentioned. Indeed, it would be more accurate to say that there are not three groups of pupils but rather a continuum, with at one end gifted pupils capable of high-calibre independent work and well motivated towards school and at the other much less able pupils, very easy prey to pressure from their contemporaries and whose work needs kindly but firm supervision and stimulating guidance all the way. For all of them we have to provide for the growth of their social, sexual, aesthetic and philosophic selves on the one hand and their vocational self on the other. Hence the need to provide advanced studies in the subject disciplines for those intending to study them at high level, and also studies at a lower level, both for those aiming at high-level work in other disciplines but needing to broaden their general education and for those whose studies will all remain at a lower level.

We have now described the pupils for whom we have to cater. Curriculum-wise, do we treat them as one group and give them all the same treatment, or as two or three groups requiring different treatments? We shall probably be wiser to think of them as individuals with their own particular emerging strengths and weaknesses. Indeed it is clear from a flood of research that individuals vary considerably both in general readiness for learning and in particular aptitudes, and this because learning readiness is determined by the interaction between genetically based maturational factors and previous experiences. Hence a vast variety of combinations of particular strengths and weaknesses in particular individuals. As a result, although we can think in terms of universal long-term aims, individual differences make it impossible to set universal immediate objectives of education for all children, and this fact has implications both for subject matter, for teaching approach and for curriculum. It does not mean that no general education is possible. The various aptitudes and interests are not usually very stable till the age of 15 or 16. It is, therefore, wise to defer curricular differentiation until the time when the line of an individual's future evolution is clear, even though we will make allowance for the impact that a pupil's general ability must make on his capacity to function with regard to all subjects in a general curriculum.

C. The Cultural Values of Technology

Before proceeding further and looking at the curricular implications of what has already been said, it will be as well to consider the implications for the curriculum of the emerging awareness among educated people of the cultural values of technology. As has already been indicated, organizational and curricular developments since 1900 have gradually had the effect of introducing working-class children to the "academic" curriculum of the middle class. However, the attempt to convince all pupils, but especially middle-class pupils, of the cultural values of technology and craftsmanship has barely begun in British schools. The traditional liberal curriculum neglected the practical and technical aptitudes of pupils. Games apart, little but lip-service was paid in academic schools to the bodily half of the tag *mens sana in corpore sano* until the twentieth century. Shameful to say, this was true in a country that should have been aware of these new cultural values,[14] since it was the first where the intellectual and practical inventiveness of artisans enabled a liberally educated middle class to live in increasing wealth and material comfort. The training of hand and eye in a practical and technical way was much neglected and, where it was practised, it was

[14] It is significant that Snow talked about the gap between the two cultures. He should have said three.

despised, as not requiring any great mental capacity. However that may be, as intelligent working-class children have moved out of the working class into the sixth forms and universities, never to darken a factory door, the supply of intelligent foremen and engineers at workshop level has shown signs of diminishing, whilst the supply of intelligent doctors moving out to America has increased. It is time for a radical reappraisal of attitudes, and there are signs that it has already begun.

The practical effect of this out-of-date mental climate was that, until recently, technical and craft subjects were taught at junior secondary level, but unless they were part of specialized vocational courses, mainly in technical schools, they often ceased at fifth-form level. More damagingly still, they were often the object of scorn by such sixth-formers as had the opportunity to continue with them in "minority subjects" time. They usually still are. But Project Technology and other schemes herald a change of heart, brought about by the increasing prestige of technology, the development of the advanced colleges of technology and their upgrading into universities, the introduction of engineering departments in universities, and by the belated realization in the first country to be industrialized, that our survival depends on our technical expertise. We have therefore every incentive to make all our pupils keenly aware of the work of technology, not merely those who will one day be technicians or technologists.

This process of generalizing elements of education once viewed as vocational skills is clearly seen in the development of Soviet polytechnical education, and the trend to enlarge the concept of general education to include manual and technical activities once regarded as vocational has even got a foothold now, perhaps somewhat unexpectedly, in France. At the same time as these subjects become part of general education they tend to change in nature from manual skills, narrowly conceived as trade training, to something much broader based, related to design as well as construction, with a creative and problem-solving approach.[15] Technology is beginning to be viewed as part of a liberal education, contributing a different mental set to those produced by the arts or by the sciences.

No one could yet say that the development of Soviet polytechnical education has been an unqualified success, but then there are precedents in other fields, notably in science, for subjects to fail when first introduced into the curriculum and gradually to succeed and be accepted as an indispensable part of it. Soviet polytechnic education attempts to integrate manual and verbal elements of pupils' personal development, to prevent their polarization on the basis of social class and to relate school activities closely to those of everyday life. At the junior secondary stage a range of basic manual skills are learned by all pupils and instruction is given in the general principles of industrial production. At the senior stage instruction is continued in school and attempts have been made to initiate all pupils, including the most intelligent, into the actual processes of production under the supervision of the technical personnel of industrial enterprises,[16] and with a view to inculcating the idea of participation in socially useful labour. This last feature, work experience, has not yet met with much success, since no one really knows how to organize it, but it needs to be watched.

This movement is also getting under way in western countries, mostly in the work experience experiments of the U.S.A., Sweden and Britain. It seems likely to become generalized,

[15] For a practical example of this approach see Robinson, C. F., Open planning in a department of art and design, in: Mason, S. C. (ed.), *In Our Experience*, Longmans, 1970.

[16] An interesting parallel, in the industrial field, of the ancient Greek practice of using the elders to provide political education for the young.

as public opinion is already favourable to it. The Schools Council Enquiry found that three-quarters of the parents of 15-year-olds, heads of schools and teachers, favoured work experience.[17] The impact of the movement is also to be seen in the development in France of the *baccalauréat technique* and the advent of our own 'A' level courses on Engineering Science.

D. Implications for the Curriculum

What does all this mean in practical terms for the curriculum of the comprehensive school in a society where *l'éducation permanente*, continual retraining, and much greater leisure are just over the horizon, and entry to the Common Market already with us?

1. *The Gifted*

First, by the time able pupils leave school they must have been provided with a range of subject disciplines at a sufficiently high level for them to move on to the next stage. At present, this means up to 'A' level, or, if the sixth-form curriculum is reformed, somewhere rather below it, as long as pupils continue to leave at 18. This does not imply, necessarily, that they will have been studying these subjects as separate disciplines since their entry into secondary education. With the "content" subjects, certainly, it is possible to group them into broader areas of study in the early years of the course, giving, for example, broad courses in the humanities[18] and the sciences, with gradually increasing specialization in the later stages. Such a policy is in many ways more respectable intellectually than the current practice of studying separate subjects, which have entered the secondary school course more or less haphazardly over the years. It leads us first to the grouping together of subjects that have relevance for each other, history illuminating the study of literature, and geography meeting biology in environmental studies, and then to their gradual interweaving. Here the experience that many secondary modern school teachers have acquired of integrating two or more subjects, of relating them to the children's interests and indeed of going further and developing the "inquiry" type of approach has much to contribute to the development of the comprehensive school curriculum. Subsequent specialization by the able will be all the better based for being thus situated in its context and those other pupils whose intellectual curiosity is soon exhausted and who, in the later stages of the course, require material more slanted to basic drives than to intellectual interests, will already have some experience of the style of learning required to further such studies.

2. *The Less Able Children*

The least able group, who are likely to go into unskilled jobs requiring no previous training, have no obvious vocational incentive in the curriculum, especially as their studies are at present authenticated by no leaving certificate. They are likely to need, none the less, a course something on the lines of Soviet polytechnical education, as previously outlined, to provide a link between school and job.[19] They also need plenty of information about such things as national insurance, sick benefits and rebates, since as grown-ups (a) they are the group most

[17] p. 129.

[18] The old classical course was in many ways an integrated course.

[19] We cannot, of course, even be sure that any jobs will be available for them in the long run, since many of those they previously filled are being automated out of existence. But this is too large a question to be considered here, especially as it may eventually affect most of the population and thus totally slant incentives for learning away from the vocational.

vulnerable to the effects of automation; (b) they have the highest sickness rates; (c) they have the lowest income rates; (d) contrary to popular belief, they take less advantage of the benefits available to them than does any other intelligence and income group, their lower intelligence being one factor that acts as a weak link in a weak chain of communication from the authorities to themselves, as the work of the Poverty Action group has shown. That link should be established during the last year at school, since the best chance for their own children to rise out of the ranks of the sick and the inadequate will exist if they know where to look for help when it is needed.

If this group has no strong vocational incentives to help them, the problem of motivating them to learning, especially in the last year of the course, is a difficult one. Moreover, their span of attention is so short that no course, however interesting, keeps their attention indefinitely. Yet their desire to leave school should tell us something. What they are perhaps looking for more than anything is adult status, and this is probably true of all pupils, their interest in future vocations being but one aspect of the search. There is a strong case for the curriculum for this group in the year, or years, immediately preceding leaving school to be generally slanted towards material and procedures which suggest their growth to adulthood and which are not confined to the school. The results of the New York Homework Helpers project, in which less able adolescents successfully helped backward elementary school children to learn to read and made significant progress themselves while doing so, may be due to the adolescent feeling of increased status. These small children would treat them as adults, or near-adults, and they would be impelled to accept the challenge. Some of the integrated courses linked to activity outside school which are being developed by individual schools, as well as by national bodies, with the raising of the school-leaving age in view, seem promising in this regard. Their scientific evaluation, once they are developed, will be an urgent task and preparations towards this end need to be set in motion now; otherwise we will be caught napping as the American "Head Start" programme was, and courses whose success owes more to the Hawthorne effect[20] of the publicity and euphoria which surrounds their introduction, and less to their actual worth, will be extended from one school to many, when they should be discarded.

It is not difficult to tap sexual incentives, which are always only just beneath the surface. They can be tapped by any means from courses in sex education, linked to a consideration of the family and its needs, homemaking, child-rearing in both its physical and psychological aspects, do-it-yourself, dressmaking and beauty-care courses with something of an accent on hygiene, to suitable courses in literature. Suitable may be the operative word in the case of the least able. There is still not enough suitable material, suitable in level of difficulty, for the less able adolescent girl.

With regard to the social (civic) and religious or philosophic growth tasks and the incentives they produce for study, these would appear to be the weakest of the four listed by Wall, for the least able and least motivated children. In addition the very fact that these children do not get beyond the Piagetian stage of concrete operations, renders the job of exploring these tasks with them all the more difficult, since the areas in question lend themselves readily to abstract statements and somewhat less readily to concrete statements. The Schools Council's suggestion[21] that the school's failure to interest pupils in the humanities,

[20] It was found in a branch of American industry that new procedures accompanied by increased notice of workers increased productivity irrespective of their actual efficiency.

[21] *Schools Council Working Paper* No. 11, p. 3.

by comparison with vocational subjects, is due to basing the work on the subject disciplines, taught without reference to the needs of pupils, has a good deal of substance in it, especially as it is backed up by experiential evidence that the schools most successful with these pupils are those which consider their needs and interests rather than the logical content of the course. At the same time there are limits to the work that can be done—whatever the approach—which derive from the level of development reached by these children. It is highly desirable that children should learn to understand our society's institutions and should acquire a system of belief and a philosophy of life, but the least able will do so at a somewhat rudimentary level. Still, we should make sure that they do not work at a level *below* their capacity. One favourable factor is that this generation has been noted for increased interest and work in community service and for increased compassion. We can use the practical experience we give them as an intellectual base, and use it to stretch them as far as they can go.

So far in the actual curriculum of the less able child, we have considered "material" which is largely "content" based, and which can be gathered from several subject disciplines.

Mainly "skill" subjects present a different sort of problem from mainly "content" subjects.[22] There is little real overspill into another subject. It is true that mathematics is often used in physics, but it is used as a tool, not as an interlocking subject, and, as with every tool, the knack of it is acquired only by doing mathematics. Some of the skills are long and difficult to acquire and it is known that "skill" subjects exhaust interest more quickly than "content" subjects.[23] It is not difficult to see why this should be so. The informational content is less and the practice element high, because the information is arranged in structures which are the key elements in the skill. There is also evidence to show that they demand a highly structured approach in teaching. It is no wonder then that interest wanes, in spite of skilful efforts to maintain it relatively to "content" subjects. There is as much difference in interest between "skill" and "content" subjects as between working on a conveyor belt and driving a bus. There is more to see when doing the latter.

The implication of this for the less able child is not difficult to divine. The less able the child and the less motivated, the fewer skills we shall expect him to acquire, the more he should concentrate on "content" material or on a more dilettante[24] sampling of skills, for example, in art. With the least able, literacy and basic mathematics are the only skills that it is really vital for him to acquire.[25] This policy may appear to be one of soft options for the less able child, but it is not really so, since any learning process is arduous for him and his courage must be husbanded. It provides the best chance of keeping him willing to try to learn and so of avoiding demoralizing unemployment when his job becomes obsolete and he needs to take retraining.

Fundamentally, the same principle will also apply with the more able child. He will certainly need and want many more skills than the less able. The questions to answer are how many does he need and how many can he carry without losing heart and without losing interest.

[22] There is, of course, no subject which is wholly "skill" or wholly "content".

[23] See Stevens, F., *The Living Tradition*, Hutchinson, 1961, p. 291. Lewis, D. G., An investigation, of subject preferences of grammar school pupils, *Durham Res. Rev.*, vol. 14, Sept. 1963, pp. 95–105. Pritchard, R., The relative popularity of secondary school subjects at various ages., *Brit. J. Educ. Psychol.*, vol. V, 1935, pp. 157–74 and pp. 229–41.

[24] The word "dilettante" has been a dirty word for too long. We are all dilettantes in some fields of experience but are too puritan to admit it. Why shouldn't we play?

[25] This does not imply that there will be anything other than a basically common curriculum in the first 3 years of the secondary course.

To return for a moment to the less able child, this does not mean that we should deprive him of the opportunity to learn French in the early stages of the secondary school course. This subject has acquired curious overtones in terms of social and academic snobbery. It is symbolic of status. To deprive a less able child of the opportunity to learn French, is, therefore, to reject him out of hand. A distinction should be made between obliging a child to continue for a time with a subject he is beginning to dislike and to fail with, and never giving him the opportunity to start it. The latter policy he will view as a slight, the former is merely an imposition. The best policy is to give him the same opportunity to start French as is given to other children and, at a later stage, the opportunity to drop it, when he has found out whether he likes it or not, for some more attractive alternative. In this way his ego can survive without too much damage. He will have rejected a subject without having been unduly rejected himself.

Perhaps the greatest need of the disadvantaged in the context of all their growth tasks is the need to widen their experience. Here the range of arts and crafts, of hobbies and sports available within the curricular and extra-curricular programmes of many secondary schools bring a plethora of experiences to them, such as the old elementary school never could have done. Indeed the increase in the range of hobbies amongst teachers has been as important a factor in promoting this development as has the greater academic and professional expertise acquired since the war by non-graduates. But, however great the range, it is still important to start from where the child is. For many children it is more necessary, if a permanent interest is to be developed, to start, for example, with pigeon-fancying, than with bird-watching. An interest in ornithology can develop from either, but whereas the latter may appear "cissy" and be rejected for that reason, pigeon-fancying is known as a strong man's hobby and is hence acceptable by boys aspiring to become strong men themselves.

It has been noted how alert and knowledgeable are the children of the air force and army personnel, who move all over the world and see many things that ordinary children never see. One of the greatest needs of the disadvantaged child is to see things outside their own milieu. The many residential courses that have been developed by schools, the disused railway stations in remote mountain fastnesses, the castles in Wales bought by the local authority for them and manned by staff, have brought many children to a better understanding of the breadth of experience available to them in the world, of what their teachers are trying to do for them and of what their teachers are like as human beings. They have thus enabled the schools to convince some less able children that their teachers were basically on their side, with happy results for their motivation and progress.[26]

If we are to tap motivation in the less able child, it will not be enough to alter curriculum and teaching methods. Perhaps as much as anything we have to alter our methods of marking work. Poor marks, week in week out, depress motivation. At present the most able pupils, who are the best motivated on the whole and need motivating least, get the best marks, and the least able, who need motivating most, get the worst. Class teaching leads to class marking, not to individual marking.

However, it is very easy to say "mark the individual against himself". Teachers need some method of doing so which will be at least moderately reliable. A first approach to obtaining a standard for each child against which to mark him would be to set four or five pieces of work at the beginning of the school year, each done in class and based on material taught in the immediately preceding lesson. These could then be corrected, without a mark being

[26] See p. 35.

given, and a photostat copy of each could be placed in a separate file for each child. The piece of work, out of the four or five done, nearest the average for each child could be taken as the "standard" by which to judge subsequent work, and a good mark be given for getting above it, a poor mark for falling below it, preferably on a five-point scale from A to E. The "standard" could be reassessed, say, every 6 months or every year. The system would keep all children up to the mark without depressing anyone and it would encourage them to real effort.

It would, of course, be necessary to keep the child's parents informed as to how he rated with reference to the whole age-group, since this affects future prospects on leaving school. A parents' meeting to explain the system, with a circular to parents who failed to attend it, and to indicate how a child rated on his current showing, would round off the scheme.

From time to time the introduction of individual forms of marking have been mooted, and scattered experiments here and there have been undertaken. Now that one of the main aims of education must be to maintain motivation to learn, a general movement towards such methods of marking would be one of the best ways to achieve this objective.

Lastly, we have now to consider whether we can continue to deprive the least able pupils of the immediate objective which entry for a public examination gives to other pupils in the last year of compulsory schooling, and whether, if we do, they will feel as rejected as 11+ failures have done. One of the most urgent tasks of ROSLA is to try and set up suitable syllabuses for say, three C.S.E. examinations covering material in the humanities, the sciences and the arts and crafts, which the less able pupils could cover, with a view to a Grade 4 C.S.E. certificate.

In short, with these pupils we have to tap motivation in every possible way and to use the energy it engenders for productive learning in relation to their adult tasks.

3. *Aesthetic Subjects*

So far we have dealt with "academic" subjects, whether "content" or "skill" subjects, and in relation first to the more able and then to the less able child. Aesthetic subjects need special consideration, since one can be both participant and audience. Along with the crafts and physical education, they provide all pupils with the most fruitful source of leisure time hobbies and pastimes, apart from those they will find in extra-curricular activities. In the early stages of the course they should provide pupils with varied opportunities to "taste" rather than to become skilled. A pupil cannot know whether he wants to take up painting or pottery as a more advanced skill until he has tried both. Most young men take out a number of girls before they hit upon their heart's desire. In providing varied opportunities to try out these skills, small schools are at a disadvantage by comparison with larger schools, with their large art and craft departments and their variety of practitioners. They need either very versatile teachers or one full-time head of department and two or three part-time teachers, perhaps shared with other schools. It is often difficult to staff these subjects really satisfactorily in small schools in any other way.

The reader will have noted that the aesthetic, craft and physical skills have been treated differently from other skills. This is because individually they are not essential to modern living, even though collectively they are, whereas the ability to read and compute are. We cannot easily get along without the latter, but it does not really signify which one of the aesthetic or craft skills is finally chosen, provided we have some outlet for hand and eye.

Even for the future craft or art specialist experience of a variety of skills in the early stages of the secondary school course is as profitable as competence in one. Thus in this group of subjects, as in the "content" subjects, it is better to start from a broad base rather than a narrow one. The same is probably true also of skills in physical education.

4. *General Considerations of Curriculum in the Last Years at School*

There would be some justification for suggesting that we should have a more common course up to the end of the fifth year than we have at present in the comprehensive school. The evidence concerning the instability of interests before the age of 16 or 17 and that showing that particular aptitudes tend to emerge more fully at present[27] around 15 suggest that one should treat the early teens as a guidance period in which a common curriculum is followed. The present habit of starting curricular choices in grammar and some comprehensive schools in the second and third year is counterproductive. Similarly, the comprehensive school custom of setting up options courses in the fourth year may also be a little too early.

At this point it will be fruitful to explore why the comprehensive school developed a regular, formal system of two-year options grouping, alongside a compulsory common core, in the fourth and fifth year, such as does not exist in either the grammar schools or perhaps even in many secondary modern schools. Historically, it would appear to be because the leaving age was 15 at the time and because the new comprehensive, in order to stand comparison with the grammar school, had to ensure that those who stayed on achieved good results. Hence many comprehensive schools pursued a policy of separating those who were staying on from the more restless leavers at the beginning of the fourth year, providing separate courses for both. Even if they later abandoned this practice the needs of some pupils to reach 'O' level standards, which they could not do without dropping some subjects, ensured the survival of subject dropping in a system where the needs of other pupils had also to be met. It will be interesting to see whether, once the effects of the raising of the leaving age are felt, it will continue to survive and whether options subject groups will start as early as the fourth year of the course. If they do, it will be more for reasons of educational inertia than for any that are rationally based.[28]

It seems, therefore, that one might seriously consider delaying the setting up of an options system as we know it till the beginning of the fifth year. Yet this is an awkward point administratively, as it leaves only a year before the end of compulsory schooling and the taking of a public examination. If the change involves a switch of teachers, a year is hardly enough for teacher and taught to adapt themselves to each other's ways and to recover from the effects of the change, in "skill" subjects particularly. The difficulty is that, with an options system from the fourth year, pupils risk making wrong decisions, as aptitudes and interest often fully emerge later than the age of 14, but if we delay till the fifth year there are teaching difficulties.

In order to resolve this dilemma, let us reflect for a moment what an options system is for. It is a system designed to make it possible to drop subjects. Therefore the way out of the dilemma may be to abandon or much reduce the dropping of subjects before the end of the

[27] See pp. 50–53. N.B. It does not follow, perhaps, that the present age of their emergence will always continue. Since aptitudes appear to arise out of experience, if there were nursery education for all and an earlier start in some subjects, conceivably aptitudes would emerge earlier. But this is speculation. One must deal with the situation as it is.

[28] In the same way as the age of 11 survived as the age of transfer. See p. 182.

fifth year. This broader curriculum would carry with it the disadvantage of some loss of standard in individual subjects, so that rather able pupils would be carrying, say, twelve C.S.E. subjects rather than eight 'O' levels. But standards as we know them are not sacrosanct. It may well be preferable to accept slightly lower standards to obtain a greater breadth of education. Certainly we ought to consider whether the system of options in the fourth or fifth year of the comprehensive school is still relevant, now the leaving age has been raised, and whether, if it is still relevant, it should involve such a large portion of the curriculum.

Should there be no differentiation in teaching method and approach to the curriculum, before the end of the fifth year? Whatever may be the case in 10 or 20 years' time, when every school is well equipped with all manner of electronic ironmongery suited to individual methods, this is hardly practical politics at the moment, in view of the differences in general intellectual capacities and motivational needs of pupils. There is a lot to be said, for this reason, rather than for any other, for differentiating the approach to the curriculum, with that for the more able being increasingly subject based and for the less able the more topic or theme based. This does not imply that traditional streaming would therefore reappear in the fourth and fifth year. Particular subjects or groups of subjects would appear on the time table at the same time as particular themes in the same field. It would then be up to the pupil to decide which he was going to choose. Because topics and subjects in the same area of knowledge would appear on the timetable at the same time, it would be possible for him to choose a subject discipline in one area of knowledge and a topic in another according to his individual needs; he might, for example, have crossed the Piagetian boundary between concrete and formal operations in one area and not in another; he might be motivated by sheer intellectual interest in one area and need work closely related to his basic drives in another. This system would guarantee maximum flexibility and ensure at the same time that pupils will continue to cover the main areas of the curriculum until the age when particular aptitudes and stable interests had fully established themselves. Within it one would also be able to allow for the fact that less able children can take only a smaller amount of academic "skill" subjects than able children and remain well motivated.

The construction of the fourth- and fifth-year timetables would clearly require a nice balancing of interests, but it would certainly be less complicated than the construction of timetables for these years in comprehensive schools as at present.[29]

A move in this direction would also have other advantages. For example, in many schools it would fit in better with the actual building provision. However educationists may theorize about the content of the curriculum, there are in practice limiting factors which prevent schools from providing exactly what they would like. The options system in comprehensive schools presupposes, even in large schools, the existence of a number of small division rooms for subjects for which there are not many takers. Where one large classroom exists, very often two or three small division rooms are needed. This situation is already causing difficulties in some schools, so that either the number of peripheral options has to be reduced, or the intake into the school has to be reduced, to release the necessary classrooms for these peripheral options classes, or minor building works have to be undertaken, or classes take place on landings and in cloakrooms.

With the raising of the school-leaving age, these difficulties may well be exacerbated under the present system. It seems that many schools will find themselves short of space and so be

[29] See Appendices II and III.

obliged to defer the start of options till the fifth year, a rather unexpected curricular result of their building provision. Hence a general movement towards a more common curriculum would ease the situation for these schools.

It would also make possible minor cuts in the cost of staffing since there would be no uneconomically small classes. Not that one should make educational changes for economic reasons. But if a justifiable educational change also reduces costs, this is an additional reason for accepting it, especially as the increasing demand for education, its increased costs and the need for development in such areas of education as nursery schools makes it more and more likely that cost-benefit analyses of policy will be made.

Such a change of policy would also help to bring this country more into line with Common Market countries. It is true that up to now Common Market countries have not felt the same need to adjust their educational policies to each other as in the case with their economic policies, but inevitably the movement towards the equivalence of degrees and certificates will gather momentum as workers increasingly work outside their own country. At that point the curricula of different countries will move towards each other. Our curricula are already much more specialized than those of any other Common Market country. If we do not begin to make adjustments soon we shall have more radical and painful readjustments to make later, and meanwhile British workers and pupils abroad will be handicapped.

Finally, previous developments in education do suggest that whenever the leaving age is raised, whenever comprehensive schooling is introduced, the start of differentiation of the curriculum is usually delayed.[30]

For all these reasons a change of policy with regard to the curriculum would seem to be advisable. It seems likely that it will be delayed unless we make radical readjustments with the sixth-form curriculum also. Other reasons for making such readjustments are suggested by the increasing cost and the increasing demand for university education. Unless we eventually move first-year university work into the sixth form the cost will become unduly burdensome. Hence the sixth form is likely to become an intermediate institution in its own right, between school and higher education.

What then should it offer? It would have received pupils very broadly educated, but to a rather lower level than formerly, in particular subjects. If it retained them for 4 years, it could provide first a 3-year course consisting of five subjects, three arts and two sciences, or vice versa, studied to an equal level, perhaps slightly below 'A' level. With such a curriculum, choice as between arts and science would not be irrevocable. If a student found he had made a wrong choice, with the aid of a conversion course in one subject in the last year, he could make the necessary switch. Universities are often exhorted to put on conversion courses, but they are not really geared to it, whereas a sixth form could be. The last year in the sixth, the fourth year, could then be devoted to first-year university work.

The policy outlined seems to offer the best prospect of achieving rational solutions to the problem of the curriculum of schools in England and Wales, without disturbing too much any of the parties involved, whether they be teachers facing the demands being made on them by the raising of the school-leaving age, heads of schools grappling with staffing problems, or universities pressurized by the advancing horizons of knowledge.

[30] As happened, for example, when the Swedish system was reorganized. N.B. Less able children would still need some small group work, if they were to leave school in a willing frame of mind, and their need for it should probably have a good measure of priority. A common baccalauréat for Europe is thought likely by Hutchins. (Hutchins, R. M., *The Learning Society*. Pall Mall Press, 1968, p. 68.)

CHAPTER 6

Size of School: Non-Curricular Aspects

THE trends in curriculum which we have so far considered, along with the social and intellectual forces which have influenced the development of the curriculum, including the movement towards comprehensive education, have certain implications for the size of schools. They are likely to increase it. Not that large schools were unknown until the recent move towards comprehensive education obliged us to reconsider the problem of size. In fact, a school of 2000 strong was run at Liège by the Brothers of the Common Life as far back as medieval times, and such schools are common enough on the Continent and in America today, but to the English the large school is in every sense foreign. Only when the comprehensive school arrived and great worry was felt as to whether it could be successful, success being evaluated in terms of a viable sixth form, were large schools set up here. It was assumed that a viable sixth form would be of about the same size as that usual in the grammar schools of the period. Implicit in the assumption was the idea, never really brought to the surface, that comprehensive school staying-on rates would be no higher than grammar school staying-on rates for the same IQ levels of pupils, and that grammar school rates themselves would not increase. Both these assumptions should have been critically reviewed in the light of the experience of American schools, for example, though it is doubtful whether at the time the idea that all pupils should be allowed to stay on if they wished to would have been acceptable to many educationists. Large comprehensive schools of up to 2000 strong were therefore built and the ideas of "comprehensive" school and of "educational factory" were equated in the public mind.

Meanwhile, almost *sub rosa*, a certain number of one- and two-stream country grammar schools were becoming first bi-lateral and then comprehensive, whatever the nomenclature bestowed on them in the L.E.A. guidebooks of the day. That, in time, the protagonists of the selective system and equally those who had worked in or organized the new large comprehensive schools should question, though for different reasons, the viability of small comprehensive schools, is perhaps an indication of the blinding power both of words themselves and of particular city- and suburbia-bound experiences. Small comprehensive schools were already in existence and functioning well. "Comprehensive" began to be redefined in terms not only of taking in whole age groups, as originally, but also of providing a vast range of subjects, as the large comprehensive schools were able to. Yet no one had really seriously questioned at an earlier stage the viability of small grammar schools as purveyors of a reasonably adequate curriculum for the children of the small communities they existed to serve, children who would otherwise have had to travel very long distances to school. These schools were able to get their students to 'O' and 'A' levels, and in the latter case in a sufficient range of subjects to allow of a reasonable choice of disciplines at university level. Three- and four-stream comprehensive schools now exist in many of these small communities. Can they do as good a job for all the children of the area from the curricular point of view and from other points of view, even as the very small grammar school did previously for the academic? Do the children of small communities have to despair, in a comprehensive system, of obtaining an education suited to their age, aptitude and ability within their own community or must they travel long distances or even board away from home during the week, in order to get it? What real difference does size, large or small, make to the education given by teachers and the education accepted by pupils? What are the relative advantages and disadvantages of large and small schools and what concrete evidence is there on the subject of size of school, other than the individual personal experiences of the protagonists, not easily subject to experimental verification?

One can look at these questions from two points of view: on the one hand the curricular and other activities offered by the school and on the other the extent of real participation in both by the pupils.

In considering both of these aspects we have to bear in mind that children are in some sense being educated every minute that they are awake, indeed as Sir Michael Sadler said, "The things that happen outside the schools are more important than those that happen inside". Moreover, even inside schools the classroom, though the locus of the school's main purposes, is not the only place where children acquire experiences that may influence them profoundly and indeed may influence what they in fact learn in the classroom. For example, a windy day, as every experienced teacher knows, disturbs children's learning, and so does bad temper induced by congestion in the corridors.

It is proposed, therefore, first of all to consider, not the curriculum, vital though this is, but the school as an organization of a given size, its impact on children's direct experiences in terms of its size and its impact on teachers' experiences and through them on the children's indirect experiences. Taking the material in this order will enable us to make use first of data in other fields, which one could not do if curriculum was considered first, since the curriculum is specific to educational institutions.

A. Non-curricular Aspects of Size: Morale and Participation

1. *The Effects of Size in Other Institutions than the School*

For a long time sociologists concentrated their efforts on determining the effects of size in the industrial and commercial field and neglected the field of education. It is only in the last 10 years or so that work has been done on this aspect of education and the data is necessarily incomplete. First, therefore, a review will be made of research evidence on the effects of size[1] of institutions in general and then the school will be looked at.

Research conducted in a variety of areas has led to the following conclusions with regard to the extent of participation, and of social interaction, and to people's reported experiences in the organizations investigated. Persons in smaller institutions[2] are absent and resign positions less often, are more punctual and more productive, are more important to the

[1] The problem of definition of "large" and "small" is a thorny one. Presthus has defined "large" as encompassing situations where face-to-face relationships amongst most members are prevented by the number of personnel involved, but this has been disputed.

[2] Campbell, W. J., School size: its influence on pupils, *J. Educ. Admin.*, vol. III, no. 1, May 1965, pp. 5–6, quoting a total of twenty-five investigations in other institutions than schools.

groups and the settings in which they find themselves, function in positions of responsibility more frequently and in a wider range of activities, are more frequently involved in roles directly relevant to the tasks of the group, have broader conceptions of their role, demonstrate more leadership, participate more frequently when participation is voluntary, and are more interested in the affairs of the group or organization. In line with the reports on participation, smaller institutions are shown to give rise to better communication and social interaction. There is greater individual participation in both communication and interaction and less centralization of communication around one or a few persons. Small groups are shown to ease communication, both through greater clarity of the material communicated and decreased difficulty in transmitting it, and to promote greater cohesiveness within the group and better relationships between members of it. Persons in smaller groups find their work more meaningful, are more familiar with the organizational arrangements and are in general more satisfied with their work. As institutions increase in size a larger, and larger relative, proportion of the activity they generate tends to be addressed to the top men and a smaller relative proportion to other members. The larger and more bureaucratically efficient the organization the greater the degradation of the individual. In this group of findings one may find some, though by no means all, of the reasons for unrest in the work situation as the size of individual firms increases. Yet as Campbell remarks,[3]

> this knowledge has had little influence upon schools, and the widespread concern for the organization man has not been accompanied by a similar concern for the organization child. On the contrary the enlargement of schools has often been accepted not as an unfortunate necessity but as a welcome educational improvement. This evaluation is usually based upon the assumption of a direct positive relationship between the properties of schools and the experiences and behaviours of their pupils, e.g. the assumption that a rich curriculum means rich experiences for students, or that a comprehensive programme of extra-curricular activities means strong individual involvement.

And Corwin says

> Learning theories in education have tended to be dominated by research into the teaching function itself and into growth and development within organizational settings, e.g. teaching methods, streaming, and non-streaming, etc., but the effect of the organization itself was taken for granted most of the time . . . except when the traditional organization was threatened by change. Usually, at these crisis periods a catalogue of idealogies, grounded in rural tradition, is suddenly announced: small classrooms and small schools are less efficient than large ones: small classrooms are more effective than larger ones. . . .[4]

The last comment is from an American familiar with American experiences, but it reads like an account of recent history in English education. Yet one must at least assume that the way schools are organized, their size, their buildings and the layout of their buildings will in some manner affect the climate of schools. None the less at present, research has not a great deal to tell us about how organizations influence the learning climate, but that they do influence it is now almost certain.[5] What evidence is there on the influence of size of school on the learning climate?

2. *Size and School Climate: Teachers*

One aspect of the learning climate is what people often refer to as the atmosphere of a school which, directly and indirectly, affects both children and teachers.

[3] *Ibid.*, p. 11.

[4] Corwin, Ronald G., Education and the sociology of complex organizations, in: Hansen, Donald A. and Gerstl, Joel E. (eds.), *On Education: Sociological Perspectives*, Wiley, 1967, p. 166.

[5] *Ibid.*, p. 166.

Those who are familiar with education can often sense the atmosphere of a school as soon as they enter the front gate and the praise or blame they feel the school merits on that account is usually laid at the head's door, as if he were the only influence on the school. Important though his role must be, it seems probable that there are other influences responsible for a school "climate". There is some research which suggests that the actual size of a school may affect its atmosphere, its "climate" as measured on a continuum from "open"[6] to "closed". It has particular reference to the reactions of teachers.

The effect of size of school on the degree to which a school has an open or a closed climate is illustrated in a study by Carver and Sergiovanni.[7] They drew together the results from several studies in which Halpin's Organizational Climate Description Questionnaire had been administered in both elementary and secondary schools, large and small. The results are incorporated in Table 1, taken from their article.

TABLE 1

Climate in Secondary Schools: a Comparison of Three Studies and the Original Development Sample
Percentage by climate type

Climate type	Halpin and Croft: elementary schools	Andrews: secondary schools	Watkins: secondary schools	Carver and Sergiovanni: secondary schools
Open	24	23	0	0
Autonomous	8	0	0	0
Controlled	18	17	11	0
Familiar	12	15	0	25
Paternal	11	15	33	3
Closed	27	30	56	72
Mean no. of teachers per school	Not available	25	52	93
No. of schools	71	47	9	36

The OCDQ had been originally constructed for use with elementary schools but Andrews' study suggested that it could also be used with secondary schools. It is clear, however, from the Watkins figures and the results of the Carver and Sergiovanni's investigation that, since we have no reason to suppose their choice of schools was defective, either the OCDQ does not validly measure the climate in large secondary schools or that large secondary schools have by nature closed climates. A closer examination of their results by Carver and Sergiovanni revealed that two of the sub-tests of the OCDQ were accounting for the major differences in the total score of different schools, the one, labelled Esprit, measuring a Group characteristic, and the other, labelled Thrust, i.e. motivation through examples, measuring a Leader characteristic. They conclude that it seems likely that *total* staff teacher–teacher

[6] An "open climate" school is defined as a school whose head has high consideration for his staff, high level of "thrust" (motivation by example) and absence of close supervision and whose staff have high "esprit" and intimacy between members of staff and perceive the school organization as helping them in their task. A "closed climate" school has a head with high aloofness, low consideration and close supervision, while the staff has a high level of disengagement from the school and perceives it as hindering their task.

[7] Carver, Fred D. and Sergiovanni, Thomas J., Some notes on the OCDQ, *J. Educ. Admin.*, vol. VII, no. 1, May 1969, p. 80.

interaction and teacher–principal interaction are so dramatically reduced, relatively, in large secondary schools that teachers are simply unable, however "open" the policy of the headmaster, to rate as "most favourable" their response to the items in these two sub-tests. Thus low Esprit and Thrust scores are inevitable and therefore "closed" climate scores result. A similar result was found by Gentry and Kenny[8] with respect to size and climate in elementary schools. To secure for the larger secondary schools the chance of rating as having an "open" climate it would probably be necessary to shift the point of reference from which individual teachers make their judgements from the school as a total unit and the head as leader, to some sub-unit such as a school department, with the head of department as leader. When teachers in large secondary schools use the school as a total unit as their point of reference, their schools' low scores on openness of climate reveal the inevitable limitations of their interpersonal interactions. They tend to see the head as remote and without drive, whether he is so by personality or not, and they tend to complain that they "do not know half the staff". There would seem to be an element of critical size of school in their reactions.

Halpin,[9] one of the main figures in the development of organization theory and in research on organization in education, puts forward the hypothesis that there is a relationship between size of school and openness of climate. It may be size which is the key issue or size in relationship to available space and he refers to Calhoun's study of rats[10] which reacted adversely under conditions of increased population density.

The effect on teachers of open climate schools as distinct from that of closed climate schools was demonstrated by Andrews.[11] He showed that teachers in open climate schools expressed greater satisfaction, greater confidence in the principal's effectiveness and greater confidence in the effectiveness of the school than did those working in closed climate schools. They also felt more committed to their schools.

Of possible relevance to the question of closed climates in large secondary schools is a study on communications in a high school by Brennan.[12] The effect of the emergence of a greater number of levels of hierarchy and responsibility on the communications network of a school can be seen from one of the results of the study. Brennan found that wherever there was a difference of opinion between two members of a school (including the head) as to whether a particular communication involved a matter of major policy or of only minor policy, the two people concerned were almost always at different levels of the school hierarchy. This finding tends to support the hypothesis that upward communication in a school staff is likely to be inaccurate and it is similar to the results of an investigation by Long[13] in other types of organizations. If the number of levels of the school hierarchy is increased because of an increase in school size, the blockages to communication and the opportunities

[8] Gentry, Harold W. and Kenny, James B., The relationship between organizational climate of elementary school and school location, school size and the economic level of the school community, *Urban Education*, vol. 3, no. 1, 1967, pp. 19–31.

[9] Halpin, Andrew W., Change and organizational climate, *J. Educ. Admin.*, vol. V, no. 1, May 1967, pp. 9–10.

[10] Calhoun, John B., Population density and social pathology, *Scientific American*, no. 206, 2 Feb. 1962, pp. 139–48.

[11] Andrews, John H. M., School organizational climate: Some validity studies of OCDQ, *Can. Educ. Res. Dig.*, vol. 5, no. 4, Dec. 1965, pp. 317–34.

[12] Brennan, Barrie, Communication in a high school staff, *J. Educ. Admin.*, vol. V. no. 2, Oct. 1967, p. 130.

[13] Long, Norton E., Administrative communication, in: Malick S. and van Ness, E. H. (eds.), *Concepts and Issues in Administrative Behavior*, Prentice Hall, Englewood Cliffs, N. J. 1962, pp. 147–9.

for misunderstandings are likely to increase[14] and adversely to affect teachers' morale. This may help to explain why the OCDQ measured large secondary schools as having closed climates.

The effect of size on other aspects of institutions can be seen in a number of other investigations. Two studies, one in education, one not, illustrate the effect of size on people's knowledge of each other. The Acton Society Trust studies[15] showed that knowledge of the names of administrators was negatively correlated with size and acceptance of rumours was positively correlated. Interest in the affairs of an organization was also negatively correlated with size. In 1965 in a study of fifteen Los Angeles high schools Monahan[16] found that teachers in schools of over 2100 students showed significantly less knowledge about their students than in those with smaller number of students.

The effect of school size on decision-making can be seen in a study by Bridges.[17] He concluded that school size tends to determine the degree of teacher participation in decision-making and that there was less participation for teachers in larger schools (defined as having 20–32 teachers) than in small schools (12–19 teachers).

One source of greater conflict and stress in the large school than in the small arises from the nature of the school as an organization staffed by professional or semi-professional people. Such people are of necessity to a greater or lesser extent specialists, with their own specialized field of knowledge, and they expect and need a considerable measure of autonomy in their own work. In many respects, though not in all, they are the best judge of the extent to which the organization of the school is helping or hindering their work. Hence a degree of conflict and stress between a head and his staff is perhaps inevitable, even in a small school. As a school increases in size, the number of levels in the hierarchy increase, and the bureaucratic or semi-bureaucratic requirements of hierarchial authority, the inevitable increase in fixed procedures and administrative rules necessary to cope with the administrative effects of size, are likely to increase the possibility of conflict between teachers and administrators.[18] Yet if the levels of hierarchy do not increase in number, problems of organizational efficiency will arise[19] (as recently in Dutch schools, due to a long tradition of professional autonomy of graduate teachers and the lack of the concept of school departments). An investigation by Brown[20] in which he used the Leadership Behaviour Description Questionnaire, constructed on the assumption that how a head really behaves is less important than how teachers perceive that he behaves, since this is what influences their own behaviour, showed that teachers' satisfaction, their confidence in the head and their belief in the effectiveness of the

[14] A study by Smith (Smith, Alfred Gond, *Communication and Status. The Dynamics of a Research Center*, Eugene Center for the Advanced Study of Educational Administration, Univ. of Oregon, 1966) of another type of institution showed that the greater the number and variety of statuses in an organization, the greater were the barriers to communication within it.

[15] Acton Society Trust, *Size and Morale*, London, 1953.

[16] Monahan, William Welsh, Teacher's knowledge of students related to urban high school size, Doctor's thesis. Berkeley: Univ. of California, 1965. Abstracted in *Dissertation Abstracts*, vol. 26, no. 2, 1966, pp. 830–1.

[17] Bridges, E. M., Teacher participation in decision-making, *Administrator's Notebook*, vol. 12, nos. 1–4, May 1964, pp. 410–43.

[18] Brown, Alan F., Research in organizational dynamics: implications for school administrators, *J. Educ. Admin.*, vol. V, no. 1, May 1967, p. 37. This view has recently been disputed.

[19] Roggema, J., *De Schoolse School. Een Orienterend Onderzoek naar kenmerken van de school als Organisatie* (The school: an explanatory inquiry into the characteristics of the school as an organization). Assem van Gorcum, 1967. This study stresses the large area of autonomy of Dutch teachers and the relative lack of power to direct and co-ordinate the professional activities of teachers in school.

[20] Brown, Alan F., Reactions to leadership, *Educ. Admin. Quart*, vol. 3, no. 1, Winter 1967, pp. 62–73.

school were in fact sensitive to their perceptions of his leadership. If their perceptions of his leadership are impeded by misunderstanding—and differences of view as between different levels of the hierarchy are shown to occur more frequently than between people on the same level—stress and lowered morale are likely to result in a large school more often than in a small school.

The open climate school has been shown to improve teacher morale. Is an improvement in teacher morale accompanied by better standards of work by the teacher? A weakness of much research in the area of teacher morale is to assume that a teacher's performance of his job is related to his satisfaction with it rather than to test out the hypothesis. Yet industrial studies have shown that workers' morale is not necessarily related to productivity. Studies in this area of educational research are few, the main one being by Gross and Herriott[21] who carried out an investigation in elementary schools in large American cities on the relationship between the degree and type of leadership provided by the principal (Executive Professional Leadership,[22] often referred to as E.P.L.) and (a) the morale of the school staff; (b) their classroom performance; (c) the academic progress of pupils. An important and technically sophisticated study, even though it has one or two methodological shortcomings,[23] it showed that E.P.L. was positively related to all three.[24] The causal link, if any, between staff morale and their classroom performance is not directly established, but at least the link between each and E.P.L. is. Moreover, there is a certain similarity between Gross's measures of E.P.L. and Halpin's measures of the behaviour of principals in open and closed climate schools. If one may therefore conclude that an open climate school leads to better classroom performance by teachers and better academic progress by pupils and if in addition teachers in large secondary schools are prevented, by the very size of the schools, from perceiving their school as having an open climate, one might then infer that academic standards might be adversely affected by this aspect of the schools' life. From inference to proof, causally established in the course of an empirical investigation, is, however, a very long way.

The effects on morale of large size may well be worse in poor socio-economic areas than in residential suburbs. A study by Nicholas[25] and others of two schools of similar low socio-economic background but different size (one school was half the size of the other) reports that they were found to have differences in atmosphere. The smaller school had a more "open" climate, the larger school had a "closed" climate, as empirically measured. The "open" school had a significantly lower frequency of behaviour problems among the pupils than the "closed" school.[26] The results of only one comparison must, of course, be treated with reserve, but Nicholas tentatively concludes that the effects of large concentrations of children in low socio-economic setting schools may need to be evaluated in terms of the

[21] Gross, N. and Herriott, R. E., *Staff Leadership in Public Schools*, Wiley, New York, 1965, pp. 34–57.

[22] Defined as the type of leadership provided in an organization staffed by professional workers, who therefore expect a degree of autonomy in their work, by a principal who in his view of his task "stresses his obligation to improve the quality of staff performance" (Gross and Herriott's own words). The amount of decision-sharing, egalitarian relationships with teachers and degree of support given were all related to the principal's E.P.L., which affected his contribution to teachers' morale, his effect on their performance of their jobs and the degree of help he gave them.

[23] See Banks, O., *The Sociology of Education*, Batsford, 1968, pp. 169–70.

[24] The study also showed, incidentally, that the stronger the professional leadership of the principal's immediate superiors, the stronger his own.

[25] Nicholas, Lynn V., Virgo, Helen E. and Wattenberg, William W., *Effect of Socio-Economic Setting and Organizational Climate on Problems Brought to Elementary School Offices*, Final Report of Cooperative Research Project No. 2394, Wayne State Univ., Detroit, Michigan, 1965. Quoted by Halpin.

[26] See also pp. 94, 99 and 126–7 for indirect evidence on discipline.

climate they create for the school organization and for pupil adjustment. With less pupil problems confronting him, the principal in the "low-open" school was free to initiate more varied activities than was possible in the "low-closed" school. He was able to devote time to drawing parents into involvement in school affairs and encouraging livelier interaction patterns with staff, outside agencies, auxiliary services and the community. Meanwhile the principal and staff of the "low-closed" school were virtually immobilized, in so far as other activities were concerned, by the flood of pupil-behaviour problems. Any attempts at initiation of new ideas by the principal may have been construed as overburdening the staff under such conditions.

With reference to British schools Eric Hoyle[27] suggests that, with the growth in size and complexity of secondary schools, bureaucratization may be increasing in our system and that we have not yet investigated the implications of such developments for teachers' morale and effectiveness and the way in which they affect the formal purposes of the school. He also refers to an article by Wilson[28] in which the latter explores possible conflicts experienced by teachers, mentioning specifically the case where the teacher finds his commitment to children thwarted by the size and complexity of the school. The latter also asked if growth in the size of schools and of increased specialization of teachers generates conflicts between commitment to children and career prospects.

One of the results of building very large schools is likely to be an increase in stress for middle rank executives directly related to the ambiguity of their roles. House[29] studied the influence structures of a single comprehensive high school and his study revealed that different influence structures functioned in relation to each of twelve different organizational tasks. Equally, the many books that describe the internal working of the large British comprehensive school indicate more complex structures, often with one person filling two roles. Yet an investigation by Kahn,[30] which analysed the stresses common to large organizations, found that one type common amongst educators, especially those at the middle level, was stress due to ambiguity in their roles. Hence an increase in the number of large schools must inevitably mean an increase of stress on senior teachers.

Moreover, the N.F.E.R. study noted an increase in hours of work for all teachers when they worked in large schools.[31]

A link between teachers' and pupils' responses is to be found in a study by Rose.[32] In an investigation of the relationship between the personal qualities of teachers and their organizational behaviour, and between their organizational behaviour and their pupils' response to school, the factor of school size was found to be an influence of some importance in altering the basic relationship and affecting pupils' attitudes and aspirations.

3. *Size of School and Pupils*

The direct effects of school size on pupils have been investigated by a number of workers.

[27] Hoyle, Eric, Organizational analysis in the field of education, *Educ. Res.*, vol. 7, Feb. 1965, pp. 97–114.

[28] Wilson, B. R., The teachers' role: a sociological analysis, *Brit. J. Sociology*, vol. XIII, no. 1, 1962, pp. 15–32.

[29] House, John H., An analysis of interpersonal influence relations within a school organization, Doctor's thesis. Edmonton, University of Alberta, 1966. Quoted *Rev. Educ. Res.*, vol. 37, no. 4, Oct. 1967, p. 409.

[30] Kahn, R. C. *et al.*, *Organizational Stress: Studies in Role Conflict and Ambiguity*, Wiley, New York, 1964.

[31] Monks, T. G. (ed.), *Comprehensive Education in Action*, N.F.E.R., 1970, p. 51.

[32] Rose, Gale W., Organizational behaviour and its concomitants, *Administrator's Notebook*, vol. 15, no. 7, 1967.

A study was undertaken by Barker[33] and his associates at the University of Kansas in the early 1960s. Barker had already done work on the effects of size in other types of institutions and used this experience to set up a complex and sophisticated series of investigations, involving a preliminary survey of a total of 218 high schools varying in size from eighteen to 2287. Thirteen of these schools were then studied intensively, and thirty-nine for special, limited investigations. The study was mainly focused on activities outside the classroom, but there is some data on academic activities.

The schools were analysed in terms of the number of behaviour settings[34] they provided. At one end of the scale, a school with 2287 pupils had 499 distinct settings, whilst at the other a school of thirty-five pupils had only sixty. The large school therefore was able to provide a much greater number of activities. If one divides the number of pupils by the number of settings to obtain the "setting density", the large school is, however, seen to have 4.58 pupils per setting and the small 0.58 pupil. The probability of pupil participation in behaviour settings is therefore much greater in the small school than the large, since a particular setting cannot survive if no one opts for it. These figures also show that school settings do not increase at the same rate as pupils. More pertinently perhaps, the varieties of settings increase relatively little. In the example given the large school had 65 times as many pupils as the small school, 8 times as many settings but only 1·5 times as many varieties of settings (forty-three compared with twenty-nine). The small-school pupil is therefore much less penalized in the range of his activities than might appear at first sight. Forty-four per cent of the varieties were common to all schools, 47 per cent or more of the behaviour settings of every school were in common varieties, and the percentages were even greater when individual large and small schools were compared, the large and one of the smallest schools sharing 77 per cent of the varieties. All of the smaller schools' and 80 per cent of the large schools' settings were common varieties.

The authors limited their focus mainly to activities outside the classroom, on the grounds that their main aim was to study motivation and participation and that it was difficult to assess either, where attendance and participation are not voluntary (a claim that one might query) and on the grounds that, in the Kansas schools they studied, the great amount of students' energies invested in extra-curricular activities and the schools' extensive support of them made them part of the total educational process.

Table 2[35] shows the student population, number of behaviour settings, the setting density and the varieties of settings in the thirteen schools studied intensively.

Table 3[36] shows the number and percentages of behaviour settings of various types in the thirteen intensively investigated schools.

A remark by Barker will serve both as a comment on this data and as an introduction to further investigations.

> We have discovered[37] that small high schools are, in fact, not so small on the inside as they are on the outside. In terms of number of behaviour settings, number of varieties of behaviour settings, and number of inhabitants per setting—interior characteristics not easily seen from the outside—small

---

[33] Barker, R. G. and Gump, P. V., *Big School, Small School*, Stanford, California, 1964.

[34] For example, mathematics classes taken by Mr. X at School Y is a behaviour setting, as is also the Art Club, or the headmaster's office. No distinction as to relative importance of behaviour settings was made in these initial calculations.

[35] Taken from Barker and Gump, *op. cit.*, table 4.3, p. 49.

[36] *Ibid.*, table 4.6, p. 54.

[37] *Ibid.*, p. 63.

TABLE 2

Student Population, Number of Behaviour Settings or Differentiation, Population/Differentiation Ratios, and Varieties of Settings in Thirteen Kansas Schools

School	Population (P)	Differentiation (D)	P/D Ratio	Varieties
Otan	35	60	0·58	29
Dorset	45	58	0·78	28
Walker	83	96	0·86	31
Malden	92	78	1·18	33
Meadow	113	94	1·20	32
Midwest	117	107	1·09	33
Vernon	151	98	1·54	29
Haven	221	154	1·44	36
Eakins	339	139	2·44	34
Booth	438	218	2·01	39
University City	945	312	3·03	36
Shereton	1,923	487	3·95	41
Capital City	2,287	499	4·58	43

TABLE 3

Number and Per Cent of Behaviour Settings within each School Which Fall into Four Variety Groupings

School	Educational		Athletic		Operating		Extra-curricular		Total
	No.	%	No.	%	No.	%	No.	%	
Otan	12	(20)	10	(17)	11	(18)	27	(45)	60
Dorset	15	(26)	12	(21)	6	(10)	25	(43)	58
Walker	17	(18)	13	(14)	11	(12)	55	(57)	96
Malden	14	(18)	13	(17)	8	(10)	43	(55)	78
Meadow	20	(21)	15	(16)	11	(12)	48	(51)	94
Midwest	18	(17)	15	(14)	13	(12)	61	(57)	107
Vernon	18	(18)	17	(17)	8	(8)	55	(56)	98
Haven	27	(18)	20	(13)	14	(9)	93	(60)	154
Eakins	40	(29)	18	(13)	14	(10)	67	(48)	139
Booth	39	(18)	22	(10)	32	(15)	125	(57)	218
University City	56	(18)	53	(17)	57	(18)	146	(47)	312
Shereton	88	(18)	54	(11)	101	(21)	244	(50)	487
Capital City	108	(22)	50	(10)	114	(23)	227	(46)	499

schools differ less from large schools than in terms of number of students and amount of space, which are perceptually salient external attributes of schools. Here is one basic of the school size illusion. But, more important, these findings raise the question of which are the stronger variables so far as the students are concerned, the inside ones or the outside ones, and how they operate upon students.

The effect of school size on pupils can be analysed more precisely by considering it from the following points of view: the degree of participation and social interaction; the level of satisfaction; the forces acting upon the pupils; and the academic offerings and results.

The effect of school size on pupils' activities and their relationship with each other was studied by Larson[38] in 1949. She reported that a higher percentage of students in small schools than in medium or large schools found it easy to make friends and liked all their

[38] Larson, Carol M., *School Size as a Factor in the Adjustment of High School Seniors*, Bulletin No. 511, Youth Series No. 6, State College of Washington.

school acquaintances. Higher percentages of students in large schools than in medium and small schools took part in no activities or only one and they experienced difficulty in getting into activities.

In 1961 Coleman[39] found that in large high schools there were smaller percentages of boys who played football or were able to name another pupil who was outstanding in certain areas. He also reported less agreement among pupils in large schools about pupils who were outstanding.

In the Barker and Gump investigation data from 218 high schools, varying in size from eighteen to 2287 pupils, showed that participation in inter-school events was more frequent in high schools within the 61–285 size range than in the smallest or the larger schools. Participation percentages for the inter-school events started at 28 in the smallest schools, rose to 45 and fell to 4 for the largest schools, even though the large schools, as schools, were the strongest supporters of inter-school activities and secured most of the prizes.

Pupils from small schools also showed more versatility in participating in inter-school activities. When the maximum score was 8, seniors from the small schools were averaging 4·8, while those from the largest schools were averaging 2·2. In the smallest school 53 per cent of the seniors scored 5 or more; in the largest schools only 4 per cent did so.[40]

Although the large schools provided a larger number and wider variety of activities outside the classroom the number of students participating was higher in small schools. The *degree* of participation was also more marked in the small school students. Almost one-half of the extra-curricular participations of students in the very small schools were performances.[41] This proportion ranged from about 40 per cent for schools in the 83–221 range, to 30 per cent for schools in the 339–438 range and to about 15 per cent in the very large schools. Small-school pupils also took part in a wider range of activities. They also held responsible and central positions in a wider variety of activities than did the large-school students and a greater percentage of them held positions of importance and responsibility. These results were confirmed by Kleinhart[42] in a study of sixty-three Michigan high schools. He found that pupil participation in school-related activities is more widely distributed in smaller schools.

4. *Forces Toward Participation in Large and Small Schools*

The Barker and Gump investigation showed that the number of persons present in behaviour settings not only alters overt behaviour in predictable ways but also determines, within limits, the nature of the psychological experience of students.[43] Students from the small schools, where there were relatively few people in any particular behaviour setting, reported more feelings of attraction[44] towards participation, more internal pressures[45] and more pressures from outside themselves[46] towards participation, than did those from large schools. Moreover, quite a large number of students in the big school experienced few, if any,

[39] Coleman, J. S., *The Adolescent Society*, Free Press of Glencoe, New York, 1961 p. 147.
[40] Campbell, *op. cit.*, p. 8.
[41] Campbell, *op. cit.*, p. 8.
[42] Kleinhart, Erwin John, Student activity participation and high school size. Doctor's thesis. Ann Arbor, University of Michigan, 1964. Abstracted in *Dissertation Abstracts*, vol. 25, no. 7, 1965, p. 3935.
[43] *Op. cit.*, pp. 133–5.
[44] e.g. "I thought that it would be lots of fun".
[45] e.g. "I had a responsibility with the activity".
[46] e.g. "I was expected to go".

forces towards participation. No such "outsiders" were to be found in the small schools. Exactly similar results came from a study of the effect of size on students' sense of responsibility and obligation. Pressures from outside the pupils' own personalities varied more with size of school than did feelings of attraction from within themselves and they correlated more highly with actual participation and involvement. It would seem therefore that it is the self-generated pressures of the behaviour settings which form the most powerful link between size of school and participation by pupils.

In certain situations, especially in rural areas, the location of large schools produce travel problems for many students, with indirect effects on participation in both school and community activities.[47]

A study by Campbell[48] showed that there were statistically significant differences between students of two small schools and one medium-sized school, a school which had developed as a result of transfer of students in small communities to a larger school, in respect of the total number of situations experienced out of school, time spent on travel (about double for commuting students), and the total number of community situations and miscellaneous activities in which they were involved. Amalgamation of schools and the resultant increase in size of school was shown to lead to a decrease in neighbourhood and community participation and to a reduction in the variety of situations and activities in which a part was taken. These results favourable to the small schools were, of course, in line generally with all the other results on participation. His study also confirmed that the medium-sized school suffered decreases in pressures, sense of responsibility, performances, participations, variety of participation and satisfactions.[49] The investigation, however, produced one result favourable to the larger school. In spite of the amount of time spent in travel, pupils averaged 80 minutes in private study per day as compared with 49 minutes for the small schools. Owing to the small number of schools investigated, it is not known whether this result is related to the issue of size of school or to individual school policies.

Two more investigations report similar results to those in Campbell's study. Maton[50] showed that distance from school is significant at the secondary level in affecting degree of participation. Korang[51] studied differences in attitude in pupils who either board at school, live at home near school or travel long distances from home. Although boarders seemed the worst placed, since they were both more dissatisfied with their leisure opportunities and felt more trouble with their studies than either of the other two groups, those who had long distances to travel felt more pressure than either boarders or those living near school and they experienced more isolation in their studies, the boarders getting help from fellow-pupils, those living near school getting help from the grown-ups at home. Presumably the time factor was the factor responsible. The author concluded that in organizing and siting schools more attention needs to be paid to the problems of distance. Marklund[52] concurred with

[47] Barker and Gump, *op. cit.*, p. 153.

[48] Campbell, W. J., Some effects of high school consolidation upon out-of-school experiences of pupils, *J. Educ. Admin.*, vol. IV, no. 2, Oct. 66, pp. 112–23.

[49] Campbell, W. J., *Ibid.*, pp. 112–23.

[50] Maton, J., Regional differences in educational participation, *Sociology of Education*, vol. 39, no. 3, 1966, pp. 276–87.

[51] Kåräng, Gösta, Bostadsförhallanden och skolanpassning (Housing conditions and adjustment to school), *Skole och Samhälle*, vol. 47, no. 4, 1966, pp. 106–13. (See *Sociology of Education Abstracts* vol. 2, no. 1, 1966, p. 131).

[52] Marklund, S., School organization, school location and student achievement, *Int. Rev. Educ.*, vol. XV, no. 3, 1969, pp. 295–320.

this view, the pupils in his investigation who lived a long way from school finding it more difficult to realize their potential than those living near school. He felt that authorities should hesitate before centralizing schools and should ensure by research that the large school does in fact make the most of the greater pedagogical facilities and possibilities. Generally similar results to those of the above studies were also found in the Barker and Gump investigation.[53] It is noteworthy that in siting new schools the French authorities bear the distance factor in mind.

The effect of increasing size of school is therefore to discourage the number, variety and depth of participations by pupils in the areas so far investigated, that is to say, in out-of-class activities, in community activities, and in "behaviour settings", including academic, generally.

Similar results are to be found in studies of pupils' satisfaction at school. A large-scale investigation by Anderson, Ladd and Smith[54] in 1954 found that the percentage of high school graduates who felt that their school experiences were very valuable and useful was negatively correlated with school size.

With regard to satisfaction associated with activities in school, in the Barker and Gump study,[55] junior students[56] from small schools reported more non-classroom activities from which they received satisfaction than did their large-school contemporaries, a larger number of satisfactions per activity mentioned and more satisfactions related to the development of physical and mental competence, to challenge, to group action and to general "uplift". Large-school juniors reported more satisfactions relating to vicarious enjoyment, to affiliation to large groups, to learning about their school's affairs and personalities, and to gaining "points" via participation. Presumably the size of their school prevented them from learning as easily about school business as small-school pupils and they took it less for granted. One might also assume perhaps that they compensated for lack of really active participation by finding satisfaction in the form of activity involved in gaining points. These differences in satisfaction between pupils of large and small schools were shown to be related to differences in the number of students who occupied more central important positions.

It is clear from the above data that small schools provide a socially different environment from large schools and that in respect of personal development it is a more favourable one. Research on child development shows that active participation is more stimulating than passive participation. It is not surprising then that small-school students experience greater satisfaction with school and that they tend to relate it to various aspects of personal development. The pressures which small schools are shown to exert more successfully than the large ones help to contribute to a sense of competence, since whether weak, strong, inept, skilful, young or experienced, each pupil really is important. Many activities cannot continue without his participation, and the increased sense of responsibility which this situation generates is likely to produce greater and earlier maturity, as well as greater capacity for leadership.

B. Other Non-curricular Aspects of Size

It is now proposed to look at features of size of school which, at first sight, do not appear to affect pupils' mental and emotional experiences, since they are related to their physical

[53] Barker and Gump, *op. cit.*, chaps. 9–11.

[54] Anderson, R. E., Ladd, G. E. and Smith, H. A., *A Study of 2,500 Kansas High School Graduates*, Kansas Studies in Education, Univ. of Kansas, no. 4, 1954.

[55] Barker and Gump, *op. cit.*, pp. 113–14.

[56] Junior students: students in the 11th grade, aged about 16.

experiences in a small or a large school. As the matter is explored, however, it will become clear that these elements connected with school size do have a bearing on experiences other than physical, indeed that they are bound up with the whole problem of pastoral care. Research evidence is largely absent. Hence part of this section will include reference to a mathematical analysis of the problem by the writer, to be published elsewhere.

1. *Size of School and Problems of Movement*

Whilst the effect of size of school on such matters as have already been discussed was not self-evident before investigations were undertaken, it is self-evident that the larger the school the longer it will take for teacher or pupil to move from class to class, unless both are restricted to one particular area of the school building, and the greater the waste of time. Actual experience in large comprehensive schools has borne this out, and there are numerous references at the anecdotal level to problems of movement, in the literature on these schools published in Britain during and since the 1950s.

One particular feature of the comprehensive school timetable makes the problem of movement even more intractable than it might otherwise be. As is well known, in comprehensive schools the fourth and fifth years are split up in many different ways according to the options subjects which pupils have chosen. Hence, for any given lesson they may be arriving at a particular classroom from as many as half a dozen or more other classrooms, of which at least one is likely to be on the other side of the campus. Since no lesson starts until every pupil, or almost every pupil, has arrived, on each of these occasions there will be maximum delay and the bigger the school the greater the delay. The options section of the fourth- and fifth-year timetable covers at least half and very often nearly two-thirds of the curriculum for these years. The amount of delay over a week is therefore likely to be considerable, and similar delays will also be encountered by the sixth form, though possibly not to the same extent. Such waste of time leads to aggravation and bad temper amongst teachers if they are stationed in their own specialist rooms, and to undue fatigue if they have to move about a great deal from room to room. The opportunities for misbehaviour by pupils on long journeys are self-evident.

Consequently, building plans which have been perfectly acceptable for smaller schools are revealed to have glaring weaknesses if adapted to large ones. For example, the linear or the cruciform types of buildings are quite unsuited to large schools if a policy of unrestricted movement around the school for all pupils is followed. Either is bound to lead to too heavy traffic at the centre of the building at changeover of lessons, unless the axes of the cruciform type or the two ends of the linear type are used for particular sections of the school population only, and unless these sections do not, generally speaking, move outside their own particular area. Such a policy cannot be pursued as an afterthought, without some loss of efficiency, because each axis is unlikely to contain the right mix of rooms for a particular section of the school, unless it has been decided at the planning stage that that section of the school will be housed there. If not, pupils will have to move out from time to time to specialist rooms available only in some other part of the building.

Equally, the siting of exit doors and paths used for moving from one area of the building to another has always to be looked at from the point of view of ease of movement.[57] This

[57] How long it can take to get the siting of a door changed can be seen in the chapter by Withington in: Halsall, Elizab eth (ed.), *Becoming Comprehensive: Case Histories*, Pergamon Press, 1970, p. 74.

seems a very trite thing to say, but it needs saying. This question does not always seem to get the consideration that it should from architects; yet it can make a great deal of difference both to teachers and pupils at the changeover of lessons, all the difference between going into a lesson in a calm, positive and hopeful frame of mind and going into it exasperated after a great "waste of spirit".

To return, however, to the main theme of movement problems, it will now be argued that they have a real influence on the effectiveness of pastoral care in the large school, especially in regard to proper supervision and control.

2. *Effects of Size of School on Problems of Pastoral Care, Supervision and Control*

The effects of the size of large comprehensive schools on pastoral care of pupils early preoccupied British educators and ways of reducing the anonymity of such institutions were soon discussed in the literature. In particular it was thought that pastoral care would be improved if the school was divided up into smaller units, and both house and year systems became characteristic features of the organization of large comprehensive schools. Though both these systems have been staunchly defended, the degree of success in improving pastoral care achieved by either has never really been fully evaluated. Although a thorough evaluation cannot be attempted here, it is none the less possible to make a fruitful analysis of the various aspects of pastoral care and of the effect on it of size of school, and of the various devices for breaking down large schools into smaller units.[58]

If a high degree of pastoral care and individual attention are to be realized certain conditions have to be present. Pupils have to come into contact with as few members of staff as possible, consonant with their having a suitably broad curriculum in relation to their age. The more teachers teach them, the more staff are "responsible" for them, the less pastoral care they get, because the teachers concerned have, over the week, too many pupils to look after to give enough really individual attention to each one, whether that attention be academic or personal.[59] It is for this reason that in many schools it is customary for teachers of the first year to teach more than one subject to the same class. Since academic teaching forms part of pastoral care in the sense that it prolongs contact and interaction this practice gives pupils more intensive pastoral care. It eases the transition to secondary school, from the primary school where the pupil has been entirely, or almost entirely, taught by one teacher and where he has been used to very intimate pastoral and academic care by one person. Similarly, even higher up the secondary school, it is quite common in streamed schools for the remedial class to be taught by one teacher for several of the basic subjects. Daily teaching contact at least once a day and preferably twice with the same teacher seems to act as a stabilizing force for children who are often not merely backward but also in some degree maladjusted.[60] Thus the younger or the less able the children, the more they appear to thrive, the more easily they appear to be socialized, when provided with this more intensive pastoral care, academic teaching itself forming part of the overall pastoral care

[58] Although the succeeding remarks are often critical of methods used to break down large comprehensive schools into smaller units, credit must be given to these schools for having thought about the problem. Grammar schools tend not to have done so, including very large grammar schools. The writer visited one very large grammar school as late as 1966, for example, to find that pastoral arrangements there were very much inferior to those of comprehensive schools of similar size.

[59] See p. 88 for evidence of teacher's knowledge of pupils in large schools.

[60] See p. 42, footnote 105.

given. As has been well said: "Teaching and pastoral care are indivisible and reciprocal."[61]

If we examine what pastoral care involves, we find that it has two aspects, a positive one and a negative. The positive aspect is that which encourages the flourishing of all those facets of a child's personality which, in society's view or on an absolute view, are deemed to be "right" or "suitable" or "worth while": the negative aspect is that which prevents the development of those facets deemed to be "wrong", "unsuitable" or "worthless".[62] If we consider for a moment the positive aspect of pastoral care, we can see that there would be a danger at secondary level in pupils being in contact with too few teachers, in relation to their age and mental capacity, since contact with too few minds and personalities might well stunt growth through lack of enough stimulation. Equally, having too many contacts would seem likely to produce rampant, uncoordinated growth, or enfeebled, distorted growth, where a child has more teachers than he can cope with mentally or emotionally. It would be difficult to spot, or to calculate exactly what the "right" or "ideal" number of teachers would be for a particular child at a particular stage of growth, but at least we can conceive of there being such an ideal number in respect of his positive development.

The negative aspects of pastoral care, on the other hand, are concerned with the degree of good control and supervision exercised, and hence are rather like the plumbing and drains of a city. Cities have produced good cultures without benefit of them, but at the expense of great discomfort and disease. Similarly, there are often pockets of excellent work in a disorganized and undisciplined school, but too much energy is wasted by teachers and taught on elbowing their way into their rights, for a high consistent level of performance, both academic and personal, to be achieved. The impact of size of school on the negative aspects of pastoral care, therefore, also merits serious study.

Before we proceed further it might be as well to consider the impact of the house and year systems of large schools, on the degree and quality of pastoral care, since these devices were introduced with the express intention of improving it. Both systems, of course, by reducing the numbers of children under the care of the house or year head to the level of the numbers of children in a small school, certainly make pastoral care easier and more possible for particular senior staff to attend to than it would be without them, other things being equal. This, however, is not quite the same thing as actually improving pastoral care for pupils.

As usually organized, the house system separates the teaching groups from the house groups. The tutor groups of the house system are frequently organized on a mixed ability, or even a mixed age, basis, whereas the teaching groups are often streamed. In such a context the children have to get to know more grown-ups than they would under the old form system. The form teacher usually taught his form, the house tutor cannot teach all of his group if the teaching groups are streamed or include several age groups. Hence he sees very little of his pupils and the possibility of his giving adequate pastoral care, or of exercising control over pupils' behaviour around the school, is thereby reduced. To organize houses on the basis of the streamed teaching groups, though it would improve individual pastoral care, would have academically and socially divisive effects that are very undesirable. It would also render interhouse co-operation or competition very difficult, since there would be "academic group" houses, "remedial group" houses and "average group" houses. To organize houses on the basis of unstreamed teaching groups produces houses which are

[61] Barnes, A., Unstreaming: two viewpoints, two strategies, in: Halsall, Elizabeth (ed.), *Becoming Comprehensive: Case Histories*, Pergamon Press, Oxford, 1970, p. 238.

[62] We will not here discuss the implications of these terms.

equal in intake as regards measured ability, but, if pastoral care is to be really good,[63] it commits the school to unstreamed teaching groups, whatever the beliefs, knowledge or lack of knowledge, on this matter of teaching such groups, of the head and the staff. Since it has been shown by the N.F.E.R. report on streaming that the attitudes of head and staff to whatever policy is followed crucially affect its success, the conclusion one must come to is that the house system in a large comprehensive school is likely to be successful in improving pastoral care, without damaging academic results, only when head and staff believe in unstreaming and have reorientated their teaching methods to suit it. Every other alternative appears likely to damage either academic results or pastoral care.

The same disadvantages would seem to appertain to the year system also, in the case where the year is streamed for teaching, but organized in mixed ability groups for other purposes. Since pastoral care occurs all the time, inside and outside the classroom, its focus is blurred in this case also. Indeed one may say that wherever the teaching groups are different from the administrative and overtly pastoral groups, the pastoral care is by definition made more difficult.

The very fact that these various stratagems for dividing up large schools into manageable units have had to be thought out is itself an indication of the difficulty of providing good pastoral care in large schools. It would therefore seem worth while to explore more deeply the relationship between size of school and effectiveness of pastoral care. Here it is proposed to confine the analysis to the negative aspects of pastoral care, that is to a discussion of overall supervision and control, though some of the initial remarks may be relevant also for the more positive aspects.

There would seem to be two factors through which size of school influences effectiveness of overall pastoral care. The first factor is the degree of teachers' acquaintance with, and knowledge of, the children. In a small school teachers know all, or nearly all, the children, even when they do not teach them. As the size of the school increases they know a smaller proportion of the total numbers.[64] The second factor would appear to be the factor of distance and accessibility. Whether a teacher takes action or checks up on a disciplinary problem, or not, will depend largely on the degree of effort involved, other things being equal. Where he is not too sure of a child's name, has too far to walk, or knows he has not much chance of finding a relevant member of staff, he is less likely to take action. These conditions are present in large schools and are likely to lead to less effective control.

However, to make such categorical but vague and unproven statements did not seem sufficient in the current analysis. It seemed possible to do better than indulge in mere theorizing and an attempt was therefore made to explore the problem mathematically. The results of this exercise[65] showed that close knowledge of children inside and outside the classroom is at most over twice as difficult to acquire in a 14-F.E. school as in a 3-F.E. school, and at the very least $1\frac{1}{2}$ times as difficult, depending on the weighting given to one intermediate factor. When indices representing degree of close knowledge of children were used along with indices related to size of building to produce overall indices of difficulty of supervision and control, it was found that, according to the weightings used, outside the classroom control is at least 3 times as difficult to exercise in a 14-F.E. school as in a 3-F.E., at most 9

[63] See Barnes' account of the reasons for unstreaming in his house-based comprehensive school in a difficult area, where the need for good pastoral care was paramount.

[64] See p. 88 for the American research on this subject.

[65] Halsall, Elizabeth, A mathematical analysis of the difficulty of disciplinary supervision and control according to size of school. (To be published.) See also *1967 A.M.A. Report on Comprehensive Schools*, p. 218.

times as difficult. Whichever index is nearer to the truth, both of them help to give those who have not worked in very large schools some idea of the "outside class" burdens of disciplinary control carried by their teachers. Small wonder that, when confronted with a pupil they do not recognize at all, guilty of a misdemeanour of some seriousness, they feel tempted to do no more than give a word of warning, and not to follow up an incident that often should be followed up. These calculations also help to explain why heads and staffs of very large schools often experience a sensation of great difficulty in pinning things down. Hence good disciplinary control is much harder to achieve in large schools than in small, as anyone who has worked in both knows. Moreover, the large school, unlike the large car firm, is processing material that is self-propelling and self-directional. In other words, it can run away!

We must therefore conclude that the interaction of large size of school buildings and large numbers of children is such as to make negative aspects of pastoral care more difficult for the teacher and to increase his burdens of control and supervision.[66] Pastoral care is therefore less likely to be effective in this respect in a large school than in a small, with all that this probably implies for the sense of security of the average pupil. What is more, a teacher overburdened by problems of control and supervision will be without sufficient time and energy to tackle positive aspects of pastoral care.

3. *Size of School and Communication Problems*

As the *Review of Educational Research* says, "in studies of communication little has been done to investigate the relationship between size and the overloading of communication channels and any ecological impediments to communication other than differences of status between members of the organization's staff and the misunderstandings due to their different attitudes and personalities". It has already been noted that in one research study[67] there were found to be impediments to communication between higher and lower levels of a school's hierarchy due to misunderstandings. Hence one could infer that the greater the number of levels, the poorer the communication, to the disadvantage of the large school.

For lack of further research data in an area that badly needs investigation we can do no more than describe from the experience of many, reported anecdotally in the literature, the differences between the communication systems and problems of small schools and those of large ones.

A day spent in the present normal-sized English school, a glance at the average staffroom noticeboard, even more years of experience of teaching in schools of this size, that is, schools of about 300–600 pupils, reveal situations in which much of the necessary communication between head and staff, head and pupils, staff with staff and staff with pupils can be made by word of mouth, or failing that, by a notice on the noticeboards inside or outside the staff-room. The twenty or thirty staff congregate in the staffroom before morning school or at breaktime or in the dinner hour. In an emergency or as a routine the head or deputy head can always slip in for a few moments consultation with one or several or all of the staff in the certainty of being almost at once in contact with all those he or she wishes to see. If the staff concerned are not in the staffroom they are not usually far to seek and if any of them are not in fact immediately accessible there are not likely to be more than one or two who

[66] For evidence on hours of work by teachers in large schools see p. 192.
[67] See p. 87 for a study by Brennan.

have to be approached separately. Hence there is less probability than in larger institutions of a slip of memory on the part of the head or the deputy that will later cause chaos or send someone into the staffroom complaining that he "hasn't been told". If the head prefers to discuss a matter privately the member of staff concerned is easily available. A notice on the staffroom noticeboard, where word of mouth has not been sufficient, is practically certain to be read by everyone in the course of the day, and if it has not been read, almost always no one is to blame but the member of staff concerned.

In the same way members of staff can easily communicate with each other. If the person looked for is not in the staffroom there is no great distance to walk to find him. Communication between the different subject departments is also easy. In general, one has to be rather deaf not to know what is going on in a school of 300–600 pupils. The staff grapevine is a reasonably efficient means of communication, and is less subject to the effects of rumour than it is in a large school.[68]

Communication with the children is also relatively simple for the head and for staff dealing with extra-curricular matters. There are notices at assembly every morning, there are noticeboards which the children are practically certain to pass in the course of the day. In a grammar school the use of very adult language at assembly is not much of a barrier to communication. In a secondary modern school where the range of ability is greater more care does have to be taken to suit the words used to the capacities of some of those listening; one therefore already finds in secondary modern school teachers and heads greater sophistication in expressing complicated ideas and instructions in simple words than one does amongst those in grammar schools.

It may be felt that the present situation in schools has been described at some length and that in any case it was superfluous so to describe it, since everyone knows exactly what it is. But it seemed worthwhile to devote some space to it precisely because in a school of 1000 pupils or more that situation no longer exists and the methods used for dealing with it are therefore often irrelevant to the new one facing head and staff. The problem is complicated by the fact that, even if they have read the literature on the subject, at first both head and staff are often unaware, at any but the most general level and rarely in respect of a particular problem as they work through it, that they are faced with a totally new situation. For this new situation their previous training and experience, which is all that they can take with them into it, provide them with no adequate guide. Their resultant criticism of each other and the tensions that arise stem as often from their own failure to understand and evaluate the new situation as from other people's failure to apply new solutions.

What is the new situation? It is that in large schools more or less informal methods of communication will no longer suffice. Where buildings are widely spaced, on the same campus or on different sites, this is especially true. If on different sites this fact is obvious, though the solutions are not so. If on the same campus the problem is less obvious but failure to deal with it produces difficulties which accumulate insidiously. Even where a large comprehensive school has been provided with good buildings within a properly restricted area the problem exists and has to be dealt with. New methods of communication have to be found and old attitudes have to be changed by the head, staff, pupils and indeed parents as well. In fact, if changes in attitude do not take place it is impossible to develop the needed changes in method. It is clearly the duty of the head to take the initiative in starting changes in methods of communication, but a head whose own attitudes have altered sufficiently for

[68] See p. 88.

him to realize the necessity for change can be hampered by staff whose attitudes have not changed. Conversely staff working under a head whose attitudes have not changed will have their working lives made uncomfortable to the point of being really unpleasant by his failure to try new methods of communication. Nothing is more needed in the early years of a large comprehensive school's existence than open-mindedness on the part of all those working in it and a constant willingness to look for new solutions. This is true for all aspects of the life of the school, but especially so as regards its methods of communication.

Why is this so? Many schools have as many as three staffrooms, ninety classrooms and division rooms, a hundred staff. Mistakes in planning the buildings may entail a walk of a couple of hundred yards for one member of staff to make contact with another or with a pupil. Such mistakes seriously affect problems of communication as much as of organization.

However, even where buildings are well planned, size produces communication difficulties. The traditional face-to-face methods of communication no longer fit, except as auxiliaries. New methods must therefore be sought. What was good enough for the corner shop will not do for Selfridge's. Methods well adapted to small schools are of limited relevance to large ones. One of the first signs that communication is breaking down is the spread amongst the staff of rumours that are really wide of the mark and which result in the creation of tension.[69]

One or two simple examples will illustrate the need for new methods of communication. Consider the large comprehensive school with one large main staffroom and 80–100 staff. To use the noticeboard in the staffroom as the only, or even the main, vehicle of communication is not to understand the problem. Eighty to a hundred staff cannot be expected to queue up to read a notice. Similarly, assembly can no longer be used as a main means of communicating with the pupils. The assembly hall is unlikely to be big enough to hold them all, assemblies for different groups of pupils may well be on different days. Only announcements of a non-urgent character can therefore be made at assembly, and all other arrangements to communicate will be more time- and energy-wasting for the communicator than would be a simple announcement at assembly. This is one of the most important aspects of the communication problems of the large school. Proportionately more time and energy have to be devoted to them than in the smaller school. As has been said in the context of other institutions, proportionately more time and energy have to be devoted to the task of maintaining the institution in the large school than in the small, and there is less time and energy available for the task of developing it.

4. *The Effects of Size on Policy, Administration and Innovation*

There is a certain amount of very general research on the effects of size on administration and policy, some of it referring to school systems rather than to schools. However, it tends to support the findings on the effect of school size on school climate. For lack of more, and better, evidence on the subject we make what sense of it we can and look for clues that may have relevance to school problems.

The effect of increases in size of school systems was studied by Terrien and Mills.[70] They showed that the number of administrators increased disproportionately with the size of the

[69] See p. 88 for the effect of large institutions on the spread of rumours.

[70] Terrien, F. C. and Mills, D. C. The effect of changing size upon the internal structure of an organization, *Amer. Sociological Rev.*, vol. 20, no. 1, 1955, pp. 11–13.

school system. Like Blau[71] they also examined the relationship between the size of the system and its organizational practices. They concluded that the larger the size the greater the likelihood that it will be bureaucratically organized[72] (i.e. in terms of promoting the erection of a fixed hierarchy, regulations, division of work, specialization, etc.). There is disagreement as to the effects of bureaucratization of institutions on their capacity to respond to necessary change. Some writers feel that with the meticulous application of detailed rules characteristic of bureaucratic institutions, there follows overconformity, rigid adherence to established routine and what sociologists term displacement of goals[73] within the system, as the top echelons of the hierarchy develop a vested interest in preserving the rules against change. Other writers have since pointed out that bureaucracies may change under competitive duress or if pressure for change comes from the top.

Blau, Heyderbrand and Stauffer[74] analysed the interrelationship among four structural attributes within small bureaucracies. It was expected that with a professional staff the need for many managers would be reduced but it was found that the need actually increased. They also suggested that although bureaucratic structure can become dysfunctional as bureaucracies increase in size, this disadvantage can be overcome by the appointment of sufficient administrative staff. It seems probable that this result may well apply also to educational organizations. It could account for the fact that over and above a certain size economies of scale cease,[75] and for Terrien and Mills' finding that the number of administrators increased disproportionately with size.

5. *Conclusion*

(a) *Large schools*. These findings may profitably be related to the general problems of setting up and administering large schools in the present reorganization of secondary education in Britain. At this point, however, we will relate them only to immediate and temporary problems. One of these is that many of the heads appointed to them have no personal experience of working in large institutions. Yet the operational characteristics of large schools are different from those of small ones. For example, there are more levels in the hierarchy and different problems of movement and communication. Hence these heads are appointed to institutions of a size for which they have no instinctive feel based on earlier experience, albeit at a lower level in the hierarchy. Yet it is known that effective decision-making correlates highly with operational knowledge of the administrative job.[76] Hence it is inevitable that such heads should spend 2 or 3 years at least making mistakes they would not otherwise have made, with the schools functioning less advantageously in consequence. The same may well be true, though less obvious, at slightly lower levels of the large schools' hierarchy. A few such people never quite make up for that lack of initial experience of what it is like to be a junior member of staff in a very large school.

[71] Blau, P. M., *Bureaucracy in Modern Society*, Random House, New York, 1956.

[72] Some recent research does, however, suggest that the character of the head has more effect on the degree of bureaucratization than school size, but it concerns primary schools. Pierce, Keith F., Interschool variation in bureaucratization, *J. Educ. Admin.*, vol. VIII, no. 2, Oct. 1970.

[73] Displacement of goals from developing the institution in line with its goals to maintaining the institution as it is.

[74] Blau, Peter M., Heyderbrand, Wolf V. and Stauffer, Robert E., The structure of small bureaucracies, *Amer. Sociological Rev.*, vol. 31, Apr. 1966, pp. 179–91.

[75] See p. 120.

[76] Antley, E. M., Creativity in educational administration, *J. Exper. Educ.*, vol. 34, Summer 1966, pp. 21–7.

Other temporary problems can also be caused when a school grows rapidly in size.

If a school is growing in size and at a considerable speed, e.g. from 400 to 1500 in 5 years or if it is changing from one type of school to another, there are additional causes of tension that will result from a combination of failures of administration and communication. A head can allow himself to be swamped by the growing amount of administration each year. Delegation of the work is only part of the answer. There is so much extra work of a new kind each year during the growth of a school that there is a clear case here for L.E.A.s to be as generous as they can within the framework of national policy with regard to staffing ratios at this stage of a school's development, to the point where the school may appear administratively top-heavy. It will be less top-heavy than it appears because during the growth of a school, relative to the number of pupils, there is more administrative and communication work than on completion of growth.[77] A set of administrative arrangements which worked well one year will be quite inadequate the next and each year sees the need to create a new framework or to effect really major alterations to the old. Every new set of arrangements will have some snags in it. These cannot be eliminated in an atmosphere of haste and overwork or with insufficient personnel to make and critically examine the arrangements. The net effect of having insufficient personnel at the top during a period of growth or the failure of a head to delegate sufficiently is a blockage in communication. A poor set of arrangements is completed in haste and communicated to the staff too late for them to have time to assimilate them and therefore apply them effectively, if indeed they are capable of being so applied. The resultant chaos does no one any good and raises the doubt in everyone's minds as to the school's viability. Local authorities who wish the change-over to this new form of school organization to take place calmly and effectively should be sensitive to this point, especially as the major effort of readjustment demanded will impose great strains on heads and staffs in other ways also.

(b) *Small schools*. By contrast the small comprehensive school has few difficulties of either administration or communication and there is a lesser need for wholesale reorientation of attitudes than is true in the large schools. At a series of small comprehensive schools visited by the writer,[78] schools of three, four and five streams, the heads tended to be of the opinion that administration did not produce problems of any considerable difficulty. The problem of communication was not difficult either, since the whole school met at assembly every day and noticeboards, both in and out of the staffroom, provided another channel. Similarly, staff meetings were not unwieldy and there were no good administrative or pastoral reasons for the introduction of the house or year system, as was the case with large schools. No breakdown into smaller units was needed. The house system's main use was of a social or sporting character. School bulletins were not reported, unless the schools were working in two small buildings on different sites. The schools, however, did encounter some movement problems, but only in the case of poor layout of buildings. Even in this size of school if the layout was elongated it could take some time to walk from one end to the other end and there tended to be bunching at the midpoint of the building at change of lessons.

[77] For example, as the school grows in size a new blueprint for the time-table is required every year, often requiring a radical rethink, whereas, except at times of radical changes of policy, a school of stable size finds less administrative energy is wasted if an old time-table analysis is adapted to suit slightly changed needs. Similarly, with increasing size, communication arrangements have to be altered each year.

[78] For further details see p. 110.

Conclusion

This investigation of the non-curricular effects of school size tends to support the view that small schools are easier to manage, have better school climates, are likely to be more innovative, other things being equal, and provide intrinsically better environments for effective pastoral care than is the case with large schools. Offsetting of these disadvantages by teachers in large schools demands great efforts and extra work, for some aspects of the effects of size. For other aspects it may be well nigh impossible to achieve.

CHAPTER 7

Size of School: Its Effect Upon Curriculum and Achievement

WHEN one considers the size of a school in relation to its academic achievements, one has two aspects of the subject to examine, on the one hand the curriculum provided, its range and its depth, and on the other the extent to which students take advantage of what is provided, in terms of their individual academic results.

A. Curriculum

There is relatively little research on the effect of the size of secondary school on the curriculum provided and much of what there is has been carried out, as is so common in the sphere of educational research, in the U.S.A., particularly after Sputnik, when standards of education became a national issue. Although conditions in the U.S.A. are different from those in England, the data do provide some suggestions as to the effect of size of school which appear to be generally applicable. Moreover, when the British data are presented, certain similarities, certain common problems appear. Hence, it is worth while to look at the American data.

Conant[1] examined the relationship between school size and curriculum in his report on the American high school in 1959, in which he pleaded for the large high school, and for a minimum size of high school, one that would produce a graduating class each year of a minimum of 100. His emphasis on the size of the graduating year rather than the entry year pinpoints the main problem. It is in the final year or years of schooling that the greatest differentiation is needed, in every country, and the greater the differentiation, the greater the need for more staff and therefore for more pupils to justify the greater numbers of staff. Conant's survey of schools led him to claim that there were greater opportunities for differentiation in the larger schools and that a school "with a graduating class of less than one hundred" cannot offer an adequate curriculum for all kinds of pupils, for example, advanced courses in mathematics, science and foreign languages for the brightest 15–20 per cent, or adequate non-academic training for the less academically gifted.

The curricular data of the Barker and Gump study is more difficult to evaluate in relation to English schools. As far as the number of educational behavioural settings is concerned, the larger schools already had the advantage with a school of 2287 pupils having 108 settings, compared with only eighteen in a school of 117 pupils.[2] Yet the small school students tended

[1] Conant, James B., *The American High School Today*, McGraw-Hill, New York, 1959, p. 77.

[2] Barker and Gump, *op. cit.*, p. 54.

to take more courses. Pupils in schools of about 300 pupils took on average six courses per year,[3] whilst those in the 1800 group took an average of five.

Subjects studied did not vary as much as one might expect as between large and small schools. The largest school had 65 times as many students, 8 times as many academic behaviour settings and only 2·3 times as many kinds of academic activities (subjects) as the smallest school.[4] The following "academic" subjects were common to schools of 220 and over: English, general maths, algebra, geometry, trigonometry, general science, chemistry, physics, general biology, botany, health, American history, American government, world history, general business, typing, shorthand and book-keeping. Art and music did not occur in schools of less than 339 students. In an English school art and music would be in the curriculum and the commercial subjects left out, in this size of school. The smaller schools tended to be individually deficient, in comparison with the larger schools, in specialized mathematics, specialized social and behavioural sciences (psychology, sociology, etc.), foreign languages or specialized business classes. The large schools were able to provide up to thirty subjects approximately. The large schools provided 4 times as many kinds of athletic activities as the small schools.

"In general, the smaller schools managed to sustain a large proportion of the *types* of offerings provided by the larger schools."[5] They did not, however, provide as many classes in each type as the larger schools and the range of subjects they were not able to cover bears out the claims by Conant in respect of the gifted academic student at least.

A limited small study of intellectually gifted children[6] showed that in the large schools, although more classes and varieties of classes were available, they were enrolled in a somewhat smaller total number of school classes. They were, however, enrolled in a somewhat greater number of academic[7] classes than their equals in the small schools. Non-academic classes made up 41 per cent of the classes taken by the small-school students and 21 per cent of those taken by the large-school students. The education received by the small-school students, as measured by classes, was relatively heavier in total and less academically specialized than the education of the large school students. No data were gathered on the quality of the classes or the depth of student participation in them.

Data on musical education in large and small schools showed that many more small school than large school pupils were receiving some formal classroom instruction in music (49 per cent compared with 13 per cent). The proportions enrolled in two music classes were more different still (20 per cent and 1·3 per cent); all these pupils also took part in extra-curricular music. However, those in the large schools who were specializing in music had a much greater degree of specialization than those specializing in it in the small schools. They also tended to dominate the school music activities to a much greater extent. To sum up, musical education and participation was much more widely distributed in smaller than in large schools, but specialization was deeper in large than in small.

The Barker and Gump study thus shows greater versatility and less specialization in small schools than in large, a greater number of subjects taken by individual pupils, fewer academic and more aesthetic and general subjects, a wider range of subjects available in small schools

[3] Subject courses usually have a larger number of periods per week than in British schools.
[4] *Ibid.*, p. 60.
[5] *Ibid.*, p. 62. N.B. See p. 92 for details of numbers in large and small schools.
[6] *Ibid.*, pp. 169–70.
[7] The list of subjects deemed academic is wider in range than in British schools, but does not include aesthetic subjects.

than one would expect, though not as many classes or as specialized in each subject as in large schools, and no evidence as to levels of achievement in any schools. One's view of the issue of school size in respect of specialization and versatility will depend on a value judgement as to which of these is the more important, in general, and at a particular stage of a pupil's school career. At a stage where a great variety of subject choice is thought to be needed the large school will have some advantage over the small school.

The use of this American material has to be approached with caution, since curricula are not exactly the same in American as in British schools, though they are more similar than would be continental curricula. At the fourth- and fifth-year level, however, curricula in British comprehensive schools have a not dissimilar pattern to those of senior classes in many American high schools. The curriculum usually has a common core of basic subjects, including English and mathematics, and a series of options subjects or options courses. Hence American data on the effects of size on curriculum might well have some bearing on British problems with the curriculum for 14- and 15-year-olds. It would have little relevance for the sixth form, with its much more specialized offerings to students. But Conant's remark about a graduating class (or year, in British terms) of a minimum of 100 could be applied at our fifth-form level, where the conditions are not dissimilar. The following timetabling analysis bears out this contention.

B. Theoretical Analysis of Timetabling

A theoretical examination of the timetable possibilities for small British comprehensive schools of two-, three-, four- and five-form entry, based on the generally agreed assumption of a common curriculum for ages 11 to 14 (with some provision for remedial work, split classes, etc.) and for the ages 14–16 a curriculum involving a common core plus a series of options, bears out the conclusions of Barker and Gump in one way and of Conant to a lesser extent in another. Timetables were worked out for small 11–18 schools on the basis of a 20:1 pupil–teacher ratio, a forty periods per week timetable and five free periods per week for each member of staff, clearly a minimum allocation.[8] A maximum of sixteen periods per year on average in the first 3 years was allowed for split classes or remedials, a maximum of forty extra periods per year for the fourth- and fifth-year options. Since staying-on rates in the sixth form are problematical, at the initial stage of calculation no allowance was made for teachers obtained due to the presence of sixth-form pupils, clearly a very limiting constraint when it was intended to see what provision of sixth-form subjects was possible in these circumstances.

On these assumptions a 2-F.E. school of 200 can meet its basic requirements only, up to and including the fifth form; by basic is meant that there would be one teacher with every class at all times and the teacher would retain his five free periods. As its classes are small the problem of split classes is minimal, but extra part-time teachers would be required to provide sets, options and remedial classes. One school of this size has, however, been reported as providing a C.S.E./G.C.E. choice of twelve subjects. It must have access to part-time teachers to provide extra help, or use the alternate years method of timetabling[9] or work

[8] Halsall, Elizabeth, *Timetable Allocations for Small Comprehensive Schools.* Univ. of Hull Institute of Education, 1968.

[9] See Halsall, Elizabeth. *The Alternate Years Method of Timetabling* (to be published).

miracles of ingenuity. A 2-F.E. school of 275 could meet the requirements for split classes, remedials and fourth- and fifth-year options with something over. The equivalent of two-thirds of a full-time teacher could be deployed, therefore, to extend the range of options nearly to that available, because of the extra class, in a three-form entry school. A 2-F.E. school of 370 pupils with forms averaging thirty-seven in size, i.e. with a graduating year of seventy-four, could provide from its total of 18½ staff facilities for a three-stream fourth and fifth year, with options as already indicated, and for a sixth form offering a few arts and science subjects, even before extra staff have been allocated according to the numbers of pupils in the sixth form. Even with only 340 pupils a school could just manage to offer a few 'A' level subjects,[10] as indeed is indicated by advertisements in the *Times Educational Supplement*. Sixth-form pupils taking non-A-level subjects would have to be taught in the fifth. Not that forms of thirty-seven are usually thought desirable;[11] but they are not unknown and, in the present circumstances of reorganization under difficult conditions, they may be preferable to running a larger school in two buildings or on two separate sites.

The small 3-F.E. school of 300+ as distinct from the large 3-F.E. school of 500 or 530 would perhaps be better run as a 2-F.E. school, with staff redeployed to give greater flexibility in the provision of split classes, remedials, sets and options. Similarly the small 4-F.E. would probably be better run as a 3-F.E. In making the calculations it is noteworthy how the provision of sets and options and of sixth-form subjects is eased once an allowance is made for the staff entitlement for pupils in the sixth form or if average class size is increased. For example, if there are forty pupils in the sixth form there are four more staff, there being a double allocation of staff for sixth formers, and therefore about eleven more subjects at 'A' level. Similarly, an average of thirty-five pupils per class instead of thirty gives three extra staff in a 3-F.E. school over and above what one gets for a school where the average class size is thirty. Experience confirms the above calculations. A 4-F.E. school in an area with one of the lowest staffing ratios in the country offered eleven subjects at 'A' level in 1966 and another 4-F.E. comprehensive school of long standing in the Isle of Man offered sixteen subjects at 'A' level out of nineteen subjects taken in the sixth. In fact, the relationship between the size of school and viability of the sixth form does not merely depend on the size of school, as was thought in the early days of comprehensive education, but also on the average size of class and on the numbers staying on in the sixth form. Moreover, the raising of the school-leaving age will increase the numbers staying on into the sixth form, and therefore the sixth-form viability of small schools.[12]

This theoretical analysis suggests that Conant's view that a graduating class of a minimum of 100 is needed is slightly conservative in the British context, though of course due allowance must be made for the fact that a theoretical timetable analysis is always somewhat more optimistic than any actual timetable, which has to cater for the realities of a world where staff are often unavailable or sick. The analysis did suggest at the same time that the smaller the school, the more its curriculum is likely to suffer in respect of a second foreign language or a full range of science subjects, somewhat in line with Conant's findings.

Subsequently a timetable analysis was made for three-, four- and five-form entry schools which included sixth forms. These latter were allotted a 20 per cent staying-on rate, a rate

[10] Whether it should do so is another matter.

[11] Yet, see pp. 155–8.

[12] For an example of a timetable for a four-stream 11–16 school, i.e. without a sixth form, see Owen, D., Timetabling in a junior comprehensive school, *Teacher in Wales*, 6 Nov. 1964, pp. 18–19.

which seems likely to develop rather quickly once the school-leaving age is raised, since staying on into the sixth and acquiring further qualifications will give students an advantage in applying for jobs. This new analysis confirmed that the smaller comprehensive school was more viable in the English context than had previously been realized.[13]

In addition, a series of visits to some rather small comprehensive schools in various parts of rural England suggested that they were able to provide a far better curricular service to their pupils than city-bound colleagues in urban comprehensive schools would ever have imagined. Moreover, evidence was available from America of success with new timetabling methods which would greatly assist them.[14]

C. Existing Small Comprehensive Schools in Rural Areas

1. *Their History*

This group of smallish comprehensive schools varying in size from 350 to 700, fascinatingly seemed to have had a very similar history, which is worth recounting, for it highlights some of the issues.

Often started in the sixteenth or seventeenth century as schools for teaching Latin and Greek, they had entered the twentieth century with forty or fifty pupils, had reached the 100+ mark in the twenties and at their best were still somewhat short of the 200 mark in the fifties, often in spite of a catchment area of, say, 400 square miles, involving a minimum of 10 miles travel for pupils furthest away. Their curricula had, of course, widened but, functioning as one-stream grammar schools, they had increasingly become non-viable, because of the expansion of knowledge in our society and the consequent pressures on their curricula. A school of 180, including twenty in the sixth form, with a staffing ratio of 20:1 (10:1 for the sixth form) would have ten full-time teachers. The basic academic subjects and P.E. could be covered by the staff (English, French, history, geography, Latin, physics, chemistry, biology, mathematics, P.E.) but, if the normal allocation of periods to subjects was followed, history and geography teachers, for example, would not have a full timetable unless they spread themselves in the sixth form. More seriously, English, French and mathematics teachers would be grossly overburdened, unless they could count on someone else to undertake some work in the lower school for them and release them for sixth-form work. It would be impossible without a versatile staff to provide the non-academic subjects (art, music, woodwork, domestic science) and in what were always mixed schools there would only be one full-time P.E. teacher. A most unfortunate feature, in many of these one-stream grammar schools some teachers would be carrying two 'A' level subjects.

The opportunity to improve this situation came with the 1944 Act. With the reorganization of the all-age school there were developed, not separate secondary modern schools, but, from the one-stream grammar schools, bilateral schools of two or three streams, able to staff a wider range of subjects. They often continued to bear their original title. It was therefore partly to preserve the grammar schools[15] as viable entities capable of producing good sixth-form courses that in the remote countryside they were transformed, first of all into two-, three- or four-stream bilaterals, often with different catchment areas for the grammar

[13] See Appendix II for evidence.

[14] See p. 160.

[15] The effect of this attitude might be demonstrated by the grammar school pupils having different school badges from the secondary modern, or the secondary modern pupils not being considered for school teams, or distinctions being made between the two staffs.

school pupils from those for the secondary modern pupils, and later into full comprehensive schools drawing on the same catchment areas for all pupils. For these schools when they were bilaterals certain difficulties arose. They were often not allowed to transfer a pupil from the grammar stream to the secondary modern or vice versa, even if a patent error of allocation had been made, because the secondary modern school which served the rest of the grammar stream catchment area would object. To provide for the brighter secondary modern children a completely separate and parallel examination course had therefore to be set up, which was very wasteful in staffing. Over time, it became apparent that the operation of options at fourth- and fifth-year level defied their separation into grammar and modern streams. Because of these difficulties, the schools often became, internally, comprehensive. Thus, the comprehensive school was in a number of country areas the solution to the problem of the one stream grammar school,[16] just as in the towns the construction of comprehensive schools that were large was thought to be the only way of producing comprehensive schools with viable sixth forms.

2. *Their Curricula*

How varied the curriculum can be in the three-stream school is well illustrated by that of one such school of 370 pupils, including twenty-six in the sixth form. In the first 3 years all three streams follow a completely parallel timetable, except that the lowest stream does not take French. The slow readers in the first and second year are withdrawn, as a combined group, five times a week for special treatment. Latin is started in the fourth year as an option. The system of options in the fourth and fifth year varies somewhat from year to year because of individual needs but the basic pattern of the curriculum is as shown in Table 1.

The greatest weaknesses of this curriculum are the inability to provide music as an examination subject, the lack of a second modern language[17] and the difficulty in catering for both physics and chemistry separately in the fourth and fifth form. Some of the options subjects in the fourth year may possibly be oversubscribed, though the average number of pupils in each year intake is only about seventy. Although, as set out, the timetable makes no specific reference to the less able, it would be possible, with a little manoeuvring as the timetable was being made and the pupils were being allocated to, or choosing, their options and sets, to cater for at least some of their needs within the framework of the curriculum, and even to provide some Newsom type block-of-time courses.

Another small rural school, with 410 as the total roll, with thirty-five in the sixth, and with a staff of twenty-one, was able to offer a wide range of 'O' level and C.S.E. subjects and had gained passes in seven 'A' level subjects in the current year. Of these seven, four were successfully taught by non-graduates.

A four-stream school was able to choose to start a limited number of options in the third year, which suggests indirectly that it was not finding it too difficult to cater, for example, for the less able. It separated stayers and leavers in the fourth year and gave the leavers' class a special course with only nine formal lessons. Such courses are almost inevitably expensive staffing-wise. For the rest of the year English and maths were common to all and the options

[16] See Woodward, R. J., Sir William Romney's School, Tetbury, in: Halsall, Elizabeth (ed.), *Becoming Comprehensive: Case Histories*, Pergamon Press, 1970, pp. 3–17. N.B. This idea had already been suggested in the Spens Report (p. 345), quoted in Rubinstein, D. and Simon, B., *The Evolution of the Comprehensive School*, Routledge & Kegan Paul, 1969, p. 19.

[17] Note the similarity with the American findings.

were approximately as follows:

1. Phys. & Chem./Hist. & Geog./Woodw. & Metalw./Dom. Sci.
2. German/Biology/Art/General Science (C.S.E.)
3. Biology/German/Music/History (C.S.E.)
4. Geog./Eng. Lit./Eng. (C.S.E.)
5. French/French/Pottery/Tech. Drawing

The chance of taking a second modern language (though there is no Latin) in two different options, of taking music, pottery and technical drawing as examination subjects (though rural studies and commerce have been lost) seem to be major gains, along with the possibility in one or two cases of picking up a desired subject in one option when it has been rejected in favour of another more desired subject in a second option.

TABLE 1

Fourth- and Fifth-Year Curriculum

	5A		5B		5M (Commercial)	
Setted across streams	English	(G.C.E.) (6)	English	(C.S.E.) (6)	English	(C.S.E.) (6)
	Mathematics	(G.C.E.) (6)	Mathematics	(C.S.E.) (6)	Mathematics	(C.S.E.) (6)
	History	(G.C.E.) (4)	History	(C.S.E.) (4)	History	(C.S.E.) (4)
	Geography	(G.C.E.) (3)	Geography	(C.S.E.) (3)	Geography	(C.S.E.) (3)
Options	French/Domestic Science/Art/Metalwork/Commerce				(6)	
	Biology/Rural Studies/Latin/Commerce				(5)	
	Physics with Chemistry/Housecraft/Woodwork				(5/6)	
	P.E.	(3)	P.E.	(3)	P.E.	(3)
	R.I.	(1)	R.I.	(1)	R.I.	(1)
	Music	(1)	Music	(1)	Music	(1)
		40		40		40

How this pattern may vary can be seen from the pattern for the fourth year concurrent with the above fifth year.

4A	4B	4C	
English	English	English	(4 sets)
Mathematics	Mathematics	Mathematics	(4 sets)
History	History	History	
Latin/Geography/Geography			
French/Domestic Science/Metalwork			
General Science/Rural Studies/Commerce			
General Science/Art/Commerce			
P.E.	P.E.	P.E.	
R.I.	R.I.	R.I.	
Music	Music	Music	

Either school could put on a curriculum leading ultimately to a wide range of university courses or giving good general training preparatory to some other vocational course. The four-stream school is able to increase the number of subjects taken as options (there are five option groups) in line with traditional English specialization, the three-stream school, being obliged to husband staff teaching periods, has a more extensive general curriculum and a reduced number of *option groups*, more in line with a continental tradition. Reducing the number of option groups helps too in the more economic use of staff. The four-stream school could put on an entirely separate course for the less able, the three-stream school would have to work in a partially separated course within the framework of the general fourth year curriculum, unless the number of *option subjects*[18] was reduced. A similar situation will be encountered at the fifth-year level with the raising of the school-leaving age.

[18] A distinction is made here between option groups and option subjects. The four-stream school described above has five option groups with three or four option subjects within each option group.

Sixth-form policy in the small school can be illustrated by the arrangements at the first three-stream school mentioned. At this school the approach was one of flexibility, of endeavouring to provide what individual pupils needed each year rather than of fitting them into an already predetermined framework. This policy would seem to be the most economic in respect of staffing in small schools as well as the most humane towards pupils. They would get most of the subjects, often all, that they asked for, even if the timetable looked less balanced in any given year than it should do ideally. The sixth-form timetable of a small school should be judged by its provisions over a number of years.

Individual timetables included such 'A' level combinations as:

Physics	Chemistry	Maths	Biology	Geography	History	Art	French	English
√	√		√					
√	√	√						
√		√		√				
			√	√				
√		√	√					
			√				√	√
					√		√	√
							√	√
						√		
				√	√		√	

The choices indicate that the subjects could be blocked on the timetable thus:

Physics	Chemistry	Mathematics	Biology
French	Geography	English	History
		Art	

The main limiting factors were that one 'A' level subject had to be taken in another school 10 miles away, that 'O' levels and 'O' level repeats had to be taken with the fifth form, that the curriculum would be mainly 'A' and 'O' level oriented and mainly academic, and that some overlap had to be accepted between the lower and upper sixth-form teaching periods. There was also no second language and no splitting up of maths. With small classes of around eight on average when the lower and upper sixth were taken together, a more tutorial approach to teaching the lower and upper sixth together for some periods would not provide serious difficulties for the sixth-form teacher in most subjects, though clearly there would be some difficulties and some need for adaptability and flexibility. The inability to offer "non-academic" 'A' levels except for art was a more serious weakness. Music, domestic science and engineering science could not be made available, the last perhaps not a serious weakness in a rural area.

Yet, in spite of these weaknesses, the school could prepare intelligent youngsters for university and other courses in a fair range of subjects. Having been a pupil at such a small school was no bar to a good career, even if there was not quite the range of choice of subject available at larger schools. And in fact the school had always sent pupils on to higher education, and it should be noted that a sixth form of twenty-six from initial entries of seventy pupils represents a sixth form staying-on rate of about 18 per cent, an expression of parental confidence in the school.

It is clear, however, that a three-stream school with a sixth form is operating under a degree of constraint.

In the four-stream schools visited, eleven or twelve subjects could be studied at 'A' level without the lower and upper sixth having to be taught together, except occasionally, perhaps for laboratory work in science. It was possible to include a second language, to split mathematics and often to make provision for either music or domestic science. Again 'O' level repeats were taken with the fifth form. Periods could be allotted for minority time subjects apart from the usual P.E. and R.E., as was also true for the 3-F.E. school.

A small school which has reported its sixth-form arrangements is Settle High School in Yorkshire.[19] This is a four-form entry school of 630 pupils in a rural area. It has forty-eight in its sixth form, which is allocated 178 teaching periods on the timetable; 134 of these are devoted to 'A' levels, twenty-five to a 1-year commercial course and nineteen to general studies. Thirty-five to forty of the students aim at 'A' levels, five to ten students at commerce, and some of both at 'O' level retakes. In addition to the commercial course the sixth-form course includes ten 'A' level subjects, which allow students to qualify for most university courses. A second modern language is difficult to provide and there are no craft or technical subjects.

One problem in small schools which is rather difficult to solve is encountered with regard to 'O' level repeat lessons. Generally these are catered for by returning the pupil to the fifth form for the appropriate lessons. For maximum timetable flexibility and administrative convenience it is often desirable that these 'O' level lessons should be put on at the same time as the first-year 'A' level lessons in the same subject. Two teachers of the relevant subject are therefore required and in a three-stream school there will be some subjects where there will only be one. Since the 'O' and the 'A' level lessons have therefore to be timetabled at different times, this adds a further constraint to the timetable.

One trap into which it is all too easy for the small school to fall is that of the temptation to deprive the first 3 years to some extent of needed reliefs in the way of split classes and remedial groups in order to extend the range of options in the fourth, fifth and sixth years. Of course, we do not even know scientifically what is the most effective mix of split classes and remedial groups in the lower school, or even whether they are really needed,[20] but in the absence of evidence we must protect the lower school from the possibility of curricular deprivation. This is not always easy to do in the small school, given the curricular pressures at the upper end of the school.

A deficiency with regard to the small school is its inability to provide a wide coverage of skills in arts and crafts. The typical art department of a large comprehensive school will have on its staff specialists in painting, pottery, fabric printing and so on. A small school will have only one or at the most two art teachers and unless they are very versatile they will not be able to cover so wide a range. A similar situation may well develop in P.E., though usually in this subject one can call on the services of non-specialists in P.E. who are interested and skilled in particular, and sometimes very diverse, sports.

It has often been thought that staff in small comprehensive schools need to be unusually versatile with regard to subjects taught. As far as four-stream schools are concerned this was shown by the survey not to be so. In one school visited only four out of the thirty staff regularly taught more than one subject. What a few staff did specially need to be, however, was both very responsible and also very competent. However desirable such traits are in teachers in all sizes of schools, the small school has a particular need of them since, in a

[19] Tucker, M., A small sixth form, *Forum*, vol. 12, no. 3, Summer 1970, pp. 100–2.

[20] From the learner's point of view split classes may not be needed (see p. 155 for evidence on size of class); from the teacher's point of view in some subjects they may well be.

3-F.E. school, for example, a few subjects will be staffed by only one teacher and the subject stands or falls accordingly. In these subjects the schools needed to offer a graded post to get a person with the right degree of experience. Since one of the 3-F.E. schools concerned had only eight graded posts this had not always been possible. Still, with a permanent staff of twenty, the school was able to provide a good range of specialist studies and to cater for remedial work, the library and careers. The development of an evening institute, besides being an excellent thing in itself, had provided one way of attracting staff of the right calibre.

A particular staffing difficulty was found by 3-F.E. schools with regard to P.E. Because of the odd number of forms it was often difficult to staff economically, without placing, say, a first- and a second-year form together, a somewhat dubious procedure for some activities. There was the additional difficulty that teachers of both sexes were required, when the staffing entitlement would only be $1\frac{1}{2}$ at most, or 1, if games were shared out to other members of staff. This made it inevitable that the second P.E. teacher at least would also teach another subject.

D. Conclusion

Clearly the small school's difficulties centre on the curriculum. Equally clearly, they are not by any means so great as used to be supposed or as was implied by the D.E.S. suggestion of a *minimum* 6-F.E. school in Circular 10/65, based as it was on anxiety about the need to provide a good range of sixth-form subjects. Indeed within a couple of years evidence had been accumulated by a group of northern H.M.I.s which showed indirectly that the small school was more viable than had been supposed. They were reported in the *Times Educational Supplement*[21] to have discovered that eight 'A' level subjects (English, history, geography, French, mathematics, physics, chemistry and biology) accounted for 80 per cent of the subjects taken. If mathematics is split into two subjects, we have nine. A similar finding was made in London, namely that 80 per cent of the choices made by sixth-form students centred on ten subjects,[22] and that if one also included seven more subjects the percentage rose to 97. Since a 3-F.E. school can provide ten 'A' level subjects and a 4-F.E. eighteen 'A' level subjects[23] the small school's curricular difficulties, though real, are not so great as has been supposed. Schools of 5-F.E. are certainly viable curricula-wise in respect of the sixth form; 4-F.E. schools experience certain constraints as regards the sixth-form curriculum, but can cover most of the demands. As 11–16 schools they are completely viable. The 3-F.E. can provide a very bare minimum at sixth-form level and experiences certain constraints in the fourth- and fifth-year curriculum. Its viability, and even more the viability of the 2-F.E. school, will depend on such diverse factors as the staffing ratio, the provision of part-time teachers, the average size of class and, if there is a sixth form, the number of pupils in it. Another factor would be the method used to timetable that part of the curriculum involving options. (See p. 160.)

The large school's advantages are confined at the sixth-form level on the whole to the provision of peripheral 'A' levels, of 'O' level repeats inside the sixth form, instead of a return for the appropriate lessons to the fifth form, and of commercial and technical courses. The latter have been found necessary for a large group of pupils in some areas, e.g. London,

[21] In early 1967.
[22] *London Comprehensive Schools*, 1966, Appendix XI, I.L.E.A., p. 127.
[23] See Appendix II.

but in the main as yet those who wish to stay on into the sixth are attracted by academic work[24] or by work[25] which can be fitted into the academic courses. The "new" sixth former comes so far in only small numbers in most places and, except where he comes in large numbers, only limited provision for him can be justified, even in large schools. The advantages of the large school at fourth- and fifth-year level centre partly on its ability to provide more peripheral subjects, partly on its ability to provide second classes in a particular optional subject. These can then be setted, or, if preferred, used as alternative sets, so that pupils who have a clash in their subject choices can get a second chance to take one of the subjects concerned. The value of setting, unless different subject material is being studied in the two sets, is at least disputed by the evidence on streaming and non-streaming, so that this is not as much of an advantage as has been supposed. The clash of subject choices could be avoided in small schools if the school day were extended and staff given appropriate time off to compensate for taking pupils after 4 o'clock. Many staff would appreciate a morning or afternoon free in return for taking pupils up to, say, 4.45 p.m. for an equivalent number of periods. Women, in particular, could get shopping done at a quiet time. But there has to be a *quid pro quo* for teaching after 4 p.m.

However that may be, what does become clear is that twelve-stream schools do not have anything like the advantage curriculum-wise, that was once supposed, as regards the ability to provide a wide curriculum. Indeed six-stream schools, the minimum size suggested by Circular 10/65, can provide all that is needed at fourth-, fifth- and sixth-form level in the way of differentiation.

E. Achievement and Outcomes

There is relatively little evidence relating school size to academic achievement or for that matter to early leaving or subsequent careers at college or university. According to Banks this is "an area in which the amount of research is inadequate to support the conclusions drawn".[26] Moreover, many of the results are contradictory.

Hoyt, in a review of the field, reported nineteen studies on the subject between 1924 and the late 1950s, with wide variations in experimental design, statistical sophistication and findings. Only four of them reported statistical tests of significance of the results. His own more sophisticated study demonstrated that the differences between students coming from various sizes of American high school in potential for college work were no larger than could have occurred by chance, although there was a slight non-significant trend for those from larger schools to get higher scores.[27] Harmon[28] showed that schools with less than 100 students in the graduating year[29] all fell below the national norm in the ultimate production of doctorates, those with more than 100 were all above it, thus confirming Conant's suppositions.

[24] Compare the Swedish finding that the vast majority of pupils in their comprehensive schools opt for academic and theoretical lines rather than for practical lines.

[25] e.g. preparation for nursing.

[26] Banks, O., *Sociology of Education*, Batsford, 1968, p. 174.

[27] Hoyt, D., Size of high school and college, *Personnel and Guidance J.* vol. XXXVII, no. 8, Apr. 1959, pp. 569–73.

[28] Harmon, Lindsay R., High school background of science doctorates, *Science*, 10 March 1961, pp. 679–88.

[29] Now that our leaving age has been raised to 16, our three-stream schools would be on the borderline between the two groups.

At the other end of the intellectual scale, Welch[30] found that the two most important determinants of quality of education for rural-farm males were the qualifications of their teachers, as reflected in their salaries, and school size (in sizes of school varying from 93 to 281). In the larger schools teachers did not have to cover large areas of the curriculum for which they were not qualified. Hence quality of schooling improved. A study by Isaacs[31] showed that the larger the school, the higher the percentage of drop-outs.

Work by Hieronymous and Feldt on the relationship between achievement, especially in basic skills, and high-school size, is reported in the *Review of Educational Research*.[32] Both studies favour schools of larger size.[33]

After an extensive investigation Coleman[34] concluded that the apparent effects of school size (the bigger, the better) vanish if various facilities and curricular differences are controlled. Higher achievement in larger schools is mainly accounted for by the additional facilities they have, such as libraries and science laboratories, and this is especially true at the secondary level. He noted urban and rural differences in effects of size. In urban downtown areas, the largest schools have no higher achievement levels than medium-sized schools and sometimes have lower; this affects disadvantaged children particularly. Coleman found teacher effects more important than size of school.

Analysis of the data from the large Project Talent Study[35] turned up no evidence of any distinct relationship between high-school size and any measure of academic output such as the percentage of students going on to higher education, the drop-out rate or scores on achievement tests. Marklund,[36] in a study of the attainments of 1800 Swedish pupils in large and small schools, showed that the prospects of pupils realizing their inherent potential was better in small schools than in large ones.

A large American study[37] showed that pupils in large schools, defined as schools of 500 and over, tended to earn more credits for graduation than those in medium or small schools, defined as schools of 200–499 and 100–199 pupils respectively. While 31 per cent of the pupils in the large schools earned $18\frac{1}{2}$ or more credits, only 19 per cent of the pupils in the small schools earned the same number. At the other end of the scale, 26 per cent of the pupils enrolled in the 500+ schools earned less than $16\frac{1}{2}$ credits and 41 per cent of those in the small schools. In the larger schools there seemed to have been a greater attempt to adjust the curricular load to the ability of the pupils than was true in the smaller schools. The I.E.A. study,[38] also, came to the conclusion that larger-sized schools promoted better academic

[30] Welch, F., Measurement of the quality of schooling, *Amer. Econ. Rev.*, vol. 56, no. 2, May 1966, pp. 379–92.

[31] Isaacs, D. A., A study of predicting high school drop-outs. Unpublished doctoral dissertation. Univ. of Kansas, 1953.

[32] Vol. 31, no. 4, Oct. 1961, p. 385.

[33] It is very important to remember in evaluating American research on this topic the existence of many very small high schools of even less than 100 pupils. Most of our "small" schools would be of medium size in American terms. Thus Feldt's study of high schools (grades 9–12, about ages 14–18) described schools of less than 100 as small, 101–200 as medium and 201+ as large.

[34] Coleman, J. S. *et al.*, *Equality of Educational Opportunity*, U.S. Department of Health, Education and Welfare, Office of Education, 1966, pp. 313–14.

[35] Flanagan, J. C., Daly, J. T., Shaycroft, M. F., Orr, D. B. and Goldberg, I., *Studies of the American High School*, Project Talent Office, University of Pittsburgh, 1962.

[36] Marklund, S., School organization, school location and student achievement, *Int. Rev. Educ.*, vol. XV, no. 3, 1969, pp. 295–320.

[37] Greer, E. S. and Harbeck, R. M., *What High School Pupils Study*, U.S. Department of Health, Education and Welfare, U.S. Government Printing Office, 1962, p. 122.

[38] *International Evaluation of Achievement Project* (*Mathematics*), vol. III. (Some of its results are contradictory.)

achievements. There was shown to be an increase in quality as school size increased, with a plateau reached at about 400.

The I.E.A. project also showed that selective academic schools of 700–1000 achieve higher scores than smaller or larger schools. In comprehensive schools the larger the school the higher the level reached, with the exception of Scotland where the smallest schools show up best in the comprehensive groups, probably because they take the whole age group. No data was given for English comprehensive schools. In general the conclusion of the I.E.A. study would be: younger students do better in schools of 800+; for older students the evidence is conflicting. One difficulty about the I.E.A. study is that some of the variables have not been controlled and may be skewing the results. Hence, maybe, the contradictions.

British studies on the effects of size of school are rare in the extreme. There is to hand one early British study on the academic effects of school size and it has to do with examination results, though in grammar, not comprehensive, schools. Lynn[39] showed that 'A' level pupils in larger sixth forms got more passes and distinctions. Unfortunately it is not too clear what one can make of this result, since there was no evidence of comparability of intelligence as between the pupils of large and small sixth forms in large and small grammar schools and no evidence of the relative calibre of the teaching staff in the different schools. If G.C.E. results at 'O' level were taken as an index of pupils' intelligence, however, the difference between the percentage of 'A' level passes obtained by pupils in large and small schools was only 8 per cent. At distinction level the difference was very much more marked, rising to 100 per cent. It was suggested that, to get open scholarships, sixth forms need to be about 150 strong. Two reasons, unexplored, were suggested for the results obtained. One reason suggested was that it was difficult for teaching to be efficiently organized in a small sixth form. Certainly if the approach to sixth-form work is that of class teaching rather than individual work, this might well be true, since for some lessons a small sixth may contain pupils from both upper and lower sixth and they may need work of a different level and approach. But it would not seem that this could be a valid reason where sixth-form work was organized on an individual basis, with the accent on the pupil learning rather than on the teacher teaching. The second reason suggested was that the larger class groups of the larger sixth form might provide a more stimulating and competitive atmosphere than would the small groups of the small sixth form. This would be in line with results obtained over many years on the effects, not of size of school, but of size of class.[40] Superior qualifications of teachers in large grammar schools might well also be contributing to the result. Welch's evidence on the effect of teacher qualification in the American context would support this view. Small schools would tend to get less well-qualified heads of departments than large schools, though the same would not be true, or not so true, for assistant teachers. The implications of this as regards the large schools would frequently be that sixth-form teaching was often given only by heads of departments, they would also do much teaching of 'A' forms, with less able children left to less able teachers; not a very satisfactory situation.

The relationship between size of school and attainment in comprehensive schools at first-, fourth- and sixth-year levels was studied in the second N.F.E.R. report.[41] The tests used concerned attainment in mathematics and the mother tongue.

[39] Lynn, R., The relation between educational achievement and school size, *Brit. J. Sociology*, vol. X no. 2, June 1959, pp. 129–36.

[40] See pp. 155–8.

[41] Monks, T. G. (ed.), *Comprehensive Education in Action*, N.F.E.R., 1970, p. 112.

TABLE 2

Total Test Scores and Size of School

	First year (NF 68) Mean	First year (NF 68) No. of schools	Fourth year (NF 68) Mean	Fourth year (NF 68) No. of schools	Sixth year (P66)	
600 and under	75·5	13	103·4	10	55·7	13
601–1200	73·4	22	96·3	20	50·8	20
1201 and over	72·7	10	97·2	10	49·3	10
All schools	73·9	45	58·1	40	51·9	43
	F = 1 N.S.		F = 2·71 N.S.		F = 2·26 N.S.	

Although the pupils in small schools scored higher on average, size was not significantly associated with test score results for any of the year groups. When the schools were divided into those of 600 or less and the rest, the fourth- and sixth-years' results just reached significance.

Staying-on into the sixth form would, from rough estimates, based on data from the N.F.E.R. study, seem not to disfavour the small comprehensive school. It may have a small sixth but at least as many stay on proportionately as in larger schools.

TABLE 3

Relationships[42] Between Size of School. How Long Established and Size of Sixth Form

Size of school	Number of schools	Number of pupils	Mean
Less than 600	39	1554	39·8
601–1000	67	3741	55·8
1000 and over	75	7095	94·6
	181	12,390	68·5

It can be roughly estimated from Table 2[43] that the average size of school in each of the groups of schools is 500?, 850?, 1350? The average staying-on rate into the sixth in each group of schools would therefore be 7·9 per cent, 6·6 per cent and 7·0 per cent respectively.

Comparable percentages from Benn and Simon[44] are as shown in Table 4.

Staying-on rates in the sixth form would not therefore appear to be to the disadvantage of the small school.

It is difficult to evaluate the evidence with regard to the effect of size of school on academic attainment, since some of it is conflicting. Probably the best verdict with regard to academic attainment is one of not proven, partly due to the lack of enough research, with the suspicion that large schools may well prove in the end to produce somewhat better academic results

[42] Monks, T. G., *Comprehensive Education in England and Wales, A Survey of Schools and their Organisation*, N.F.E.R., 1968, p. 97.

[43] *Ibid.*, p. 88.

[44] Benn, C. and Simon B., *Half Way There*, McGraw-Hill, 1970, p. 130.

TABLE 4

Size of School and Sixth Form Staying-on Rotes

Size of schools	Average size of sixth forms	Staying-on rate into sixth forms
		%
201–400	18	6·0
401–600	32	6·5
601–800	50	7·3
801–1000	48	5·3
1001–1200	72	6·5
1201–1400	82	6·3
1401–1600	100	6·6
1601–1800	130	7·6
1801–2000	132	6·9
2001–2200	138	6·2
2201–2400	184	8·3[45]

than small schools, large being defined as consisting of 400 or 500 pupils or more. An important factor may well be (see Coleman's finding on teacher effects) whether *a school is big enough to employ at least one specialist teacher at the right level of qualification in each of the subjects needed for its curriculum.* With regard to staying-on rates the evidence would appear to be neutral in respect of size, though American evidence suggests very large schools produce a larger percentage of dropouts.

The above evidence also needs to be evaluated against a background of data as to the actual proportions of the variation in students' achievement that is due to the organizational characteristics of a school. Such data is to be found in a systems analysis by Greenfield.[46] In view of the indirect nature of the relationship between the organizational characteristics of a school and the achievements of its pupils, the school as an organization could not really expect to claim more than a small portion of the achievement variance. Greenfield found that this assumption is correct. The variation in achievement of 2069 pupils from eighty-eight classrooms of forty-four schools in twenty-two districts was divided up as follows: 19 per cent of the variation between pupils was due to the class, 68 per cent to the individual pupil, 10 per cent to the district and 3 per cent to the school. Coleman came to similar conclusions.[47] *Perhaps we should not worry too much about the effects of school size on academic achievement.*

F. School Size and Costs

Riew[48] studied the relation between school size and the cost per pupil in Wisconsin and found evidence of significant economies of scale in school operation. He found that when crude controls for school quality are introduced, increases in enrolment are accompanied by decreases in per-pupil expenditure, increases in number of courses offered, and increases in the percentage of teaching staff with higher qualifications.[49] The decline in expenditure

[45] In view of the small numbers of schools of the size, this result could arise by chance.

[46] Greenfield, Thomas B., Administrations and systems analysis, *Can. Admin.*, no. 3, April 1964, pp. 25–30.

[47] *Op. cit.*, p. 316.

[48] Riew, J., Economics of scale in high school operation, *Rev. Econ. Stat.*, vol. 48, Aug. 1966, pp. 280–8.

[49] A finding confirmed by Danowski and Finch. Danowski, Charles E. and Finch, James N., Teacher prepa ation and numerical adequacy: an historical comparison, *I.A.R. Res. Bull.*, no. 6, June 1966, pp. 7–10. Whe er it is wise to allow the best qualified teachers to congregate in certain schools is a point for discussion.

per pupil levels off in schools of 1600 and above but the proportion of teaching staff with higher qualifications and the number of courses offered both continue to increase. Riew decided, however, that more research was needed with samples including more large schools.

G. Synoptic Evidence

Two other more general studies are reported in the literature. In a study of the relationship between high school size and five qualitative and quantitative factors of educational import Gray,[50] using four different sizes of schools, found that schools in the size 400–999 pupils were placed highest or near the top on all five factors.[51] There appeared to be an increase in quality as school size increased, but a plateau was reached at about 400 pupils. Smith[52] also found, in a study relating school size to twenty-one selected cost, pupil, teacher, administrative and institutional factors, that high schools with fewer than 200 pupils were paying a premium for an inferior programme. When all factors were considered a size range of 800–1200 pupils was the one at which favourable factors approached a maximum and unfavourable factors a minimum. It is clear from these studies that a school can be too large as well as too small, and the data suggests that for a school to be really viable on purely educational grounds it can be smaller than if cost and administrative factors are also considered.

H. Conclusion

The results of this survey of the relationship between size of school and such factors as (a) curriculum, academic output and staying-on rates; (b) participation, satisfaction and development of leadership amongst pupils; (c) organization and finance, suggest that schools can be too large as well as too small, and that there is some conflict as to ideal size, according to whether one uses measures of cost, width of curriculum, academic output or personal development. The larger schools can provide a wider measure of curricular choice than small schools, though not to the extent thought previously. Some of the research suggested that academic quality rose with the size of the school but that a plateau was reached when a school's size reached 400; other research suggested a higher figure. It was not completely clear whether this was due to size alone or to factors associated with size though Coleman's study suggested the latter. At the same time the smaller schools scored by their contribution to personal development and did not appear to have such high drop-out rates as large schools. The ideal size would appear to be between 400 and 1000 when purely educational factors are considered; when administrative and cost factors are also included, the ideal size would be between 800 and 1200.

If small schools provide the best opportunities for personal development and large schools provide a wider curricular choice and possibly slightly higher levels of attainment, as well as, up to a certain size, economies of scale, we may ask the following question: Would the campus school be the right one, with students grouped in semi-autonomous units for most studies

[50] Gray, S. C., A study of the relationship between size and number of qualitative and quantitative factors of education in four sizes of secondary school in Iowa. Thesis, Iowa State University 1961. Abstracted in *Dissertation Abstracts*, vol. 22, no. 8, 1962, p. 2631.

[51] The writer's timetabling analysis would confirm this finding in respect of curriculum. Recent work by Curtis shows that the 16 most popular subjects *always* appear in the curriculum of schools of 800 and over.

[52] Smith, C. B., A study of the optimum size of secondary school. Doctoral thesis, Columbus, Ohio State University. Abstracted in *Dissertation Abstracts*, vol. 21, no. 8, 1961, pp. 2181–2.

and activities, but with access to the whole school for more peripheral studies and activities? The campus school, if thus organized, would provide for continued association between the same teachers and students, which leads to closer social bonds, according to Plath,[53] and, so one might think, would combine the academic and economic advantages of the larger school and the social advantages of the small.

But the social values of the small school, as investigated by Barker and Gump, depend to a considerable extent on "low population per setting, a condition difficult or impossible to achieve" in the large school. "What seems to happen is that as schools get larger and settings inevitably become more heavily populated, more of the students are less needed; they become superfluous, redundant." "A school should be sufficiently small that all of its students are needed for its enterprises. A school should be small enough that students are not redundant."[54] Campbell[55] hazards a guess that once a school passes the 400 mark it is probably difficult to ensure that students do not become redundant. A scientific answer, he says, would probably be expressed in terms of the ratio of students to settings, and, although no conclusive data are available, this ratio probably should not exceed 2·5 : 1.[56] This implies a size no greater than 750 probably. It would seem likely therefore that the campus school would provide only a partial solution to the dilemma of reconciling the needs of personal development with the criteria on ideal size of school. Probably the best guess would be to accept schools in the range 400–1000 as being within the ideal range. The latter size is that recommended as a minimum size for the 11–18 school, namely, a six-stream school, in Circular 10/65 of the Department of Education and Science. It would then depend on what factors were considered to be most important on the continuum from personal development to economic cost, important generally and in the particular circumstances, which size of school was opted for in new building programmes.

[53] See pp. 125–7, especially p. 127.
[54] Barker and Gump, *op. cit.*, p. 202.
[55] Campbell, W. J., School size: its influence on pupils, *J. Educ. Admin.*, vol. III, no. 1, May 1965, pp. 5–11.
[56] See p. 92, Table 2, P/D Ratio.

CHAPTER 8

The Large School: Offsetting Its Disadvantages

It is clear that very small schools and very large schools both have their disadvantages as well as their advantages, and reasonably clear that the ideal size of school at secondary level, when only educational considerations are borne in mind, lies somewhere between 400 and 1000, when administrative and cost factors, are included, somewhere between 800 and 1200. In terms of the 11–18 school we might plump for the five- or six-stream school on one site as being the ideal, since it would produce numbers of pupils between 800 and 1000, if we wish to reconcile both sets of factors. If we think only educational considerations should be borne in mind the four-stream school would also be justifiable, and certainly up to fifth-form level; its sixth form would, however, be small, at least until sixth-form staying-on rates increase materially, as they may very well do after the raising of the school-leaving age.

However, we do not live in an ideal world and cannot rebuild all our schools to fit in with ideal considerations. What then can we do to offset the disadvantages of the over-small or over-large schools which already exist?

THE LARGE SCHOOL

In view of the reported defects of the larger school with respect to pupil participation and satisfaction, it is gratifying to think that the British, with their deep-rooted attachment to all that is personal in education, intuitively realized, from the beginning of experimentation with comprehensive schools, the need to break down the larger schools into smaller units if the personal touch was to be maintained. An early report in the 1950s suggested that large comprehensive schools might take a leaf out of the book of boarding schools and make use of a house system. The Coventry authorities took a lead and built house systems into the very design of their schools. Some schools, though not purpose-built for it, tried, with greater or lesser success, to work a house system. Other schools, like Mayfield, for example, used a year system on the grounds that the design of their buildings precluded any effective use of the house system, and others again found their salvation in a junior-, middle- and upper-school arrangement. In each case appropriate administrative and other personnel were appointed to each unit and in the early days at least each system, in almost every school, functioned in a context of fine streaming. Yet material from America and also the material developed by the present writer suggest that the systems we have evolved have not been sufficiently thought through in many cases.

A. Systems of Decentralization in the U.S.A.

It is of interest to find that variations on the house and year systems have been in operation in a few American schools since just after the First World War, that is in the period when the American high school was becoming fully developed as a school for all the children of a community. One school began what Plath refers to as a "school within a school" type of organization as far back as 1919, another followed in 1924, and a further half dozen in the 1930s and 1940s. By 1960 about fifty schools had decentralized their form of organization, whether horizontally, vertically or by a combination of both, and by the end of the 1950s educationists were beginning to investigate the characteristics of these new types of organization, as compared with those of the more common large educational institutions which were monolithic.

To what extent is American experience of the "school within a school" relevant to the English situation? Have we not already catered for the effects of size in our large comprehensive schools with such decentralizing devices as year systems and house systems? It is true, of course, that American practice of the school within a school idea varies, just as our year and house systems vary, but an examination of the best American practice seems to have relevance for our own, as will be seen from a comparison of the two.

Three main research studies on these schools were made by Hodgson, York and Plath and are reported by Plath.[1] All of them were more in the nature of surveys, rather than sophisticated investigations like that of Barker and Gump. A further study also mentioned by Plath was undertaken by Michigan State University College of Education, with a preliminary visit to 300 secondary schools, and an intensive study of thirty of them.

In the smaller units into which the schools are divided enrolments are known to vary from 125 to 1100. Most are in the 400 to 600 range. Such large differences must have considerable consequences for their effectiveness, but these do not appear to have been evaluated in any of the studies named.

The decentralization of these large schools took the form of dividing the schools up into smaller *territorial* units, in which certain administrative duties were placed closer to those immediately affected by them and *the pupils had more classes within a limited geographical area than formerly*.

The division of these schools into smaller units had as one of its main aims the improvement of personal relationships and participation and greater knowledge of the pupils. Indeed, in the case of one school, catastrophe had played a very large part in motivating a move to a school-within-a-school plan.[2] A senior boy had been killed at a party away from the school and when police requested information about him from the school no teacher

[1] (a) Hodgson, John H., The schools within a school plan. Unpublished Doctor of Education project report, Teachers' College, Columbia University, 1958. (b) York, William J., The schools within a school: a study of selected secondary schools which embody this plan of organization. Unpublished Doctor of Education project report, Teachers' College, Columbia University, 1958. (c) Plath, Karl R., The school within a school: a study of the organization of selected senior high schools, with possible applications for Evanston Township high school. Unpublished Doctor of Education project report, Teachers' College, Columbia University, 1961. (All three studies are reported in Plath, Karl R., *Schools within Schools. A Study of High School Organization*, Secondary School Administration Series, Teachers' College, Columbia, New York, 1965.)

[2] Plath, *op. cit.*, p. 20.

could be found who was well acquainted with him.[3] In another large school there were 120 cases of persistent behaviour problems involving long-term suspension before decentralization. The staff felt that the size of the school and the supervision of student control by a few administrators who could not know the students had contributed to the situation. After the school was decentralized into "little schools" and the onus for discipline was placed on administrators operating within each unit, the total of persistent major behaviour problems dropped to nine.

This decentralization with a view to improved personal relationships has implications for the way in which the curriculum is to be organized. "Ideally, to gain the greatest advantages of personal relationships a pupil's classes in a school within a school should all be scheduled with students and teachers in his unit."[4] Two factors can prevent this, highly refined ability grouping and a large number of elective subjects.[5]

Where ability grouping is strongly emphasized a school may have to assign all lessons schoolwide in order to refine the groups to the greatest extent, and the pupil will have few lessons within the little school. The advantages in terms of personal development that accrue with close relationships between teachers and pupils and with limiting of pupils to certain geographical areas of the school are therefore lost. If a large school wishes to work a school-within-a-school organization in any real sense, very refined ability grouping has to be discarded.[6]

The second factor, the large number of elective subjects, results from the explosion of knowledge, the increasing specialization of the curriculum and the increasing differentiation of choice as pupils move up the school. The greater the number of elective subjects, reports Plath, the greater the difficulty in keeping the pupil within his own little school. Thus over-specialization of the curriculum can impede pastoral care and diminish pupil participation and satisfaction by preventing or hindering proper decentralization.

At the junior level these two issues are relatively minor ones, because the amount of ability grouping may be limited or even non-existent and because the curriculum is more general at this stage. At a vertically organized junior high school, for example, Plath found that lessons for all academic[7] subjects, plus art and vocal music, took place within the pupil's own "little school", each of which contained 340 pupils. At the senior level the position is different. At one senior high school which was horizontally organized on a "school-within-a-school" basis he found that pupils took their compulsory courses within their own unit, their elective courses outside it. At another senior high school, 66 per cent of first years, 50 per cent of second years, 44 per cent of third years and 18 per cent of fourth years had half or more of their classes within their own unit. This school was vertically organized. Plath comments that schools that do attempt to timetable a pupil's lessons within the little-school unit realize that a pupil will leave his unit for more lessons as he progresses up the school and studies more elective subjects. The normal policy in such schools is to give each pupil the curriculum most suited to his own individual needs and wishes, disregarding at the individual level the number of classes he will have within his own unit.

[3] See p. 88 for the evidence from Monahan's study of the effect of schools of over 2000 on teachers' knowledge of children.

[4] Plath, *ibid.*, p. 24.

[5] In British terms options groups subjects.

[6] It is interesting to see how large British comprehensive schools gradually moved away from highly refined ability grouping.

[7] Academic subjects as defined by Americans include commercial but not aesthetic subjects.

This will reduce, but not eliminate, for the individual pupil the effects of the size of the large school. It would also explain a finding by Campbell[8] in a research project on the effects of school size, which happened by chance to include one of the schools mentioned by Plath. The "little-school" organization of a large school, at least as far as this one school of 2000 pupils was concerned—hence conclusions must be tentative—proved to be still at a disadvantage in the matter of pupil participation and development when compared with the genuine small school. He further comments, however, that as we have large schools, it is encouraging to see that ways are being explored of minimizing their disadvantages. Plath's remark[9] that timetabling by computer may push large schools towards reducing the amount of time pupils spend within their own unit, i.e. towards maximizing their disadvantages in respect of personal development, should serve as a warning to take proper precautions in using these devices.[10]

The conflict between the personal needs of the pupil to be in a small unit and his curricular needs for access to a wide variety of subjects and subject choices, in the later years especially, often catered for by setting up large schools and therefore large school-wide departments, is well illustrated by arrangements in which little school units are constructed within large schools. Such arrangements enable pupils to get the best of both worlds but they complicate the task of heads of subject departments, as Plath reports. The subject departments are organized on a schoolwide basis but they must be able to function at the "little school" level. He therefore stresses the importance of co-ordination between the departments and the "little school" to avoid duplication of effort, to insure communication of ideas and practice and to fix responsibilities for various phases of curriculum development.[11] There was a need within the little school for both vertical co-ordination of curriculum within a department and horizontal curriculum integration among departments.

Clearly heads of departments in these schools, with their subject teachers and classrooms scattered over the whole group of buildings in many cases, will need to be very good co-ordinators of the activities for which they hold the chief responsibility and to have adequate time allotted for the achievement of these objectives. If adequate time for this work cannot be given, another possible solution is more decentralization and delegation of authority and responsibility within the departments, to match that which has already taken place in the general administrative and policy structure of the school as a whole.

The effect of decentralization on the general administrative structure of the schools studied is also reported by Plath. The three investigators all found that the main functions of the head of the little school were administration within the unit and control of students. Pupils' records tended to be kept in the office of the little school and preventive discipline was more possible than in a school where those in charge of discipline were further removed from students. The head of the little school's closer knowledge of the pupils' capacities and his assignment of them to more suitable classes had led, in one school, to a reduction of the failure rate by 20 per cent in the year after the school was divided into smaller units.

The reactions of students[12] at one school after 1 year's experience of the school-within-a-school organization, i.e. when the impact of the new arrangements was fresh in their minds,

[8] Mentioned by him in a review of Plath's book in the *J. Educ. Admin.*, vol. II, no. 1, May 1964, pp. 138–9.
[9] *Op cit.*, p. 25.
[10] The day of their common use is not distant. See Egner, W. E., *Education*, 17 Dec. 1971, pp. 543–4.
[11] Plath, *op. cit.*, p. 15; quoting Hodgson, p. 186.
[12] Plath, *ibid.*, p. 68.

can be gauged from the following remarks, including one unfavourable one:

> "Now you go to an administrator who knows you when you are in difficulties rather than to a building organizer who may never have seen you and is too busy to talk to you."
>
> "They know you now. You can't get away with as much as before, so you don't try it. You know Mr. X will be calling home."
>
> "Activity participation is much more important and is done more. We can win trophies for our house."
>
> "House dances are a flop. Very few attend."
>
> "There is more opportunity for participation in student activities and with it some individual recognition. The top jobs used to seem impossible to reach."

In spite of the occasional jargon, the message is clear. Only in respect of dancing partners was the new arrangement defective.

As a result of decentralization several advantages[13] accrued to pupils, varying from school to school according to the degree and type of decentralization arranged.

(a) The pupils have closer relationships with their teachers, relationships that continue over a longer period.
(b) Within the little school, individual abilities are recognized earlier and developed, co-operation between members of staff increases on behalf of individual pupils, and behaviour problems are recognized earlier.
(c) Where lessons are timetabled to take place within a pupil's own unit, the continuity and integration of subject matter are improved.
(d) Student activities increase as a result of increased opportunities in the little school for immediate participation and socialization, and more opportunities for leadership.
(e) Maintaining pupils mainly in particular areas of the building helps to develop a sense of belonging in the pupils.

Other advantages accrued to the staff:

(a) The principal of the school is relieved of administrative routine and can concentrate on policy.
(b) Because the pupil feels he is known, there is more effective control of pupils and the problem pupils and situations are recognized more easily by the administrator, who has a better knowledge of pupils, parents and home backgrounds. There is consequent improvement in counselling.
(c) Within the little school the guidance of inexperienced teachers improves, as their introduction into the school is thereby eased.
(d) Because the principal is more available, general supervision is improved.
(e) School policies with regard to curricula, teaching methods and administration improve as does also staff morale, because of better communication and personal relationships than in the monolithic institutions and because of increased attention to the views of teachers in the policy-making process.
(f) Because it is easier to try out a new policy in a small school of 300 rather than a large school of 2000, a particular little school can be used for a pilot study. Hence change and innovation become easier in the school as a whole.

[13] Plath, pp. 15, 45, 66–7.

B. Systems of Decentralization in Britain

The research by Plath and his associates on the decentralization of large schools in the U.S.A. suggests that it is important to decentralize not only administratively, as we have done,[14] but also academically, that is to say, it is important for a particular group of pupils to be confined to one particular area of the school for teaching purposes, as far as is possible in the context of ever-widening curricular choice in the later years of schooling. It also suggests, perhaps, at first sight, unexpectedly, that the greater the success in achieving geographical decentralization, the greater the improvement in pastoral care and in a number of other aspects of school life.

Our own attempts in Britain at decentralization do not appear in many cases to meet the criteria and conditions of success that this finding implies, since the geographical aspect of decentralization has not usually been emphasized enough.

1. *House Systems*

So far most of our house systems have been mainly social devices. In most of them the social structure of the school is separated from the teaching and working structure. Pupils are placed in houses according to some practice which ensures that a similar spread of ability is to be found in each house and in each tutor group. Typically, pupils meet in each house block for registration, for assembly, for break, for school dinner and for such extra-curricular activities as are organized on a house basis. Their working units are usually quite different, however, from their social units. A few schools, it is true, organize their teaching groups on a mixed ability basis and can therefore make these coincidental with their house groups, but these are still rather rare. Most schools which are run according to a house system still organize their teaching by either finely, or more often coarsely, graded streaming or banding; therefore their social and their teaching units do not coincide and, moreover, pupils go to classes all over the building. Even in schools whose house groups and teaching groups do coincide, pupils still go to classes all over the building.

Where house groups and teaching groups do not coincide, pupils often do not meet their house tutors as teachers. The consequences of this split in roles can be seen from Barnes' account[15] of the results of a policy of separating the teaching and the pastoral role in a socially difficult neighbourhood, i.e. a school where the social and psychological consequences of such a policy inevitably stand out most clearly.

> Before any of our earliest pupils had left school we noticed that friendship grouping among them did not correlate closely with house membership and that pupils often appeared to be influenced more by teachers who taught them or met them for some extra-curricular activity, than by those charged, under the house system, with a special pastoral responsibility. Although the housemasters were themselves influential, for from the beginning Ruffwood had teachers of outstanding ability to fill this role, many of the staff, especially the less experienced, found it hard to make much of the role of house tutor, especially in the case of pupils whom they did not meet in lessons. House-based extra-curricular activities, also, were hard to vitalize, partly because pupils wanted to participate in activities with friends not in the same house.

In an area where the socialization of children was as important as, indeed often an essential

[14] Even in our purpose-built house-based comprehensive schools, pupils are confined to one area of the school for social and administrative purposes only. For lessons they may go all over the school.

[15] Halsall, Elizabeth (ed.), *op. cit.*, p. 235.

preliminary to, their education, the separation of the pastoral from the teaching role, of the social group from the teaching group, brought difficulties to a school which had in fact been purpose-built for the house system. As a result over a period of years the school moved gradually to a position in which the two were brought together again, with pupils taught in house groups, practically unstreamed.[16] Until this happened, the prime purpose of the house system, namely to improve pastoral care, was not fulfilled.

In the few schools, however, where mixed ability groups do coincide with house groups, i.e. where the working and the social groups coincide, the pupils are not in current practice usually confined, for their working and social life, to one area of the school. The whole school in practice is their parish. Their timetable ensures that they move all over it. In a school of 1500 or 2000 this means that individual pupils are in the same situation as had formerly been the American adolescents who made comments in one of the research studies referred to by Plath.[17] These students were very perceptive about the differences to their contacts with administrators, their behaviour and their participation in school activities which resulted from the total decentralization of their working and social life, i.e. their confinement mainly to one area of their school. Their evidence suggests that when pupils are mainly restricted to one area they are at least much nearer to the happier psychological situation of pupils in small schools, as described by Barker and the other research workers who have explored the effects of size of school on pupils. They were clearly feeling greater internal incentives and greater external pressures to participate in activities than before and they were appreciating both knowing and being better known than before. It is not, of course, clear from Plath's account whether the number of behaviour settings, as defined by Barker and Gump, increased with decentralization. Nor can we assume that it did, especially in view of Campbell's comment[18] about one decentralized large school which had formed part of his research study. But the increased and more intimate contact with fewer people which resulted from being confined to one area of the school was clearly having an effect and a very beneficial one. We have underestimated the importance of the concept of *territoriality*. Perhaps here we have something to learn from the birds!

2. *Year Systems*

Our year systems do not, like most of our house systems, usually involve any split between the working and the social life of pupils within the school. Whether pupils are separated according to fine streaming, coarse streaming or banding, the teaching and the social units are the same. Where they are separated into mixed ability groups there is some divergence of practice. In some schools mixed ability grouping is as much a teaching device as a social one. There are, however, a number of schools where mixed ability grouping for social purposes, such as registration, is carried on alongside teaching in a streamed situation with many pupils not meeting their tutor as a teacher at all. On the whole, however, our year systems at present tend to some form of coarse streaming or banding and also tend to keep the pastoral and the teaching role united. But often the year system and its fellow, the junior/middle and senior system demand excessive movement by either teachers or by pupils, if specialist teachers are to get an adequate variety of teaching. If the whole

[16] *Ibid.*, pp. 242–6.
[17] See p. 127.
[18] See p. 126.

of the first year of a large school, for example, is stationed in a particular area of the school the pupils of that year can move mainly to the teachers also stationed in this area. If they do the teachers will be condemned to teach all of the classes of the year mainly the same material. In this situation, the only way of giving staff adequate variety is to give them a few classes from other years. This cannot be done without excessive movement by either the teachers themselves or the pupils of the other years.

The effects of such a policy both on the teaching organization of the school and on staff and pupil morale are well delineated by Withington[19] who describes its effects in a school consisting of three rather spread-out buildings organized on a junior/middle/senior system.

> Some movement of staff and/or pupils was inevitable if staff were not to be restricted to teaching only those pupils who were based in the same building as themselves: that had to be accepted. So that it would be accepted with good grace, every journey that could be avoided had to be avoided or reduced. This meant that every form had to be based, wherever possible, in the building where most of its periods could be spent. . . . Teachers also had to be based according to their teaching programme: teachers with an appreciable number of senior teaching periods were generally based in C, those with a few periods were based in B, those with fewer still in A, and those with none in the annexe. Conversely, building A tended to get more inexperienced young teachers and the annexe the more experienced non-senior teachers.

That this result is more or less inevitable is confirmed by the writer's experience, also in a three building school, unsuited to the house system and which was therefore worked on a junior/middle/senior system. One could not place young inexperienced teachers in the middle school building, since they had enough difficulty in establishing themselves with junior pupils without throwing them to the lions of the middle school; hence, it was inevitable that the junior building would have a disproportionate number of inexperienced teachers, that the more experienced teachers in the building would carry too heavy a burden in respect of the enforcement of reasonable order and discipline and that, despite their efforts, the general good order would suffer.

There is a further acute comment by Withington[20] on the effects of excessive movement which might affect individual teachers or individual forms in such a large school. "If anyone, pupil or teacher, was given a timetable with frequent inter-building movement . . . their morale suffered and they took longer and longer to make each journey." Yet it is also clear from his accounts that efforts to prevent overmuch interbuilding movement were a major preoccupation of the school's hierarchy, for it had an elongated linear school to cope with. One may therefore perhaps trace a connection between Withington's experiences and the comments of Plath's adolescents and infer that a type of decentralization which includes a reduction of movement of pupils about the whole school campus is an important factor in promoting pupil morale.

3. *Conclusion and Comment*

The year system or the junior/middle/senior system either restricts teachers too much to teaching only one section of the school, stationed in their own geographical area, and confines too many inexperienced teachers to the junior section of the school, or, if this restriction is not accepted, it involves teachers or pupils in too much movement, with unfortunate consequences for their morale.

[19] Halsall, Elizabeth (ed.), *op. cit.*, p. 77.
[20] *Ibid.*, pp. 76–7.

At the same time, unless the teaching organization of the school as well as its social organization is based on mixed ability groups, the house system results in the separation of these two aspects of the life of the school and a consequent blurring of the responsibility for, and a decline in the effectiveness of, pastoral care. Yet if teachers are not convinced of the value of mixed ability groups and adjust their methods to them, they do not teach them well.[21]

Is it therefore inevitable that in a large school, whatever system is used for breaking it down into smaller organizational units, there should be serious disadvantages of one kind or another for the life and well-being of the school? Or have we not thought through far enough all the organizational implications of decentralization in the school context? It is the writer's purpose to demonstrate that we have not.

One may speculate as to the reasons why our systems of decentralization have not yet been completely successful. One possible reason is especially worth discussing since it can act as a lead to better policies. Historically, the development of our large schools took place at a time when the British thought that the more finely streamed children were the more effective the teaching and that even in the primary school streaming was beneficial. At the same time the protagonists of the comprehensive school were anxious to prove, in the élitist atmosphere of the period, that bright children could do at least as well in comprehensive schools as they did in grammar schools. Indeed, it was essential for their survival that they should do so. They were therefore very anxious that no step should be taken which might worsen, or even appear to worsen, the academic prospects of these children. Now, however, that children are frequently "banded" or placed in coarsely streamed classes or even in mixed ability groups, and teachers find these classes acceptable as teaching units, more flexible arrangements are possible within a whole year group, for example, than formerly. In a twelve-stream school, instead of an inflexible system of streaming, in descending order of ability, thus:

(a) A B C D E F G H I J K L

one can find an arrangement on the following lines:

(b)

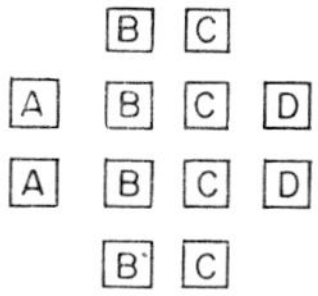

B C
A B C D
A B C D
B C

This arrangement, as can easily be seen from the diagram, allows for a division of the year into two groups, including in each group one A, two B, two C and one D stream(s).

Another possible arrangement in a coarse-streaming situation would be as follows:

(c)

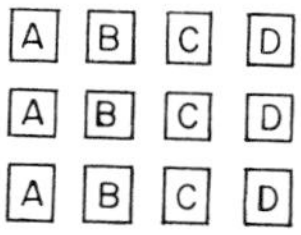

A B C D
A B C D
A B C D

[21] See evidence on p. 15.

In this scheme the whole of a year would be divided into three groups, each containing one A, one B, one C and one D form.

Protagonists of even coarser streaming, who do not however feel able to go the whole way towards mixed ability grouping, might even find the following arrangement acceptable for teaching purposes:

(d)

A	B	C
A	B	C
A	B	C
A	B	C

Here the whole year would be divided up into four groups of three forms each.

Variations on the above themes are possible where a school contains fewer, or even more, than twelve streams.

As we shall hope to show presently, these new arrangements are pregnant with possibilities for improving pastoral care and reducing movement without at the same time reducing the variety of teaching for the individual teacher. (See pp. 137–9.)

C. Prelude to a More Detailed Analysis of Decentralization

This review of practice in some large American schools and the review and critique of current general practice in large British comprehensive schools can now be linked with the mathematical analysis of the difficulties of disciplinary control and supervision in large schools, as compared with small schools, which was reported in Chapter 6. A more detailed review and analysis of current British practice in the light of this other evidence will enable us to see what changes could be made in our present systems of decentralization in large schools which would help to eliminate, or at least reduce, the difficulties encountered.

One unmentioned assumption underlying the mathematical analysis is the assumption that any pupil may move about anywhere in the school, or may be so moved about by the timetable. It is this which brings him into contact with so many comparative strangers on the staff, thus making his behaviour so difficult to control. In a large comprehensive school there is nothing to prevent any pupil from moving about anywhere in the school, unless positive attempts are made on the timetable to restrict movement on some rational principle. Of course, every good timetable-maker, other things being equal, attempts to restrict movement between lessons and, of two rooms equally suitable for a particular subject, chooses the nearest to whatever class requires a lesson in that subject, so as to prevent congestion on corridors or waste of time on long journeys.[22] But apart from this, the bigger the school, and the very fact of having more staff in a particular department to choose from to teach a particular subject, the longer the distances to travel. Even when strenuous efforts to reduce movement have been made, it needs only one member of staff to leave at Christmas and the attempt to fit into the existing timetable the replacement teacher—unless his strengths are exactly the same as those of the leaving teacher—can destroy elaborate

[22] N.B. Hence any attempt to ensure all rooms are in use all the time, as in the Glasgow research, inevitably results in some loss of time, since the only available room may be at the other end of the campus. On a large campus one either wastes space or wastes teachers' and pupils' time.

arrangements to keep movement to a minimum, in a way that cannot happen in a smaller school.[23] Hence, for all these reasons there are often long distances for pupils to travel in large schools. It is on these long journeys that there is the greatest opportunity for hanging around or for getting into more mischief than is tolerable or in the interests of reasonable order and on the same long journeys that there is least risk of pupils being recognized when so engaged.

It is for this reason that consideration should be given to a policy of restricting the movement of a particular class or groups of classes between lessons to a given territorial area; consideration should also be given to the principles on which such a policy should be based. In planning new buildings far greater attention should be given to layouts which would enable the timetable-maker and the policy-maker to reduce movement over large areas. To put the matter more accurately, some such consideration should be given, since almost none has been in the past. Personally, I believe that the plans for a large school should never be passed by the Department of Education and Science until they have been vetted by a small committee of two or three people who have had experience in organizing large schools. No other group of people has any real feeling for the snags that may be encountered. They do not sense the difficulties that a particular plan may produce.

In an existing school the policy of restricting movement can be carried out only in the context of the available buildings and facilities, and their layout, which may be counterproductive. The extent to which movement can be cut down will determine, other things being equal, the degree of difficulty of disciplinary control relative to the indices which have been reported in Chapter 6. If classes move within a very narrow area for half of their time, for example, the index of difficulty of disciplinary control will be halved relative to the school's theoretical index.

How high a priority the policy of restricting movement so as to promote good discipline and control will have in the overall policy of the school will be strongly influenced by the sort of area and clientèle the school serves. In a suburban middle-class area, with children who are already highly socialized, such a policy will be desirable; in a twilight area or in any other area of great social difficulty and delinquescence it will be imperative, since the clientèle of the school is on the whole prey to greater temptations. Yet it is on council housing estates rather than in middle-class residential areas that very large comprehensive schools have frequently been built; and they have been built with no real thought for the problems of movement and for their effect on discipline and socialization in a group of children that badly need both, before academic work of any value or calibre can be expected from most of them.

D. A Detailed Analysis of Current Decentralization Practices

Since a high proportion of contacts with staff who are comparative strangers to them is the source of much bad behaviour in many pupils, since large schools promote such contacts, we must seek for rational principles of avoiding or reducing them by reducing movement over a wide area. An examination of where, when and in what context movement occurs ought to help us to formulate these principles.

First, there are three main times at which movement occurs in a school: between lessons,

[23] The writer is speaking from personal experience in a school that grew from small to very large, and from other experience in small schools.

between registration and assembly or lessons, between assembly and registration or lessons.

The "between lessons" movement is the most vital to consider since it occurs most often. Movement at break-time will not be considered as a source of waste time, because break-time itself can be used for movement, but it may well produce contacts with strange staff. Secondly, there are two organizational contexts in large schools in which such movement takes place; that is, as has already been said, large schools are run either on the basis of houses or of years. The junior, middle and senior type of organization may be looked on as a variant of the latter. Thirdly, classes themselves are internally organized on a streamed or an unstreamed basis.

1. *Current Practice in the First Three Years of the School Course*

Let us take, first of all, a school operating a year system and streamed classes and consider the movement patterns of the classes of the first 3 years.[24] Such a school can operate a form system in the traditional way with minimum movement and minimum splitting up into smaller groups, at least in so far as we have yet considered the restriction of movement.[25] Movement from registration to the teaching classroom will normally be undertaken by the whole class; there will be no splitting up except for such subjects as P.E. and crafts. Movement to assembly will normally be movement to the hall nearest to the particular year groups' area of the school, unless there is only one assembly hall. However, between lessons movements may be considerable in some circumstances. For example, if the year group has been placed all over the school and not restricted to a particular area, or has to be so placed because of an inconvenient building layout, or if the classes of the year group have teachers whose subject rooms are situated all over the campus there will be excessive movement between lessons. The amount of movement from classroom to classroom between lessons will thus depend on whether the year group has been, or can be, mainly allotted to staff teaching in the year group area. If the school is a twelve-stream school the allotment to staff teaching in a particular area will not be too difficult, provided the area has a craft room and a laboratory, since the curriculum for the first 3 years is not likely to contain more than about twelve subjects and there would be twelve teachers stationed for subject teaching in the twelve form rooms. If the school is an eight-stream school such an arrangement will be possible for all subjects not needing laboratories or craft rooms. It does, however, imply, as we have already said, that the member of staff concerned with a particular subject and stationed in the year group area will teach all or many of the classes of the group. If a teacher is to maintain enthusiasm for his subject such a practice is undesirable. The different intelligence levels of the various classes in the year group will require different teaching approaches, it is true, but the material taught will be similar in all the classes. We will return to the implications of this fact later. Meanwhile, it will suffice to say that the teacher who can teach more than one subject in the junior part of the school has a better chance of varied teaching than his more specialized colleague; yet even he is likely to get bored if he teaches two subjects requiring three periods each to the classes of only one year. The require-

[24] The movement patterns of the fourth, fifth and subsequent years are complex in all types of organization because of the complexity of subject choices. We will therefore leave aside these years for the moment.

[25] Appendix IV gives charted basic movement patterns relating to a variety of comprehensive school situations and will clarify the discussion in the following pages.

ments of reduced movement on the one hand and inspired teaching on the other seem, at first sight, incompatible.

Where a streamed-teaching year system has been combined, not with a traditional form system of pastoral care based on the teaching group, but with a mixed ability tutor group system, the result is both diluted pastoral care and splitting up and excessive movement by individuals at registration and assembly times, as pupils go from their tutor group base to any one of a dozen different teaching classrooms within the year group area, or possibly outside it. Excessive splitting-up itself wastes time, and should therefore not be accepted, except for good pastoral or educational reasons, because no class starts till its last pupil arrives from the farthest away point. A time-wasting recheck that all pupils are present may also often be required. Every class is so affected whenever there is a changeover from an unstreamed tutor group base to a streamed teaching classroom. Where there is no changeover and so no splitting up, only the class which has farthest to go starts as late as all the classes in the year do when there is such a changeover and splitting-up. Moreover, in the latter case it is all the more important to restrict the year-groups area as much as possible and not spread its tutor bases or teaching classrooms all over the campus.

If an unstreamed tutor-group system has been combined with an unstreamed teaching system in the context of a "year" type of organization, there will be no more movement or delay at registration or assembly times than for streamed classes operating the traditional form system. In both cases the teaching and the social groups coincide. Whether there is excessive movement between lessons will depend on the same factors as have already been referred to for the previous category, for example whether or not the tutor bases and teaching classrooms of a particular year have been spread all over the campus or not.

One further point. In practice the year system frequently operates within the context of a school divided into junior, middle and upper sections. If it does so operate and if each section is mainly confined to a particular geographical area, each area contains double the number of rooms that a single year area would contain, since each section consists of two school years. It will be necessary therefore for pupils to move around in an area of 24+ classrooms rather than 12+, or 16+ rather than 8+, in a 12-F.E. or 8-F.E. school. The greater distances to walk are not excessive, being equivalent to those in a 5- or 6-F.E. or 3- or 4-F.E. school operating a 5-year course. In addition, staff have the opportunity to teach the 2 years within the section area rather than only one, a great advantage for teachers who have only one subject.

We can now turn to a consideration of movement problems in a school organized on a house basis. Let us assume for a moment that the school is also finely streamed and that the streams do not coincide with the house tutor groups, which are organized on a mixed-ability or mixed-age basis. The work groups and the social groups do not coincide and, as in all cases where this is so, extra movement and delay at the changeover from tutor group to streamed class is built into the system. No teaching class will start after registration until the last pupil from the furthest tutor group has arrived. Where the house tutor groups include pupils of all ages, such movement will take place from any point on the campus to any other point and the amount of delay will be considerable, especially if the architect has spread the buildings over a wide area. Where the house tutor groups include children of only one age group, it should be possible to reduce the movement of a particular year mainly to one particular area of the school, so that they arrive with maximum speed at their teaching classrooms. This can be achieved as long as the area inhabited by the house groups of that year is the same as that inhabited by the teaching groups. Where an existing building has been adapted to the house system, it may be possible to arrange this. Where a school has been purpose built for the house system, it will probably be impossible to do so; in purpose-built schools the house buildings are often scattered all round the perimeter. Even if it is possible to keep the house groups of different houses of a particular year close together in one area of the building, it could be argued that to separate the tutor groups of a house from each other all over the building, which this arrangement would imply, is to diminish the impact of the house on the children. Moreover, individual pupils will, in this case also, be moving in all directions from their tutor group to their teaching group, even if the movement is confined to their own year-group area. One cannot then rely on the group forces within a particular group of thirty children to get them reasonably quickly to their destination since, momentarily, no group exists. Only if the tutor group is the main teaching group and there is no changeover from the one to the other, i.e. only if the teaching group is unstreamed, will there normally be movement as a group from registration to teaching and not a movement of separate individuals, with different members of the tutor group going to different teaching groups. Hence where a school is operating a house system and at the same time teaching groups are streamed, splitting with consequent movement and excessive delay is inevitable at registration time.

Movement to assembly also presents a problem, if it does not occur immediately before or after registration. Again pupils will be obliged to walk to assembly in a number of different house assembly rooms from any point on the campus, or vice versa. It may be possible to reduce this waste of time by organizing junior house assemblies or senior house assemblies in appropriate parts of the building, but this arrangement lessens the contact between the junior and the senior parts of the houses, even supposing there are enough rooms of a suitable size to hold even a partial house assembly comfortably.

The fact that the tutor group is different from the teaching group in the category we are dealing with will have least impact on movement once lessons have begun and the pupils are moving round mainly in their normal teaching groups. Even so, in a large school, there will be advantages in reducing the amount of movement made by a particular set of teaching groups by confining it to a given area, as in the year system. Since every teaching group includes pupils from all houses, we cannot select the groups to be stationed in a particular area on a house basis. More or less inevitably the groups will have to be selected on a year basis, or on a junior school, or middle school basis. If they are not, it is likely that the criteria of selection will be ability, with, for example, all the groups of able children in the first 3 years together in a particular area of the building, the least able in another area and so on. Hence, if we wish to avoid élitist practices, where a house system operates in conjunction with finely streamed classes we are more or less obliged to make the decision that the teaching groups of a particular year will be stationed together in the same area of the building. This strengthens the "year" element at the expense of the "house" element.

If the teaching groups are unstreamed, however, they can be organized on a house basis, and the work groups will then coincide with the social groups. Splitting up after registration will disappear, and with it the extra delay in starting lessons resulting from waiting for the last pupil from the furthest group. As regards movement between lessons, it is again possible to reduce it by confining particular classes to certain areas of the school. However, instead of having to select classes to be stationed in a particular area from 1 year, or at the most 2 years, with all that this implies for teachers in the way of repetition of their lessons and consequent boredom, it is possible, and advantageous, to use the house as a basis for selection of classes. In this case, teaching groups from the same house but different years can be selected to inhabit a particular teaching area of the school. Though, for reasons which will be referred to later, the selection of groups must be confined to the first 3 years of the school, the variety of teaching for the staff is notably increased and at the same time, with movement confined mainly to a particular area and the teaching and tutorial groups coinciding, pastoral care is improved. These are major advantages, provided the staff is convinced of the value of mixed ability group teaching.

2. *Improvement of Decentralization Practices in the First* 3 *Years*

Our analysis shows fairly clearly that, with respect to the first 3 years of the course, the year system maximizes pastoral care and can minimize movement—provided the classes of a particular year are mainly confined to a particular area—if the groups are streamed, in both the work and the social situations, or if they are unstreamed in both. Where classes are streamed for teaching purposes but unstreamed for social purposes pastoral care is blurred and movement increased. By contrast the house system maximizes pastoral care and can minimize movement only if the classes are unstreamed in both work and social situations. At the same time, unfortunately, the year system and even the junior and middle system, if the classes are confined to a particular area, reduce the variety of teaching available to the staff. We must now ask whether there is any system which maximizes pastoral care and minimizes movement for the first 3 years of the school, without committing the head and staff in advance to either streaming or unstreaming, and which at the same time gives the staff a greater variety of teaching. The criteria of judgement of school organization we are now setting up would not be satisfied by a system which minimized movement (for example, at changeover from pastoral to teaching groups, say, after registration) by making the pastoral and the teaching groups consist of the same pupils, but which did not improve pastoral care by restricting the area in which they moved and thus reducing the number of staff they met, whom they did not know, as they moved around. Both criteria of judgement must be satisfied.

In considering the question a moment's reflection will remind us that so far we have spoken of the streamed school only in the context of fine streaming, which many schools have now abandoned in favour of "coarse" streaming or "banding". Fine streaming was thought necessary in the early days of the comprehensive school, in order to enable, so it was supposed, the bright pupil to go ahead at his own pace. Hence the large size of the early urban comprehensive schools; hence, as a consequence, the house system, the year system and the junior/middle/senior system. In some ways these are all anachronisms from the early days, in the sense that, on the assumptions then current, any other arrangements would have been difficult to make. It is now generally thought that, even if streaming is accepted, we do not need such fine streaming. We may therefore find, for example, a 12-F.E. school divided, in each of the first 3 years of the school course, into two blocks of six forms or three blocks of four forms, with each block containing the full range of ability, and the forms within each block streamed according to ability or, if such is the policy, left unstreamed. For schools with a larger or somewhat smaller entry similar arrangements can be made. Thus in a 10-F.E. school each year may be divided into two blocks of five forms each, a 14-F.E. school into three blocks of five, five and four forms respectively. This organization may be used to restrict movement, by placing the classes of each year of each block within the same geographical area and stationing most of its teachers within the same area. Each lower school area in a 12-F.E. school will thus contain four first-year forms, four second-year forms and four third-year forms, twelve in all, stationed close to each other. There will be twelve teachers of appropriate subjects using particular form bases as their subject rooms, and they will teach mainly, though not exclusively, within the area. They will cover most or all of the subjects required in the first 3 years of the course, provided appropriate specialist rooms are available within the area. Blocks of fewer than four forms per year should be avoided if it is hoped to furnish enough teachers stationed within the block area to staff about a dozen subjects. If craft and science rooms are not available in the block area, three forms per year group will furnish nine subject teachers to be stationed there. One will then, however, have to decide whether in a streamed situation streamed-type teaching methods will be adequate for such broad bands of ability. (See p. 131.)

With such, or similar, arrangements one could restrict the movement of the pupils of a particular block mainly to a particular area of the school, with consequent saving of time. Pastoral care would also be improved, simply because teachers would be better acquainted with the children they did not teach, for only a restricted number of pupils would normally circulate in the area where their classroom was situated, and not usually pupils from all over the school. Since in a 12-F.E. school only twelve forms, four from each of the first 3 years, would circulate within the area, at least as a rule, there would be only 360 children for the staff to get to know. Since on average the teachers would teach 270 of them,[26] there would be only 190 children whom they did not teach. The index of their acquaintance with the children would be the same as for a 5-year 3-F.E. school, namely 11·6,[27] and the index of difficulty of control would be better than that of a 3-F.E. school, since only twelve rooms are contained in the area, not eighteen.[28] These indices would, however, probably give a rather more favourable impression of the real situation than was warranted by the facts. They leave out of consideration the fact that (a) the children in the block would sometimes leave the area for physical education or a craft, for example, or to give teachers in the upper school a chance of teaching lower school children, that (b) *some* pupils from the upper part of the school would come into the area every day, if the staff were not to be confined to teaching only the first 3 years, and that (c) it is unlikely that any particular area of an existing school would have exactly the right mix of specially equipped subject rooms for twelve forms. None the less, setting out the ideal theoretical case does reveal how greatly disciplinary control and pastoral care are facilitated by confining the movement of a particular group of children mainly to a particular area. At the same time the policy outlined allows for reasonable variety of teaching within one subject for highly specialized staff, if necessary, and does not commit the school in advance to either streaming or unstreaming. Suitably adapted, it can be followed in a variety of situations, for example, in schools where there is more than one building on the campus,[29] or in some types of split-site situation, or where the existing building is very elongated and therefore subject to great congestion at midpoint, if classes are not confined to a particular area. The chief impediment to its unmodified adoption is the placing of such rooms as

[26] As calculated in a forthcoming article. See p. 99.
[27] *Ibid*.
[28] *Ibid*.
[29] See Halsall, Elizabeth, Organization on a comprehensive campus, *Education*, vol. 6, May 1966, pp. 951–2.

science laboratories or art rooms. If art rooms, for example, are placed together *en suite* in a separate part of the building, as has been increasingly the custom of recent years, the policy has to be modified, though it need not be abandoned. Even so, a modified policy will greatly improve disciplinary control and negative aspects of pastoral care, by comparison with a policy of allowing movement all over the campus, and there will be happy results for the general tone of the school. The comments of a group of pupils quoted by Plath[30] provide evidence as to the improvement achieved.

A further advantage of this system, by comparison with the junior/middle system, for example, is that pupils can keep the same teachers for 3 years, if such a policy is advisable, as it probably is in such sequential subjects as mathematics or French. With the junior/middle system, if one is to restrict movement adequately, a change of teacher is necessary at the end of the second year when pupils move on to the middle building. A change of teacher for many subjects is almost inevitable at present for most pupils at the end of the third year, when they make their choice amongst a variety of options subjects or courses. Under the junior/middle system, there would then be two changes of teachers in two successive years, which is much to be deplored.

The system we have described also avoids one of the major pitfalls of the junior/middle system. As we have already indicated[31] of necessity, the junior building tends to accumulate a large number of inexperienced teachers. When an area of the school accommodates forms from 3 years it contains a higher proportion of experienced teachers.

The chief disadvantage of the system advocated is that subject department heads carry a heavier burden than normally,[32] since their subject rooms are scattered over the whole building rather than grouped together in subject areas. Movement of books or other equipment is more difficult in such a case and general administration of the department is heavier, unless heads of departments learn what the head and deputy head of a large school have to learn in any case, if the school is to be run efficiently, namely how to decentralize and to delegate.

In any school policy there is a balance of advantages and disadvantages and, apart from the advantages already listed, there is one which might well reconcile a head of department to this necessary readjustment of his role. Where subject rooms are scattered over the whole of a very large building, as a result of organizing the school in smaller units, rather than grouped together in subject areas, the organization of integrated studies is much facilitated.[33] A geography room may well be next door to a history room instead of two flights of stairs away in the geography suite and the science laboratory may be down the passage instead of across the quadrangle in a separate building. The more subject rooms are grouped together in one subject area, the more committed to a specialized approach the teaching policy must be. At best there can be integration only with closely allied subjects whose subject rooms are placed close by; for example, there might be integration between mathematics and science subjects. When, however, a number of rooms allotted to different subjects are to be found within the same immediate area, greater flexibility of policy is possible. They may be used either for an integrated approach or for a specialized approach, though how far a really specialized approach is valid before the end of the first 3 years of the secondary course is increasingly questioned.

[30] See p. 127.
[31] See p. 130.
[32] See p. 126.
[33] This result was noted by Plath. See p. 127.

3. *The Fourth and Fifth Years*

So much for the first 3 years of the secondary school course in large schools. They aim at providing a solid base of general education through which children can explore their strengths and their weaknesses and begin to develop their interests. Since this implies a more or less common curriculum for all, without the added complication of many subject choices, division of the populations of these 3 years into smaller working units does not involve insuperable problems. The last 2 years[34] of the comprehensive school course, however, at present have different objectives. They aim to develop pupils' strengths and interests by providing a great variety of options subjects and the maximum freedom of choice between them. The number of possible combinations of subjects in a really flexible comprehensive school fourth-year timetable is considerable, and one would not wish it otherwise at some stage of schooling since modern society makes many varied and complex demands on pupils as soon as they leave school or go into the sixth. But every policy has its price, and the price of the present policy is that there is no serious alternative to a good deal of movement and splitting up and re-forming of teaching groups from lesson to lesson. One can, of course, restrict movement to some extent. If one assumes that the fourth and fifth years inhabit the same area of the building as the sixth form, a 12-F.E. school will have in that area about 800 pupils or so. If the sixth has its own quarters there will be about 700. If the fourth and fifth years never leave their own area they will be as well known to the teachers also located in that area as the pupils of a 5-F.E. 5-year school would be to their teachers and the index of difficulty of control will be the same as that of a 5-F.E. or 6-F.E. school.[35] However, in actuality classes in the fourth and fifth year will have to be taught in part by some teachers stationed in one or other of the sections of the building devoted to the lower school, even if they are mainly taught in their own area. Because of the complexity of the timetable and its choices the effect of often moving out of their own area is to produce greater movement and greater delays than is the case for the lower school. "Between lessons" movement of the lower school classes is largely movement of whole classes; "between lessons" movement of fourth- and fifth-year classes is mainly the movement of groups which are splitting up to form new groups, according to whether particular pupils have opted for French or biology or technical drawing or whatever, after having opted in the previous lesson for history or physics or art and so on. The new group's lesson will not start till the last pupil from the furthest group of the previous lesson has arrived. There will be longish delays for all classes, instead of for only one or two classes. Where the move involves a transfer to an area of the school other than the fourth- and fifth-year area, the delay will be at its maximum. It is a common enough practice to arrange the lessons for the options groups subjects in double periods, because one or more of the subjects in a particular group can only be taught in double periods, and the other subjects in the group have to fit in to this pattern. But even if this were not so, it seems probable that it would be necessary to use double periods for the fourth and fifth year anyway. This avoids waste of time between lessons by placing the necessary movement at break time or at the beginning or end of the session and it eliminates half the total contact with staff who are comparative strangers, thus improving pastoral care. Even so, it is likely that the degree of disciplinary control achieved with the

[34] See p. 80 for a query as to whether we shall continue to organize the last 2 years as an entity.

[35] See p. 99.

fourth and fifth year will be less than that achieved with the lower school, quite apart from the differences resulting from age and attitudes, because the whole population inevitably is larger than for the lower school and the groups are for ever splitting up.[36] Perhaps this has to be accepted for the sake of the variety of choice it brings to pupils, at this stage a greater priority on the whole than intensity of pastoral care, for all except the most disturbed, and it would seem advisable that a policy of using double periods should be followed to help to diminish movement and delay.

At what point the advantage gained by having a wide variety of subjects to choose from is offset by the disadvantages resulting from too much movement and delay, and less effective disciplinary control and pastoral care is a nice question, and the answer to it will not coincide from school to school. Probably, as has already been said in another context, the answer will depend in part on the character of the area served by the school and on the degree of socialization already achieved by the pupils. A high rate of absenteeism and discipline problems would indicate the desirability of reducing the amount of movement and, with it, the amount of choice.

E. Implications for the Design of New Large Schools

The above discussion has certain implications for the design of new schools. It would seem advisable that new schools which are large[37] should be so designed as to produce a number of smaller areas,[38] much as council housing estates, new towns and new residential areas generally, now tend to be divided up into a number of smaller communities. The more that integrated studies and individualized instruction are introduced, the more necessary it will be to restrict movement to a particular area in the way suggested, so as to combine maximum fluidity and flexibility with maximum pastoral care. It would also seem necessary perhaps to abandon building schools on the house system, since schools so built are less flexible and promote pastoral care less effectively, unless unstreamed. A large comprehensive school should probably contain two or three smaller units, each housing a section of the lower school and having within it classes from each of the first 3 years, another section housing the fourth and fifth year[39] and a sixth-form unit. Ideally, there would be science, art, craft and domestic subjects rooms within each unit. Possibly, it would be necessary to accept that, for reasons of expense, such specially equipped rooms would have to be housed together in the same separate unit. If this were so, the limitations on effective pastoral care that seem to result from pupils having access to too wide areas of the school, might also have to be accepted—unless more effective school designs could be formulated—though, of course, lower school pupils would normally not circulate outside their own

[36] Each fourth and fifth year of a 12-F.E. school could, however, be split into two, making a total of twelve forms in each area rather than twenty-four. But only the compulsory subjects could be taken in the block's own area. The options subjects would have to be available to the whole year unless choice was to be limited and therefore movement would be necessary over the whole territory of the fourth and fifth year. If the choice of options was thus limited, the pupils in each of the two blocks would have the same amount of choice as fourth- and fifth-year pupils in a 6-F.E. school. It is axiomatic that the more choice you have, the more movement you have and the less effective the pastoral care. The choice available in a 6-F.E. school is considerable. See Appendix II for the choice available in a 5-F.E. school.

[37] It would seem inadvisable to build any more 12-F.E. schools but one cannot really be sure that local circumstances will always prevent this.

[38] The building of comprehensive schools on the house principle was the first attempt to produce smaller units. Unfortunately, the house concept does not quite fit the realities of the situation.

[39] Or two sections, if the fourth year was divided into two and the fifth likewise.

specified area, the science and craft block, and the physical education area. This does not imply, however, that the remaining areas of the school would be placed out of bounds to them. Such a policy would be unworkable. It implies simply that school arrangements would ensure that normally pupils would circulate in as restricted an area as could be managed without damaging their curriculum.

Ease of access for all pupils to the science and craft block would be very important, if movement delays were not to occur or unless all such lessons took place in double periods. If the latter were not the case[40] it would need to occupy a central position on the campus so as to minimize walking distances. This should not imply that science and craft rooms could be used as throughways, a feature of the design of one recently erected comprehensive school. It implies, however, that the science and craft block, with the exception of noisy

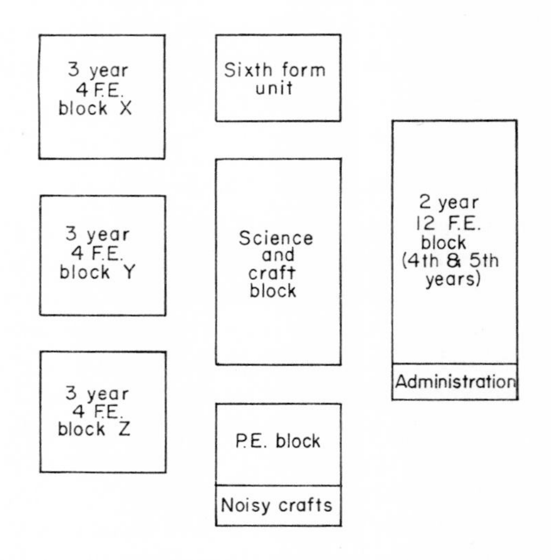

FIG. 1. Building layout.

rooms, should be as near to the other blocks as is consonant with adequate circulation space. Noisy rooms would have to be placed on the periphery.

Perhaps the diagram in Fig. 1 will give some idea of the layout of a 12-F.E. school building that seems to fit the requirements set out in the preceding pages. Entrances to the ordinary teaching blocks would have to be placed as near to the entrances of the science and craft block as is consonant with other requirements. What difference a misplacing of a block on a plan to the general good order of the school can make will be seen if we remove the P.E. block from its present position and place it to the left of block Y of the lower school. This would probably ensure that the fourth and fifth years would use the corridors of the science and craft block, and maybe of block Y also, if they were sited horizontal to the plan, as ways of getting to the P.E. block, thus causing congestion. On the present plan only the sixth form would be tempted so to do—if the corridors were sited vertical to the plan—and

[40] It would seem important that a school design should not commit a head and staff beforehand to a decision to rely on double periods to reduce movement problems, without considering the teaching needs of particular subjects.

the sixth form is at present a smaller group. For the rest of the school the quickest route is by way of the open air. Adequate covered ways should be provided and can be at little extra cost, as long as services are carried on top of them instead of underground.

Another possible arrangement for a 12-F.E. school would be that of the double square or quadrangle, which would allow: (a) science and craft rooms to be placed in close proximity to the area any particular group of pupils inhabited and (b) most of the science and craft rooms to be placed together.

Let us assume for a moment that craft and science lessons are usually given in double or treble periods and that therefore movement to the appropriate rooms will not occur "between lessons", but only after assembly, registration or break times. If one is thinking

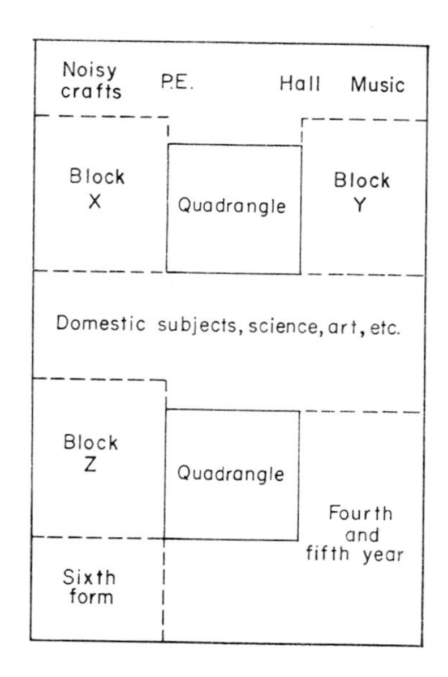

FIG. 2. Building layout.

only in terms of reducing movement and waste of time, one can then place the craft and science block somewhere, say, on the periphery of the school building. The movement and pastoral situation for most pupils would therefore be like that of shoppers in a residential suburb or on a council estate, who buy their groceries from the local shops but go into town to purchase clothes or furniture. But the previous discussion indicates that we are not thinking in terms of waste of time only. We are interested in the reduction of movement as a means also of reducing the number of comparative strangers on the staff that pupils meet, with a view to intensifying pastoral care. From this angle the double square is of special interest. By placing all the craft, science and aesthetic subject rooms all together in the centre (noisy crafts, music and P.E. areas being sited at the end of the building) one has first of all the advantage of reduced costs of building. At the same time one could arrange the blocks in such a way that the art, domestic subjects and science rooms serving block X could be placed close to it, those serving block Y close to block Y, those serving block Z and the fourth and fifth year respectively also close to their own blocks. Yet all the science rooms would be within easy reach of each other in the same block, all the art rooms similarly and so on. Only the sixth form would need to move any distance for the sciences and crafts. Only for music, some crafts, drama and P.E. would it be necessary for children to move long distances and also for those lessons where lower school children were taught by teachers whose main classes were in the upper school or vice versa. Heads of departments in the science and crafts block would find their departments easier to organize, for even though their rooms were not *en suite*, but sited individually near to the block they served, as a group they would be within relatively easy reach of each other. Again it would be important to ensure that the science and craft block did not serve as throughways from one area of the school to another.

For 9-F.E. and 10-F.E. schools arrangements would probably involve lopping off the end of one of the squares, since there would be two lower school blocks to cater for instead of three, and readjusting the plan. The design could also be adapted to other sizes of large school.

There have been suggestions that the lower school should be further broken up, with the first year hived off into a separate unit,[41] the second and third year remaining still together as one unit. The aim is partly to reduce the size of each unit, partly to allow for the first year to continue with more class teaching and primary school-type methods than has been the practice in the secondary school. This plan has merits for the treatment of first-year pupils, and does allow for variety of teaching for the first-year teachers, since they would take several subjects, but it reduces the variety of teaching for those specialist teachers mainly engaged in the rest of the lower school. If, to compensate, we then give them proportionately more upper school teaching than on the suggested 3-year lower school unit plan, we induce far more movement, and reduce pastoral care far more, than when they taught the first year. The reason is that, as has already been said, by the nature of the case, problems of movement are always greater in the upper school. Even within the 3-year lower school system it is still possible to allow for special treatment for the first year on primary school lines.

Even if the present suggestions are disputed as not yet verified by experimental proof, one small piece of research has now been done which demonstrates the importance of improved layout in reducing movement problems at least. An operational research study by Hinchliffe,[42] the first scientific British study of movement problems, has shown that a more compact design of buildings, which had resulted from suggestions drawn from the experience of existing heads of large comprehensive schools, resulted in shorter movement times. He found that a useful guiding principle, for a school built according to a traditional house system design, is to try to keep the house blocks as near as possible to the main teaching blocks and to position the latter in a central position.

F. Implications for Existing Large Schools

For a head and staff already working in a large and not particularly well-designed school the above discussion may well appear of purely academic interest. At the same time it does

[41] According to a recent London project.

[42] Hinchliffe, P., Operational Research in Comprehensive Schools, M.Sc. Operational Research Project, Univ. of Hull, 1971. Reported in: *Comprehensive Education*, no. 21, Summer 1972, pp. 10–12.

indicate the principles which should underlie the organization of the school plant, principles which point the way to the most effective use of available space, even if ideal solutions to the school's problems can never be reached.

It may also be argued that the principles set out above and illustrated by the diagrams take no account of one important aim in the life and management of a school, namely, the school's unity, and not much account of a second, the legitimate desires of many teachers in the lower school blocks to get some upper school teaching, and for those stationed in the upper school areas to get some lower school teaching. With regard to the first, it seems unrealistic to place the unity of the school at the top of the list of priorities in a very large school. Avoidance of impossible burdens for teachers—whether they result from considerable movement by themselves or from coping with the effects of considerable movement by pupils—and promotion of more effective pastoral care are more important objectives of policy than the maintenance of the school's unity, a fact sometimes overlooked by heads in the first year or so of a large school's existence. Decentralization and delegation are inevitable if health, efficiency and morale are not to be impaired. Inevitably, the unity of the school will be to some extent reduced; there is no alternative but to accept this.

With regard to the second point it has already been said that in large schools only a more limited provision can be made for a wide variety of teaching for specialist teachers than is the case in small schools. Small schools suffer in the context of the present curriculum of comprehensive schools, by not being able to offer *pupils* quite the variety of subjects a large school can offer, unless they make use of correspondence courses. They can, however, offer a wide variety of teaching to *teachers*, from the first year to the sixth, in fact the more versatile teachers are the better in a small school. Large schools can offer a wide variety of subjects to pupils, but, if specialist teachers want a *full* variety of teaching they must suffer the inconvenience of either moving long distances themselves or of waiting a long time for children to arrive, with all that this implies of lack of adequate supervision, and their own exasperation. To give pupils in a large school adequate pastoral care involves teachers in *some* reduction in variety of teaching. They simply cannot teach every year in the school as small-school teachers often do, without considerable inconvenience.

G. Conclusion

These two differing disadvantages of small and large schools, and the other advantages and disadvantages discussed in recent chapters, arise from the expansion of the curriculum as we at present organize it, as well as from reorganization on comprehensive lines. We have introduced more and more subjects into the school course as new disciplines have arisen—and trained more and more specialist teachers—until now the curriculum is bursting at the seams. It requires a larger number of teachers to staff it and therefore a larger number of pupils in any particular school to enable them to be used economically. The larger size of school produces serious problems of internal organization and pastoral care, the smaller school problems of adequate staffing of the curriculum. These problems are likely to continue, and even to get worse, unless we undertake a radical rethink of the curriculum or of teacher training[43] or both. Until that day arrives we have to do the best we can—unless

[43] We could, for example, do as the Belgians have done since the 1920s, and train teachers capable of teaching three of the traditional subjects to children of up to the age of 14–15. From such teachers as they would make we might secure that radical rethink of the curriculum which gets right down to the grass roots and does not affect merely the reformers themselves and a few teachers in their immediate entourage.

we undertake a major rebuilding programme the country cannot afford—with the small schools and the large schools that we already have, to offset their respective disadvantages.

H. Communication

No survey of the difficulties of the large school and the ways of circumventing them would be complete without some reference to the changes in methods of communication required. A short summary of the main issues and the main possible approaches is therefore included here. Since little research has been done on the best ways of mitigating the difficulties of communication of large schools that were described in Chapter 6, this present section consists mainly of a somewhat "feeling" account of what one person found to be partial or complete solutions to problems encountered, evaluated in the light of others' similar experiences and the solutions they discovered.

Since there is about as much similarity between running a very small and a very large school as there is between organizing a corner shop and organizing Selfridge's, methods of communication must take account of this fact and of the fact that it is not enough formally to organize one-way communication. In a small school it is often sufficient to organize one-way communication since two-way communication takes place very easily in an informal way through face-to-face discussion. In a large school the faces do not necessarily meet.

Because the school is so large full staff meetings are now too unwieldy for administrative decisions to be taken at them, in the main, however useful they may be for airing ideas and grievances and putting forward suggestions. Decisions therefore tend to be taken at smaller meetings such as the meetings of heads of departments or year mistresses or house masters. These decisions must be communicated to the rest of the staff. There are several methods of communicating such decisions and other information. Minutes of the meetings can be circulated. School routine, for example the general procedure to be followed for dinner duty or assembly, can be explained in a set of staff notes, which should cover all the school's routine arrangements and which should be in the possession of every member of staff. Without such notes new teachers tend to flounder for about 3 months in a large school. Alterations in arrangements can be communicated on separate sheets as "addenda" or "corrigenda". Arrangements for particular events, e.g. prize day, examinations, beginning and end of term likewise need duplicated sheets. Warnings of the next week's activities, school matches, club meetings, school visits and staff duties that alter from week to week are best given in two types of weekly bulletin, the staff bulletin and the form bulletin. Without them the staff and pupils, and occasionally the head, feel that they do not know what is happening in the school, as indeed they do not. The bulletins help everyone to maintain contact with the school's life, to retain a sense of its identity and of their own links with what would otherwise be an amorphous and anonymous institution. The bulletins do not merely help the head of the school. They provide the youngest recruit to the staff, or indeed the secretaries of the Stamp or Chess Clubs, with a means of communicating easily and effectively to all concerned what needs to be publicized about a particular event, be it only the time and place of the next meeting. They also stimulate other ideas and activities amongst staff and pupils generally, and they provide training for children in organizing their own affairs.

There remains the problem of the urgent notice about some unforeseen or unforeseeable circumstance. Announcements at assembly may have only a limited value as far as rather urgent notices are concerned, since in many large schools it is impossible for the whole school to meet together for an assembly every day. In this case a note slipped into the staff register which in many schools members of staff sign on arriving in the morning will often meet the need. To those not used to it, as indeed originally to the writer, a staff register may smack of clocking-in at the factory gate. Here is a clear case for the reorientation of attitudes, since the register serves everyone's interests. In a large building, especially if it is not decentralized, it provides the quickest means, for whoever is in charge of replacing absent staff, to discover whether anyone is absent and to prevent a class from having half a period of unsupervized bedlam, that will try the patience of those working in nearby rooms and ruin the class's attitude to work for the rest of the day. One member of staff absent in a staff of twenty is remarked almost at once; not so in a staff of eighty, and there will be more absences to deal with. A staff register promotes speedy and effective adjustment to the situation. This is especially true where the building does not allow for members of the same department working in adjacent rooms and replacements therefore being organized by the head of the department; or where, alternatively and more appropriately, the building is not suited to being administered in smaller units of the kind described in this chapter.

If an emergency requiring immediate attention occurs during the day there are various methods of communication. Some schools use a system of runners, usually taken from the leavers' classes, each pupil being allotted a day in turn or the more reliable pupils being chosen more regularly. The system has the advantage that it can be used as one of the means to give this group of pupils prestige and the compiler of testimonials some idea of how they will react to the world of work and responsibility outside. It has the disadvantage that it may in the end result in the best pupils being away from their lessons too often or, if every pupil gets a turn, it may result in inefficiency on the days when less reliable pupils are acting as runners. It also provides the administration with a continual temptation to interrupt classes for trivial reasons. At its worst it furnishes the less conscientious pupils with an opportunity to get out of class and idle their way through one errand after another. For this reason it is probably not to be recommended as a permanent feature of the communications system, but it has its uses as a temporary tool if for any reason more sophisticated methods are lacking. As a temporary tool it is also a prestige builder for the leavers who, when it is first introduced, look upon the post of runner as conferring status. If the system is used, a set of duplicated slips needs to be made, containing a space for the insertion of the name and room number of the member of staff to whom the message is being sent and a space for the message itself. Even where the system is not in use throughout the day it proves helpful for sending out chits requesting teachers to take the place of those absent. Where the staff-room is distant from the main teaching block its use is almost inevitable, since the staff are less likely to go to the staff room than when it is near. A staff replacement list on the staff-room noticeboard may therefore go unread, though it should be posted for reference in emergency. Although it is desirable that people should visit the staffroom regularly there are cases in a large school where it would be unreasonable, not to stay unwise, to insist on it. A staff replacement chit needs, in addition to the spaces already indicated, space also for the name, lesson and room number of the form to be taken. Unfortunately there is no way of adding to it a friendly smile, which can often lessen the impact of an unpleasant request when it is made orally. Hence some of the misunderstandings reported by Brennan in Chapter 6.[44]

A Tannoy loudspeaker system is also used in large schools as a means of communication.

[44] See p. 87.

If it is used only at registration times, break, the dinner hour or the end of the afternoon or immediately before or during special events such as the sports day or the Christmas celebrations, it can be a great boon to everyone. A certain initial distaste for Big Brother will have to be overcome by the individualists in the school. It is especially valuable to a school unable to provide assembly for all classes every day for lack of enough accommodation. Instructions which cannot wait longer than the next morning and which would otherwise have to be sent round by messenger, with consequent interruption of lessons, can easily be given over the public-address system to the whole school during the registration period at the beginning of the morning or afternoon, or after the bell has rung at the end of the morning or afternoon. In addition, members of staff, for example the P.E. staff in charge of a school team playing away, may need to make an announcement at a late stage. In a small school all that is needed is to ask form teachers, for example in the staffroom at lunch time, to announce changed arrangements to their class at the beginning of the afternoon. In a school with seventy to a hundred staff, scattered in two or three staffrooms or in their own units or taking clubs in the dinner hour anywhere in any of several wings or blocks, this is no longer possible. Members of staff also therefore need access to the Tannoy loudspeaker system. However, the system can be seriously abused and some limitation must be placed on its use. It is better to specify the times at which it may be used rather than to insist on permission being sought for its use on each particular occasion. In the latter case the person from whom permission has to be sought may well not be findable or available at the time when the member of staff is free and can seek permission. It is also essential that the head and deputy should restrict themselves in their use of it to the same times as everyone else. Only the most serious emergency excuses the interruption of lessons, especially since the announcement has to be made to the whole building even if it concerns only one child. It is possible, of course, to arrange a Tannoy system in such a way as to make communication possible with one classroom only. However, the expense of its installation is much greater and, according to the information available to the writer, the instrument is more liable to breakdown. Only when there is so much delicate electrical equipment in a school as to justify the employment of a full-time or part-time electrician will the more sophisticated instrument be also the more convenient one. In addition to the uses of the public-address system that have already been mentioned, one may cite the following possible uses, among many: (1) for controlling the departure of classes from classrooms and their entry in the right order into the hall for the school play or other event; (2) for giving out instructions for the voting procedure for election to the school council; (3) for common prayers for classes not going to assembly.

The Tannoy can also be used for communication with the whole or part of the staff, where whatever message has to be given is such that it can be given in the hearing of the children; for example, change of room for a staff meeting. One notice in a staffroom for seventy staff does not fill the bill; they would have to queue up to read it. Three notices for each of three scattered staffrooms require either a runner to take them round or an efficient internal telephone system. The unforgivable sin, however, is to give over the public-address system a notice which the staff feel should be heard by the staff only! The Tannoy is as good as one's use of it makes it. To employ it to interrupt lessons for trivial reasons or to allow other people to do so is evidence of bad management. None the less anyone who has worked as a member of staff in a very large school with a public-address system and has also worked in a similar school without one knows only too well the vast difference that the

Tannoy, properly used, can make to the smooth and efficient running of a school and so to the working conditions and good temper of everyone in it.

Probably the most flexible mechanical aid to communication in a large school is a good internal telephone system. There needs to be a telephone in the room occupied by each person concerned in administration, the head, the deputy head, the heads of buildings or year, house or hall masters or mistresses, according to the way the school is organized, and also one in each staffroom and such critical places in the building as the gymnasium, science or practical blocks. The latter areas need easy access to a telephone because of the possibility of accidents and, in a large school, they may well be some distance from the main administrative block. Telephones are also required, of course, in the office or offices and allowance needs to be made for the fact that one of the school secretaries must spend a proportion of her time attending to the switchboard. It is quite normal for a large comprehensive school to have as many as ten telephone points. What is not always appreciated is that in a school so equipped there is the possibility of joint consultation over the telephone in which more than two can take part. An internal telephone system also eases follow-up of pupils involved in discipline difficulties, contact between members of staff in the same department who may be obliged to work in different buildings and so on. One further point: a school big enough to require ten internal telephone points needs more than one external line. Otherwise an urgent request for an ambulance from the physical education area is liable to be blocked by an incoming call for the headmaster.

So far the discussion has centred either on problems of communication downwards or on problems of two-way communication. Before we proceed to discuss the problems of communication upwards it is perhaps worth recalling in passing that the staff-pigeonhole, that interesting survival from a pre-technological age, still has its uses, especially if a twice-daily postal system is organized by the office staff. Equally arrangements must also be made for easy access for staff to report books and to record cards and files that contain plenty of information and are kept up to date.

What then of communication upwards? Of course the full staff meeting has its value in allowing ideas to be put forward by even the youngest member of staff in the presence of all, but a young teacher is less willing to speak up before such a formidable assembly. Yet he or she may have a worth-while idea. It is still possible to take a matter to the head, though this is more difficult than in a smaller school, because of increased distances to walk, more staff seeking interviews and the possibility of a fruitless journey. In spite of the greater formality it may well be, in a particular school's circumstances, that an appointments system provides the best method of ensuring that staff do get opportunities to consult the head at a time convenient to both. This degree of formalization will often also help to ensure that when staff need to see the head in an emergency they will make the effort to do so, as they are not discouraged from trying by previous failures. It also makes it easier for the head to make provision for such emergency interviews.

However, many of the routine problems which in a smaller school would be taken to the head are dealt with by the deputy head, assistant heads or other suitable people in a large comprehensive school. Role definition is therefore essential. It is vital that the staff notes should state exactly who deals with a particular type of problem and that everyone concerned should get used to this new situation. If the staff take the habits acquired in smaller schools with them into large schools and consult the head on relatively trivial and routine matters they will take up so much of his time and energy that he has none to devote to essentials such as policy-making and the furtherance of good relationships at all levels. Similarly, if the head does not delegate, he will be swamped by the volume of administration.

Other vehicles for the transmission of information both upwards and downwards, as well as for the appropriate level of decision-making, are the meetings of heads of year, house or block groups and heads of department meetings. The people concerned in these meetings organize in their turn meetings of staff who work in their department, year or house. However, it is possible for there to be a blockage in the flow of information[45] upwards if the head of department, year, house or block is not sufficiently alive to the need for him to transmit ideas upwards as well as decisions downwards and, moreover, if he is not sensitive to people's needs. He has a key role to play here which is insufficiently appreciated, often even by himself. He is in regular and informal contact with those working with him in a way that the head or deputy cannot be. Unless he transmits suggestions upwards the potential of a young member of staff with a particular problem or idea, who has not sufficient self-confidence to speak up in a staff meeting of eighty or a hundred or to approach the head in person, will not be properly exploited. In these circumstances frustrations can develop for particular individuals that can easily remain unnoticed by the head, unless he takes steps to guard against the possibility of such a situation arising. A suggestions book or box can be helpful in solving this problem and also in transmitting ideas upwards at times when there are no meetings taking place. There needs to be a feedback with reference to decisions taken for or against ideas put forward, after discussion of the suggestions at the appropriate level.

It is clear that the larger the school the greater the amount of paper work.[46] It is easier for the head to write a note to a member of staff on the opposite side of the building and not within easy reach of the telephone than to go and see him or send for him. It is easier for staff to drop notes in each other's pigeonholes. The difficulty is, however, that it is much more likely that the written word will be misinterpreted than the spoken word, which can convey at least half the meaning through the tone of voice. There is no substitute, therefore, for personal contact. One of the most important tasks of the head and deputy is to provide ways for regular, informal contact with and between the staff. The coffee break should be spent in a different staffroom and school dinner taken by the head and deputy with a different group of staff each day. These informal contacts, besides being valuable in themselves, either uncover difficulties or help to create the atmosphere in which the staff will bring them to the head's or deputy head's notice before they begin to poison relationships. It is equally important to provide opportunities for staff who rarely meet each other, who may in fact work and eat in different buildings, to make contact with each other. Here schools with a good catering section to their housecraft department have a definite advantage. A well-cooked, even though more expensive, lunch provided by the catering group draws staff inured to school dinner like a magnet and provides those who rarely see each other except at meetings with a chance for informal contact and discussion. But with or without a catering department the opportunity must be created and it must be a real one, not an imposed one, an opportunity the staff themselves will want to take advantage of. A sound educational policy, backed by a sense of authority and effectiveness at the top, is very important but a good policy can be wrecked by poor relationships.

Very large institutions tend to foster poor relationships more easily than they foster

[45] See pp. 87–8 for research findings on this topic.

[46] One of the reasons for the increased relative running costs of very large schools? See pp. 120–1.

good ones, because there are enough levels in the hierarchy[47] to promote distortion of communication and to increase rumour. Institutions in a period of growth are also subject to tensions relatively rare in established ones. Comprehensive schools have this problem in an acute form during their early stages of growth because they take in teachers whose training and experience have been acquired in two different settings, the grammar school and the secondary modern, one of which is held to be inferior to the other. These disparate groups have to be welded together into an effective, because co-operating, teaching force. Of course, no policy with reference to improving contact, collaboration, understanding and mutual respect between graduates and non-graduates has a chance of succeeding without a wise promotion policy that gives recognition to the distinctive but valuable gifts of both. This having been looked to, however, much remains to be done. The individual gifts of the staff need an opportunity to be revealed to their colleagues. They cannot as a rule see each other at work in the classroom, unless the school pursues a policy of team teaching, though if they are very inefficient or lacking in conscientiousness their colleagues will soon know it. Capacity in the usual duties outside the classroom will also be noted quickly. More slowly through informal talk in the staffrooms different types of experience can be shared. This process can be quickened and many difficult problems of organization, often outside the experience of most of those concerned, can be solved at the same time by the introduction of group dynamics sessions. For these sessions the various areas of policy-making are mapped out by the head and listed. Staff are then free to attend any of the meetings dealing with problems in which they are particularly interested or by which they are affected. The group elects its own chairman, the problems to be discussed are thrashed out at one or more meetings and recommendations are eventually made. This procedure has the effect of throwing up a number of good ideas for consideration by the head, it gives everyone a better understanding of what policy-making involves and of the difficulties of finding solutions with no drawbacks, it gives chairmen particularly a greater insight into problems of deciding and carrying out policies in face of differences of opinion, and it reveals more quickly than would otherwise be the case the individual qualities of teachers, graduate or non-graduate, to other members of the staff. The reappraisal of each other that takes place tends to blur the distinction between the graduate and the non-graduate and to encourage evaluation of individuals rather than alignment along "party" lines. Only as this process takes place does the staff become an entity, a group functioning really well as a body. It is not suggested that without group dynamics sessions the staff will not acquire corporate feeling, merely that such sessions speed up the process. It may be argued that the heads of departments' meetings and the other groups described can act in a similar way, and they do, but there is something about a meeting to which one is not obliged to go which creates interest and a feeling of goodwill and this is half the battle. Needless to say, when such sessions are in progress pressure must be taken off the staff in other ways and the usual meetings abandoned.

I. Conclusion

The large school's problems of pastoral care, of movement and of communication can be reduced, though not eliminated, by careful organization. In the case of the first the British have always been keenly aware of the need for delegation and decentralization. Hence

[47] See pp. 87–8.

house and year systems. We have not, however, been sufficiently aware of the importance of teaching groups and social groups being one and the same. Nor have we sufficiently realized the relevance of the concept of territoriality and, where we have done so, we have not usually managed to combine restriction to a particular school area for children with an adequate variety of teaching for teachers, unless the latter moved all over the building. It has been the purpose of this section to indicate some measures by which this complex problem could be tackled, so as to provide adequate care for the children without producing utter exhaustion in teachers. In the case of problems of communication it is clear that the large school has to rely to a large extent on measures which do not involve face-to-face contact and which often take a lot of contriving. Hence greater possibilities of misunderstanding, hence greater costs in typing and duplicating, and in the provision and maintenance of sophisticated equipment. Hence, in part, also the rather longer hours of work reported by teachers in large schools.[48]

The complex problems of the large school require complex, and sometimes expensive, solutions. So far, research suggests that they do not quite make up for the losses in personal contact and personal development that go with increased size, but that the effort and expense involved is necessary cannot be questioned.

[48] Monks, T. G. (ed.), *Comprehensive Education in Action*, N.F.E.R., 1970, p. 51.

CHAPTER 9

The Small School: Offsetting Its Disadvantages

If we must look to ways of offsetting the social and personal disadvantages of the large school we must in justice try to do the same for the academic disadvantages of the small school, especially the small 11–18 school.

These would appear to stem from two sources, one national, the other specific to the size of school. Until recently in Britain there has been a serious shortage of teachers, and even now the shortage in some fields, especially in mathematics and science,[1] is still serious. Nor do we have any guarantee that the shortage of teachers will not recur, especially as the raising of the school-leaving age will take up much of the slack. The specific source of disadvantage also has to do with teachers. The smaller the school, the fewer the teachers and the greater the chance of difficulty in staffing peripheral subjects, and sometimes in staffing major subjects such as mathematics, at least as far as 'A' level is concerned.

It is not our main business here to consider what administrative and educational measures might be taken to ensure that there are enough mathematics and science teachers in the schools generally; still, one might make some comment on the policy of drift and *laissez-faire* which brought us to our recent desperate position. The numbers of college of education trained mathematics teachers have gone down steadily since the old School Certificate and matriculation examination, which was group based, was replaced by the single subject G.C.E. examination. The reason is obvious. Many intending teachers who, under the old dispensation, would have gone to college with a qualification in mathematics, even if it had been difficult to get, now drop the subject at the beginning of the fourth or fifth year. As the subject is so "sequence-based" they cannot then take it up again on their arrival at the college of education. Nor is any general effort made to induce waverers entering the sixth form to study mathematics, for example, by limiting the numbers who may enter the arts sixth or by providing monetary incentives to study subjects where there is a shortfall in takers. Similar comments might be made with regard to the universities. There is a general wringing of hands, and very little action taken. The wishes of the student are to be paramount and the needs of the body politic are not to be considered. It is forgotten that the wishes of the student now and his needs in 5 years' time may be vastly different, and that we do little as yet to help the student to understand what they will be, as our vocational counselling services are rather poor. Not that one would wish to underestimate the plight of pupils under the old dispensation who had, say, a mental block-

[1] Of teachers emerging from colleges of education recently, six times as many had arts 'A' levels as science 'A' levels.

age with regard to mathematics and who tried for 3 years in succession to get matriculation and failed for lack of a pass in this subject. Good careers were completely blocked in consequence. But, if it were compulsory to take mathematics the first time a pupil sat a public examination, if it were compulsory also to re-sit the subject once in case of failure, many more pupils would acquire a qualification in it than do so at present. The solution to the shortage lies not in blocking pupils' futures completely, but in structuring the situation to ensure that a maximum number will qualify. Another approach to the problem is now increasingly possible, an approach which should be particularly helpful in subjects of a sequential type, because absence during any particular sequence renders future progress problematical. The increasing availability of programmed learning sequences that can be offered to pupils who, for whatever reason, are performing at a level below that required, should go far towards preventing the development of subject phobias. These latter often develop in the absence of remedial help, available as soon as difficulty arises; so failure breeds failure and finally the emotional expectation of it. Energetic development and use of such sequences in the early years of schooling particularly would help to produce a larger supply of people competent in subjects where there is a shortfall.

It is therefore contended that the shortages of teachers in some subjects since the war stem from a lack of sufficiently vigorous and well-thought-out and persistent action at various levels, a lack of leadership in the face of vested interest and ill-thought-out concern for the individual pupil, amounting almost to a lack of nerve. It is not much of an excuse to say that these shortages afflict some other Western countries besides our own. To date, historically, no problem of staffing has remained permanently intractable when enough resources have been devoted to it and proper administrative policies followed. There is no reason why this staffing problem should be different from any other. We have just not looked at it radically enough. We have all failed, because we have not tried hard enough, and in the end the children are the losers, not us.

Apart from the general shortage of teachers in certain subjects, the difficulty that affects a small school specifically is, of course, the lack of enough teachers to staff peripheral subjects, because the number of pupils in the school entitle it to only a certain number of staff. This difficulty affected the small one-stream grammar school more seriously than it affects the small three- or four-stream comprehensive school. The number of teachers in the one-stream grammar school was so small that as the curriculum expanded between the wars, individual teachers had frequently to take more than one common subject up to 'A' level standard. Indeed here was the rationale for the development in the countryside of small bi-lateral, eventually comprehensive, schools, after the war, and the wholehearted support often offered by Conservative county councils to this development. The three- or four-stream comprehensive school is not so seriously affected by the expansion of the curriculum as was the one-stream grammar school. The latter might be entitled only to eight teachers, the three-stream comprehensive to twenty-three, on a staffing ratio of 20:1 (sixth form not included). None the less, the fact that no one objected to the one-stream grammar school is no excuse for failing to consider the curricular problems of the small comprehensive school. Indeed, if the appropriate authorities had been more willing to consider the problems of the former between the wars, we would now be better oriented in our attitudes towards considering the problems of the latter. These problems will always exist so long as we have a countryside, but the British, unlike, for example, the Swedes or the Australians, have never seriously considered them except at the local level and in the most piecemeal way. In spite of our professed love of the countryside, in education we are urban in our approach.

A fact which would seem likely to improve the prospects of the small school to provide an adequate curriculum is the increased staying-on rate in the sixth form. With regard to this point, it is noteworthy that Benn and Simon[2] report from 30 to 50 per cent staying on into the sixth in some of the comprehensive schools they visited. It seems likely that many more schools will reach similar startling percentages as the effects of the school-leaving age begin to be felt.[3] The Crowther Report itself pointed out that, after the school-leaving age is raised, the trend towards increased staying on becomes more marked. Benn and Simon warn us, moreover, that all forecasts have fallen short of actual targets when predicting demand for education and that the present forecast by the D.E.S. of 36 per cent of 17-year-olds in full-time school only by 1990 may well be doing the same.

The effects of an increased staying-on rate in the sixth form, in practice, can be seen from the following calculations. If the staying-on rate is 30 per cent in a three-stream school, there will be fifty to sixty in its sixth form. At a staffing ratio of 10:1 (the staffing allocation for the sixth form is double that for the rest of the school) we have the equivalent of five to six full-time teachers; this gives a minimum of thirteen subjects on the timetable, without skimping in any way or borrowing periods from the rest of the school. A similar staying-on rate in a four stream school would produce seventeen subjects. A 40 per cent staying-on rate produces sixteen to seventeen subjects in a three-stream school, twenty-one to twenty-two in a four-stream school. The capacity of the small school to produce an adequate sixth-form curriculum is directly related to the staying-on rate. Previous experience in this country and abroad should warn us to expect it to escalate.

What is more, these calculations have been made according to current assumptions about what the sixth-form curriculum should be like, that is very specialized and with almost complete freedom of choice and consequently very expensive in staffing. Arrangements to make the sixth-form curriculum rather more general, as has been suggested by various reports, is likely to improve the viability of the small school at the sixth-form level.

However, since the preceding paragraphs are somewhat speculative, it is now proposed to look at ways and means by which the small comprehensive school can offset deficiencies of staffing and of subject provision as matters now stand. Measures that seem appropriate fall roughly under two headings: (a) internal administrative measures and (b) measures of various kinds that come to us from outside the school.

A. Administrative Measures

1. *Size of Class*

In making our calculations on the curricular problems of the small 11–18 comprehensive school we have already noted that a small 3-F.E. school of 380+ would be better run as a 2-F.E. school, or the small 4-F.E. run as a 3-F.E., with staff redeployed to give greater flexibility in the provision of split classes and remedials in the lower school; in this way more staff time would be made available for extending the range of options in the fourth and fifth year and, where there is a sixth form, in the sixth. Since such an administrative decision inevitably produces large classes in the junior section of the school, are we justified in taking it, against the weight of much professional opinion as to the desirability of the large class?

[2] Benn and Simon, *op. cit.*, p. 119.

[3] Britain is behind many continental countries in its staying-on rates for 16–18-year-olds.

A review of the research suggests that we are. Moreover, many of the early research results were gathered in the teeth of the investigator's own original opinion that large classes had adverse effects on children.

As far back as 1902–3 Rice concluded from his studies of the effect of class size on the attainments of 6000 children in arithmetic and language, that there was no relationship between size of class and academic results achieved. In the 1920 and early 1930s a very large number of research reports appeared, based on investigations of varying degrees of sophistication and competence in research design. Otto van Borgersrode in 1941 reported a total of 267 studies carried out in schools and colleges, which it was possible to trace. A summary of some of the earlier studies by Fleming[4] showed that high school classes varying in size from three to seventy had shown no significant variation in achievement in English, mathematics, physics and history;[5] or the results were contradictory.

Incidentally acquired data also present the same picture. Data on the effect of size of class obtained incidentally during an N.F.E.R. survey on another subject in the late 1950s showed no significant difference between the average performances of more than 4000 pupils in classes of various sizes in the primary schools. A study by Morris[6] on reading in the primary schools about the same time and another by Daniels and Diack[7] even produced significantly rather more favourable results for pupils in the larger classes. Conversely, a study by Lundberg produced more favourable results in smaller classes.

In a series of technically sophisticated experiments Eastburn[8] divided up 360 pupils of about 16 years old arranged as one class of sixty and two classes of thirty at each of three ability levels. At the end of a year of teaching, the same methods being used for each class, the average scores of small classes on standardized tests did not differ significantly from those of large classes in either English or history at the lower level and the upper level or in history at the middle level; but scores were significantly higher in the larger classes in English at the middle level. A test of attitude showed no significant differences between classes either, nor did behaviour appear to be affected by class size. A second study threw equal doubt on the assumption that pupils of lower ability should necessarily be taught in smaller groups than those of middle or upper ability.

In a study by Marklund[9] of two samples of classes, totalling in all 4924 pupils, aged 13, in 189 classes, similar results were reported. Class sizes were respectively 16–20, 21–25, 26–30, 31–35; 281 comparisons were made of attainment between pupils in larger and smaller classes. Thirty-seven favoured the larger classes, twenty-two the smaller and in the remainder the differences were not significant. Differences attributable to class size failed to appear even when such factors as level and homogeneity of intelligence, social pattern, etc., were controlled.

[4] Fleming, C. M., Class size as a variable in the teaching situation, *Educ. Res.* vol. 1, no. 2, Feb. 1959, pp. 35–48.

[5] The variations in size of classes for individual subjects occurred within the range given.

[6] Morris, J. M., *Reading in the Primary School*, N.F.E.R., Newnes, 1959, pp. 124–7.

[7] Daniels, J. C. and Diack, H., *Progress in Reading*, University of Nottingham Institute of Education, 1956, p. 8, p. 28. N.B. The larger class was taught by a different method.

[8] Eastburn, L. A., The relative efficiency of instruction in large and small classes at three ability levels, *J. Exper. Educ.*, vol. VI, 1936, pp. 17–22. Eastburn, L. A., Report of class size investigations in the Phoenix Union High School, 1933–4 to 1935–6, *J. Educ. Res.*, vol. XXXI, no. 2, 1937, pp. 107–17.

[9] Marklund, S., Scholastic attainments as related to size and homogeneity of classes, *Educ. Res.*, vol. VI, no. 1, Nov. 1963, pp. 63–7. Abstract prepared by N. Postlethwaite from Marklund, Sixten. *Stockholm Studies in Educational Psychology* no. 6, Almqvist & Wiksell, Stockholm, 1962. Text in Swedish with an English summary.

Marklund also refers to several previous studies, involving both the more and the less intelligent pupils, which show that size of class is not conclusively related to their well-being, mental health or social adjustment.

In a paper critical of many of the earlier investigations of the effects of class size Cecco[10] states that frequently they have measured nothing beyond the recall or recognition of material learnt on a particular course and have therefore not measured other elements in cognitive behaviour change. Very few have used a random assignment of students to the various sizes of class, the more sophisticated studies have used instead groups matched for aptitude and achievement. Lastly the co-ordination of materials of instruction between the classes often did not extend beyond the use of a common text and the test being used as a measure of the criterion of success. In other words, many of the studies, especially the earlier ones, have not fully measured up to the stringent requirements of educational psychologists.

He then gives an account of a series of studies undertaken since World War II by different workers, of college- and university-level classes, which have more or less successfully attempted to relate class size to cognitive change—beyond the mere acquisition of information—as described in Bloom's *Taxonomy of Educational Objectives*. These include attitude change, increased awareness, critical thinking and so on. Generally speaking, the investigations showed no significant differences between classes of different sizes in respect of any of these or in respect of acquisition of information. Nor do the results of Cecco's own even more sophisticated study, in which students were randomly assigned to three types of groups (large-experimental, small-experimental and small-control) and instructional materials and assignments were closely co-ordinated for the first two groups. In the main there were no significant differences in achievement or preferences. Students, however, consistently preferred the smaller class when asked directly about this factor, although other responses were not consistent with this attitude and it was suggested that stereotypic thinking might be playing some part in this expression of preference.

Corroboration of previous research by many workers on the effect of class size was given in 1966 in a large study by Coleman and others.[11] They showed that pupil–teacher ratios in instruction "showed a consistent lack of relation to achievement among all groups under all conditions".

Another suggestion which may explain the apparent lack of relationship between class size and students' achievement has been made by McKeachie.[12] He proposes that it may be due to two effects working in opposite directions. On the one hand, increasing size increases the resources of the class (for example, the total amount of information available, the number of different approaches to the problem in hand, the opportunities for providing feedback from one member of the class to another). On the other hand, the possibility of getting the maximum contribution from all members decreases.

One can sum up the results of these many studies, whether sophisticated in research design and techniques or not, in the words of C. M. Fleming:[13]

[10] Cecco, J. P., Class size and coordinated instruction, *Brit. J. Educ. Psychol.*, vol. XXXIV, no. 1., Feb. 1964, pp. 65–74.

[11] Coleman, J. S. *et al.*, *Equality of Educational Opportunity*, U.S. Department of Health, Education and Welfare, Office of Education, 1966, p. 312.

[12] McKeachie, W. J. Procedures and techniques of teaching. A survey of experimental studies. In: Sanford, N. (ed.), *The American College*, Wiley, New York, 1962, pp. 312–64.

[13] *Op. cit.*, p. 38.

> There have been many investigations, but, with few exceptions, it has had to be reported that, under typical conditions class size in itself appears to be an unimportant factor. The benefits of small classes, though commonly taken for granted by theorists, are as yet largely undemonstrated in the pages of accredited research reports. This conclusion has been reached at every level from infant-room to university lecture-theatre. It has been formulated in relation to many subjects; and it is supported both by test results and by assessments of various types.

One might add that the increasing sophistication of research techniques should by this time have revealed any hidden variable that favoured small classes if any such variable existed.

Another reason for these unexpected results may lie in a suggestion made by Marklund to explain what differences of class size mean for pupils' attainment. He points out that we have been influenced by the idea that pupils must in some way share out the teacher's instruction between them and that the larger the class the less instruction a pupil will get. In the debate about streaming and non-streaming, on the contrary, those in favour of homogeneous grouping have assumed on their part that the teacher's instruction is essentially of a collective nature, adapted to the class average; the more any one pupil deviates from the average, the "poorer" the teaching he will receive.

> According to the theory of class size the teacher imparts instruction individually and to the theory of class homogeneity, he does so collectively. These theories are based on what the teacher imparts and not on what the pupils learn, but in the final analysis it is the pupil who teaches himself and it is the teacher's task to arrange a total situation from which the pupil learns through his own efforts. Learning is fostered and manifested by actions which learning theories usually subsume under the term "reinforcement". If pupil activity and reinforcement are regarded as determinants of learning, the theories on the importance of class size and class homogeneity acquire another and less self-evident character. What becomes decisive instead is the extent to which class size and homogeneity simplify, impede or otherwise affect pupil activity and reinforcement. A teacher's methods of instruction and the pupil's methods of study will become the cruxes.

What implications have these results for the small school? The small school is faced with the fact that, on an equal staffing ratio to that of the larger school, it cannot provide the variety of subjects in the option groups from the fourth year onwards. In order to increase the range of these subjects it may try to save up sufficient staff periods by decreasing the number and increasing the size of all the classes in any or all of the age groups in the lower school, and in the compulsory subjects from the fourth year onwards. In so doing, is it damaging the interests of the children in these larger groups? The evidence from these many research studies overwhelmingly answers that it is not. If anything, and very unexpectedly, the research tends to favour the larger class.

However, the children are not the only groups to be considered. What of the teachers? What evidence is there of the effect on them of larger classes? Marklund suggests that in one respect research has provided evidence of a clear-cut tendency: the larger classes are, the heavier is the teaching load. In other words, the teacher rises, or by the nature of the situation, has to rise, to the challenge which a larger class presents. It would not therefore be just or wise for the head of a small school to give a teacher nothing but larger classes without adjusting the number of free periods. If he were carrying along with a few larger classes some small classes in the options groups, there would of course be no need to adjust the number of his free periods, and this is precisely what is needed if the number of curricular offerings in the options groups is to be maximized.

2. *Other Administrative Measures*

Another administrative device of service to small schools with a broad band of ability in its classes, classes which may be large and which may be taught by teachers unconvinced of the value of unstreaming or unable to adjust their methods to it, would be the old-fashioned stratagem of skipping a class by able pupils. In the last 30 or 40 years we have promoted solely by age, but the Continent has pursued a policy of promoting by standard reached. There is some evidence, moreover, which suggests—one cannot be more definite than that—that promotion by standard reached produces better standards.[14] A mixed system of age and grade promotion would enable the high flyer in a very small but still streamed comprehensive school to proceed at his own rate, with the possibility, for example, of 6-monthly transfer if progress warranted it. There is evidence to show that such a practice is not inimical to the high flyers.[15]

Of course such a system would produce a wider range in ages in a particular class, but this does not lead to the emotional difficulties it has been thought to. Taylor[16] demonstrated that social acceptance by other children of pupils older or younger than themselves is more related to mental age than to chronological age.

In point of fact, during the survey mentioned in Chapter 7, the writer came across one three-stream school where prejudice against skipping a class had been allowed to die. Six able children had been promoted at the end of the third year straight into form five, so doing certain 'O' level subjects earlier. No emotional difficulties had been encountered, there had been good integration, and the group had gained twenty-one 'O' level successes between them before going on to the sixth form. Promotion had in fact been decided on the standard of work reached and the high flyers allowed to proceed at their own rate.

With regard to the question of minority time subjects in the sixth form, one 3-F.E. school the writer saw had hit upon a happy stratagem. It had always had a minority time allocation of periods, since it felt the need to open windows for pupils whose environment provided little general stimulus. To do so it had used whatever staff were available, without over-burdening any one of them, to cater for a wide range of topics. When the J.M.B. General Studies paper was introduced it was able to enter any pupils from this general course who so wished, for an additional 'A' level subject, and this made the difference for some pupils between having two 'A' levels and having three, or between having three and having four. There were thus several advantages: pupils could take an 'A' or 'O' level in General Studies or take no exam; the course provided another examination subject without demanding a major portion of the time of any one teacher which it might have been difficult to allocate; it also provided an intellectual meeting point for the upper and lower sixth.

Another device which is of assistance to the small school is that of subject-sharing with other schools; for example, a sixth-form subject in little demand can be taught by only one school in the neighbourhood and pupils from other schools can go for the relevant periods to that school. This procedure involves inconvenience for the timetable maker and negotiation with other schools, less easy in our system, where the head of a school has an autonomous position, than it would be elsewhere. It also involves problems of transport and would therefore seem not very suited for the small rural school. In point of fact it is often so used by them. The writer came across schools collaborating as regards 'A' levels which were 10 to 15 miles apart. Woodward, too, in his account of the evolution of Sir William Romney's School, Tetbury,[17] indicates that some of his pupils went to Stroud for their commercial

[14] Unesco Institute of Education, Hamburg, *International Evaluation of Achievement Project: Educational Attainments of Thirteen-Year-Olds in Twelve Countries*, 1963. Chapter by Pidgeon.

[15] See p. 72.

[16] *J. Educat. Psychol.*, vol. 43, no. 5, 1952.

[17] In: Halsall, Elizabeth (ed.) (1970), p. 16.

subjects. From such beginnings have developed the linked courses which are now increasingly advocated as a way of broadening curricular offerings and ensuring maximum use of expensive equipment.

So much for the sixth form and the high flyers,[18] and for ways of economizing on staff time without affecting their interests. Other procedures can help the rest of the school.

A curriculum device used by three-stream schools in order to get the advantage of split classes for practical subjects in the lower school without waste of staff time is the device of rotation. It is the usual practice to consider that twenty is a suitable number of pupils for practical subjects. To split a class in half provides only fifteen. If one takes the whole of the year in a three-stream school one gets from ninety children four groups of 20+. However, in no subject would there be four teachers available in a three stream school, often there will be only one. The device of rotation involves taking four different specialist teachers of practical or craft subjects and dividing the four groups between them at any one time. Each group moves to each specialist teacher in turn. It involves some constraint on the timetable, since the whole of a particular year has to be kept together for sufficient periods of time to cover the four subjects, but it is a useful device for the small school with an odd number of entry (e.g. 3-F.E.) particularly.

Another way of economizing on staff at the fourth- and fifth-year level is to ensure that practical and art subjects which, as has been said, require these smaller numbers of pupils, form part of the options groups on the timetable, as indeed one would expect them to do so from the "educationally desirable" point of view. It is in the options groups section of the timetable that we find, because of the range of choice provided, classes whose numbers approximate to those required by these subjects. If this precaution is taken there is no waste of scarce teaching time in a way that serves no particular educational purpose.

Another device which also has an educational as well as an administration rationale, is to allow both boys and girls to take domestic science and woodwork. In these days of congruence of sexual roles there is far more to be said for this arrangement than there would have been 50 years ago.

Perhaps the most effective of all timetabling methods for helping the small school to solve its curricular problems is that of the alternate years method, reported in the *International Review of Education*.[19] What is termed the alternate years curriculum has been very effective in increasing the number of subjects on offer in relation to the size of school. By crossing year lines and by teaching even multiple section courses in alternate years the curricular offering of some small American high schools has been doubled. In one of three schools reporting success with this timetable design the number of option subjects was doubled. This claim has been verified by the writer[20] and has also been shown to be an effective way of doubling the size of uneconomic small classes in the options groups section of small British comprehensive schools timetables.

B. Non-administrative Measures

The use of other media of instruction than the teacher would seem to be one way by which small schools could increase their curricular range. The decision whether or not to use such

[18] See also p. 116 for a way of avoiding subject clashes in the sixth-form timetable.

[19] Bush, R. N. and Delay, D. H., Making the school schedule by computer, *Int. Rev. Educ.*, vol. XIV, no. 2, 1968, pp. 173–4.

[20] An article by the writer on the adaptation of the method to the problems of small British comprehensive schools, is to be published.

media would depend on three factors: namely, (a) whether the given medium was as, or nearly as, effective as the teacher or had its own peculiar strengths; (b) whether or not it was more, or less, expensive to install and operate than the equivalent full or "part-time" teacher's salary; and (c) whether or not there was sufficient material available in a particular medium to justify the policy of using it as a substitute for a teacher, for the whole or part of his time. If the medium under review was more expensive than, or as expensive as, a teacher, its adoption could be justified only if no teacher in the given subject could be obtained by the small school. Otherwise it would be simpler to increase the staffing ratio to allow for the appointment of extra full or part-time teachers to improve the curricular range. Equally, if there were insufficient material available in the medium for the subject concerned it would be impossible to use it as a significant element in the course.

With regard to other media of instruction than the teacher, the small school would do well to look to such devices as correspondence courses, educational television, programmed learning courses and, eventually, computerized learning, as aids to widening its curriculum. It is therefore worthwhile at this stage to review, as briefly as is consonant with accuracy, what each of these various devices can offer to the small school, now and in the future. This can hardly be done without some reference first to their general possibilities, before we can estimate what they can offer, now and ultimately, to the small school.

1. *Correspondence Courses*

Other countries have made considerable use of correspondence courses as a way of helping the small school. Sweden, in particular, has a very well-thought-out scheme.

Provision for academically able pupils in the sparsely populated far north has had to be made through the development of correspondence courses in subjects for which specialist teaching could not be economically provided. The Hermods' correspondence college at Malmö was put in charge of this task.[21] Two-thirds of many pupils' time, including both classwork and homework, in fourteen very small state secondary schools was devoted to work on correspondence courses, under the general supervision of a non-specialist class teacher, and for the remaining third of his time he was taught in the normal way. In his first gymnasium year he concentrated on the three or four subjects of least interest to himself, taking Hermods' courses and returning exercises to the college. After an oral and written examination at the end of the first year, he concentrated on his four main subjects for the remaining 2 years, with a month's residence at Malmö in the second year and two in the third, in addition to his correspondence courses, before leaving school. These courses were found to be very effective with older boys and girls, neither significantly better nor significantly worse in overall results, according to a study by Dr. Broden,[22] than normal teaching. Where the teachers, who were general class teachers, did more direct teaching than Hermods recommended, the results were less satisfactory; where they followed instructions explicitly, the results were better than for traditional teaching. The emotional adjustment of the children concerned was shown to be equal to that of other children.

Since the introduction of a reorganized secondary education system in Sweden attempts have been made to adapt this system of correspondence courses to the non-academic pupil

[21] Glatter, R. and Wedell, E. G., *Study by Correspondence*, Longmans, 1971, pp. 164–6. The main Swedish writer on the subject is Holmberg.

[22] Taylor, L. C., *Resources for Learning*, Penguin Education Specials, 1971, p. 260.

also. The Swedish Board of Education has sponsored new individualized courses in mathematics, German, English, history, R.E., ethics, civics, and general studies. Remedial courses in reading, writing and mathematics are also being developed.[23]

Although Britain has been very tepid in its approach to the use of correspondence courses, Lumby and Jackson reported in 1967 that seventy-five secondary schools were using the National Extension College courses in the mid-sixties.[24] Thirty-four courses and 275 children were involved and the schools concerned used the courses either to cope with the problem of no staff, to help pupils who had got behind or who had changed schools or to widen the choice of subjects, especially in the sixth form. If every small 11–18 comprehensive school was allowed by its L.E.A. to have access to a maximum of five correspondence courses at 'A' level each year, five pupils in its relatively small sixth form would have the possibility of choosing one subject outside the school's own curriculum. As most of these schools manage to provide eleven or twelve 'A' level subjects, from their own staffing, this would provide a total maximum of sixteen or seventeen 'A' levels, ensuring that, according to one study, 97 per cent of subject choices made on average by sixth formers would be covered,[25] instead of the 80 per cent of choices these schools manage to cater for already with their eleven or twelve 'A' levels. Moreover, it seems likely that to use correspondence courses in this way could reduce costs. Another study by the National Extension College showed that a joint TV and correspondence course was much cheaper than an equivalent course in a technical college. Probably the same would be equally true at the secondary level, even for courses in the less common subjects. The use of correspondence courses would, in addition, help us to tap one source of trained teaching expertise temporarily unable to teach in schools, namely the young married woman at home with small children. It would enable her to use her training with profit both to herself and the country and keep her in touch with educational developments in preparation for the time when she returned to the secondary school. At present we waste her talents and expertise during the period she spends at home.

The correspondence course is perhaps the oldest device for offsetting the deficiencies of educational systems. It has encountered much prejudice in Britain. It needs to get a fair trial.

2. *ETV and Film*

A newer, less print-based medium of instruction is the television programme and its predecessor the film. Are they as effective and as economic as the teacher? Are there sufficient programmes available to act as full-time or part-time substitutes for specialist teachers in short supply? Could they help a teacher with relatively slight specialist expertise to cover adequately specialist subjects at given levels?

With regard to the relative effectiveness of TV and direct instruction Stickell[26] reviewed 250 comparison studies in 1963. As usual with so much of educational research[27] he found

[23] *Ibid.*, p. 260. See also: Spolton, Lewis, *The Upper Secondary School*, Pergamon Press, 1967, p. 183, for Japanese developments. (Pupils can combine correspondence, part-time and full-time education to build up complete courses.)

[24] One small school visited by the writer occasionally used a correspondence course for an 'A' level subject for which a teacher was not available; the cost was about £15.

[25] See p. 115.

[26] *Rev. Educ. Res.*, vol. 38, no. 2, April 1968, p. 118. Similar results were obtained by a further review of comparative studies by Dubin and Hedley in 1969.

[27] Many of these studies are surveys, made by people without research expertise, and should not really be classified as research.

217 of these studies uninterpretable and twenty-three partly uninterpretable due to defects of experimental design. The ten which, according to his stringent criteria, were interpretable all showed no significant difference between the effectiveness of TV and that of direct instruction. Speaking more generally, more than 90 per cent of comparison studies show no significant difference between TV and conventional classroom methods in teaching a given topic.[28] At the same time it would appear that there are probably differences between subjects in their ability to adapt to ETV and that probably in some it is impossible to eliminate the subject teacher completely. It was found by Gropper[29] in 1967 that, when science concepts were being taught to junior secondary pupils by TV, some method of ensuring active responding was also needed if they were to acquire, retain and transfer these concepts and principles. Gordon, Engar and Shape[30] likewise showed that control groups learning elementary Russian by direct instruction did better than TV groups. At the same time a teacher without knowledge of the language concerned[31] could learn to manage well a combination of language activities built round TV, according to a study on elementary Spanish.[32]

The effectiveness of TV in conjunction with correspondence teaching has also been demonstrated[33] by one piece of research and denied by another.[34] The latter study suggested correspondence courses were more effective on their own. Clearly, more research is needed on this particular issue.

All these findings are relevant to policy-making decisions with regard to the use of TV as a partial or total substitute for a specialist teacher.

From a more general viewpoint it is clear that TV has much to offer. Research has shown that pupils' achievements *can* improve significantly when TV is used consistently, that TV accelerates teachers' professional growth and provides enrichment in, for example, geography and mathematics, and that its operational costs can be met from within the existing budget.

The bulk of studies of pupils' attitudes to ETV show neutral to negative feelings. Westley and Jacobson, for example, showed that groups of students using TV tended to rate their teachers and textbooks higher than did control groups without TV.[35] This finding is a warning against overuse of the medium.

The genesis for these negative or neutral feelings might be that TV is even less adjusted to the individual child's needs than a teacher teaching to a whole class, but on this there appears to be no evidence.

ETV, in the form of closed-circuit television, has already been used to overcome shortages of teachers and to upgrade in some measure the capacities of those available; for example,

[28] This does not imply that any TV programme will do as long as it is generally related to the topic, but rather that, if a TV programme is slanted to a specific objective and well constructed, it can be as effective as a teacher.

[29] *Ibid.*, p. 137.

[30] *Ibid.*, p. 137.

[31] Similarly, where good work in French has been done in our primary schools some of it has been done by teachers who knew little French but were supported by film strips and tape-recorder material.

[32] The content of instructional TV: summary report of research findings, the Denver–Stanford Project. (Abstract) *Audio-Visual Commun. Rev.*, vol. 13, Summer 1965, pp. 237–8.

[33] Perraton, H., Correspondence teaching and television. (Abstract) *Audio-Visual Commun. Rev.*, vol. 15, Summer 1967, p. 227.

[34] Holmberg, Booje, *Correspondence Education*, Malmö, Hermöds-NKI, 1967, p. 26, quoting a study by Childs (*I.C.C.E. Proceedings*, 1965, p. 81).

[35] Westley, B. H. and Jacobson, H. K., Instructional television and student attitudes towards teacher, course and medium, *Audio-Visual Commun. Rev.*, vol. 11, May–June 1963, pp. 47–60.

it has been so used in Glasgow and in Hull. Shortages of mathematics teachers, especially those qualified in modern mathematics, and of French teachers in primary schools, have to some extent been overcome by this means.

It is clear, however, that critical factors in the usefulness of educational television are financing the improvement of programmes, the increase in the number of programmes available and the availability, whether at a school or at a central depot, of a video-tape recorder for the recording of programmes which can later be used by a school at a time convenient to it. Programmes will not improve in quality until research has been done into what ETV's unique contribution can be in a particular subject, as well as its general contribution, and into practical ways of involving its audiences sufficiently.

One must therefore conclude that at present the possibility of television making a significant contribution to the solution of the small school's problems in the short run is rather slight,[36] though its potential is considerable and the need for development urgent, for both the small and the larger school. It may help a teacher to provide material in areas of a discipline on which he lacks deep knowledge, but it cannot as yet act as a substitute for a specialist teacher working at a high level in a subject where there is a shortage of well-qualified staff or in a subject for which the school has so little demand that it cannot afford to appoint a full or part-time teacher. Until ETV can teach a full course in a scarce subject at fifth- or sixth-form level, it cannot on its own do much to help the small school.

3. *Film*

It seems very unlikely that instruction by film could ever be used by itself as a substitute for a teacher. Although one could, conceivably, put the whole of the instructional, as opposed to the learning, part of a year's course in a given subject on film, film does not have the flexibility of use that educational television has, provided one has a videotape recorder. Films have to be ordered and returned, and heavy hire and postal charges paid. The video-tape copy can be retained on the premises for further use.

None the less it would appear that more use could be made of film to offset the lack of high expertise or broad knowledge, in a teacher, if the example of Surrey was followed in setting up an audio-visual store with technicians attached. In Surrey not only is faulty equipment replaced on breakdown, whilst a school's model is being repaired, not only are architects briefed to equip new buildings with audio-visual teaching in mind, but films are delivered and collected weekly from its film library. In view of the high cost of hiring and postage, this practice is economic. It also increases accessibility of material since one can check by telephone whether particular material is available. Teachers who are well serviced in this way do not have to waste time and energy on procuring films that would be better spent on teaching. Until such services become general there is little incentive for the teacher to take advantage of the peculiar attribute of the film medium, namely its ability to furnish a particular type of experience and material otherwise inaccessible.

Research on films report that "films are not intrinsically different from lectures or other instructional methods".[37] Hour-long viewing sessions are as effective as shorter periods,

[36] Yet, to be fair, one must note that Japan now has 370 ETV stations and, presumably, is making an economic and efficient use of them (Taylor, L. C., *op. cit.*, pp. 156–7). This judgement may therefore be outpaced by events.

[37] Rigg, R. P., *Audio-visual Aids and Techniques in Managerial and Supervisory Training*, Hamish Hamilton, 1969, p. 11, quoting evidence from Instructional Film Research 1918–50. Department of Commerce, Office of Technical Services, Washington D.C.

but after each 10 minutes of presentation a change of pace or technique must be introduced to refocus attention. This fact is said to back up the idea that films could be used as an exclusive means of instruction, and perhaps with additional teaching material in the way of still visuals, books and worksheets they could,[38] but the time when the teacher could be disposed with would appear to be a long way off.

The need for revision and criticism of existing educational films is demonstrated by an investigation which showed that revisions in introductions, summaries, outlines, diagrams, titles and commentaries appreciably increased learning of content.[39]

4. *Language Laboratories*

Could one use a language laboratory,[40] without the intervention of a teacher, to teach a scarce language in a small school? One would first have to justify the equipping of a small school with a language laboratory. If one assumes that a language laboratory is used regularly by children in the first 3 years of a language course, and intermittently afterwards, a four-stream school would have twelve classes requiring regular use of the laboratory. Since it has been demonstrated that once a week use of the laboratory is no better than non-use[41] one cannot justify its use for less than two periods per week per class. This means that it would be regularly employed for twenty-four periods out of thirty-five or forty. The eight forms in the fourth and fifth year plus the sixth would furnish further groups requiring some use of the language laboratory for practice of the school's main foreign language. The few remaining periods when the language laboratory was not in use could well be devoted to machine teaching of a second foreign language at the elementary stage, say, for sixth formers, if a suitable course were available.

Two studies bear on this last point. They showed that speaking and understanding of limited material in a foreign language could be effectively taught without human instruction provided lessons were prepared and sequenced according to the principles of programmed learning. The authors felt their research demonstrated the possibility of machine teaching a full-scale modern language course.[42] Moreover, a new machine, the "oreille électronique",

[38] (a) Roberts, P. and Parchott, R. (Do Worksheets Improve Film Utilization?, *Audio-Visual Commun. Rev.*, vol. 10, Mar.–Apr. 1962, pp. 106–9) found using worksheets with films to establish clear-cut viewing aims resulted in significant gains if the worksheets contained objective questions. (b) Wittich, W. A. and Fowlkes, J. G. (*Audio-Visual Paths to Learning*, Harper & Row, 1946) showed that pupils gave a greater response to a film accompanied by an introduction than to a film alone, and the greatest response of all to an introduction, the film and a review of the film, a finding which is indirectly relevant. N.B. *Multi*-media instruction has been shown to produce greater learning gains and greater retention than conventional methods of instruction and to be preferred by students.

[39] Van der Meer, A. W., Morrison, J. and Smith, P., An investigation of educational motion pictures and a derivation of principles relating to the effectiveness of these media, *Audio-Visual Commun. Rev.*, vol. 13, Winter 1965, p. 465.

[40] N.B. If one wished to justify from research the use of a language laboratory at all in any school, one had to wait till the middle sixties for the production of scientifically acceptable research on this issue. Before this time the research on this subject was poor. The research in the mid-sixties is of better quality and does validate the language laboratory as a teaching tool. (Large, D., Foreign language instruction, *Rev. Educ. Res.*, vol. 37, Apr. 1967, pp. 186–99.)

[41] Large, D., The relative effectiveness of four types of language laboratory experiences. (Abstract) *Audio-Visual Commun. Rev.*, vol. 12, no. 1, Spring 1964, pp. 107–8.

[42] Rocklyn, E. H. and Moren, R. I., A special machine taught oral–aural Russian language course: a feasibility study, *Audio-Visual Commun. Rev.*, vol. 10, Mar.–Apr. 1962, pp. 132–6. And: Rocklyn and Moren, A feasibility study of a special machine-taught oral–aural Russian language course. (Abstract) *Audio-Visual Commun. Rev.*, vol. 14, Spring 1966, pp. 147–8.

taught accent-free French to an experimental group in a quarter of the time required by a control group.[43]

5. *Programmed Learning*

As far as programmed learning is concerned, obviously it has a great future, even if present performance is not yet adequate to what is needed in the way of output of courses. Basically, it attempts to put into practice in the classroom the experimental findings of psychology and to use modern industrial techniques such as task analysis, job evaluation and data processing to find the most efficient path for learning.[44] It could be defined as an attempt to devise a systematic technology of instruction, by stating objectives, taking into account the capacity and level of knowledge of the pupils concerned, using step-by-step procedures and evaluating each item included in every segment of a programme for its teaching efficiency. Programming therefore subjects teaching to a searching operational analysis and has resulted in savings of time varying from 20 to 50 per cent in a number of instances.[45] It has even been suggested that weaker students in a class "will probably do better with a programme written at an appropriate level than with conventional instruction in large groups."[46] Even the most sceptical cannot dispute that it is at least equally as effective as traditional methods. If this is so, any school is entitled to use the technique in appropriate circumstances or in case of staffing difficulties without fear of injuring academic results.

To how many subjects programmed learning techniques can be applied is a matter of some debate. They are obviously applicable to factual areas of knowledge in all subjects, and it has been assumed that any subject which can be taught can be programmed, but it depends on what one means by taught. How could one programme for the appreciation of English literature, music or art?

Another factor which also needs consideration is the question of how far children can, and should, work in the personal isolation that programmed learning implies, and, indeed, to what extent variety of approach is needed in teaching if interest is to be retained. Studies of relevance to the latter indicate that programmed learning has a saturation effect and one study showed that, as negative attitudes develop, achievement declines.[47]

As an example of what can be done, that is of relevance to the small school, a British experiment in the use of programmed learning is worth describing. It shows how the time of

[43] Bauer, Eric W., New avenues of international co-operation in audio-visual language teaching, *Audio-Visual Commun. Rev.*, vol. 11, Sept.–Oct. 1963, pp. 200–6.

[44] Callender, P., *Programmed Learning*, Longmans, 1969, p. 1.

[45] Goodman, R., *Programmed Learning and Teaching Machines*, E.U.P., 1967, p. 11. N.B. Most studies of the relative effects of programmed learning and traditional teaching leave something to be desired in their research design, the number of students tested and so on. Hartley in his comprehensive review of 112 studies, involving 16,000 pupils, makes these and other criticisms but outlines the following results of the investigation. Ninety of the studies recorded the time taken to complete the task set: forty-seven programmed groups took a shorter time than the traditionally taught groups, six took longer and for the remaining thirty-seven the time taken was not significantly different for either group. One hundred and ten of the studies recorded the test results: forty-one programmed groups got significantly better results, fifteen significantly worse and fifty-four not significantly different. Thirty-three studies recorded retest results: six of the programmed groups got significantly better results, three significantly worse, and there was no significant difference between the groups in the other twenty-four studies. (Hartley, J., *New Education*, vol. 2, 1966, pp. 29–35).

[46] Leedham, J. and Unwin, D., *Programmed Learning in the Schools*, Longmans, 1965, p. 93.

[47] *Rev. Educ. Res.*, vol. 38, no. 2, 1968, p. 130 and Hartley, J., Social factors in programmed instruction: a review. *Programmed Learning*, vol. 3, no. 1, Feb. 1966, pp. 5–9.

scarce personnel could be saved. A three-stream 11–16 school only able to find one mathematics teacher, for example, when it needed two,[48] could adapt its arrangements to cope with this difficult situation by employing programmed learning techniques and non-specialized supervision.

Ovenden School, Halifax,[49] a 5-F.E. secondary modern school, has built up a simple linear machine over a 3-year period, the Bingley Tutor. The hall is used for up to eighty children on 2 days a week, with machines, programmes and desks in continual use. One teacher supervizes the pupils working there. A microphone is used to settle them and no disciplinary problems appear to have been encountered because of the highly motivated, self-controlled learning situation. Of the pupils' five mathematics periods two are used for programmed learning, three for normal class work. Study of a programmed topic starts with normal class teaching to introduce the topic and is completed by programmed learning work in the hall. Further discussion and follow-up work is also undertaken in the ordinary classroom. Ovenden's investment in machines and programmes cost £650. Apart from an initial grant of £150, the cost of the project has been met from the normal expenditure of the mathematics department, transferred from books to programmes. Another £350 would provide enough programmes to keep the machine room fully utilized for 3 days a week.[50]

Clearly, the use of a programmed learning approach makes it possible to economize on staff time, to make the best use of scarce personnel and to train teachers other than those who have specialized in a particular scarce subject to give assistance with it. As more programmes become available in more subjects, the small school's difficulties will be greatly minimized, and that day is not far off.

To sum up, programmed instruction will be useful to all schools, and, *ipso facto*, especially to the small school, for all kinds of reasons. It is at least as effective in appropriate situations as conventional methods and probably more effective on balance. It is an appropriate technique in mixed ability classes. It can bring up to date children who have been absent, who have changed schools or who need remedial teaching. It can also give the able the opportunity to go beyond the prescribed syllabus. It can be used in subjects where there is a teacher shortage, especially in mathematics and science, where there is much material suitable for programming, in subjects for which a small school cannot afford to allot a teacher, or in those where there are new developments for which teachers have not been trained.

At the same time we have come to realize that, for the present, especially in the current dearth of programmes, much individually tailored ancillary material has to be given to pupils, including practice work, extension to variations on the main theme, and revision work. And the task of the teacher remains, the need to foster methodical habits of work, self-reliance and persistence and to maintain confidence and interest. Teachers are well aware that this task is uniquely theirs. Meanwhile they could do with more, and better, programmes.[51]

[48] At five periods per class in a forty-period week, it would require for mathematics around seventy-five periods per week if every class took the subject, and therefore 2+ teachers.

[49] *Programmed Learning*, vol. 4, no. 2, April 1967, pp. 164–7. For other examples of use in schools see: A series of case histories of the use of programmed learning, *Occasional Paper* 16. National Committee for Audio-Visual Aids in Education, 1969.

[50] For examples of other experiments undertaken see also: *Programmed Learning and Educational Technology*, vol. 4, no. 2, Apr. 1967, pp. 113–20; *New Education*, Sept. 1966, pp. 28–31.

[51] For a survey of local authorities using or investigating programmed learning see: *Programmed Learning*, vol. 5, no. 2, Apr. 1968, pp. 157–86, and for programmes in print, *ibid.*, vol. 7, no. 2, Apr. 1970, pp. 157–71.

6. Learning by Computer

What assistance will computerized learning eventually be able to give to the small school? Of course in approaching this subject we are looking into the future, but that future is not so far distant as one might be inclined to believe. The combined effects of the development of programmed learning and electronic data processing and especially of the introduction of the time-sharing system which wedded them both, have led to the development of computerized learning. In less than 10 years, indeed by 1967–8, several thousand American pupils at every level from primary school to university were receiving a significant portion of their education in at least one subject by computer.[52] The Philadelphia and New York school systems moved into C.A.I., the most sophisticated form of computerized learning, by the late sixties, at both primary and secondary level for mathematics, reading and biology; other school districts did so by 1970. A comment by Patrick Suppes[53] indicates its potential. "If the potentials of computer technology are properly realized, the character and nature of education during the course of our lifetime will be radically changed. Perhaps the most important aspect of computerized instructional devices is that the kind of individualized instruction once possible only for a few members of the aristocracy can be made available to all students at all levels of ability." He further predicts that within the next decade many children will use the "drill and practice" types of systems[54] at primary school level for 20–30 per cent of their time, that by the time they reach secondary school tutorial systems will be available and that their children may use dialogue systems throughout their school experience.

Another contribution to the same book expresses the opinion that, though computer-aided instruction is not yet a practical instructional tool ready for widespread installation in schools, the rate of development of on-line computer usage for individual instruction is so rapid that it deserves serious attention by school planners.[55]

One factor which tended for a time to hold up the development of computerized learning was the problem of how teachers were to insert new material into the computer when it became clear that further material was needed. This problem of communication with the computer appeared to be a thorny one because of the difficulty of most computer languages. A new language, PLANIT, now allows a teacher to insert instructional material into the machine with great ease, for subsequent presentation to the students. It is organized in multiple-choice form, so that the teacher merely responds to the machine's prompting concerning what is expected next. It is said to be easy to learn, very powerful and flexible.

We have also to consider the question of cost of computer-assisted instruction. At present, evaluation of costs is difficult, indeed it is probably premature, as hardware manu-

[52] Atkinson, R. C. and Wilson, H. A. (ed.) *Computer-assisted Instruction: a Book of Readings*, Academic Press, New York, 1969.

[53] Atkinson and Wilson, *op. cit.*, p. 41.

[54] Drill and practice system of linear type: new concepts are introduced by the teacher conventionally, and the computer provides practice on an individualized basis according to ability. This system suits the elementary stages of mathematics, science and modern languages. Tutorial system: new concepts are presented by the system and the skill practised. Existing tutorial systems use the branching approach, according to pupil's responses, and have enough flexibility to prevent failure in the slow child and boredom in the bright. Dialogue system: student will be able to speak to computer, and will have almost complete control of the sequence of learning. At present the system exists in theory rather than in practice. A large 200-terminal computer could handle 6000 students daily. Soon computers will exist with 1000 terminals, which could handle 3000 students per day (Atkinson and Wilson, pp. 43–4).

[55] Silbermann, Harry F., Applications of computers in education, in: Atkinson and Wilson, *op. cit.*, p. 50.

facturers are only beginning the transition from development to production. However, Kopstein and Seidel[56] believe it will not be long before it will be available in America at a cost per student of 0·11 dollars per hour, that is, in American terms, at approximately the cost per student for instruction by teachers in 1959–60, for the same level of efficiency of instruction. Even if this estimate is an optimistic one, clearly the pressure to develop programmes for different subjects at different standards will become very considerable as the cost approaches an economic level compared with teachers' salaries. Two points need to be remembered in evaluating the prospects of C.A.I. Telephone-line charges are important items in costs when maintaining terminals at remote locations. The cost of the initial hardware would make it desirable that it should be in use for more hours than the length of the normal school day, so that any system would need to be linked to further education institutions to keep down costs. As far as the actual courses are concerned, as with all programming, production is very expensive. One hour's course may require as many as 200 hours' preparation, and will at present certainly require 50–100 hours, including tryouts, but once it is completed, it can be used by thousands of pupils, located anywhere.

In Britain, Professor J. Black[57] has suggested that computer-based learning can be provided at a cost which is two to four times the current cost of conventional teaching at the secondary school. In 10 years' time the relative cost will be reduced by half for large systems, but on present trends it will take 40 years to equalize costs for secondary schools. He suggests that for large systems of about 1000 type A terminals "computer-based learning is not entirely to be dismissed as an unjustifiable expense", and that it should be tried out with Newsom children who find relationships with teachers difficult, with sixth-form teaching, and in mathematics where there is a shortage of teachers. A pessimistic view?

The possible impact of computerized learning, especially of computer-aided instruction, can best be grasped if we consider what it adds to programmed learning.

Programmed learning makes it possible for pupils to proceed at their own pace, be given continuous opportunities to test themselves and immediate confirmation of results, and it frees teachers from repetitive teaching. The computer adds the following facilities: a wider variety of responses can be accepted including some degree of constructed response and multiple choice answers; a route can be chosen through well-designed programme sequences for a student according to his ability and his past history of success; access to files for updating and rewriting the programmes can be provided in a way impossible with conventional programmed texts.

Various practical points are worthy of mention since they will eventually affect decision-making by schools.

(a) C.A.I. has had most effect on the curriculum in mathematics and science. Both subjects being well defined and logically organized, they lend themselves to systems analysis and programming.

(b) Most experimentation with C.A.I. so far has been with the age groups 16 to 21,[58] but a wider use is envisaged with the further technological development of "peripherals". In this country a new town, Milton Keynes, has already been wired to accept lines direct to computerized services.

[56] In Atkinson and Wilson, *op. cit.*, p. 354.

[57] National Council for Educational Technology, *Computers for Education. Report of Working Party*, Working Paper no. 1, N.C.E.T., 1969, p. 33.

[58] Richmond, W. K., *The Concept of Educational Technology*, Weidenfeld and Nicolson, 1970, p. 166.

(c) Of relevance to the problems of all schools is the fact that eventually the computer could be used to improve the schools' resources. The explosion of knowledge is making the teacher inefficient at transferring information; therefore the ability to guide pupils to sources of information will become valuable. The computer can store a vast amount and produce it quickly and it is all the more useful because it can be employed by many operators at the same time without them interfering with one another. Computers could be located in particular areas to serve the schools in them and they could be linked to a national grid of computers. From them packaged projects containing both material and references to sources of all kinds could be obtained. How much greater would be the range of stimuli available to students in these circumstances is obvious.

(d) One of the problems of non-streaming or of teaching across a broad ability band, such as one gets in the small school, is that it bears heavily upon the teacher. When each pupil works at his own rate and experiences learning problems peculiar to himself, which often have to be dealt with by the teacher, the latter soon reaches his maximum bearable load. It seems likely that in the future the computer will come increasingly to his aid and in this regard it is worth describing a system which is already beginning to be developed, known as the Computer Based Instructional Management System (C.B.I.M.).

Initially the pupil takes a pretest and on the basis of his results is assigned either by his teacher or the computer to a specific learning task which might, for example, take a total of 2 weeks to accomplish but would be subdivided into 2-hour units. At various points during the accomplishment of the task he may take diagnostic or progress tests marked by the computer. The teacher gets a printed report after each test, from which he can deduce what points need additional attention by the pupil and additional teaching by himself. Once this work is completed the pupil goes on to the next task. This approach eases the transition from class instruction to individual learning and the available conventional textbooks and other instructional material can be used.[59] The use of the computer for marking and diagnosis reduces the burdens on the teacher.

This system sounds rather like a watered-down form of computer-aided instruction, but it appears more likely that both will develop side by side, each performing different tasks for the teacher. In both cases, however, promise far exceeds their present accomplishments.[60]

An opinion as to the capability of educational technology to resolve dilemmas in comprehensive reorganization is to be found in *Towards More Effective Learning: the Report of the National Council for Educational Technology for 1967–8*. It has particular relevance to the problems of small schools. Quite apart from the fact that the individualized learning promoted by some forms of educational technology will eventually take the heat out of the streaming/non-streaming controversy, the wealth of new teaching materials and the more flexible staff deployment they make possible makes the increasing numbers of small sixth forms and the decreasing numbers of highly qualified specialist teachers less daunting. As ways are found to help pupils learn effectively without constant resource to a human instructor we shall be able to make better use of both time and space. N.C.E.T.'s research and development committee has sponsored research into computer-based learning systems and materials packages.

Research results as to the effectiveness of computerized learning look promising. Limited experience to date of C.A.I. indicates that pupils cover the course material, skills and under-

[59] The best known of these systems is PLAN (Program for Learning in Accordance with Needs).
[60] *Review of Educational Research*, vol. 41, no. 1, Feb. 1971, pp. 53–7.

standing as well as content, faster than in ordinary classes, with better mastery and retention.[61] Of particular interest for the small school is an experiment with German.

An evaluation of an experiment contrasting German[62] taught by teachers according to a direct-oral method and German taught by computer-aided instruction, to two groups, each of which contained more than 100 students of equal linguistic aptitude, showed that the C.A.I. course was more efficient in the development of reading and writing skills, equally efficient in developing listening skills and nearly as efficient in teaching speech. Attitudes to C.A.I. were as favourable as to ordinary teaching.

This C.A.I. course used a typewriter-type keyboard for written communication between the student and the machine, a tape recorder by which the computer could present pre-recorded aural messages in any order or could permit the student to record and hear his own voice, and a projector for the projection of any one of eighty still pictures.

Whatever may be the ultimate implications of the computer, hard-headed administrators, heads of schools and teaching staffs must be mainly preoccupied with their present possibilities and prospects in the near future. At present computers are not sufficiently refined in development, of peripherals and remote access particularly, to be of much use for teaching or for the storage of learning material[63] in the near future and they are also too expensive as yet. Yet it does not do to be myopic. Twenty-one years ago there were a mere 300 16-mm projectors in schools—now there are over 40,000 and over 50,000 film strip projectors. In 1957 the tape recorder and schools television were introduced—now there are about 40,000 tape recorders and 15,000 school television receivers. The language laboratory was first introduced in 1961—now we have 1200 installations and there are, too, 12,600 teaching machines. We ought now to be making some preparations for the day of the school computer.

The most important current use of C.A.I. would, however, appear to be its use for the improvement of programmed learning courses, as they are designed, at a much faster rate than is possible by traditional methods. The computer can collect and analyse the responses by pupils to items in the course at a very fast rate. The very rapid rejection of poor items which ensues makes it possible for courses to be developed in considerably less time than formerly. The consequent benefits to schools, in the way of rapid proliferation of efficient programmes, will be immense.

To sum up the implications of the computer for education, one can see that it will increase the advantages offered by programmed learning and the two together will oblige the teacher to undertake a more careful review of his aims and the means of accomplishing them. He will thus gain a clearer understanding of his task. It will enable pupils to proceed at their own pace. It will enable subjects where there is a teacher shortage to continue to be studied and help small schools to extend their curriculum. It will also change the concept of the teacher and the school, because it shifts the onus for learning "from the classroom teacher (in the role of the man-who-knows-telling-those-who-don't) to the learner himself".[64] The school will then become a resources-for-learning centre and the teacher will become its librarian, with easy access through a computer to a vast treasure chest of knowledge of all kinds.

[61] Atkinson and Wilson, *op. cit.*, p. 29. For a somewhat less confident opinion from another contributor see p. 60.

[62] Atkinson and Wilson, *op. cit.*, pp. 204–5, 174–5.

[63] For school timetabling and for counselling data the prospects are more immediate. See p. 63 and p. 126, footnote 10.

[64] Richmond, *op. cit.*, p. 169.

In case we should be over-sanguine about the prospect before us, Hutchins[65] points out that the programmed learning plus computer approach may well lead to increased standardization and centralization; because really effective and efficient programmes are expensive to produce there will be fewer of them than there are styles of teaching amongst individual teachers. He also thinks the new approach will extend training, rote learning and the transmission of mere information, diminish the attention given to reasoning and judgement, because these aims are difficult to adapt to teaching machines, reduce discussion, because it is difficult to talk back to machinery, and dehumanize a process whose aim is humanization.[66] As this may be a danger, it would appear to be a school's task to consider how much of the curriculum should be taught by these methods and how much by face-to-face interchange, if we are not to involve children in the predicament of the young monkeys who were reared without their mothers. The problem of the pupil learning in virtual solitude in a crowd is one we should never forget.

On the other hand, the computer will give us access to a vast range of learning materials at a moment's notice. This implies that one of its greatest potentials is to make learning more personalized, since it can suit the interests of each learner better than the teacher standing in front of a whole class. As yet we do not really know how diverse we want education to be for individual students or even whether we want it to be diverse. This is a question of educational philosophy. But if we do want diversity, just as the invention of the printed book freed serious students from the over-simple methods of oral recitation and from the drudgery of copying, computers can free pupils from the drudgery of doing exactly similar things untailored to their individual needs.

C. Conclusion

The small comprehensive school's defects are curricular and academic, but they are not beyond solution. Even without the aids which new educational technologies and new "resource-based" approaches to learning can provide for the small school, there are a number of administrative and timetabling devices which can be brought to bear on its problems, as well as the use of correspondence courses and other packaged material. For a long time the large comprehensive school received but grudging help with the solution of its problems of organization and communication. They were not understood by administrators and the latter objected to the large school's proportionately increased costs with regard to paper work and communication, although research was to show that beyond a certain size economies of scale cease.[67] In the same way the problems of the small school have been insufficiently understood, or rather its problems were understood,[68] but the relatively small cost of remedying some of them was not realized, in part because of the long-standing and gen-

[65] Hutchins, R. M., *The Learning Society*, Pall Mall Press, 1968, pp. 82–3.

[66] In considering such a statement we would do well to refer back to that other period of apocalyptic change, the Renaissance, and consider the reaction to the printed book. Intelligent people at that time deplored the way in which the printed book had become a substitute for inquiry, dialogue and debate, for conversation and reflection, with passive assimilation of information taking the place of face-to-face confrontation of issues. We now no longer associate inquiry and reflection with person-to-person interchange and expect reading of a book to be accompanied by active evaluation of it.

[67] See pp. 120–1.

[68] To be fair, staffing ratios tend on the whole, though not invariably, to be better in small schools than in medium or large schools, but a more effective approach would have allowed also for some limited use of correspondence courses, for example, in fringe subjects at sixth-form and possibly fifth-form level.

eral prejudice in Britain against the use of correspondence courses. That prejudice is beginning to break down, with the development of packaged materials of all kinds. Large schools now get much more understanding and more financial help, in the way of procuring and servicing technical aids, than they did formerly. It is now time that the small school got the extra minimal assistance that it needs from correspondence courses and from programmed learning, where material is available.

To conclude, "the current method of broadening educational offerings by moving hundreds of bodies to a central spot may be both unnecessary and old-fashioned" since the school must be radically affected by current and future developments in educational technology. Moreover, Barker and Gump's research and "all other research known to us, indicates that the negative relationship between institutional size and individual participation is deeply based and difficult, if not impossible, to avoid. It may be easier to bring specialized and varied behaviour settings into the small school than to raise the level of participation in the large school."

CHAPTER 10

The Relative Advantages and Disadvantages of Different Forms of Comprehensive Reorganization

ONE of the main purposes of this book has been to gather evidence on such factors as the size of school or the provision in school for the gifted and the disadvantaged child, and to discuss at some length issues connected with the curriculum, so as to be able to evaluate the relevance of the reorganization schemes suggested by Circular 10/65 in the light of these findings and of the conclusions reached with regard to the curriculum. It is now proposed to look at other evidence bearing directly on the appropriateness of the particular schemes, to relate the two sets of findings, to try to come to some conclusions about the advantages and disadvantages of the various schemes, according to certain criteria with regard to both efficient schooling and to the objectives of comprehensive schooling, and finally to suggest the probable pattern of evolution for the future.

As a preliminary to setting out the criteria to be used as a yardstick in an evaluation of the different schemes we will first look at the objectives of comprehensive education as set out by the N.F.E.R. survey of 1968 and the Comprehensive Schools Committee survey of 1967.

The former body stated them as follows:

1. To eliminate separation in post-primary education by gathering pupils of the whole ability range in one school so that by their association pupils may benefit each other and that easy readjustments in grouping and in subjects studied may be made as pupils themselves change and develop.
2. To collect pupils representing a cross-section of society in one school, so that good academic and social standards, an integrated school society and a gradual contribution to an integrated community beyond the school may be developed out of this amalgam of varying abilities and social environments.
3. To concentrate teachers, accommodation and equipment so that pupils of all ability groups may be offered a wide variety of educational opportunity and that scarce resources may be used economically.[1]

The survey by the Comprehensive Schools Committee stipulated as well that any scheme of reorganization should have its timing and physical arrangements thoroughly and rationally worked out, that it should begin its operation with the present school generation, include

[1] Monks, T. G. (ed.), *Comprehensive Education in England and Wales. A Survey of Schools and their Organisation*, N.F.E.R., 1968, p. xi.

all publicly supported secondary schools within its area and, taking account of local conditions, should afford "the maxim umopportunity to the maximum number to stay at school for the maximum length of time and to have, equally in each school, as full and satisfactory a choice of courses as is possible under local circumstances".[2]

In the event the timing and the orderliness of the reorganization scheme have left much to be desired at the national level and some of the assumptions underlying the stated objectives have not always been spelt out at the local level. The political in-fighting and practical and economic difficulties that have accompanied reorganization locally and the comparative lack of planned research support from the centre, such as was available in Sweden, have not left much room for the careful consideration of objectives and their underlying assumptions and values, nor for the tidy setting-out of "ideal" schemes, though research is beginning to produce some tentative guidelines. Hence the "messy" nature of some reorganization schemes, hence the chaotic character of reorganization nationally. Yet careful consideration of the objectives of comprehensive education in the light of what research could tell us as to the most effective ways of implementing them is well worth while. Since we now have considerable experience of reorganization schemes, and reorganization itself seems to have lost its first momentum, it seems a suitable time for taking stock.

The objectives listed above are, as they stand, too vague to enable anyone to make rational choices, amongst the schemes set out in Circular 10/65, as to the "best" scheme nationally or in a particular local situation. For convenience, one can group the various schemes into three basic ones:[3] the all-through school (11 or 12 to 18); the tiered schemes, where there are in effect three stages in education; and the sixth-form college-type scheme, with either 11–16 schools followed by a sixth-form college or a junior college, or 11–16 schools coexisting with an 11–18 school, the latter providing the sixth form for all of them.[4]

A. Criteria of Evaluation

The more detailed criteria we need for evaluation of the various schemes might be set out in the following questions:

1. Which form of comprehensive reorganization promotes the highest staying-on rate, including amongst working-class pupils?
2. Which form of comprehensive reorganization has the highest success rate
   (a) at 'O' and C.S.E. level;
   (b) at 'A' level?
3. Which form best promotes personal development of pupils?
4. Which makes the best use of buildings?
5. Which makes for the most rational deployment of teachers?
6. Which puts the smallest organizational and administrative burdens on teachers, so that they can concentrate their energies on their teaching task?

[2] Comprehensive Schools Committee, *Comprehensive Education: Secondary Reorganization in England and Wales*, Survey No. 1, 1966–7.

[3] It is not proposed to consider in any detail "interim" schemes which involve segregation of pupils at some particular stage. They are, by definition, "interim" even if we do not know how long "interim" means.

[4] In 1968 about 40 per cent of reorganization schemes were being planned as "all through" schemes, 25 per cent as tiered schemes and 35 per cent as sixth-form schemes. (Benn, C., *Survey of Comprehensive Reorganization*, 1971, p. i). The average size of school was somewhere between 800 and 1000, the most usual size being just below 800 (Monks, 1970, p. 176). About one-third of fully developed 11–18 schools had less than 600 pupils on roll (Monks, 1968, p. 56).

7. Which form of organization produces the least staffing turnover—in these days when salary structures force teachers to move, anyway, more frequently than is good for children?
8. Which form is the most economic, without prejudice to educational efficiency?

It is proposed to take each of these questions in turn and to see what evidence there is that relates to them.

1. *Staying-on Rates*

The emphasis by the Comprehensive Schools Committee on the promotion of higher staying-on rates needs justifying. It is, of course, in line with the demands of social justice for the individual in societies which are broadly egalitarian, as western nations have become during the present century. Perhaps more urgently, higher staying-on rates would take youth off the labour market as increasingly improved technologies reduce the numbers of people who can be maintained in employment. Since employers prefer more mature workers when they can get them, the very young, and the elderly, are the first to become unemployed. Moreover, we have more to fear from social disturbance arising out of teenage unemployment than was the case a generation ago. Unemployment amongst present teenage youth is much more likely to lead to social unrest, than was teenage unemployment during the 1930s, since this generation is more spirited. There are three ways of solving unemployment problems apart from retiring the elderly: one is to get growth in the economy, another is to keep the young compulsorily at school a year longer and a third is to make whatever other arrangements one can to induce them to stay on at school. In practice, governments, now generally aware of the desirability of economic planning in a technological world and of keeping the educational system in step with the economy, are likely to try all three solutions. Britain, unfortunately, seems to have been less successful than others in Western Europe, as far as the third alternative is concerned. The second report of the Public Schools Commission (Newsom II) noted that "the most striking feature of the British system, when compared with those of other countries, is the heavy loss of pupils at the minimum leaving age". The D.E.S. still estimate that even by 1980 only 25 per cent of pupils will remain in school after 16, whereas 70–80 per cent are staying on in Sweden already. Probably the D.E.S. estimate is much too conservative, but the need to stimulate the staying-on rate in Great Britain is beyond dispute. The only other alternative, unless society can think of some better scheme, is teenage unemployment.

If reasonable social stability is a prime objective, the necessary condition of everything else, for without it the individual is as much adversely affected as society, then schemes of reorganization which really promote longer staying-on are more valuable than those which are less effective in this respect.

The survey by Benn and Simon showed the differences in holding power between the different types of comprehensive school (Table 1). The advantage is to the 14–18 school.

Data in the N.F.E.R. Survey[5] supplies confirmatory evidence as between 11–18 and 13–18 age range schools. The proportions leaving school in these two types of school are shown in Table 2.

A higher proportion also left from the 13–18 school to go on to further education to

[5] Monks (ed.), *op. cit.*, 1968, table VII: School Leavers 1964–5, p. 38.

TABLE 1
Staying-on Rates, 'O' and 'A' Levels

Age range[a] of school	No. of schools	Average size of school	Percentage of average intake in top 20% of ability	Percentage of pupils staying on beyond statutory leaving age	Average no. of 'O' level subject groups offered by school	Average no. of 'A' level subject groups offered
11 (or 12)–18	389	950	14	55	14	7
11 (or 12)–18 Type II*	31	1081	25	62	15	9
11 (or 12)–16	154	586	13	37	7	—
13–18	34	538	25	63	14	8
14–18[b]	16	587	17	76	15	9

[a] Benn, C. and Simon, B., *Half Way There*, McGraw-Hill, 1970, Abstract from Table 5.2, p. 72.
[b] N.B. The 14–18 schools also allow the largest proportion of pupils to enter the sixth form without 'A' levels (*ibid*., p. 189).
* Schools which allow entry into the sixth form from other schools.

TABLE 2
Staying-on Rates

School year	Percentage leaving 11–18	Percentage leaving 13–18
4	46·4	26·2
5	57·6	51·0
6	45·4	29·7
7 and 8	86·1	88·8

follow 'A' level courses, probably under the influence of a long-standing grammar school tradition, which may not survive.

The highest staying-on rate is to be found in the 14–18 school. The small numbers of schools involved in the 14–18 school sample must reduce the degree of confidence one can place in their results, but the difference in staying-on rates between this and other types of comprehensive school is too great to ignore.

How great the difference is in holding power can be seen especially if one compares this school with either the 11–18 or the 11–16 schools. Both of these types of school approach the 14–18 school in the intellectual calibre of their intake, 14 and 13 per cent respectively by comparison with 17 per cent of their pupils being in the top 20 per cent of the ability range. Yet their staying-on rates are only 55 and 37 per cent by comparison with 76 per cent. One must, however, allow for the fact that many of the 11–16 and 11–18 schools are either former secondary modern schools or are on council housing estates, whereas the 13/14–18 schools are usually former grammar schools with a long tradition of staying on. The staying-on rates of 11–16 and 11–18 schools will therefore be adversely affected by the social-class factor and by too low expectations on the part of teachers. Even so, one would not expect a discrepancy of this magnitude in the percentages of pupils staying on.

If one compares the 14–18 school with the 13–18 school one finds that the former has a higher percentage of its pupils staying on, though it has a lower percentage in the top ability range. The 13–18 schools have so far tended to be schools where some selection has already taken place, through the operation of "guided" choice schemes,[6] and where one ought therefore to expect the survivors to have high incentives or aspirations to stay on.

On a superficial view one would expect the 14–18 school, likely to appear to its early leavers and even its 'O' level pupils as only a very temporary resting place, to lose more of its pupils early than the other types. Yet in fact evidence so far suggests that it holds its pupils. Why? The curricular structure of the English comprehensive system would seem likely to be responsible for its holding-power. At 14, the general curriculum ends and the options groups begin. At this point it is imperative, in the 14–18 school as in no other, that the staff of the upper school collaborate with the staff of the lower school. Only through the latter can they set out their wares, publicize the various courses and choices available to the pupils at the upper school, arrange course and subject-choice conferences and individual interviews with parents and children. The whole timetabling operation for the upper school depends on a vast public relations and communications exercise with the lower school. If the staff and pupils of the lower school do not understand what is on offer there will be so much muddle in the upper school in the following September that its staff have every incentive to make the effort to communicate. If they, in their turn, are not to be blamed for a muddle, the staff of the lower school have every incentive to respond. School pride and prestige on both sides are involved, in a way that they are not inside one school, whether of the 13–18 or the 11–18 variety. The vast communications exercise is more likely to make every pupil and parent aware of all the opportunities available to those who stay on than in the case of an internal exercise. At the same time the 14–18 school has only 2 years in which to prepare pupils for public examinations and liaison at the level of department and syllabus is even more necessary than it is internally or externally, for example, in the case of the 13–18 school. In no other type of comprehensive system would there seem to be so much incentive for liaison between the staff of upper and lower schools. This hypothesis would help to account for the apparently considerable difference in the holding power of the 13–18 and the 14–18 schools. It needs testing by research.

Another factor which appears to affect the staying-on rate is the method of grouping pupils adopted by schools. Benn and Simon analyse the schools in their survey into eight different groups according to whether they are streamed, setted, both streamed and setted or in varying measure unstreamed. Their results show a definite trend for more pupils to stay on in unstreamed schools. (Table 3.) Similar evidence is available from Denmark.[7]

In Table 3 mixed ability group (iii) is something of a maverick in that the group has by far the highest percentage of pupils in the top 20 per cent of the ability range. That this 27 per cent should markedly affect the percentage of pupils staying on is more than likely and the relatively small numbers of schools involved may possibly affect the reliability of the results. If we leave this group on one side, it is still clear that non-streaming in the first year

[6] Benn and Simon, *op. cit.*, pp. 110–11.

[7] Torpe, H., *Control and Estimation of Experiments with the Undivided 9-year School at Frederiksborg Educational System*, Paedagogiske Streiftog, Copenhagen, 1960.

TABLE 3

Method of Grouping, Staying-on Rates and Percentages in Top 20 per cent of Ability Range

Method of grouping[8]	Percentage in top 20 per cent of ability range	Average per cent staying-on beyond school-leaving age in 1968 in schools with 13–16 age range	Total number of schools
1. In streams	13	43	130
2. In broad ability bands	16	52	210
3. In sets	14	52	36
4. Combination of streams and sets	14	50	96
5. Mixed ability (i) (two subjects setted)	16	55	42
6. Mixed ability (ii) (remedial pupils separated)	14	55	80
7. Mixed ability (iii) (for all subjects and pupils)	27	63	29
8. Other method	14	51	43

of the secondary course tends to increase the staying-on rate at the end of the course, not markedly, but to an extent we should not ignore. Moreover, the acceptance of a common curriculum[9] appears to make it easier for teachers to consider unstreaming.

There is one research finding as regards staying-on rates which tells against the sixth-form college type of reorganization scheme. Eggleston has established that, when the decision to continue at school also requires a decision to transfer to another school then there is an unnecessarily large fall-out.[10] Similar evidence is available from the Continent. This is precisely the situation of children in 11–16 schools after the raising of the leaving age.

Whether a school operates on one site or two appears not to affect staying-on rates significantly. Benn and Simon[11] showed that the average percentage staying on beyond the leaving age of 15 in one- and two-site schools was the same. The average size of sixth form was somewhat higher in the two-site schools, although the average percentage of the intake pupils who were in the top 20 per cent of the ability range was the same in both types of schools. No data was given on the size of the schools but it seems probable that the two-site schools would on average be bigger than the one-site schools, so that this second result is probably of no significance in respect of differences in staying-on rate at sixth-form level between one- and two-site schools.

As between large "all-through" schools and small "all-through" schools there appears probably to be no significant difference in staying-on rates.[12]

With regard to staying-on rates amongst working-class children the Advisory Centre for Education found that "guided-choice" schemes could operate to discourage them from staying on even more than selection at 11+. The same was true for the less able. Increased staying-on rates of pupils generally, however, have been experienced, for example, in the "guided-choice" Louth Plan. They have occurred mainly in the junior high schools and

[8] Benn and Simon, *op. cit.*, table 9.3, p. 152.
[9] *Ibid.*, p. 153.
[10] Eggleston, J. F., Environment and comprehensives, *Education*, no. 127, 28 Jan. 1966, p. 195.
[11] *Op. cit.*, p. 91.
[12] See p. 119.

relatively little in the grammar (upper) school. One cannot say whether the rate would have been higher or lower if everyone had been transferred to the upper school.

These findings suggest, though they do not conclusively prove, that, if we gave national priority to high staying-on rates, we would plump for tiered reorganization schemes, with an unstreamed junior high school and a senior high school, with free-choice entry, covering the years 14–18. They also suggest that at present the sixth-form college-type scheme fulfils this objective least well.

2. *Success Rates in Different Types of Comprehensive School*

Evidence with regard to attainment levels in different types of comprehensive school, though not plentiful, has been gathered during the survey conducted by the N.F.E.R., a body better placed than any individual to collect such material. It suggests that there is no significant difference in attainment levels between two types of comprehensive school systems. The average test scores are to be found in Table 4.

TABLE 4

Attainment Levels in Different Types of Comprehensive School[13]

	First Year		Fourth Year		Sixth Year	
	Mean	No. of schools	Mean	No. of schools	Mean	No. of schools
Junior high schools	74·0	7	85·3	6	—	—
Senior high schools	—	—	101·6	3	52·7	3
11–18 schools	73·8	38	98·0	37	51·8	40
All schools	73·9	45	96·6	46	51·9	43
	$t < 1$		$F = 5{\cdot}00$			
	N.S.		$p < 0{\cdot}05$			

At the first-year level there is no statistically significant difference, at the fourth year there is, but it is probably due to the residue of pupils staying on in the junior high school in some tiered schemes and not transferring. The difference at sixth-form level is so small and the number of senior high schools so small, that it was not worth while to calculate the statistical difference. Yet 11–18 schools tend to get a lower percentage of able pupils than other types of school, somewhat less so according to Benn and Simon,[14] markedly less so according to Monks.[15] This suggests that 11–18 schools have a higher success rate, with level of pupils' ability held constant, than do junior high–senior high systems. Staffing ratios probably worked out at about the same for each group of schools, since 11–13/14/15/16 schools had staffing ratios averaging 19:8, 13/14–18 schools 17:4 and 11–18 schools 18:1, with the average for the whole groups 18:2.[16] Hence this result could not be due to more favourable staffing ratios in the 11–18 schools. It might very well be due to the break at 13 or 14 and the imperfect liaison between the junior and senior high schools reported else-

[13] Monks, T. G. (ed.), *Comprehensive Education in Action*, N.F.E.R., 1970, table 4.7, pp. 108–9.
[14] *Op. cit.*, p. 72.
[15] Monks, *op. cit.*, 1968, p. 227.
[16] *Ibid.*, p. 150.

where.[17] However, we cannot state categorically that there is a real difference in the success rates of 11–18 schools and of the junior high–senior high type of arrangements because of the very small number of the latter which took part in the N.F.E.R. attainment survey. All that we have is a clue.

Is it better from the point of view of academic results to have a split-site school for pupils of 11–18 or a tiered arrangement? This is often the only choice open to a local authority. As far as the writer is aware, there is no direct evidence on this point. There is, however, some indirect evidence. Benn and Simon show that schools on two sites,[18] with the same average percentage intake of the top 20 per cent of ability as schools on one site, have the same staying-on rate beyond the leaving age, a rather bigger sixth form (no doubt because split-site schools tend to be bigger on average than single-site schools) and a slightly larger number of 'O' and 'A' level subjects (probably for the same reason), in other words the split-site school is not disadvantaged in these respects. If it is also true that academic results of all-through schools are, if anything, slightly better than those for tiered arrangements,[19] one could perhaps opt tentatively for split-site schools rather than for junior high–senior high or middle school schemes. However, the evidence is somewhat tenuous and certainly not strong enough to base a decision on, especially in situations where there might be other local contraindicative factors.

The results obtained by Lynn[20] with regard to academic results in large and small sixth forms of large and small grammar schools might well be used to justify the development of sixth form colleges in an area where the size of existing urban 11–18 schools does not permit the development of large sixth forms. At the same time it should be remembered that the size of sixth forms is increasing year by year and that the raising of the school-leaving age is likely to result in further expansion, which would produce sixth forms of the requisite size in smaller schools than formerly. Arguments as to any consequent overall reduction in intellectual calibre and therefore as to the numbers capable of truly academic work in these enlarged sixth forms need to be treated with great caution. There is data in many places on the numbers of pupils still not going on to the sixth form, who could certainly do 'A' level work, in view of their measured ability in terms of IQ, and who are more likely to be tempted to stay on after the school leaving age is raised.[21]

With regard to academic results in different types of comprehensive schools we must therefore conclude that there is no strong evidence that any type is superior.

An advantage specific to the middle school,[22] which might eventually affect success rates, is that it enables young children to stay on longer in their first school and so get a better grounding in basic skills such as reading, and that it allows the changes in content and method visible in the junior school to work their way further up the age range. It also prevents the downward pressure of public examinations and enables the 11-year-old children to go to a school whose size they can cope with, mentally and emotionally. It is not yet clear what the eventual results of this will be.

One of the middle school's great disadvantages is that neither the D.E.S. nor such a local

[17] See pp. 185–6.
[18] Benn and Simon, *op. cit.*, p. 91.
[19] See p. 180.
[20] See p. 118.
[21] See Halsey, A. H. (ed.), *Ability and Educational Opportunity*, O.E.C.D. Paris, 1961, pp. 103, 125–6, 167–75, and Crowther Report.
[22] Existing or pending in sixty-three authorities by July 1970. (*Towards the Middle School*, H.M.S.O., 1970, pp. 30–1.)

authority as the West Riding[23] which favours the middle school seem to have much idea as to how it will develop. Both tend to suggest the trying of various approaches, thus throwing the main onus on the teachers. At present the approach used tends to depend on whether a particular school was previously a primary school, in which case a flexible primary approach tends to be used, or a secondary school, in which case the approach is more specialized and more rigid. Until the middle school acquires its own personality and its own specific approach it is difficult to speculate on what its eventual success rates will be or indeed what effect it will specifically have on the personal development of children.

3. *Personal Development of Pupils*

With regard to personal development of pupils it is clear from Barker and Gump's research[24] and from research in other fields producing similar results that the smaller the school, the greater the participation, the greater the satisfaction and the greater the opportunities to develop leadership. Hence, tiered schools, which tend to be smaller than "all-through" schools, would have the edge on these points. In Benn and Simon's survey they tended to be about half the size:[25]

11 (or 12)–18 Type I	970
11 (or 12)–18 Type II	1137
11 (or 12)–16	587
11–13	341
11–14/15	503
13–18	538
14–18	587
16–18 or Sixth form College	582

Not dissimilar figures are found in the second N.F.E.R. report, with "all-through" schools averaging 943 pupils, junior high schools 475, and senior high 600.[26] Small "all-through" schools would have the same advantage as tiered schools.

4. *Reorganization Schemes and the Best Age for Transfer*

An issue which affects decisions as to what type of comprehensive school shall be chosen is that of the optimum age for transfer.

The age of 11 has been the age of transfer in state schools since the beginning of the century and for many years it went unquestioned. Yet, originally, the choice of 11 was purely a matter of practical convenience.[27] In the closing years of the last century the leaving age was 12 for those pupils intelligent enough to pass the Standard VII exam. at that age. Hence these pupils' last chance to sit the grammar school entrance examination occurred at the age of 11. In addition, the 1904 Regulations stipulated that the secondary school course was to be of a minimum of 4 years. If the transfer was delayed till the age of 12 the grammar school course could not terminate till 16. This increased the likelihood of larger percentages of poor scholarship pupils leaving before completing the course. Already 20 per cent did leave early. Hence the age of 11 was chosen as the age for transfer. Later the choice was

[23] West Riding County Council Education Committee, *Middle Schools*, 1968, pp. 3–4.
[24] See pp. 84–5, and 90–5.
[25] Abstracted from their table A.1, p. 372.
[26] Monks, T. G. (ed.), 1970, p. 193.
[27] Lawton, D., A hundred years of curriculum change, *Trends in Education*, Feb. 1970, pp. 18–26. Lowndes, C. A. N., *The Silent Social Revolution*, 2nd ed., Oxford Univ. Press, 1969, p. 297.

rationalized by the Hadow and subsequent reports as the best age for transfer from the point of view of psychological development of pupils.

There is little evidence from the psychological field to justify the choice of 11, or, for that matter, of any other age. It is true that the shift from the Piagetian phase of concrete operations to that of formal operations occurs in many pupils at around 12 or 13, but there is such variability in the age at which this happens, because of the variability in intelligence, that it is not a particularly sound basis for deciding the age of transfer. A report by Nisbet and Entwistle[28] concludes that individual differences in the rates of children's physical, social and emotional growth, as well as intellectual, make it impossible to choose any one year as the correct age for transfer. From this point of view therefore all the types of comprehensive reorganization listed by the D.E.S. are equally acceptable.

Other research by the same workers,[29] however, showed that children from poorer homes, and younger children, experience great difficulty in adjusting to change and those who have moved twice are at a disadvantage compared with those who have moved once. This result would tell against those forms of comprehensive reorganization which involve children in the greatest number of moves, and the earliest moves, during their school life.

Another factor which has relevance to the age of transfer is the point in the comprehensive school curriculum at which the general curriculum ceases and the choice of subjects in different options begins. Traditionally—and one can already speak of tradition in respect of the comprehensive school[30]—this has occurred at the end of the third year. The reason why this particular point was chosen was connected with the age of leaving just as earlier the choice of the age for transfer had been. Practical experience in the early comprehensive schools of the need for somewhat different curricula, syllabuses and teaching methods for stayers and leavers, the fear that without separation of the two, comprehensive schools would get poorer academic results than the grammar schools—since leavers in a particular class would work less hard than the stayers and so impede the class's work—and some justified fear in schools in poor socio-economic areas of the leavers unsettling the stayers and so inclining them to become leavers, were all factors which impelled many early comprehensive schools to separate leavers and stayers. Even for those leavers who would be staying till the end of the academic year and who could therefore be entered for certain available public or local examinations, if it was so desired, it was often a matter of practical politics to hive them off for part of the time, because of major differences of syllabus in some subjects between the different examining bodies. Hence the comprehensive school curriculum, which tended to be more general, and indeed more universal in range, in the first 3 years, than the grammar school curriculum, developed a series of options in the fourth year which sometimes gave pupils a rather more limited curriculum[31] from the fourth year onwards than was true of the fourth-year curriculum of the grammar school. In the latter, dropping of subjects, though it occurred any time from the third year onwards, mainly took place at the beginning of the fifth year.

Now the leaving age has been raised, the conditions which promoted the setting-up of

[28] Nisbet, J. D. and Entwistle, N. J., *The Age of Transfer to Secondary Education*, Univ. of London Press, 1966, p. 89.
[29] Nisbet, J. D. and Entwistle, N. J., *The Transition to Secondary Education*, Scottish Council for Research in Education, Univ. of London Press, 1969, p. 81.
[30] Monks (ed.), 1970, p. 74.
[31] However, there were ways of getting round this for specially able pupils. See Cole, Roger, *Comprehensive Schools in Action*, Longbourne, 1964, p. 123.

options groups in the fourth year no longer apply. It therefore behoves us to re-examine the layout of the fourth-year curriculum and to decide whether it needs changing. We should not be satisfied to let things go on as they are without questioning their rationale, as was done for many years with the age of transfer. Would a delay of the options groups to the fifth year prove a better policy?

One advantage would certainly be that pupils would have a year longer of a more general education. In principle this would appear to be very desirable. In practice, it is difficult to be sure beforehand whether some pupils can continue for another year with subjects they do not much care for, though it should be remembered that at 14–15 interests are still notoriously unstable,[32] often depend on whether a popular teacher takes the subject in question and may very well change with increasing maturity and increasing knowledge of the subject. Hence in principle one would like to continue with another year of general education. Practical politics also suggests that this might be a wise policy in the general context of educational developments. There is evidence to show that the raising of the school-leaving age has tended in the past to delay the onset of specialization.[33] It may well do so again.

Another advantage would be that it would be somewhat more economic in staffing and housing. The options groups draw rather heavily on staff time, since they provide a great variety of choices. Delay of specialization would also make easier the use of existing buildings, without alteration, for the housing of options groups. The latter tend to require a large number of small division rooms, except in the case of subjects for which there are many takers. They are therefore less economic from the point of view of available spaces than is the case with the compulsory subjects of the fourth and fifth year or with the general curriculum of the first three years. Of course, it is true that, apart from the existing options groups in the fourth year, there have always been options groups in the fifth year also. The raising of the leaving age will certainly make the fifth-year subjects in which there are at present few takers more economic to staff and to house, since there will be more pupils available to opt for them and the resultant classes will be larger. At the same time it will necessitate the introduction of new subjects or integrated study courses for which there may, again, be relatively few takers. Such subjects will require more division rooms; in fact, in total, if the fourth-year curriculum still continues to be arranged partly in options groups, there may be a need for more rooms than a school has. It will then either have to teach some of its pupils in cloakrooms and on landings, badger its local authority to divide large classrooms into two, or increase the generality of the fourth-year curriculum, concentrating the options groups in the fifth year, and so reduce the number of rooms needed. It is very difficult indeed to predict what will eventually happen. For what the opinion of the writer is worth, bearing in mind the prospect of the unification of the public examination system at the fifth-year level, and also remembering what is known about the stability of pupils' interests in the early teens and the age of emergence of particular aptitudes,[34] it it seems not unlikely that, over time, the age of choice of subject options will be delayed till the beginning of the fifth year.

What has all this to do with the age of transfer? In some circumstances it has a good deal.

[32] See pp. 52–3.
[33] *World Survey of Education*. Vol. III: *Secondary Education*, Unesco, 1961. Introduction by Parkijn, G. W., p. 131.
[34] See pp. 50–2.

The tiered arrangement of comprehensive schooling may encounter difficulties according to the age of choice of subject options. With the present practice of choosing options in the fourth year of the secondary course, tiered arrangements which transfer pupils at 13, i.e. at the end of the second year of the secondary course, may severely handicap them,[35] especially the less able pupils. They are taught by a particular group of teachers for one year in the upper school and then their choice of subject options at the end of the year will oblige them in a number of subjects to change teachers. Two changes of teachers, as well as one change of school, in so short a time, is good for no one and especially not for the less able,[36] who thrive on stability. This is, in all probability, a much greater handicap than transferring at 14 and remaining steadily with the same group of teachers for 2 years before the taking of a public examination. Such quandaries as pupils may face, with transfer at 14, because of uncertainties as to the right subject choices in the upper school, are easier to get over, if there is energetic action and collaboration between the staff of the two schools with regard to careers, conferences and subject choice meetings, than are the difficulties arising from two changes of teacher in so short a time.

If, however, over time the choice of subject options is delayed to the fifth year, it is the tiered schemes which transfer at 14 which will handicap pupils. The 13-year-old transfers will have had 2 years' stable teaching before choice of options obliges them to change teachers in some subjects.

The ambiguity which surrounds future policies on age of subject choice and its effects on pupils transferred at 13 or 14 would therefore justify a belief that tiered schemes have serious disadvantages.

5. *Problems of Liaison*

As junior high and senior high school systems have been set up, reports have circulated of many difficulties arising from the need to coordinate courses and syllabuses between schools. Benn and Simon's survey,[37] for example, showed that this was the main cause of complaint against such systems. In Leicestershire from the earliest days of reorganization efforts were made to deal with this problem[38] by having joint annual meetings of staff, as well as meetings of subject specialists. The intractability of the problem is indicated by the more recent setting up of a working party whose aim is to find ways of improving contacts between schools and to study the feasibility of exchanging teachers for certain periods.[39]

Elsewhere it has been found that after frequent meetings, both formal and informal, between heads of departments, a broad working agreement on syllabuses might be reached, but this was no guarantee that anything would result from it.[40] Moreover, organization inside a school, for example the method of grouping pupils, and individual teachers' teaching methods can rarely, if ever, be discussed, yet they too affect the pupil on his transfer from one school to another.

[35] This may be one reason for their poorer staying-on rate reported by Benn and Simon.

[36] See p. 183.

[37] Benn and Simon, *op. cit.*, p. 110.

[38] Lycett, P. M. in Halsall, Elizabeth, *Becoming Comprehensive: Case Histories*, Pergamon Press, 1970, p. 143.

[39] Harris, C. in Mason, S. C. (ed.), *In Our Experience. Education Today*, Longmans, 1970, p. 120.

[40] Benn and Simon indicate that even this degree of planning does not take place in some areas and contrast the situation unfavourably by comparison with the amalgamation of schools on two sites, where planning was often very careful. Yet physically the "tiered" individual schools might be just as close and would take the same age ranges as the amalgamated individual schools (p. 63).

Elsewhere, again, the problems of transfer have been identified as a lack of a common curriculum policy, and variation in teaching method and in structuring the timetable. These problems are compounded where pupils transfer from a great many schools.

Transfer at 14, and perhaps even at 13, puts pressure on the upper school with regard to examination work, since in certain subjects skill is the result of development and practice over a number of years. The upper school either tries to put pressure on the lower school and succeeds, so that curriculum, syllabus and even teaching methods are brought into line, at the cost of much resentment; or, more frequently, it fails. In the latter case, teachers in the upper school grapple with difficulties arising because different junior high schools have different syllabuses in the same subjects and sometimes do not study the same curriculum, for example, the same second language. With only 2, or at the most 3 years to public examinations, teachers in sequential subjects particularly have an unenviable task, if one of their feeder schools is performing at a level below an acceptable minimum.

Nor does the U.S.A., with half a century of experience of the junior high school, appear to have found an acceptable *modus vivendi* with regard to liaison. A relevant report from America shows that discontinuity of curriculum content is one of the chief problems in the transition from junior high to senior high school. One school used as many as twelve liaison committees in as many subject fields.[41] One would imagine that, after 50 years of experience, if it had been possible to iron out the difficulties of articulating courses and syllabuses as between one school and another, a way would have now been found. Moreover, in the U.S.A. the headmaster and teachers have much less autonomy than is the case in England, for the district superintendent or his advisers usually decide the curriculum and syllabuses of all schools. If America has not been able to solve this problem in these favourable circumstances, it seems very unlikely that, in a country where professional autonomy is considerable and no chief education officer or local organizer would feel able to decide any aspect of a school's internal policy, success in liaison will be achieved.

Whether or not the autonomy of the individual school will ever be eroded in the British system is a matter for conjecture, though there are signs that perhaps it should be, at least to some extent;[42] if it is not, the tiered system must encounter serious difficulties. One would expect them to be of such a kind as to affect academic results. Research on the subject of whether they have done so is lacking, though one may note the very tentative indirect evidence that has already been quoted.

6. "*Guided-choice*" *Schemes*

There is already beginning to be some evidence that "guided-choice" schemes are being used as a way of maintaining an academic grammar-type upper school,[43] with selection at 13 or 14, instead of at 11. In such cases, the increase in staying-on rates occurs not in the upper school but in the lower, as courses are put on for the unsatisfied customers left behind there. Thus at Louth about half the yearly intake are now staying on in the lower school to take C.S.E. courses. Cardiff's experience is somewhat similar. From all the evidence on the

[41] Michael, L. S., Articulation problems with lower school and higher education, *Bulletin of the National Association of Secondary School Principals*, vol. 43, Feb. 1959, p. 51–5.

[42] As workers move more and their children have to adjust to changes in curriculum arising from school autonomy.

[43] See R. E. Presswood's description of the Cardiff scheme in Maclure, S. (ed.), *Comprehensive Planning*. Councils and Education Press, 1965, p. 26, Benn and Simon, *op. cit.*, p. 111, and Whalley, G. E., hinder parenta choice. *Trends in Education*, no. 18, April 1970, pp. 28–34.

relationship between measures of intelligence and social class, one would expect a social bias in the intake into the upper school. One would also expect greater inaccuracies in selection than in the 11+ because suitable standardized tests are not so readily available for the 13+ group.

Moreover, "guided-choice" schemes do not have the advantage of "parental-choice" schemes, such as the Leicestershire Plan, that of gradually accustoming academic staff to adapt their teaching methods to suit less able children. When the decision as to transfer is left to parents and pupils, one can expect a gradual rise in the numbers electing to stay on, and therefore an easier readjustment over a longer period for grammar school staff. Hence, when "guided-choice" schemes become fully comprehensive, as they will eventually, such staff will be suddenly faced with the problem of the less able child. Though this, inevitably, is what has happened to most academic staff involved in reorganization, one can see the point of a scheme which eases them in gently in the way that the Leicestershire Plan has done. That must be counted as one of the notable advantages of the "parental-choice" scheme. One of its disadvantages, administratively, is that, as increasing numbers of pupils opt to transfer to the upper school, the number and types of courses that can be put on for those left behind must diminish. When the transfer rate approaches 70 to 80 per cent there is not much alternative to transferring everyone.[44] Another disadvantage is that those left behind, though not necessarily the least intelligent, are likely to be the least motivated and to provide the younger pupils with less suitable models with which to identify.

7. *Deployment of Teachers and Reorganization*

(a) *Scarce personnel.* Though there are other issues connected with the efficient deployment of teachers, the issue which has been mainly debated in connection with reorganization schemes has been the effective use of scarce personnel, especially the use of graduates in mathematics and science. It has been particularly debated in relation to size and type of comprehensive school.

Egner,[45] for example, calculated that if "all-through" comprehensives were instituted everywhere and their size averaged out at 833 pupils, there would be 3382 such schools in the country. For each of these schools there would be available 2 graduate modern language teachers, $1\frac{1}{2}$ historians, $1\frac{1}{2}$ English teachers, $\frac{2}{3}$ of a mathematician, $\frac{1}{3}$ of a physicist and $\frac{1}{4}$ of a chemist. Figures for East Sussex and Renfrewshire bear out these views.[46]

Taylor[47] in his study of the situation in science demonstrated the decline in the numbers of pupils taking 'A' levels in this group of subjects:

	1963	1964	1965	1966
Pupils taking only science	53,700	58,480	60,200	58,200
Pupils taking no science at all	58,200	70,000	78,300	81,500

[44] Thus in the Oadby/Wigston and Burstall areas of Leicestershire the switch to total transfer took place when the transfer rate had reached 71 and 72 per cent respectively. N.B. 13–18 schools are usually still highly selective, unlike 14–18 schools. They are usually smaller (Benn and Simon, p. 111).

[45] Egner, W. E., Sixth form dilemma, *Education*, no. 132, 1 Nov. 1968, p. 523.

[46] Taylor, L. C., *Resources for Learning*, Penguin Education Specials, 1971, p. 43.

[47] Taylor, G., School science crisis, *New Society*, 23 Feb. 1967, pp. 273–4.

and he has related it to the decreasing proportion of good science graduates entering teaching:

	1960	1961	1962	1963	1964	1965
Entering higher education and research	2410	2480	2540	2870	3350	3850
Entering teaching	1560	1500	1730	1830	1950	1750

The scarcity of well-qualified teachers in certain fields has therefore led a number of authorities to opt for systems in which 11–16 schools are combined with a sixth-form college, or for some variant of that scheme, with non-graduates concentrating on work up to 'O' level in the 11–16 school, and graduates working in the sixth-form college. How far the latter can use its teachers efficiently has been a matter of some dispute.[48] It has been argued that in some subjects there will not be enough work to fill a teacher's timetable, in a course which takes only 2 years or at most 3. Egner[49] even claimed that, for efficient use of the time of all teachers and for an effective response to the curricular demands of pupils, as evidenced by national figures on choices of subjects in the sixth form, a sixth-form college would need to have about 1000 students. No college of this size has been built, 500 being the figure aimed at in most plans, and only experience over several years in a number of sixth-form colleges, experience so far lacking on the whole, can show how flexibly they can deploy teachers. The general trend over time towards the "open" sixth-form college, where 'O' level, C.S.E. and other examinations can be taken, should in itself help to ensure the more effective deployment of teachers, since more varied demands on their time, within their own specialism, makes it more possible to fill up their timetables. A statutory 3-year course in the sixth would, however, do this more effectively still, as well as having the advantage of transforming the college from a transit camp between school and university into an institution with which the teenager would have time to identify himself. It would also help to ensure that the college did not become too large. Instead of having to draft in another group of students, who might mostly stay 2 years, so as to fill up a teacher's timetable, extending the course by 1 year would fill up a timetable but would increase the size of the college by only one-half, instead of doubling it. Moreover, there are many arguments in favour of extending the sixth-form course by one year, as entries to higher education, and their accompanying expense, increase. We shall consider this point later.

To return, however, to the debate on the relative scarcity of well-qualified graduates in a comprehensive system, economic recession has now ensued and will temporarily ease the problem, since it releases graduates from industry and turns newly qualified graduates towards a career in education. Some, perhaps many, of these will constitute a permanent gain to the supply of graduate teachers. If the current setbacks in industry prove only temporary, however, the old situation of shortage will re-establish itself, unless radical measures are pursued. Hence we would have the choice of employing non-graduates in the sixth form or of conserving scarce talent by opting for the sixth-form college. In view of the likelihood that schemes for 11–16 schools plus a sixth form college will depress staying-on rates and in view of the timetabling problems already mentioned, we must at least look at the possibility of employing non-graduates in the sixth forms of other reorganization schemes.

Whereas in the 1950s it would have been practically unthinkable for non-graduates to

[48] Corbett, A., Sixth form college, *Comprehensive Education*, No. 11, Spring 1969, p. 23.
[49] Egner, W. E., Sixth form dilemma, *Education*, no. 132, 1 Nov. 1968, p. 523.

teach 'A' level courses, with the possible exception of domestic science, the 1960s have seen an increasing number of them do so. Yet for a long time it was not even thought possible that they could teach 'O' level courses. At 'O' level, however, three out of four pupils are now taught by non-graduates in secondary modern schools, one in five in grammar schools. As far as secondary modern school sixth forms are concerned, 55 per cent of the teaching of 'A' levels is done by non-graduates, only 3·1 per cent in grammar schools, and in comprehensive schools 18·6 per cent. There is a growing acceptance of non-graduates as 'A' level teachers, especially in mathematics and science.

However, it is a long way from stating what is happening to agreeing that it is desirable and, though few will now object to non-graduate teaching at 'O' level, many would at 'A' level. It is worth while therefore to consider certain developments within the non-graduate teaching force. Two-thirds of college of education entrants now have one to four 'A' levels and nearly all follow a 3-year course that contains one or two main subjects going beyond 'A' level. In 1969 the output of teachers holding the B.Ed. was 1400. Furthermore, in-service training is increasingly being aimed at retraining the non-graduate for work in the comprehensive school, including at sixth-form level. Bristol Institute of Education has run courses, for example, in technical and engineering drawing.

Moreover, the motivation for non-graduates to work for a degree has increased as a result of the reorganization of secondary education. For a while, having greater experience than graduates with the more difficult children, they were better qualified than graduates for house masterships or heads of year posts. Now, increasingly, graduates are acquiring this experience, and the additional qualification of a degree is beginning to tell in the race for promotion. It is therefore not surprising that an N.F.E.R. inquiry showed that 80,000 teachers wished to take a degree and that the Open University started out with 25,000 students, mainly teachers. The ability of many of them to take a degree can hardly be questioned, if one considers the small proportion of grammar school pupils in the 1950s or earlier going on to university, or the evidence of the Crowther Report on the proportions of people in the population capable of taking 'A' levels, and so of going on to university, who had not done so. It seems likely that a national conversion process similar to that taking place in Sweden will gradually develop and that we shall end, as the United States has done, with a graduate profession.

How far this will help studies in mathematics and science is not clear. When one remembers the lower standards required by universities for science subjects, which have the effect of channelling science students away from training colleges, the evidence on 'A' levels quoted from Taylor suggests that teachers trained in the 1960s will be mainly qualified in arts subjects and this is borne out by the figures available.[50] The likelihood of their switching to science is minimal, since they will have dropped science as soon as they entered the sixth form, and the gap to bridge is therefore greater than it would be in continental countries. Because studies in the sixth form are so specialized, the standard reached in a given subject is high and requires highly specialized teachers. Because mathematics and science are now being taught by less able teachers than is the case in arts subjects, because these subjects are also looked upon as "hard" rather than "soft" options, perhaps also because of other reasons, these subjects are dropped by more people than are arts subjects. Because mathematicians and scientists have been relatively scarce and are needed in industry, the gap between the salaries they get in industry and those available in education ensures that

[50] See pp. 187–8.

the best qualified do not mainly go into teaching, and are not therefore available for the sixth-form studies which require very advanced teaching. We have here a vicious circle. The strenuous efforts of the last decade to break it by reforming the sixth-form curriculum and making it more general, have met with little or no success, beyond the universal acknowledgement that something must be done. It has proved singularly difficult to reconcile the various interests involved, and it looks as if, with such entrenched positions being held, the situation will have to advance beyond crisis point to the point of catastrophe, before all those concerned will come to an agreement. Until they do so, the 11–16 school plus sixth-form college scheme may well prove, not the ideal solution, since it will depress staying-on rates and so increase unemployment, but rather the only way out. Over-specialization in the sixth form, going back over many years, will therefore have promoted the sixth form college solution, and promoted it at the very point where, with entry into the Common Market, realignment of national institutions, to fit into continental patterns where necessary, is beginning to take place. Today, other Common Market countries have not had to make readjustments in their educational systems. But the pattern of studies for pupils of 16+ is so different here from what it is elsewhere that readjustment seems inevitable, once the movement to make national degrees, diplomas and certificates internationally equivalent gets under way. We could have saved ourselves a lot of trouble, in reorganization schemes now as well as in readjustment to continental requirements later, if we had reformed our sixth-form curriculum in the sixties and made it more general. Until we do so we cannot make it easy for students to switch to mathematics and science courses at university, as they begin to perceive the better career prospects they offer, or for mature students to retrain later. Meanwhile the shortage of mathematics and science teachers will continue and our room for manoeuvre in taking decisions on reorganization schemes will continue to be limited.

(b) *Tiered schemes*. There is some evidence with regard to the deployment of teachers which has particular relevance to tiered schemes.

Monks[51] notes that in schools with a spread of age from 11 to 17 at least, 25 per cent of teachers taught mainly younger pupils, 15 per cent mainly older pupils, and the remainder taught all age ranges. In the survey of all schools the respective figures were 33 per cent, 17 per cent and 50 per cent, the variation being due to types of comprehensive school other than the all-through type having more restricted age ranges.

Unqualified, part-time and inexperienced teachers tended to take younger and less able pupils, graduates and experienced teachers the older age groups. As many experienced as inexperienced teachers taught the less able, probably because their numbers also include the most disturbed and the most disturbing pupils. If such pupils did not get at least a measure of experienced teaching they would become an even greater problem for a school than they already are.

The concentration of experienced teachers on teaching the older age groups might perhaps lead us to infer that tiered schemes would spread experience more widely over the whole range of pupils, thus benefitting the younger pupils. Experienced teachers could not be moved from teaching the younger pupils, as they frequently are in 11–18 schools, if they were stationed in a separate school. On this point, however, there seems to be no really firm evidence, although experience has shown in some places that non-graduates move into

[51] Monks, 1968, pp. 71–2.

the middle or junior high school because of better prospects of promotion to headships there than in the senior high. It may be that too many experienced non-graduates are doing so for the well-being of the senior high.

Tiered schemes would also appear to share with "all-through" schemes the anxiety about the provision of sixth-form teachers.

The middle school also faces staffing problems peculiar to itself. Bestraddling the primary–secondary age range, it needs both versatile class teachers for the younger pupils and more specialized teachers in some subjects for the older ones. Provision of both is difficult within the usual staffing ratios.[52] Either the training establishments must provide teachers trained in general class subjects along primary school method lines and also in one specialism, or heads will agitate for increases in the sizes of their schools, so as to provide both types of teacher within the staffing ratio, or they will agitate for a better staffing ratio. If none of these things happen, either specialist teaching will develop from the age of 9 or general class teaching will continue, without specialist teaching, till the age of 13. Either solution is to be deplored. The first puts too great an emotional pressure on young children, the second stretches the average class teacher beyond what he can possibly accomplish, especially for the most able children. A third possible solution, which is being tried in some schools, is to group the humanities subjects together and environmental subjects together and appoint teachers in pairs to cover the two groups at middle school level. Arts and crafts would form a third group. Heavy crafts, home economics and modern language would probably require individual specialist teaching. Again there are new implications for the training of teachers. How soon all middle schools will have teachers specifically trained to their needs is problematical. Meanwhile some caution in opting for such schemes is appropriate.

There are in tiered systems difficulties for ex-grammar school staff which are specific to these systems. Of course, all grammar school staff are likely to experience difficulties when they first meet the less able, just as secondary modern staff worry about whether they can stretch the most able. However, in "all-through" schools or 11–16 schools graduates are usually given the chance to try their hand out with the younger less able children and can gain experience with them before tackling the more difficult older children in the middle school years. To meet difficulties with the less able when they are already 13 or 14 and going through the changes associated with puberty is a greater problem than that encountered by graduates in the "all-through" schools or the 11–16 school. The latter therefore have a slight edge by comparison with junior high–senior high schemes, as they also have in variety of teaching.

8. *Effects of Different Schemes on Efficiency of Teachers*

Different types of reorganization schemes impose on teachers different sorts of strains, some transitional, as when grammar school teachers go through a rather painful period of adjustment to the needs of the less able, some permanent and intrinsic to the type. *A priori*, one would expect them to have varying effects on the capacity of the teacher to sustain his main tasks, those of teaching and pastoral care.

Yet there does not seem to be much evidence, so far as the writer is aware, on the *relative*

[52] Suggested staffing ratios for the middle school vary from 23:1 to 29:1 (*Towards the Middle School*, H.M.S.O., 1970, p. 22).

effects on teachers of coping with the strains of movement and communication problems characteristic of very large school and split-site school or with the stress of liaison problems specific to tiered schools. Yet there must, somewhere, be data on illness and breakdown rates of teachers in such schools which would repay study and which would give some indication of how effectively and efficiently teachers in these different types of schools can apply themselves to purely educational and pastoral tasks. Equally there must now be teachers who have experience in two or even three of these types and who could therefore rate them according to the degree of stress they imposed. Clearly in tiered schools, especially in the senior schools, the main stress experienced will be in the classroom, as teachers grapple with the situation in which pupils from different schools have been taught from different syllabuses, a situation they are bound to meet unless liaison arrangements have been very effective indeed. The stress for teachers in the other schools must occur mainly outside the classroom or at the beginning or ends of lessons.

The only evidence that we have with regard to stress in teachers working in comprehensive schools is concerned with the number of hours worked per week. This suggests that size of school rather than type is the factor related to stress, if stress and number of hours of work coincide, which they probably do not do entirely.

The way in which size of school is correlated with amount of work is shown by figures from the second N.F.E.R. survey.[53] Large schools demand somewhat more of a teacher's time on average. In schools of less than 750 pupils teachers worked 41 hours per week on average, those in the range 751–1250 worked 42 hours and those in schools of above 1250 worked 45 hours. The differences were statistically significant. Smaller schools tend to have a smaller turnover of staff.[54] Whether there is any connection between the two phenomena is not clear.[55] In the larger schools teachers spent on average nearly 1 hour more on welfare-directed activities and over 1 hour less teaching than in the small schools, but it was also not clear whether this particular difference was related to size of school or to urban problems, since most large schools are situated in urban areas.[56]

The movement and communication problems of the large school are compounded in the split-site school, with probable consequent increase of stress for teachers. Often the problems are worse in a school on two nearby sites than they are in a school on two distant ones, contrary to popular belief. In the latter the only economic and fair solution, in terms of teacher efficiency, is almost to run the two buildings as if they were separate schools and reduce movement by staff and pupils drastically. In the former it is tempting for the timetable-maker to allow more changeovers from building to building than is good for the health of teachers, in order to gain some timetable advantage.

The organizational problems of split-site schools have been well described elsewhere[57] and the need for the streamlining of procedures and for maximum efficiency within the situation is self-evident, since the alternative to efficiency is chaos. The burden this places on the timetable-maker is shown by the experience of one such school of 1000 pupils,[58] whose senior staff spent 700 hours in making the timetable. The school then approached the Local Authority Operational Research Unit at Reading with a request to do a timetabling exercise.

[53] Monks (ed.), 1970, pp. 49–52.
[54] *Ibid.*, p. 59.
[55] It seems not unlikely, in view of the very intensive and exhausting character of the teaching task.
[56] See Monks, p. 52.
[57] See articles by O'Connell and Hoyles in Halsall, Elizabeth (ed.), *op. cit.*, 1970, pp. 37–70.
[58] Private information.

The unit found it well-nigh impossible, and certainly extremely difficult, to set up a computer programme that would cater successfully for the school's problems.

At present, then, such evidence as there is suggests that large schools and split-site schools put more pressure on teachers than do "tiered" schools. Again our conclusions can be no more than tentative. Here again there is room for research. Perhaps the techniques of operational research might help us to evaluate the relative pressures imposed on teachers by different reorganization schemes.

9. *Use of Existing Buildings*

Clearly, any scheme which can cut down costs by making use of existing buildings is going to appeal both to the local authorities and to the Department of Education and Science. Indeed, one of the reasons for the introduction of the Leicestershire scheme was that it could be implemented without building any of the large schools that were thought necessary for an "all-through" school. According to Benn and Simon,[59] for example, the average size of the 11–14/15 school in this survey was 497, 355 in cities and villages, 616 in the suburbs, probably not very different from the sizes of the original schools before they became junior high schools.

Of the various tiered schemes, that which appears to make best use of existing buildings is the scheme where transfer takes place at 14. As Sir Alec Clegg himself has remarked,[60] the old secondary modern school can provide accommodation for about the right numbers of pupils for a junior high school, or at least for the numbers in a feasible scheme, and similarly the grammar school can do so for the senior high. If the transfer is made at 13, however, the numbers of pupils for the junior high will fall short of the numbers the school building can house by a quarter; if it takes place at 12, by a half. Extending the number of forms entering the school must then be considered. Meanwhile, the senior high school will be overcrowded by a quarter or by a half of the total numbers and will have to consider reducing its annual intake. Yet of the two schools the senior high has the greater need to maintain or to extend the number of forms entering, so as to provide a variety of subject choice in the fourth, fifth and subsequent years. Hence, logistically, the junior high–senior high scheme with transfer at 13 and the middle school have less to recommend them, from the point of view of buildings, than the junior high–senior high system with transfer at 14. In a particular area it is likely to cause more problems in respect of buildings than the latter. It is clear also from various investigations that the internal organization of schools is more affected by the buildings available than by any other factor.[61] This finding must clearly have repercussions on the type of reorganization that proves efficient.

However, transformation of former secondary modern schools into junior high schools and former grammar schools into senior high schools does not just involve a different set of children being drafted into the existing number of rooms. Rooms and equipment have to be altered often at great expense. Even for Leicestershire data from Oldham, Lycett, Hetherington and Elliott[62] suggests that there was much remodelling and new building, although of course some of the latter would be undertaken so as to house the

[59] *Op. cit.*, p. 110.

[60] Clegg, Sir Alec, in Maclure, S. (ed.), *Comprehensive Planning*, Councils and Education Press, 1965, p. 77.

[61] e.g. Monks (1970), *op. cit.*, pp. 39–40.

[62] Elliott, B., The implementation of the Leicestershire Plan, *Forum*, vol. 12, no. 3, Summer 1970, pp. 76–8. Oldham, F. and Lycett, P.M. in Halsall, Elizabeth (ed.), *Becoming Comprehensive: Case Histories*, Pergamon Press, 1970, pp. 123–4 and 140–1.

greater number of pupils that stay on in reorganized schools. At Louth £230,000 has had to be spent on remodelling old buildings and building new ones for a total secondary school population of about 1500, a cost of about £150 per pupil on average. As alterations to buildings in some circumstances work out nearly as expensive as construction of new ones, sometimes the expense factor ought ideally not to be the prime consideration.

The middle school requires in many cases more alteration of buildings and waste of existing equipment than does the junior high–senior high scheme. Apart from the disadvantages already noted in respect of use of buildings in terms of sheer space, ex-secondary schools, converted into middle schools have too much expensive domestic science and heavy craft space and equipment, and have fixed benches in science laboratories, when what is needed is less and more flexible equipment. Ex-primary schools converted into middle schools need accommodation for science, art, crafts and domestic science, such as is provided by the "conversion units" in use at Hull, installed at a cost of £18,000 per unit.[63]

The 11–16 school plus sixth-form college would seem to have a lot to recommend it buildings-wise. The old secondary modern schools adapt well to 11–16 comprehensive schools, especially as with the earlier development of courses leading to public examinations provision of laboratory space and equipment has often been sufficiently extended already. The existing grammar school which is not to become a sixth-form college also adapts well. The main alterations have to be made in the building that forms the new sixth-form college. This scheme would appear to make the best use of already existing buildings, of all the types permitted by Circular 10/65, with the possible exception of the small "all-through" school.

10. *Economic Provision*

(a i) *Type of school and sixth-form provision.* Debate on the extent to which different types of reorganized school are economic, centres mainly on sixth-form provision of subjects in relation to numbers of pupils in the sixth. It does so because provision at this level is much more expensive than at any other level. Up to a point the provision of a wide variety of subjects in the sixth depends on the numbers of pupils[64] who stay on into it. Hence any type of reorganized school which generates large sixth forms, other things being equal, will be more economic than a type which does not.

Monks[65] shows that size of sixth form in 13–18 schools is greater than in 11–18 schools, 13–18 schools averaging 112 pupils, 11–18 schools 68·5. This result is to be expected, since where two schools of the same size, one 11–18, one 13–18, exist, the 13–18 must have the bigger yearly intake and therefore the bigger sixth form. Since, in addition, sixth form pupils get double the allocation of teachers that pupils in the rest of a school get, it is clear that for both reasons a 13–18 or 14–18 school can put on a greater variety of subjects and/or a greater number of sets than can the 11–18 school of the same size, or alternatively, it can have an equal number of subjects or/and sets, with the sets consisting of larger groups of pupils. Its sixth-form provision is therefore more economic.

For similar reasons one would also expect the sixth-form college to be more economic in this respect than any other type, but there are not enough of them yet in being for the hypothesis to be empirically verified.

[63] Hobson, S., Kingston upon Hull's past decade of achievement, *Education*, vol. 136, no. 14, 2 Oct. 1970, pp. 315–17.

[64] Yet there are ways round this. See p. 160.

[65] Monks (1968), table 10A, p. 96, and also Benn and Simon, p. 129.

(a ii) *Size of school and sixth-form provision.* So much for the present position with regard to sixth forms in different types of comprehensive school. But we have looked at this problem from a static point of view. An examination of the dynamics of the situation reveals a more promising future for those of the 11–18 schools whose sixth forms are at present small. Even if we apply the stringent criteria of economic provision of sixth-form subjects stated in the I.L.E.A. report *Sixth Form Opportunities in Inner London* it is clear that by 1980, and probably well before, the size of sixth forms in quite small comprehensive schools will be economic. The report estimates that to offer a minimum of ten 'A' level subjects economically, that is to say, so as to get groups of pupils of not less than five, the sixth form should number not less than forty.

The 1968 N.F.E.R. report states, however, that while the average size of sixth forms in 11–18 comprehensive schools was around seventy, to be precise 68·5,[66] one-third of the 187 schools studied had less than fifty pupils and the average for schools of less than 600 pupils (3-F.E.) was only forty. Even if the numbers in the last group are low, in a dynamic situation there are other considerations to be taken into account.

The age group reaching 17 in the mid and late 1970s is exceptionally large and the raising of the school-leaving age to 16 is likely to encourage an increased rate of staying-on into the sixth form, perhaps a much increased staying-on rate. The actual numbers of 17-year-olds will increase considerably in the decade 1970–80 and the relevant percentages of pupils staying on into the sixth move from below 20 up to 25 or 26.[67] We could therefore expect the average size of sixth forms for schools of at present less than 600 to be around eighty pupils by 1980, as these schools expand and the sixth form staying-on rate expands also. We could also expect the maintenance of such numbers thereafter because of increased staying-on rates in the 1980s. The numbers in the sixth forms of these schools would therefore be economic according to the criteria of the I.L.E.A. It could, of course, happen that with the increased percentage of pupils staying on there would be a number who were capable of taking only non-'A'-level courses and that these schools would experience constraint in providing them. No doubt there will be some such pupils but experience both at home and abroad[68] suggests that most of the increased percentage would aim at 'A' level and could do so successfully. Thus figures gathered from a North of Ireland school recently show that whereas pupils who were "qualified" on entry (i.e. were "selective" pupils) gained on average 2·73 'A' levels, non-qualified pupils (i.e. "non-selective") gained 1·8 'A' levels with some of the latter passing in three or even four subjects.[69] Similarly in certain London schools surveyed in 1964–5, with sixth forms of from thirty-three to 102 pupils, and a total of 547 pupils in the sixth, there was not a single selective pupil.[70] Yet 'A' level courses still developed. The 1970 N.F.E.R. survey demonstrated that sixth formers usually fell into ability groups 1 and 2, more rarely into group 3 and almost never into groups 4 or 5,

[66] Benn and Simon found an average of seventy-seven for 11–18 schools 2 years later (p. 127). The difference may possibly have been due to a difference in sample.

[67] *Statistics of Education* 1970, vol. 1, H.M.S.O., pp. 10–11. N.B. Benn and Simon found sixth forms with staying-on rates of 30, 40 and 50 per cent (p. 119).

[68] Swedish experience suggests that most pupils staying on opt for academic courses. The Crowther Report showed that many pupils capable of taking 'A' level were not then staying on.

[69] Donaghy, T., Northern Ireland's comprehensive schools, *Comprehensive Education*, No. 18, Summer 1971, p. 23. He also concludes from his survey that 11–18 comprehensive schools do not need to be very large to be viable. A number of the schools studied were well under 1000 in numbers.

[70] Benn and Simon, *op. cit.*, p. 188.

out of the five groups into which the total intake at 11+ was divided.[71] Ability group 2 is the top non-selective group, which has been shown to be capable of taking 'A' levels. Therefore the main increase in students in the next 10 years or so is likely to be amongst those capable of taking 'A' levels, though this would not necessarily happen, of course, in all localities.

Schools with eighty pupils in the sixth form can provide about eighteen 'A' level subjects in their curriculum or the equivalent of that number in mixed 'A' level, 'O' level, C.S.E. and other examination courses. They could do so without borrowing periods from lower down the school, as is frequently done today, or without sharing some periods between the upper and lower sixth.

Since it is known that on balance pupils are more willing to stay on into the sixth form in the school where they already are than if they must move to another school, if we wish to improve staying-on rates, there is more to be said for developing the small sixth form of a small school than for hiving it off to another school. Up to a certain point growth is always uneconomic, but if we want to maximize growth we have to bear with this. Yet it seems probable that we should not have to bear with it for long and that small schools will soon have sixth forms which are economic according to the criteria set up by the I.L.E.A., that is to say, whose classes for particular subjects consist of not less than five pupils.[72]

(b) *Size of school and economic provision* There is more evidence with regard to size of school than to type in respect of economic provision, and some of it, mainly from America, has already been given.[73] It shows that up to a point the larger the school, the more economic the provision, though there is a cut-off point at which the extra administrative costs demanded by large schools begin to outweigh the savings produced by economics of scale,[74] and proportionately more time and money has to be spent on non-educational tasks than in schools of smaller size.

In England also Monks[75] found that larger schools tend to devote a larger proportion of special responsibility allowances to staff undertaking administrative tasks and to those engaged on pupil welfare. Small schools, proportionately, do not have so many administrative tasks, pupil welfare is undertaken more informally and to a larger extent by the form teacher, and the schools are not subdivided into units for this pastoral task or for administrative tasks. In so far as one would wish teachers to concentrate on the tasks for which they were trained, the small school would appear to have the advantage educationally, but there appears to be no published evidence in England as to the point at which either the large or the small comprehensive school becomes financially "uneconomic" in its largeness or in its smallness.

The N.F.E.R. report[76] did, however, give indications of the interaction between size and organizational pattern of a school and its economic attractiveness to senior staff.

As we know, the size and the buildings decide to a large extent the organizational pattern of the school. When a school reaches about 800 pupils it becomes too big for traditional arrangements to be adequate for pastoral care. Other arrangements have to be made.

[71] Monks (ed.), *op. cit.*, 1970, p. 153.
[72] See *Sixth Form Opportunities in Inner London*. I.L.E.A., 1969.
[73] See p. 120.
[74] See p. 121.
[75] Monks, 1970, pp. 31–2, 35, 59.
[76] *Ibid.*, p. 39.

But up to about 1100 pupils certain economic difficulties in sub-dividing the school are encountered. If the school is a mixed school and has four to five houses or year groups, requiring eight to ten teachers, both men and women, to head these units, the allowances and extra free periods available for these people have to be spread thin because there are not enough to man these units without borrowing from academic departments. The school's capacity to deal successfully with this problem may depend on the layout of its buildings. If it is such as to allow the school to concentrate the extra allowances and the reduced teaching load on one or two positions, such as the headship of lower school or middle school, all is well. If not and the extra money and periods must be subdivided amongst ten year heads and year assistant heads, they will be short on both counts. Such schools will still be economic for local authorities, but they will be less attractive to well-qualified and experienced staffs, except for short stays to get administrative experience.

It would appear that, in the English context at present, the senior high school and the sixth-form college-type schemes are the most economic, because the heavy expenditure on the sixth form gives an advantage to types likely to generate large sixth forms. This situation will change as higher staying-on rates increase the size of sixth forms in 11–18 schools. In other respects, and *mutatis mutandis*, the large school is more economic, but not beyond a certain point. Around 1600 pupils economies of scale cease in American schools and perhaps also in ours.

B. Conclusions

1. If a high staying-on rate is being sought the 11–16+ sixth-form college scheme has poor prospects.

2. The little evidence there is on success rates in different types of comprehensive school does not provide grounds for making a definite statement on the subject.

3. With regard to participation of pupils in school activities, their satisfaction with school, and their incentives and opportunities to develop leadership, any type of reorganization scheme which reduces the size of school is to be preferred.

4. There are no grounds in the psychological development of pupils for preferring one age of transfer rather than another, but the ambiguity which surrounds future policies on the age of subject choice and its effects on pupils transferred at 13 or 14 justify a belief that tiered schemes have serious disadvantages.

5. Owing to the unusual degree of autonomy enjoyed by British schools, the tiered schemes produce problems of liaison more difficult to resolve than in any other country; this difficulty is likely to be intractable and to be a permanent one. The tiered schemes do not fit our situation, in the context of the deeply based attitudes of British heads and teachers.

6. "Guided-choice" schemes merely lead to the perpetuation of the 11+ at a later age of transfer.

7. (a) The sixth form college scheme makes the most effective use of well-qualified teachers in subjects where there are enough classes to be taught for timetables to be filled up. In subjects where there are few takers, e.g. music, it is probably wasteful. Over time there are likely to be large numbers of non-graduate teachers taking degree courses successfully, but, owing to school policies made possible by the G.C.E., these are likely to include relatively few mathematicians and scientists. Hence, any other scheme than the sixth-form college applied universally over a period would possibly cause a shortage of such staff of catastro-

phic proportions. This factor will probably force us into the adoption of the sixth-form college scheme, in spite of its weakness with regard to the promotion of high staying-on rates. A change in examinations and curriculum policies might prevent this.

(b) It seems possible that tiered schemes will lead non-graduate teachers to congregate in the junior high or the middle school; this will be to the detriment of the senior high, as long as graduates in the latter have little experience of teaching the less able.

8. Such evidence as there is suggests that size of school, rather than type, is the factor most likely to produce overwork in teachers and therefore reduced efficiency. It is also likely to increase the proportion of time spent in non-teaching tasks.

9. The schemes which appear to make the best use of existing buildings are the 11–14 and 14–18 type and the 11–16 plus sixth-form college, the latter probably having a slight advantage. More evidence is required on this point.

10. (a) Because of the heavy expenditure on sixth-form provision the schemes which generate large enough sixth forms to justify it are at present the tiered schemes and the sixth-form college. The exceptionally large age groups reaching 17 in the next few years and the increased staying-on rate into the sixth that will follow the raising of the school-leaving age will probably raise the size of sixth forms in small 11–18 schools to an economic level, according to the stringent criteria set out by the I.L.E.A.

(b) Up to a point there are economies of scale in large schools; beyond that point costs rise and an increasing proportion of teachers' time is devoted to non-educational tasks.

C. Some Further Comments

1. One factor, which makes it difficult to combine a high staying-on rate amongst pupils with the best use of scarce teaching talent in the context of the present reorganization, is the current practice of having a 5-year course up to a first public examination followed by a 2-year course. Now that the leaving age has been raised to 16, many pupils who formerly left at 15 will be able to take a public examination, though the examinations we now have automatically exclude those in greatest need of incentive. But they will have disincentives for staying on at school after 16 in sixth-form college-type reorganization schemes, since, as has already been indicated, when a change of course also involves a change of school fewer pupils stay on.[77] Yet sixth-form colleges probably make best use of scarce teaching talent. We thus cannot combine the best use of scarce teaching talent with the highest staying-on rate in the context of public examinations at 16. If they were held at the age of 15 and the leaving age was 16 many pupils, having started on a further course might become so interested in it that they would stay on after 16. Equally if the leaving age were 17 and all pupils had already transferred to the sixth form college at 16, greater numbers of them would stay on.

2. There appear to be four main demands we are trying to make on the comprehensive school, apart from the traditional desire to give every child the fullest opportunity for education:

(a) If the state is to remain stable and to avoid social disturbance it must either pursue policies which will encourage high staying-on rates in school, or find some other solution to the problem of inevitable teenage unemployment.

(b) If it is to maintain high rates in the production of educated talent, especially scarce

[77] See p. 179.

talent, it must husband its resources of such talent in the educational field and make strenuous efforts to increase the numbers of those who have it.

(c) In the process of fulfilling such objectives it must also aim to maximize opportunities for personal development, participation, satisfaction and leadership in school life as a prelude to a fruitful and meaningful adult involvement in communities where there are too many chances of becoming no more than an anonymous cypher. It must do this for all pupils, if possible, and not merely for the most intelligent.

(d) It must maintain enough continuity in teaching for subjects that proceed on a sequential basis for them not to be hobbled by too frequent changes of school or staff.

It is patent that no reorganization scheme can at present fulfil all these essential aims. The 11–16 plus sixth-form college scheme husbands scarce teaching talent, allows for good personal development and makes sequential teaching possible, but it depresses staying-on rates, a very serious weakness. The tiered schemes produce large, economic sixth forms as does the sixth-form college, are small enough to encourage good personal development and participation, and one scheme appears to promote a high staying-on rate; but they all fail on the issue of liaison, with its effect on sequential teaching. Large "all-through" schools make an economic use of scarce teaching talent in their larger sixth forms, maintain continuity of teaching better than any other type of reorganization, have reasonable staying-on rates and run serious risks of failing in the field of personal development and participation. Small "all-through" schools maintain continuity of teaching, have reasonable staying-on rates, promote personal development and participation, but are less economic in their use of scarce personnel than the other types. Since no type succeeds on all counts, in the absence of a uniform centrally defined policy, all that local authorities can do is to choose the alternative that suits local conditions best, as they grapple with the various vested interests involved and the buildings they have already built.

But is this really good enough? Surely not. One obvious consequence, and a serious one as with increasing speed of obsolescence and change in jobs men move about the country, taking their families with them, is that children will have to readjust to a new reorganization scheme, perhaps the very year after an earlier change of school, necessitated by the pattern of the reorganization scheme in the previous area where they were living. The degree of handicap they will experience can be grasped from the findings of Entwistle and Nesbit.[78] The only thing that can be said in favour of the present situation is that, in spite of everything, it is still better than continuing with a selective system, since it will still throw up more talent than the latter. But we ought not to be satisfied with such a negative result. An industry that ran its affairs on such a conflicting set of principles would go bankrupt if it did not find means of reconciling them and take steps to make them fit in with each other. So for that matter would an icecream parlour.

If one examines the reasons why we have failed so miserably, it becomes clear that there are two basic causes. The first is the failure to take radical enough action to promote a steady flow of recruits to the teaching profession, who are well qualified in fields where talent is at present scarce, notably in mathematics and science, but also to some extent in English, and, as modern languages extend into the curriculum of all pupils, in French as well. Hence shortages of teachers at sixth-form level. In the circumstances that we have had since the war, with high salaries in industry for mathematicians and scientists, we could not

[78] See p. 183.

produce a steady flow of recruits to the profession without policies which would increase staying-on rates, for example, entry into the sixth form without a minimum of four or five 'O' levels. Such policies would have had to be combined with some measures designed to increase the number of passes at 'O' level in mathematics and science, for example, the prevention of the dropping of subjects, or at least of certain subjects. We need not have gone back to the old School Certificate grouping policy in order to take such measures. We could have merely required one or two re-sits for a pupil failing to pass in these subjects before he was allowed to proceed. This policy would have produced many more passes in mathematics and science. In addition, a more general course to 'A' level would have made it easier for pupils to switch to science and mathematics when they became more aware of career possibilities in these subjects.[79] But we would have had, in that case, to alter our whole concept of the sixth form and its level of study. The failure to do so is the second cause of the present chaos in secondary reorganization.

It is quite clear that the whole of secondary reorganization has been bedevilled, right since the 1950s and even before, by our concept of the sixth form as a unit in which the pupil narrows down his field of learning considerably, in fact more so than anywhere else in Western Europe, and works at a really advanced level. Narrowing the field so much is expensive in staffing. Hence the Ministry of Education Circular 144 of 16 June 1947 argued that large comprehensive schools would be necessary so as to ensure a viable and economic sixth form.[80] The Ministry's insistence on large schools and therefore on inordinate expense if L.E.A.s were to reorganize completely led to the introduction of the Leicestershire scheme as a way of circumventing this dilemma.[81] It also led to the creation of split-site schools, so as to produce the necessary numbers. Hence both tiered systems and split-site schools have resulted from our concept of the function of the sixth form and our undue caution with regard to future staying-on rates in the sixth. How tenacious that conception is can be gauged from the number of alternative schemes suggested for the curriculum of the sixth form in the last dozen years and the icy reception they have severally received in one quarter or another. How inappropriate the degree of caution with regard to staying-on rates has been can be seen from all the statistics gathered about such rates in the comprehensive schools and indeed in the national system as a whole. The D.E.S. projections are still too cautious, in spite of all the evidence that has accumulated against caution. For both these reasons we are still worrying about the size of the sixth form and therefore about size of school, and inevitably our anxieties on this point have influenced the whole structure of the comprehensive school and particularly the structure of the options in the fourth and fifth year. It is because the work in the sixth is so specialized that the options groups in the fourth and fifth year are so elaborate and often so uneconomic. Otherwise we could not ensure that pupils will have had the chance to prepare themselves in any subject they will wish to specialize in at 'A' level later.

Rather than revise our concept of the sixth form we have preferred to accept one or other of several difficult alternatives: the building of large and expensive new schools which, in

[79] It is not denied that other countries pursuing more general courses to 18 have had their difficulties with regard to mathematics and science. But we have gone out of our way to invite them. Nor is it suggested that such a switch in policy would have been enough. Evidence from Keele shows that students often switch away from science after a general course. We have to make it worth their while not to.

[80] Rubinstein, D. and Simon, B., *The Evolution of the Comprehensive School*, Routledge and Kegan Paul, 1969, p. 45.

[81] Benn, C. and Simon, B., *op. cit.*, p. 126.

part because we have no sophisticated knowledge of the appropriate layout of large educational institutions, have produced serious problems of movement; the setting-up of split-site schools even more handicapped by problems of movement and communication; the construction of tiered schemes where the chief problem is that of liaison and articulation of courses. All of these alternatives have drained the energies of teachers in one way or another on tasks that were administrative rather than educational or pastoral. And yet it seems not unlikely that entry into the Common Market will drive us eventually to widen the sixth-form curriculum, so as to bring it more into line with equivalent courses in Western Europe, even if the whole idea of the sixth form is not altered still earlier by other pressures.

No one can deny the attractiveness of study in depth at sixth-form level, nor its educational power. What we have omitted to do is to pursue that level of study along a broad enough front. We cannot do so without extending the sixth-form course by 1 year, so as to allow for a study of five 'A' levels over a period of 3 years, with two of the subjects to come from areas outside the main field of interest in arts or science. This would allow for a possible switch later. The only alternative if we keep a 2-year course of a more general kind is to study at a more superficial level. Even that would be preferable to seeing the supply of mathematicians and scientists for schools eventually dry up; and this is what we are risking by our failure to revise our concept of the sixth form as much as by our failure to promote staying-on rates to a level that will ensure an adequate supply of teachers, coming out of universities and colleges of education well qualified in appropriate subjects. Meanwhile, we shall have to put up with varying schemes of reorganization which fail on at least one important criterion.

D. The Future

Much of this book has been somewhat myopically concentrated on the problems of reorganization as they present themselves in British schools now. It would not be complete without some consideration of probable future trends. Yet it would be of limited value to consider such trends merely in the context of the British system and without reference to what is going on elsewhere. This much is clear from the evidence of the first chapter, which showed how certain developments took place in education during past centuries in many countries at roughly the same time, though not necessarily at the same pace, nor encountering precisely the same resistances or the same encouragements. It was a long pondering over this evidence from past centuries and the casual observation of new trends in Denmark and Sweden in the middle fifties, already paralleled by similar developments in the U.S.A. and the U.S.S.R. in the 1920s and 1930s, which led the writer to deduce that reorganization along comprehensive lines would gather momentum in the rest of Western Europe in the 1960s and that it was personally essential to get experience in comprehensive schools. Perhaps I may now be allowed to get my crystal ball out again.

It seems pretty clear that in the long term, whatever its present disadvantages in depressing staying-on rates, the sixth-form college catering for all pupils will emerge as a significant type of educational institution, probably in urban areas the only type, for pupils of 16+. Moreover, there are signs of similar institutions developing also in other countries. One does not need to consider the personal advantages to students who are young adults of hiving them off into a separate institution. These are self-evident. What is perhaps less clear is that, as staying-on rates increase, there will be such pressure on higher education, that it will be too expensive to allow everyone to procure their higher education away from home for all of the course and that this will have repercussions on the secondary system. The first year of university work will then move back into the secondary system; or rather it will find its ideal niche in an intermediate institution, the sixth-form college or junior college, or whatever name attaches itself to the "genre", with a 3- or 4-year course which will be economic to man, where full use will be made of those academic talents among teaching staff which are in short supply, where young adults will be able to mature without the constraints they experience in institutions catering also for younger pupils, and where a broader course of at least the same depth as in the old sixth form will enable many of them to emerge into the world both more truly educated and better able to adapt to the varying vocational and personal pressures they will experience.

Select Bibliography

Comprehensive Education

BENN, CAROLINE, *Survey of Comprehensive Reorganisation*, Comprehensive Schools-Committee, 1968.
BENN, CAROLINE (ed.), *Comprehensive Reorganisation Survey*, 1969 and continued.
BENN, CAROLINE (ed.), *Comprehensive Schools in 1972: Reorganisation Plans to 1975*, Comprehensive Schools Committee, 1972.
BENN, CAROLINE and SIMON, BRIAN, *Half Way There*, McGraw-Hill, 1970.
BUNTON, W. J., *Comprehensive Education: a Select Annotated Bibliography*, N.F.E.R., 1971.
CLEGG, Sir ALEC *et al.*, *The Middle School: a Symposium*, Schoolmaster Publishing Co., 1967.
COLE, ROGER, *Comprehensive Schools in Action*, Longbourne, 1964.
COMPREHENSIVE SCHOOLS COMMITTEE, *Comprehensive Education Survey No. 1, 1966–7*, 1967.
CORBETT, ANNE, Sixth form college, *Comprehensive Education*, no. 11, Spring 1969, pp. 19–24.
DEPARTMENT OF EDUCATION AND SCIENCE, *Towards the Middle School*, H.M.S.O., 1970.
DONAGHY, T., Northern Ireland's comprehensive schools, *Comprehensive Education*, no. 18, Summer 1971, pp. 23–4.
EGGLESTON, J. F., Environment and comprehensives, *Education*, no. 127, 28 Jan. 1966, pp. 194–6.
EGNER, W. E., Sixth form dilemma, *Education*, no. 132, 1 Nov. 1968, pp. 522–3, and 8 Nov. 1968, p. 550.
ELLIOTT, B., The implementation of the Leicestershire Plan, *Forum*, vol. 12, no. 3, Summer 1970, pp. 76–8.
FORD, JULIENNE, *Social Class and the Comprehensive School*, Routledge & Kegan Paul, 1969.
GRIFFIN, A., Selective and non-selective secondary schools, their relative effects on ability, attainment and attitudes, *Research in Education*, No. 1, 1969, pp. 15–19.
GRIFFITHS, A. *Secondary School Reorganisation in England and Wales*, Routledge, 1971.
HALSALL, ELIZABETH (ed.), *Becoming Comprehensive: Case Histories*, Pergamon Press, 1970.
HARRIS, C., Eight years' experience of an upper school, in MASON, S. C. (ed.), *In Our Experience*, Longmans, 1970.
HINCHLIFFE, P. D., Operational research in comprehensive schools, M.Sc. Operational Research Project, Univ. of Hull, 1971. Reported in: *Comprehensive Education*, no. 21, Summer 1972, pp. 10–12.
HOBSON, S., Kingston upon Hull's past decade of achievement, *Education*, no. 36, 2 Oct. 1970, pp. 315–17.
HOLLY, D. N., Profiting from a comprehensive school: class, sex and ability, *Brit. J. Sociology*, vol. XVI, no. 2, June 1965, pp. 150–8.
HOYLES, E. M., The two-site school, in: HALSALL, ELIZABETH (ed.), *Becoming Comprehensive: Case Histories*, Pergamon Press, 1970.
INCORPORATED ASSOCIATION OF ASSISTANT MASTERS, *Teaching in Comprehensive Schools: a second report*, Cambridge Univ. Press, 1967.
INNER LONDON EDUCATION AUTHORITY, *London Comprehensive Schools 1966*, I.L.E.A., 1967.
KING, R. W., *The English Sixth Form College*, Pergamon Press, 1968.
LONDON COUNTY COUNCIL, *London Comprehensive Schools 1961*, L.C.C., 1962.
LYCETT, P. M., The Leicestershire Plan, in: HALSALL, ELIZABETH (ed.), *Becoming Comprehensive: Case Histories*, Pergamon Press, 1970.
MACLURE, S. (ed.), *Comprehensive Planning*, Councils and Education Press, 1965.
MARLAND, M., *Leading a Department in a Comprehensive School*, Heinemann, 1971.
MASON, S. C. (ed.), *In Our Experience*, Longmans, 1970.
MICHAEL, L. S., Articulation problems with lower school and higher education, *Bulletin of the National Association of Secondary School Principals*, vol. 43, Feb. 1959, pp. 51–5.
MILLER, T. W. G., *Values in the Comprehensive School*, Oliver & Boyd, 1961.
MONKS, T. G., *Comprehensive Education in England and Wales, A Survey of Schools and their Organisation*, N.F.E.R., 1968.
MONKS, T. G. (ed.), *Comprehensive Education in Action*, N.F.E.R., 1970.
NATIONAL ASSOCIATION OF SCHOOLMASTERS, *The Comprehensive School: an Appraisal from Within*, N.A.S., 1964.
NATIONAL UNION OF TEACHERS, *Inside the Comprehensive School*, Schoolmaster Publishing Co., 1958.

NELSON, M., One school on two sites (computer and a timetable), *Education*, no. 131, 15 Mar. 1968, pp. 382–3.
NISBET, J. D. and ENTWISTLE, N. J., *The Age of Transfer to Secondary Education*, Univ. of London Press, 1966.
NISBET, J. D. and ENTWISTLE, N. J., *The Transition to Secondary Education*, Scottish Council for Research in Education, Univ. of London Press, 1969.
O'CONNELL, P. J., The two-site school, in: HALSALL, ELIZABETH (ed.), *Becoming Comprehensive: Case Histories*, Pergamon Press, 1970.
OLDHAM, F., The Leicestershire Plan, in: HALSALL, ELIZABETH (ed.), *Becoming Comprehensive: Case Histories*, Pergamon Press, 1970.
PEARCE, J. J., The expansion of sixth forms, *University Quarterly*, vol. 23, no. 1, Dec. 1968, pp. 46–55.
PEDLEY, R., *The Comprehensive School*, Penguin, 1963.
POSTLETHWAITE, N., *School Organization and Student Achievement*, Almqvist & Wiksell, Stockholm, 1967.
RUBINSTEIN, D. and SIMON, B., *The Evolution of the Comprehensive School*, Routledge & Kegan Paul, 1969.
SCHOOLS COUNCIL WORKING PAPER, No. 22, *The Middle Years of Schooling*, H.M.S.O., 1969.
WEST RIDING COUNTY COUNCIL EDUCATION COMMITTEE, *Middle Schools*, 1968.

Periodicals specially concerned with reorganization:
Forum.
Comprehensive Education.

Secondary Education Abroad

BORGHI, L., Italy's Ten Year Education Plan, *Comparative Education Review*, vol. IV, no. 1, June 1960.
CAPELLE, JEAN, *Tomorrow's Education: the French Experience*, Pergamon Press, 1967.
CONANT, J. B., *The American High School Today*, McGraw-Hill, 1959.
CONANT, J. B., *The Comprehensive High School*, McGraw-Hill, 1967.
COUNCIL FOR CULTURAL CO-OPERATION, COUNCIL OF EUROPE, *Education in Europe: School Systems, a Guide*, Strasbourg, 1965.
CROS, LOUIS, *The Explosion in the Schools*, S.E.V.P.E.N., Paris, 1963.
DAHLÖF, URBAN, Recent reforms of secondary education in Sweden, *Comparative Education*, vol. 2, no. 1, Mar. 1966, pp. 71–92.
DIXON, C. W., *Society, Schools and Progress in Scandinavia*, Pergamon Press, 1965.
GRANDIA, J. H. N., Rotterdam and its educational reforms, in: *World Year Book of Education*, Evans, 1970.
GRANT, NIGEL, *Soviet Education*, Penguin, 1964.
GRANT, NIGEL, *Society, Schools and Progress in Eastern Europe*, Pergamon Press, 1969.
HALLS, W. D., *Society, Schools and Progress in France*, Pergamon Press, 1965.
HOWARD, A. V. and STORUMBIS, G. C., *The Junior High and Middle School*, International Textbook Company, Scranton, U.S.A., 1970.
HUSÉN, T., Responsiveness and resistance in the educational system to changing needs of society: some Swedish experiences, *Int. Rev. Educ.*, vol. XV, no. 4, 1969, pp. 476–86.
KANDEL, I. L., *History of Secondary Education*, Houghton Miflin, Boston, 1930.
KING, E. J., *Education and Development in Western Europe*, Addison-Wesley, Massachusetts, 1969.
KING, E. J., *Society, Schools and Progress in the U.S.A.*, Pergamon Press, 1965.
MARKLUND, S. and SODERBERG, P., *The Swedish Comprehensive School*, Longmans, 1967.
MICHAEL, L. S., Articulation problems with lower school and higher education, *Bulletin of the National Association of Secondary School Principals*, vol. 43, no. 1, Feb. 1959, pp. 51–55.
MOLYNEUX, F. H. and LINKER, G., Schools in transition: the Dutch approach, *Trends in Education*, No. 17, Jan. 1970, pp. 46–53.
ORGANISATION FOR ECONOMIC CO-OPERATION AND DEVELOPMENT, *Development of Secondary Education: Trends and Implications*, Paris, 1969.
PAULSTON, R. G., *Educational Change in Sweden*, New York Teachers College, Columbia Press, 1968.
POIGNANT, R., *Education and Development in Western Europe, the United States and the U.S.S.R.*, New York Teachers' College, Columbia Press, 1969.
ROSSI, N. and COLE, T., School of Barbiana, *Letter to a Teacher*, Penguin Press, 1970.
ROSENKRANZ, W. *et al.*, *Polytechnical Education for All*, Verlag Zeit im Bild, Dresden, 1966.
ROTHERA, H., Reorganization in France, *Trends in Education*, no. 6, Apr. 1967, pp. 21–27.
SCHULTZE, W. and FUHR, C., *Schools in the Federal Republic of Germany*, Julius Beltz, Weinheim, 1967.
SPOLTON, L., *The Upper Secondary School: a Comparative Survey*, Pergamon Press, 1967.
SPOLTON, LEWIS, A case study in comparative education: comprehensive education in the U.S. and Britain, *Brit. J. of Educational Studies*, Feb. 1969, pp. 16–25.
TORPE, H., *Control and Estimation of Experiments with the Undivided 9-year School at Frederiksborg Educational System*, Paedagogiske Streiftog, Copenhagen, 1960.

VAN GELDER, L., The Bridge Year; an aid to adaptation from elementary to secondary education in the Netherlands, *Int. Rev. Educ.*, vol. VI, no. 4, Dec. 1960, pp. 468–71.
World Survey of Education: vol. III. *Secondary Education*, Unesco, 1961.

Periodicals:
Comparative Education.
Comparative Education Review.
International Review of Education.

Streaming and Unstreaming

BARNES, A. R., Unstreaming: two viewpoints, two strategies, in: HALSALL, ELIZABETH (ed.), *Becoming Comprehensive: Case Histories*, Pergamon Press, 1970.
BLANDFORD, J. S., Standardised tests in junior schools with special reference to the effects of streaming on the constancy of results, *Brit. J. Educ. Psychol.*, vol. XXVIII, no. 2, June 1958, pp. 170–3.
DAHLÖF, U., *Ability Grouping, Content Validity and Curriculum Process Analysis*, Univ. of Gotheborg, 1969.
DANIELS, J. C., The effects of streaming in the primary school, *Brit. J. Educ. Psychol.*, vol. XXXI, no. 2, June 1961, pp. 119–22.
DOUGLAS, J. W. B., *The Home and the School*, MacGibbon & Kee, 1964.
GUNN, S. E., Teaching groups in secondary schools, *Trends in Education*, no. 19, July 1970, pp. 3–8.
HALSALL, ELIZABETH, Intelligence, school and social context: some European comparisons, *Comparative Education*, vol. 2, no. 3, 1966, pp. 181–95.
HUSÉN, T. (ed.), *International Study of Achievement in Mathematics*, Wiley, 1967.
HUSÉN, T. and SVENSSON, N. E., Pedagogic milieu and development of intellectual skills, *School Rev.*, vol. LXVIII, 1960, pp. 36–51.
International Evaluation of Achievement, *Educational Achievements of 13 year olds in 12 Countries*, Unesco Institute of Education, Hamburg, 1962.
LUNN, J. C. BARKER, *Streaming in the Primary School*, N.F.E.R., 1970.
PAPE, G. V., The duds of summer, *Education*, no. 116, 18 Nov. 1960, pp. 952–3.
PEARCE, R. A., Streaming: a sociometric study, *Educ. Rev.*, vol. 10, no. 1, Jan. 1958, pp. 248–51.
PIDGEON, D. A., Date of birth and scholastic performance, *Educ. Res.*, vol. 8, no. 1, 1965–6, pp. 3–7.
POSTLETHWAITE, N., *School Organisation and Student Achievement*, Almqvist & Wiksell, Stockholm, 1967.
ROUSE, S., The effect upon attainment levels in mathematics and English of unstreaming, *Univ. of Manchester School of Education Gazette*, vol. 13, 1969, pp. 12–14.
SVENSSON, N. E., *Ability Grouping and Scholastic Achievement*, Almqvist & Wiksell, Uppsala, 1962.
TAYLOR, E. A., *J. Educ. Psychol.*, vol. 43, no. 5, 1952. Some factors relating to social acceptance in eighth grade classes, pp. 257–72.
THOMPSON, D., Unstreaming: two viewpoints, two strategies, in: HALSALL, ELIZABETH (ed.), *Becoming Comprehensive: Case Histories*, Pergamon Press, 1970.
WATTS, A. F., PIDGEON, D. A. and YATES, A., *Secondary School Entrance Examinations*, N.F.E.R., 1952.
YATES, A. (ed.), *Grouping in Education*, Almqvist & Wiksell, Uppsala, 1966.
YATES, A., *The Organization of Schooling*, Routledge & Kegan Paul, 1971.
YOUNG, M. and ARMSTRONG, M., The flexible school: ways to establish streaming in a comprehensive, *Where*, Supplement no. 5, Autumn 1965.

Periodicals:
Comprehensive Education.
Forum.

Cultural Deprivation

ANDERSON, H. H. and BREWER, J. E., Studies of teachers' classroom personalities, *Applied Psychology Monographs* 1946, no. 6.
ANDREWS, J. H., School organizational climate: some validity studies of O.C.D.Q., *Can. Educ. Res. Dig.*, vol. 5, 1965, pp. 317–34.
BARNES, D., *Language, the learner and the school*, Penguin, 1969.
BENSON, R. C., and BLOCKER, D. H., Evaluation of developmental counseling with groups of low achievers in a high school setting, *The School Counselor*, vol. 14, 1967, pp. 215–20.
BEREITER, C. and ENGELMANN, S., *Teaching Disadvantaged Children in the Pre-School Environment*, Prentice Hall, Englewood Cliffs, N.J., 1966.

BERNSTEIN, B., Social structure, language and learning, *Educ. Res.*, vol. 3, no. 3, 1961, pp. 163–76.

BERNSTEIN, B., Social class, linguistic codes and grammatical elements, *Language and Speech*, vol. 5, pp. 221–40.

BLOOM, B. S., *Stability and Change in Human Characteristics*, Wiley, New York, 1964.

BLOOM, B. S., DAVIES, A. and HESS, R., *Compensatory Education for the Culturally Deprived*, Holt, Rinehart & Winston, New York, 1965.

BRAHAM, M., Peer group deterrents in intellectual development during adolescence, *Educational Theory*, vol. 34, Winter 1964, pp. 3–21.

BROOKOVER, W. B. *et al.*, *Self-concept of Ability and School Achievement*, East Lansing Bureau of Educational Research Services, Michigan State University, 1965.

BUNDA, R. and MAZZAU, J., The effects of a work experience program on the performance of potential dropouts, *The School Counselor*, vol. 15, 1968, pp. 272–4.

BURCHILL, G. W., *Work Study Programs for Alienated Youth: a Casebook*, Science Research Abstracts, Chicago, 1962.

CENTRAL ADVISORY COUNCIL FOR EDUCATION, *Half Our Future*, The Newsom Report, 1963.

CHAZAN, M., The relationship between maladjustment and backwardness, *Educ. Rev.*, vol. 15, Nov. 1962, pp. 54–61.

CHAZAN, M. and DOWNES, G., *Compensatory Education and the New Media*, Swansea University College Dept. of Education (Schools Council Occasional Publication No. 3), 1971.

CLARKE, A. M. and CLARKE, A. D. B., Recovery from the effects of deprivation, *J. Midland Mental Deficiency Soc.*, vol. 4, 1957, pp. 58–62.

CLEGG, SIR ALEC and MEGSON, B., *Children in Distress*, Penguin, 1968.

CLEMENTS, B. E., Transitional adolescent anxiety and group counselling, *Personnel and Guidance J.*, vol. 45, 1966, pp. 67–71.

CLOWOOD, R. A. and JONES, J. A., Social class: educational attitudes and participation in education, In: PASSOW, A. H. (ed.), *Education in Depressed Areas*, Teachers' College, Columbia, New York, 1963.

COLEMAN, J. S., *The Adolescent Society*, Free Press of Glencoe, New York, 1961.

COLEMAN, J. S. *et al.*, *Equality of Educational Opportunity*, U.S. Dept. of Health, Education and Welfare, Office of Education, 1966.

Comprehensive Education. Various articles in issue of Autumn 1968.

CULLEN, K., *School and Family. Social Factors in Educational Attainment*, Gill & Macmillan, Dublin, 1969.

DAY, ALISON, Work experience, *Times Educ. Suppl.*, 8 Oct. 1971, p. 34.

DENTLER, R. A. and WARSHAUER, M. E., *Big City Dropouts and Illiterates*, Special Studies in U.S. Economic & Social Development, Praeger, 1968.

DEPARTMENT OF EDUCATION AND SCIENCE, *Education under Social Handicap*, H.M.S.O., 1965.

DICKINSON, W. A. and TRUAX, C. B., Group counseling with college underachievers, *Personnel and Guidance J.*, vol. 45, 1966, pp. 245–7.

DOUGLAS, J. W. B., *The Home and the School*, MacGibbon & Kee, 1964.

DOUGLAS, J. W. B. *et al.*, *All Our Future: a Longitudinal Study of Secondary Education*, Report of National Survey of Health and Development, Davies, 1968.

FLOUD, J., HALSEY, A. H. and MARTIN, F. M., *Social Class and Educational Opportunity*, Heinemann, 1957.

GILLILAND, B. C., Small group counseling with Negro adolescents in a public high school, *J. Counseling Psychol.*, vol. 15, 1968, pp. 147–52.

HALSEY, A. H. (ed.), *Ability and Educational Opportunity*, O.E.C.D., Paris, 1961.

HALSEY, A. H., FLOUD, J. and ANDERSON, C. A. (eds.), *Education, Economy and Society*, Free Press of Glencoe, New York, 1961.

HAWKRIDGE, D. G., TALLMADGE, G. R. and LARSEN, J. K., *Foundations for Success in Educating Disadvantaged Children*, U.S. Office of Education, 1968.

HERNDON, J., *The Way It Spozed to Be*, Hentoff, The New Republic, 1969.

HESS, R. D. and SHIPMAN, V. C., Early experience and the socialization of cognitive modes in children, *Child Development*, vol. 36, no. 4, Dec. 1965, pp. 869–86.

HIERONYMOUS, A. N., A study of social class motivation relationships between anxiety for education and certain socio-economic and intellectual variables, *J. Educ. Psychol.*, vol. 42, no. 4, Apr. 1951, pp. 193–205.

HOLLIS, T. H. B., Teachers' attitudes to children's behaviour. M.Ed. thesis M/C.

HUNT, J. McV., *Intelligence and Experience*, Ronald, New York, 1967.

HUSÉN, T. (ed.), *International Study of Achievement in Mathematics*, Wiley, 1967.

JACKSON, B. and MARSDEN, D., *Education and the Working Class*, Routledge & Kegan Paul, 1962.

KATZ, P. and ZIGLER, E., Self-image disparity: a developmental approach, *J. Personality and Social Psychol.* vol. 5, 1967, pp. 186–95.

LAWTON, D., *Social Class, Language and Education*, Routledge, 1968.

LEWIN, K., LIPPITT, R. and WHITE, R. K., Patterns of aggressive behaviour in experimentally created social climates, *J. Social Psychol.*, vol. 10, 1939, pp. 271–99.

LITTLE, A. and WESTERGAARD, J., The trend of class differentials in educational opportunity in England and Wales, *Brit. J. Sociology*, vol. XV, no. 4, pp. 301–16.

LJUNG, B. O., *The Adolescent Spurt in Mental Growth*, Stockholm Studies in Educational Psychology No. 8, Almqvist & Wiksell, Stockholm, 1965.

MAYESKE, G. W., *Educational Achievement among Mexican Indians*, U.S. Dept. of Health, Education and Welfare, Office of Education, Technological Note No. 22, Washington D.C.

MAYS, J. B., *Education and the Urban Child*, Univ. of Liverpool Press, 1962.

MCARTHUR, R. and ELLEY, W. B., The reduction of socio-economic bias in intelligence testing, *Brit. J. Educ. Psychol.*, vol. 33, pt. 2, June 1963, pp. 107–19.

MCDILL, E. L., RIGBY, L. C. and MEYERS, E. D., Educational climates of high schools: their effects and sources, *Amer. J. Sociology*, vol. 74, 1969, pp. 567–86.

MCDILL, E. L., MCDILL, M. S. and SPREHE, J. T., *Strategies for Success in Compensatory Education. An Appraisal of Evaluation Research*, Johns Hopkins, Baltimore, 1969.

MCGOWAN, R. J., The effect of brief contact interviews with low ability, low achieving students, *The School Counselor*, vol. 15, 1968, pp. 386–9.

MORRIS, J. M., *Standards and Progress in Reading*, N.F.E.R., Slough, 1966.

MUSGROVE, F., *Youth and the Social Order*, Routledge & Kegan Paul, 1964.

OLIM, E. G., HESS, R. D. and SHIPMAN, V. C., *Relationship between Mothers' Language Style and Cognitive Styles of Urban Pre-school Children*, Urban Child Study Center, Chicago, 1965.

PASSOW, A. H., *Education in Depressed Areas*, Teachers' College, Columbia, New York, 1963.

PASSOW, A. H., *Deprivation and Disadvantage: Nature and Manifestation*, Unesco Institute of Education, Hamburg, 1970.

PLOWDEN REPORT, Department of Education and Science, *Children and their Primary Schools*, vol. 2, H.M.S.O., 1967.

POSNER, J., *Evaluation of "Successful" Projects in Compensatory Education*, U.S. Office of Education, Office of Planning and Evaluation, Occasional Paper no. 8, 1968.

PRINGLE, M. L. K., *Deprivation and Education*, Longmans, 1971.

Review of Educational Research, vol. 35, no. 5, Dec. 1965; vol. 34, no. 4, Oct. 1966; vol. 40, no. 1, Feb. 1970.

RIESSMANN, F., *The Culturally Deprived Child*, Harper, New York, 1962.

ROBSON, T. B., *Urban Analysis. A Study of City Structure*, Cambridge Univ. Press, 1969.

ROSENTHAL, R. and JACOBSON, L., *Pygmalion in the Classroom*, Holt, Rinehart & Winston, New York, 1968.

RUPP, J. C. C., *Helping the Child to Cope with the School: a study of the importance of parent-child relationships with regard to primary school success* [Opvoeding tot schoolweerbaarheid], Wolters-Noordhoff, Groningen, 1969.

RUSK, B. A., *An Evaluation of a Six-week Headstart Program Using an Academically Oriented Curriculum*, Canton, 1967. A.E.R.A., Los Angeles.

SARASON, G. *et al.*, The effect of differential instructions on anxiety and learning, *J. Abnormal and Social Psychol.*, vol. 47, 1952, pp. 561–5.

SCHOOLS COUNCIL WORKING PAPER NO. 27, *Crossed with Adversity*, Evans Methuen, 1970.

SCHOOLS COUNCIL WORKING PAPER NO. 33, *Choosing a Curriculum for the Young School Leaver*, Evans Methuen, 1971.

STEIN, Z. A. and SUSSER, M., Mild mental subnormality: social and epidemiological studies, *Social Psychiatry*, Baltimore, 1969.

STROM, R. D., *Teaching in the Slum School*, Merrill, Columbus, Ohio, 1965.

SUSSER, M., *Community Psychiatry: Epidemiology and Social Themes*, Random House, New York, 1968.

SVENSSON A., *Relative Achievement: School Performance in Relation to Intelligence, Sex and Home Environment*, Almqvist & Wiksell, 1971.

VERNON, P. E., A new look at intelligence testing, *Educ. Res.*, vol. 1, no. 1, 1958, pp. 3–12.

WALL, W. D., The wish to learn, *Educ. Res.*, vol. 1, no. 1, 1958, pp. 23–37.

WALL, W. D., *Adolescents in School and Society*, N.F.E.R. Occasional Publication no. 17, 1968.

WALL, W. D., SCHONELL, F. J. and OLSEN, W. C., *Failure in School*, Unesco Institute of Education, Hamburg, 1962.

WHITE, W. F., *Psychosocial Principles Applied to Classroom Teaching*, McGraw-Hill, 1969.

ZIGLER, E., Social class and the socialization process, *Rev. Educ. Res.*, vol. 40, no. 1, Feb. 1970, pp. 87–110.

Guidance and Counselling

ALLPORT, G., *Pattern and Growth of Personality*. Rinehart and Winston, New York, 1961.

BENSON, R. C. and BLOCKER, D. H., Evaluation of developmental counseling with groups of low achievers in a high school setting, *The School Counselor*, vol. 14, 1967, pp. 215–20.

BIESTECK, F., *The Casework Relationship*, Allen and Unwin, 1961.

BONNANDEL, R., Evolution des liaisons entre les réussites et les diverses matières scolaires, *Journal de Psychologie Normale et Pathologique*, vol. 44, 1951, pp. 438–71.

CARTER, M. P., *Home, School and Work*, Pergamon Press, 1962.

CHOWN, S. M., The foundation of occupational choice amongst grammar school pupils, *Occupational Psychology*, vol. 32, no. 3, 1958, pp. 171–82.

DAWS, P. P., *A Good Start in Life*, C.R.A.C., 1968.

DEPARTMENT OF EDUCATION AND SCIENCE, *Careers Guidance in Schools*, H.M.S.O., 1965.

DICKENSON, W. A. and TRUAX, C. B., Group counseling with college underachievers, *Personnel and Guidance J.*, vol. 45, 1966, pp. 243–7.

FULLER, J. B., School counselling: a first enquiry, *Educ. Res.*, vol. 9, no. 2, Feb. 1967, pp. 135–6.

GILLILAND, B. C., Small group counseling with negro adolescents in a public high school, *J. Counseling Psychol.*, vol. 15, 1968, pp. 147–52.

GINSBERG, S. W. *et al.*, *Occupational Choice: an Approach to a General Theory*, Univ. of Columbia Press, 1957.

GRIBBONS, W. D. and LOHNES, P. R., *Emerging Careers*, Teachers' College, Columbia, New York, 1968.

HILL, G. B., Choice of career by grammar school boys, *Occupational Psychology*, vol. 39, no. 4, Oct. 1965, pp. 279–87.

HOLDEN, A., *Counselling in Secondary Schools*, Constable, 1971.

HUSÉN, T. and HENRYSSON, S., *Differentiation and Guidance in the Comprehensive School*, Almqvist & Wiksell, Stockholm, 1958.

INSTITUTE OF CAREERS OFFICERS, *Work Experience in British Secondary Schools*, Bromsgrove I.L.O., 1971.

JAHODA, G., Job attitudes and job choice among secondary school leavers, *Occupational Psychology*, vol. 26, nos. 3 and 4, 1952.

JONES, ANNE, *School Counselling in Practice*, Ward Lock Educ. Press, 1970.

KENNEDY, W. A., School phobia: rapid treatment of 50 cases, *J. of Abnormal Psychology*, vol. 70, 1965, pp. 285–9.

LANGIER, H. and WEINBERG, D., *Recherches sur la solidarité et l'indépendance des aptitudes intellectuelles d'après les examens écrits du Baccalauréat*, Imprimerie Chantenay, Paris, 1938.

LJUNG, B. O., *The Adolescent Spurt in Mental Growth*, Stockholm Studies in Educational Psychology No. 8, Almqvist & Wiksell, Stockholm, 1965.

LYTTON, H. and CROFT, M. (eds.), *Guidance and Counselling in British Schools*, Arnold, 1969.

MACFARLANE SMITH, I., *Spatial Ability*, Univ. of London Press, 1964.

MAIZELS, J., *Adolescent Needs and the Transition from School to Work*, Univ. of London Press, 1970.

MALLINSON, G. G. and CRUMBINE, C., An investigation of the stability of interests in high school students, *J. Educ. Res.*, vol. 45, Jan. 1952, pp. 369–83.

MCGOWAN, R. J., The effect of brief contact interviews with low ability, low achieving students, *The School Counselor*, vol. 15, 1968, pp. 386–9.

MEYERS, C. E. *et al.*, *Primary Abilities at Mental Age 6*, Monograph Soc. for Res. Child Devel., no. 82, 1962.

MOORE, B. M., *Guidance in Comprehensive Schools*, N.F.E.R., 1970.

MORRISON, A. and MCINTYRE, D., *Schools and Socialization*, Penguin Books, 1971.

MUSGRAVE, P. W., Towards a sociological theory of occupational choice, *Sociological Rev.*, vol. 15, no. 1, 1967, pp. 33–46.

NATIONAL ASSOCIATION FOR MENTAL HEALTH, *Report of Working Party on School Counselling*, 1970.

NATIONAL SWEDISH BOARD OF EDUCATION. Fack S–104 22 Stockholm 22 Informatsionssektionen:

1. *Aims, Tasks and Theoretical Principles of Professional Guidance.*
2. *Summary of P.M. Worked out in the Board of Education re Study and Vocational Orientation.*
3. *The New Practical Vocational Orientation.*

PEEL, E. A., Evidence of a practical factor at age 11, *Brit. J. Educ. Psychol.*, vol. XIX, no. 1, 1949, pp. 1–15.

REUCHLIN, M., *Pupil Guidance*, Council for Cultural Co-operation, Strasbourg, 1964.

Review of Educational Research, vol. 39, no. 2: Guidance and Counselling, April 1969.

ROGERS, C., *On Becoming a Person*, Houghton Miflin, New York.

SCHOOLS COUNCIL ENQUIRY No. 1. *Young School Leavers*, H.M.S.O., 1968.

SCHOOLS COUNCIL WORKING PAPER No. 15, *Counselling in Schools*, H.M.S.O., 1967.

SCHOOLS COUNCIL WORKING PAPER No. 40, *Careers Education in the 1970s. Transition from School to Work*, Evans Methuen, 1972.

SCIENCE POLICY STUDIES No. 2, *Occupational Choice*, Department of Education and Science, 1968.

THURSTONE, L. L., *The Differential Growth Rate of Mental Abilities*, Paper No. 14, Psychometric Laboratory, Univ. of North Carolina, 1955.

VAN KAAM, A. L. *Existential Foundations of Psychology*, Doubleday, New York, 1969.

VERNON, P. E., *The Structure of Human Abilities*, Methuen, 1961.

WALL, W. D., *Adolescents in School and Society*, N.F.E.R. Occasional Publications No. 17, 1968.
WILSON, M. D., The vocational preferences of secondary modern school children, *Brit. J. Educ. Psychol.* vol. XXIII, nos. 2 and 3, 1953, pp. 97–113 and 163–79.
YEAR BOOK OF EDUCATION, *Guidance and Counselling*, Evans, 1955.

The Secondary School Curriculum

BRUNER, J. S., *The Process of Education*, Harvard Univ. Press, 1960.
DE SIMONE, D. V. (ed.), *Education for Innovation*, Pergamon Press, 1968.
GALLAGHER, J. J., *Teaching the Gifted Child*, Alleyn & Bacon, Englewood Cliffs, N.J., 1964.
GOLDSMITHS COLLEGE, *New Roles for the Learner. Report of the 5th Pilot Course for Experienced Teachers*, Univ. of London Press, 1969.
HALSALL, ELIZABETH, Education and technological change, *Trends in Education*, no. 17, Jan. 1970, pp. 24–29.
HAYWOOD, R., The humanities curriculum project in practice, *Forum*, Autumn 1970, pp. 29–31.
HIRST, B. H. and PETERS, R. S., *The Logic of Education*, Routledge, 1970.
HUTCHINS, R. M., *The Learning Society*, Pall Mall Press, 1968.
JAMES, CHARITY, *Young Lives at Stake: a Reappraisal of Secondary Schools*. Collins, 1968.
KERR, J. F. (ed.), *Changing the Curriculum*, Univ. of London Press, 1968.
KLAUSMEIER, H. J., Effect of accelerating bright older elementary pupils: a follow-up. *J. Educ. Psychol.*, vol. 54, 1963, pp. 165–71.
LAWTON, D., The idea of an integrated curriculum. *Bull. Univ. of London Institute of Education*, no. 19, Autumn 1969.
LAWTON, D., A hundred years of curriculum change, *Trends in Education*, Feb. 1970, pp. 18–26.
LUCITO, L. J., Independence–conformity behaviour as a function of intellect; bright and dull children, *Exceptional Children* no. 31, 1964, p. 5013.
MACLURE, J. S. (ed.), *Curriculum Innovation in Practice*, International Curriculum Conference, H.M.S.O., 1968.
NATIONAL SOCIETY FOR THE STUDY OF EDUCATION, *70th Yearbook*, Part 1: *The Curriculum: retrospect and prospect*, MCCLURE, R. M. (ed.), Univ. of Chicago, 1971.
ORGANISATION FOR ECONOMIC CO-OPERATION AND DEVELOPMENT, *Curriculum Improvement and Educational Development*, Paris, 1966.
PRING, R. A., Curriculum Integration, *Bull. Univ. of London Institute of Education*, no. 20, Spring, 1970.
RICHMOND, W. KENNETH, *The Teaching Revolution*, Education Paperbacks, Methuen, 1967.
RICHMOND, W. KENNETH, *The School Curriculum*, Methuen, 1971.
ROSENKRANZ, W. *et al.*, *Polytechnical Education for All*, Verlag Zeit im Bild, Dresden, 1966.
SCHOOLS COUNCIL, *The New Curriculum*, H.M.S.O., 1967.
SCHOOLS COUNCIL FIELD REPORT, No. 3, *Technology in Schools*, H.M.S.O., 1966.
SCHOOLS COUNCIL WORKING PAPER No. 11, *Society and the Young School Leaver*, H.M.S.O., 1967.
SCHOOLS COUNCIL WORKING PAPER No. 33, *Choosing a Curriculum for the Young School Leaver*, Evans Methuen, 1971.
SEARS, P. S., *The Effect of Classroom Conditions on the Strength on Achievement Motive and Work Output of Elementary School Children*, U.S. Dept. of Health, Education and Welfare, Office of Educ. Cooperative Research Project No. 873, California Univ. Press, Stanford, 1963.
SMITH, D. C., *Personal and Social Adjustment of Gifted Children*, Council on Exceptional Children Research Monograph No. 4, National Education Association, Washington D.C., 1962.
TABA, H., *Curriculum Development: Theory and Practice*, Harcourt Brace, New York, 1962.
TERMAN, LEWIS M. and ODEN, M. H., *The Gifted Group at Mid-life*, Stanford Univ. Press, 1959.
THOMAS, R. M. *et al.*, *Strategies for Curriculum Change: Thirteen Nations*, International Text Book Co. Scranton, 1968.
TIBBLE, J. W. (ed.), *The Extra Year: the Raising of the School Leaving Age*, Routledge, 1970.
WALL, W. D., *Adolescents in School and Society*, N.F.E.R. Occasional Publications No. 17, 1968.
WALTON, J. (ed.), *The Integrated Day in Theory and Practice*, Ward Lock, 1971.
WHEELER, D. K., *Curriculum Process*, Univ. of London Press, 1967.

Periodical:
J. of Curriculum Studies.

Size of School

ACTON SOCIETY TRUST, *Size and Morale*, London, 1953.
ANDERSON, R. E., LADD, G. E. and SMITH, H. A., *A Study of 2,500 Kansas High School Graduates*, Kansas Studies in Education, Univ. of Kansas, No. 4, 1954.

ANTLEY, E. M., Creativity in educational administration, *J. Exper. Educ.*, vol. 34, Summer 1966, pp. 21–7.
BANKS, O., *The Sociology of Education*, Batsford, 1968.
BARKER, C., The small comprehensive school—Westmorland, *Trends in Education*, No. 23, July 1971, pp. 23–6.
BARKER, R. G. and GUMP, P. V. *Big School, Small School*, Stanford, California, 1964.
BLAU, P. M., *Bureaucracy in Modern Society*, Random House, New York, 1956.
BLAU, P. M., HEYDERBRAND, WOLF M. and STAUFFER, R. E., The structure of small bureaucracies, *Amer. Sociological Rev.*, vol. 31, Apr. 1966, pp. 179–91.
BRENNAN, BARRIE, Communication in a high school staff, *J. Educ. Admin.*, vol. V, no. 2, Oct. 1967, p. 130.
BRIDGES, E. M., Teacher participation in decision making, *Administrator's Notebook*, vol. 12, nos. 1–4, May 1964, pp. 410–43.
BROWN, ALAN F., Reactions to leadership, *Educ. Admin. Quart.*, vol. 3, no. 1, Winter 1967, pp. 62–73.
BROWN, ALAN F., Research in organizational dynamics: Implications for school administrators, *J. Educ. Admin.*, vol. V, no. 1, May 1967, pp. 86–88.
CALHOUN, JOHN B., Population density and social pathology, *Scientific American*, no. 206,j 2 Feb. 1962, pp. 139–48.
CAMPBELL, W. J., Some effects of high school consolidation upon out-of-school experiences of pupils, *J. Educ. Admin.*, vol. IV, no. 2, Oct. 1966, pp. 112–23.
CAMPBELL, W. J., School size: Its influence on pupils, *J. Educ. Admin.*, vol. III, no. 1, May 1965, pp. 5–11.
CARVER, FRED D. and SERGIOVANNI, THOMAS J., Some notes on the OCDQ, *J. Educ. Admin.*, vol. VII, no. 1, May 1969, pp. 78–81.
COLEMAN, J. S., *The Adolescent Society*, Free Press of Glencoe, New York, 1961.
COLEMAN, J. S. *et al.*, *Equality of Educational Opportunity*, U.S. Dept. of Health, Education and Welfare, Office of Education, 1966.
CONANT, J. B., *The American High School Today*, McGraw-Hill, New York, 1959.
CORWIN, RONALD G., Education and the sociology of complex organisations, in: HANSEN, DONALD A. and GERSTL, JOEL E. (eds.), *On Education: Sociological Perspectives*, Wiley, 1967.
DANOWSKI, CHARLES E. and FINCH, JAMES N., Teacher preparation and numerical adequacy: an historical comparison, *I.A.R. Res. Bull.* no. 6, June 1966, pp. 7–10.
DAVIES, T. I., The minimum size of school, *Trends in Education*, no. 23, July 1971, pp. 15–22.
EASTBURN, L. A., The relative efficiency of instruction in large and small classes at three ability levels. *J. Exper. Educ.*, vol. VI, 1936, pp. 17–22.
EASTBURN, L. A., Report of class size investigations in the Phoenix Union High School, 1933–4 to 1935–6, *J. Educ. Res.*, vol. XXXI, no. 2, 1937, pp. 107–17.
FLANAGAN, J. C., DALY, J. T., SHAYCROFT, M. F., ORR, D. B. and GOLDBERG, I., *Studies of the American High School*, Project Talent Office, Univ. of Pittsburgh, 1962.
FLEMING, C. M., Class size as a variable in the teaching situation, *Educ. Res.* vol. 1, no. 2, Feb. 1959, pp. 35–48.
GENTRY, HAROLD W. and KENNY, JAMES B., The relationship between organizational climate of elementary school and school location, school size and the economic level of the school community, *Urban Education*, vol. 3, no. 1, 1967, pp. 19–31.
GRAY, S. C., A study of the relationship between size and a number of qualitative and quantitative factors of education in four sizes of secondary schools in Iowa. Thesis, Iowa State University 1961. Abstracted in *Dissertation Abstracts*, vol. 22, no. 8, 1962, p. 2631.
GREENFIELD, THOMAS B., Administration and systems analysis. *Can. Admin.* no. 3, Apr. 1964, pp. 25–30.
GREER, E. S. and HARBECK, R. M., *What High School Pupils Study*, U.S. Department of Health, Education and Welfare, U.S. Government Printing Office, 1962.
GROSS, N. and HERRIOT, R. E., *Staff Leadership in Public Schools*, Wiley, New York, 1965.
HALPIN, ANDREW W., Change and organizational climate, *J. Educ. Admin.*, vol. V, no. 1, May 1967, pp. 5–25.
HALSALL, ELIZABETH, The small comprehensive school. *Comprehensive Education*, no. 8, 1968.
HALSALL, ELIZABETH, *Timetable Allocations for Small Comprehensive Schools*. Univ. of Hull Institute of Education, 1968.
HALSALL, ELIZABETH, The small comprehensive school. *Trends in Education*, no. 22, Apr. 1971, pp. 12–17.
HARMON, LINDSAY R., High school background of science doctorates, *Science*, 10 Mar. 1961, pp. 679–88.
HINCHLIFFE, P. D., Operational Research in comprehensive schools, Operational Research Project, Univ. of Hull, 1971. Reported in: *Comprehensive Education*, no. 21, Summer 1972, pp. 10–12.
HOYLE, E., Organizational analysis in the field of education, *Educ. Res.*, vol. 7, no. 1, Feb. 1965, pp. 97–114.
HOYT, D., Size of high school and college. *Personnel and Guidance J.*, vol. 37, no. 8, Apr. 1959, pp. 569–73.
HUGHES, M. G., *Secondary School Administration*, Pergamon Press, 1970.
HUSÉN, T. (ed.), *International Study of Achievement in Mathematics*, Wiley, 1967.

INNER LONDON EDUCATIONAL AUTHORITY, *London Comprehensive Schools*, 1967.

International Evaluation of Achievement, Educational Attainments of 13 year olds in 12 countries, Unesco Institute of Education, Hamburg, 1963.

ISAACS, D. A., A study of predicting high school drop-outs. Unpubl. doctoral dissert., Univ. of Kansas. 1953.

KAHN, R. C. *et al.*, *Organizational Stress: Studies in Role Conflict and Ambiguity*, Wiley, New York, 1964.

KÅRÄNG, GÖSTA, Bostadsförhållanden och skolanpassning (Housing conditions and adjustment to school), *Skole ôch Samhälle*, vol. 47, no. 4, 1966, pp. 106–13. (See *Sociology of Education Abstracts*, vol. 2: no. 1, 1966, p. 131.)

KLEINHART, ERWIN J., Student activity participation and high school size. Doctor's thesis. Ann Arbor, Univ. of Michigan, 1964. Abstracted in *Dissertation Abstracts*, vol. 25, no. 7, 1965, p. 3935.

LARSON, CAROL M., *School Size as a Factor in the Adjustment of High School Seniors*, Bulletin No. 511, Youth Series No. 6, State College of Washington.

LONG, NORTON E., Administrative communication, in: MALICK, S. and VAN NESS, E. H. (eds.), *Concepts and Issues in Administrative Behaviour*, Prentice Hall, Englewood Cliffs, N.J., 1962.

LYNN, R., The relation between educational achievement and school size, *Brit. J. Sociology*, vol. X, no. 2, June 1959, pp. 129–36.

MARKLUND, S., School organization, school location and student achievement, *Int. Rev. Educ.*, vol. XV, no. 3, 1969, pp. 293–320.

MARKLUND, S., Scholastic attainments as related to size and homogeneity of classes, *Educ. Res.*, vol. 6, no. 1, Nov. 1963, pp. 63–7. (Abstract by POSTLETHWAITE, N.).

MATON, J., Regional differences in educational participation, *Sociology of Education*, vol. 39, no. 3, 1966, pp. 276–87.

MCKEACHIE, W. J., Procedures and techniques of teaching, in: SANFORD, N. (ed.), *The American College*, Wiley, New York, 1962.

MONAHAN, WILLIAM W., Teachers' knowledge of students related to urban high school size. Doctor's thesis, Berkeley, Univ. of California, 1965. Abstracted in *Dissertation Abstracts*, vol. 26, no. 2, 1966, pp. 830–1.

MONKS, T. G., *Comprehensive Education in England and Wales. A Survey of Schools and their Organisation*, N.F.E.R., 1968.

MONKS, T. G. (ed.), *Comprehensive Education in Action*, N.F.E.R., 1970.

MORRIS, J. M., *Reading in the Primary School*, N.F.E.R., Newnes, 1959.

MUSGRAVE, P. W., *The School as an Organization*, Macmillan, 1968.

OWEN, D., Timetabling in a junior comprehensive school, *Teacher in Wales*, 6 Nov. 1964, pp. 18–19.

PLATH, KARL R., *Schools within Schools. A Study of High School Organisation*, Secondary School Administration Series, Teachers' College, Columbia, New York, 1965.

PUNCH, KEITH F., Interschool variation in bureaucratization, *J. Educ. Admin.*, vol. VIII, no. 2, Oct. 1970, pp. 124–34.

Review of Educational Research, vol. 31, no. 4, Oct. 1961, and vol. 37, no. 4, Oct. 1967.

RIEW, J., Economies of scale in high school operation, *Rev. Econ. Stat.*, vol. 48, Aug. 1966, pp. 280–8.

ROGGEMA, J., *De Schoolse School. Een Orienterend Onderzoek naar Kenmerken van de school als Organisatie*, (The school: an explanatory inquiry into the characteristics of the school organization). Assem van Gorcum, 1967.

ROSE, GALE W., Organizational behaviour and its concomitants, *Administrator's Notebook*, vol. 15, no. 7, 1967.

SMITH, ALFRED G., *Communication and Status. The Dynamics of a Research Center*, Eugene Center for the Advanced Study of Educational Administration, Univ. of Oregon, 1966.

SMITH, C. B., A study of the optimum size of secondary school. Doctoral thesis, Columbus, Ohio State University. Abstracted in *Dissertation Abstracts*, vol. 21, no. 8, 1961, pp. 2181–2.

TUCKER, M., A small sixth form, *Forum*, vol. 12, no. 3, Summer 1970, pp. 100–3.

WELCH, F., Measurement of the quality of schooling, *Amer. Econ. Rev.*, vol. 56, no. 2, May 1966, pp. 379–92.

WILSON, B. R., The teacher's role: a sociological analysis. *Brit. J. Sociology*, vol. XIII, no. 1, 1962, pp. 15–32.

WOODWARD, R. J., Sir William Romney's School, Tetbury, in: HALSALL, ELIZABETH (ed.), *Becoming Comprehensive: Case Histories*, Pergamon Press, 1970.

Educational Technology and Resources

ATKINSON, R. C. and WILSON, H. A. (eds.), *Computer-assisted Instruction: a Book of Readings*, Academic Press, New York, 1969.

BAUER, ERIC W., New avenues of international cooperation in audio-visual language teaching, *Audio-Visual Commun. Rev.*, vol. 11, Sept.–Oct. 1963, pp. 200–6.

BUSH, R. N. and DELAY, D. H., Making the school schedule by computer, *Int. Rev. Educ.*, vol. XIV, no. 2, 1968, pp. 169–81.

CALLENDER, P., *Programmed Learning*, Longmans, 1969.

DENVER–STANFORD PROJECT, The Content of Instructional TV: Summary report of research findings (Abstract). *Audio-Visual Commun. Rev.*, Vol. 13, Summer 1965, pp. 237–8.

GLATTER, R. and WEDELL, E. G., *Study by Correspondence*, Longmans, 1971.

GOODMAN, R., *Programmed Learning and Teaching Machines*, E.U.P., 1967.

GUNDY, J. and JACKSON, B., Correspondence courses in schools, *Where*, May 1969.

HARTLEY, J., Social factors in programmed instruction: a review, *Programmed Learning*, vol. 3, no. 1, Feb. 1966, pp. 5–9.

HOLMBERG, BOOJE, Tuition by Correspondence in Swedish Schools (1959) and How Can Correspondence Instruction be Utilized in an Overburdened School Situation (1965), *I.C.C.E. Proceedings*.

HOLMBERG, BOOJE, *Correspondence Education*, Malmö, Hermöds NKI, 1967.

HUTCHINS, R. M., *The Learning Society*, Pall Mall Press, 1968.

KENT, G., *Blackboard to Computer*, Ward-Lock, 1969.

LARGE, D., The relative effectiveness of four types of language laboratory experiences (Abstract), *Audio-Visual Commun. Rev.*, vol. 12, no. 1, Spring 1964, pp. 107–8.

LEEDHAM, J. and UNWIN, D., *Programmed Learning in the Schools*, Longmans, 1965.

LOVELL, K., *Team Teaching*, Leeds Univ., Institute of Education, 1967.

NATIONAL COMMITTEE FOR AUDIO-VISUAL AIDS IN EDUCATION, A series of case histories in the use of programmed learning. Occasional Paper No. 16, 1969.

NATIONAL COUNCIL FOR EDUCATIONAL TECHNOLOGY, *Computers for Education. Report of Working Party*, Working Paper no. 1, N.C.E.T., 1969.

Nuffield Foundation Resources for Learning Project, Nuffield Foundation, 1967.

OETTINGER, A. G., *Run, Computer, Run*, Harvard Univ. Press, 1969.

PERRATON, H., Correspondence teaching and television (Abstract), *Audio-Visual Commun. Rev.*, vol. 15, Summer 1967.

Programmed Learning and Educational Technology, vol. 4, no. 2. Apr. 1967, Apr. 1968, Apr. 1970.

Review of Educational Research, vol. 38, no. 2, Apr. 1968, and vol. 41, no. 1, Feb. 1971.

RICHMOND, W. K., *The Concept of Educational Technology*, Weidenfeld and Nicolson, 1970.

RICHMOND, W. K., *The Teaching Revolution*, Methuen, 1967.

RIGG, R. P., *Audio-visual Aids and Techniques in Managerial and Supervisory Training*, Hamish Hamilton, 1969.

ROBERTS P. and PARCHOT, R. Do worksheets improve film utilization?, *Audio-Visual Commun. Rev.* vol. 10, Mar.–Apr. 1962, pp. 106–9.

ROCKLYN, E. H. and MOREN, R. I., A special machine taught oral-aural Russian language course: a feasibility study, *Audio-Visual Commun. Rev.*, vol. 10, Mar.–Apr. 1962, pp. 132–6. See also vol. 14, Spring 1966, pp. 147–8.

SHAPLIN, J. F. and OLDS H. F. (eds.), *Team Teaching*, Harper Row, New York, 1964.

SILBERMANN, HARRY F., Applications of computers in education, in: ATKINSON, R. C. and WILSON, H. A. (eds.), *Computer-assisted Instruction*, Academic Press, New York, 1969.

SMITH, S. M. (ed.), *The Organisation of Audio-Visual Resources for Learning in an L.E.A.*, National Committee for Audio-Visual Aids in Education, 1970.

TAYLOR, L. C., *Resources for Learning*, Penguin Education Specials, 1971.

UNESCO, *New Methods and Techniques in Education*, 1963.

VAN DER MEER, A. W., MORRISON, J. and SMITH, P., An investigation of educational motion pictures and a derivation of principles relating to the effectiveness of these media, *Audio-Visual Commun. Rev.*, vol. 13, Winter 1965, p. 465.

WESTLEY, B. H. and JACOBSON, H. K. Instructional television and student attitudes towards teacher, course and medium, *Audio-Visual Commun. Rev.*, vol. 11, May–June 1963, pp. 47–60.

WITTICH, W. A. and FOWLKES, J. G., *Audio-Visual Paths to Learning*, Harper & Row, 1946.

APPENDIX I

Current Guidance and Counselling Techniques Used in the U.S.A.

Analysis of Individual

1. *Identifying data gained from school entrance interview.* Name, address of pupil, status with reference to siblings, marital status, and occupations of parents, language spoken at home; in some states race and religion.

2. *Data on previous school performance.* Academic achievement, attendance pattern, kind and extent of his participation in extra-curricular activities; use of cumulative record card to this end (emphasis on development of individual) and need to keep up to date and to delete information no longer appropriate (so as not to prejudice teacher).

3. *Tests and inventories.* Tests (intelligence, aptitude and achievement) are standardized. Inventories are not standardized but valuable because they deal with such areas, difficult to standardize, as e.g. interests, adjustment problems, personality development and study skills. N.B. Need to administer particular test at time when most meaningful.

4. *Information from students themselves.*
(a) Autobiography done as class composition in English lesson, on e.g. "My Friends", "My Home".
(b) Personal rating sheet of two types: (1) students asked to read a brief behavioural description and then to indicate how like it is to them or to what they would like to be; (2) students asked to place a tick at a point on a suitable behaviour continuum that describes them.

5. *Information from others.* Teacher-rated devices and peer-rated devices.

Teacher-rated devices: (a) anecdotal record (put in cumulative record file) that is purely factual as regards particular incidents, not interpretative; (b) behaviour rating schedule: standardized form in which teacher asked to indicate, for example, whether pupil always works hard, usually, often, sometimes, seldom.

Peer-rated devices, derived from socio-metric techniques, e.g. sociogram—students asked, for example, who their best two friends are in class. Consequent identification of class leaders, rejected students and social isolates. *Skilfully* used very valuable.

Normal way of recording all the information is by the cumulative record card or folder.

It should be so organized that it will be possible to:

1. identify individuals who need counselling;
2. understand the behaviour of individuals.

Practical experience has shown it is necessary at the end of a pupil's school career to keep cumulative record folders intact for 5 years; at end of 5 years, all material not part of printed folder should be destroyed; at end of 10 years entire folder should be destroyed after actual administrative information has been transferred to a small file card.

Use of cumulative record to show developmental pattern of individual, identify physical or intellectual weakness (with suitable remedial work) or emotional instability, relationship between difficult family background or behaviour or other difficulties, trace personality characteristics and their development, help older pupils re vocation and counsellors re guidance, keep teacher informed of methods used to solve former problems.

APPENDIX II

Timetable Allocation for a Three-form Entry Comprehensive School (Mixed)

Pupils.

Years 1 to 4:	4 × 90 =	360
Year 5:	1 × 90 =	90
Years 6 and 7:	20 + 20 =	40
Total		490 pupils

Staff.

Allocation at 20:1	= 24·5
Addition for double allocation for sixth form	= 2·0
TOTAL	26·5

Available periods. If staff have 5 free periods (in a 40-period week): 26·5 × 35 = 928. If staff have 6 free periods (in a 40 period week): 26·5 × 34 = 901.

Basic periods required	*Extra periods*[1] Remedials	Split classes
Year 1: 3 × 40 = 120	8–20	4 (+ 3 for P.E.?)
Year 2: 3 × 40 = 120	4–8	4 (+ 3 for P.E.?)
Year 3: 3 × 40 = 120	4–5	4 (+ 3 for P.E.?)
	Options	
Year 4: 3 × 40 = 120	45	(+ 3 for P.E.?)
Year 5: 3 × 40 = 120	47	(+ 3 for P.E.?)
600	108–125	12 (+15 for P.E.?)

Years 1 to 5 Total Periods 720–737 (+15 for P.E.?)[1] = 735 – 752?

Periods available for sixth form: 149–193.

[1] See Notes.

Programme for Form 4

G.C.E.				*C.S.E.*				*Newsom*			
R.E.	2			R.E.	2			R.E.	2		
Eng.	6			Eng.	7			Eng.	7		
Maths	6			Maths.	6			Maths.	6		
Music	3	Art	3	Geog.	3			Art and des.	3	Light craft	3
Physics	4	Hist.	4	Science	5	Commerce	5	Science	5		
Chem.	4	Geog.	4	Woodwork	4	Needlew.	4	Woodwork	4	Needlew.	4
Biology	4	Latin	4	Metalwork	4	Housecraft	4	Metalwork	4	Housecraft	4
French	6	Commerce	6	Tech. draw.	4			History	4		
P.E.	3			P.E.	3			P.E.	3		
Music	2			Music	2			Music	2		
	40		21		40		13		40		11

Total number of periods = 165

Eng. and Maths. setted; options on at the same time; R.E., P.E. taken as forms. See Notes.

Programme for Form 5

R.E.	2			R.E.	2			R.E.	2	(1)	
English	6			English	7			English	7	(incl. Drama)	
Maths.	6			Maths.	6			Maths	6		
Music	3	Art	3	Geog.	3			Art and des.	3	Light craft	3
Physics	4	Hist.	4	Science	5	Commerce	5	Science	4	Needlework	3
Chem.	4	Geog.	4	Woodwork	4	Needlew.	4	Woodwork	4	Housecraft	4
Biology	4	Latin	4	Metalcraft	4	Housecraft	4	Metalwork	4		
French	6	Commerce	6	Tech. draw.	4			History	2		
								Music	1		
								Retail sales distribution 1st ½ year	2	First aid and home nursing 1st term	2
								Motorcycle maintenance 2nd ½ year		Beauty culture 2nd term	
										Mothercraft 3rd term	
Music	2			Music	2			Newsom w.	2		
P.E.	3			P.E.	3			P.E.	3		
	40		21		40		13		40		13

Total number of periods = 167.

See Notes for Form 4.

Programme for Sixth Form

149–193 periods available

1. Assume only 149 periods available and 12 periods (6 + 6) allotted to each subject. Gives 11 subjects + 17 periods for R.E., P.E. and Minor Subjects.

English, French, History, Geography, Latin, Art or Music, Pure Maths., Applied Maths., Physics, Chemistry, Biology.

2. Assume only 149 periods available and 10 periods (6 + 6, with overlap between Upper and Lower Sixth) allotted to each subject.

Gives 13 subjects + 19 periods for R.E., P.E. and Minor Subjects.

3. Assume 193 periods available and 12 periods (6 + 6) allotted to each subject.
Gives 15 subjects and 13 periods for R.E., P.E., etc.

4. Assume 193 periods available and 10 periods (6 + 6, with overlap between Upper and Lower Sixth) allotted to each subject.
Gives 18 subjects and 13 periods for R.E., P.E., etc.

5. Assume 149 periods available and 14 (7 + 7) allotted to each subject.
Gives 10 subjects and 9 periods over; with 12 periods per subject (7 + 7, with overlap), see (1).

6. Assume 193 periods available and 14 periods allotted. Gives 13 subjects and 11 periods over; with 12 (7 + 7, with overlap), see (3).

NOTES

Years 1 to 3, Practical subjects. Small allocation for split-classes achieved as follows:
Split whole year into four groups (90/4 = 22·5 per group, approx. 20·00 allowing for absences) and rotate subjects from year to year as follows.

	Girls	*Boys*
Year 1	Art, Needlework	Art, Woodwork
Year 2	Housecraft, Art	Extra Science, Art
Year 3	Needlework, Housecraft	Woodwork, Extra Science (cont.)

Allowing 3 periods per subject, each year gives 4 × 4 = 16. As there are 4 groups (instead of 3 forms) the extra allotment for splitting is only 4 periods. Each class would get 8 periods per subject over the 3 years, instead of 3 per subject per year.

P.E. The problem of split classes for P.E. in a three-stream mixed school (uneconomic splitting of classes into 2 groups of 15 each) might be solved as follows:

Year 1: 2 of the 3 forms take P.E. together and split sexes: the remaining form join one of year 2 forms for P.E.?
Year 3 and 4: repeat as for years 1 and 2.

Clearly there are objections to mixing age groups; but it could be done if necessary.

Fourth and fifth year timetables. The timetable for both compulsory subjects, e.g. English, and options, e.g. Chemistry, Geography, Woodwork, Needlework, would be setted across the three forms. Hence it would be possible to produce a very large number of combinations of subjects, e.g. one pupil might choose Physics, Geography, Metalwork and Technical Drawing or Commerce (1), Needlework, Housecraft and Commerce (2) if capable of taking these subjects at the particular level available.

The problem of double periods in, for example, French could be palliated by sending the French group to P.E. with the C.S.E. form and placing one or more of the French lessons on the timetable at the same time as P.E. for the C.S.E. form. More manoeuvring of this kind would reduce the impact of double periods in academic arts subjects, a problem in all comprehensive school timetables in the options blocks.

Provision of periods for sixth form. There is research evidence to show that varying the number of periods within the above ranges makes no significant difference to results, except for Chemistry.

Integrated courses for Newsom children. These could be set up for humanities and for environmental studies within the framework of this timetable.

Class size. This schedule assumes average form size to be 30 and there to be no part-time teachers. If average form size rose to 32, 1·5 extra teachers would be available (3·4 extra 'A' level subjects), if it rose to 35, 3·75 extra teachers (about 10 extra subjects).

Five-form Entry Comprehensive (Mixed)

Pupils.

Year 1 to 4:	4 × 150 =	600
Year 5:	1 × 150 =	150
Years 6 and 7:	33 and 33 =	66
Total		816

Staff.

Allocation at 20:1	41
Addition for double allocation for sixth form	3
Total	44

Available periods. If staff have 5 free periods in a 40-period week: 44 × 35 = 1540 periods. If staff have 6 free periods in a 40-period week: 44 × 34 = 1496 periods.

Basic periods required		*Extra periods required*
	Remedials	Split classes
Year 1: 5 × 40 = 200	8–20	8 (+ 3 for P.E.?)
Year 2: 5 × 40 = 200	4–10	8 (+ 3 for P.E.?)
Year 3: 5 × 40 = 200	4– 5	8 (+ 3 for P.E.?)
	Options	
Year 4: 5 × 40 = 200	52	(+ 3 for P.E.?)
Year 5: 5 × 40 = 200	52	(+ 3 for P.E.?)
1000	120–139	24 (+ 15 for P.E.?)

Years 1 to 5: Total periods required 1144–1163 (+ 15 for P.E.?) = 1159–1178
Periods available for sixth form 318–381

Programme for Form 4

G.C.E.				*G.C.E./C.S.E.*		*C.S.E.*				*C.S.E./Newsom*				*Newsom*			
R.E.	2			R.E.	2	R.E.	2			R.E.	2			R.E.	2		
Eng.	6			Eng.	7	Eng.	7			Eng.	7			Eng.	7		
Maths	6			Maths	6	Maths	6			Maths	6			Maths	6		
Music	3	Art	3	Geog.	3	Civics	3	Art and des.	3	Light craft	3	Pottery	3	Light craft	3	Art and des.	3
Phys.	4	Hist.	4	Commercial subjects including office practice	17	Science	5	French	5	Science	4	Rur. Sc.	4	Science	4		
Chem.	4	Geog.	4			Woodw.	4	Needlework	4	Woodwork	4			Needlework	4		
Biol.	4	German	4			Metalw.	4	Housecraft	4	Metalwork	4			Housecraft	4		
French	6	Latin	4			Tech. dr.	4	History	4	History	2			History	2		
Music	2			Music	2	Music	2			Music	2			Music	2		
										Newsom W.	3			Newsom W.	3		
P.E.	3			P.E.	3	P.E.	3	P.E.	3	P.E.	3			P.E.	3		
	40		19		40		40		23		40		7		40		3

Total number of periods = 252

Eng. and Maths. could be setted: options on at same time; R.E., Music and P.E. taken as forms.

T.C.S.—H

Programme for Form 5

G.C.E.				*G.C.E./C.S.E.*		*C.S.E.*				*C.S.E./Newsom*				*Newsom*			
R.E.	2			R.E.	2	R.E.	2			R.E.	2			R.E.	2		
Eng.	6			Eng.	7	Eng.	7			Eng.	7			Eng.	7		
Maths	6			Maths	6	Maths	6			Maths	6			Maths	6		
Music	3	Art	3	Geog.	3	Civics	3	Art and des.	3	Light craft	3	Pottery	3	Light craft	3	Art and des.	3
Phys.	4	Hist.	4	Commercial subjects including office practice	17	Science	5	French	5	Science	4	Rur. Sc.	4	Science	4		
Chem.	4	Geog.	4			Woodw.	4	Needlework	4	Woodwork	4			Needlework	4		
Biol.	4	German	4			Metalw.	4	Housecraft	4	Metalwork	4			Housecraft	4		
French	6	Latin	4			Tech. dr.	4	History	4	History	4			Newsom W.	4		
Music	2			Music	2	Music	2			Music	1			Music	1		
										RSD	2			F.A. and H.N.	2		
										MCM (half year each)	2			Beauty cult.	2		
														Mothercraft	2 (one each term)		
P.E.	3			P.E.	3	P.E.	3	P.E.	3	P.E.	3			P.E.	3		
	40		19		40		40		23		40		7		40		3

Total number of periods = 252

Subjects setted: options on at same time; R.E., Music and P.E. as forms.

Programme for Sixth Form

318–381 periods available

1. Assume only 318 periods available and 12 periods allotted for each subject.

Gives 20 subjects + 18 periods for R.E., P.E., and Minor Subjects.

English, French, History, Geography, Latin/Pure Maths, Applied Maths, Physics, Chemistry, Biology, German, Art, Music, Anatomy and Physiology.

Commerce Course (counts as two subjects), Catering Course (counts as two subjects), Technical Drawing, Engineering Science.

40 periods for 'O' level and C.S.E. Increase staff free periods.

2. Assume 381 periods available and 12 periods allotted for each subject.

Gives 22 subjects + 22 periods for R.E., P.E., and Minor Subjects.

English, French, History, Geography, Latin/Pure Maths, Applied Maths, Physics, Chemistry, Biology, German, Art, Music, Anatomy and Physiology, 2 out of Economics, Geology, Sociology, Greek.

Commerce Course, Catering Course, Technical Drawing, Engineering Science.

40 periods for 'O' level and C.S.E.

Increase number of staff free periods? Separate provision for Third Year Sixth aiming at Oxbridge? Increase provision for split classes in lower school?

3. Assume only 318 periods available and 14 periods allotted.

Choice between retaining 20 subjects and deleting some 'O' levels and having 17–18 subjects and retaining 'O' level.

4. Assume 381 periods and 14 periods allotted.

Gives 20 subjects, 16 periods for R.E., P.E., and Minor Subjects, 40 periods for 'O' level and C.S.E. Increase number of staff free periods, etc?

5. Assume 381 periods and 12 periods (7 + 7 with overlap) allotted (see (2)).

APPENDIX III

A More Generalized Curriculum for the Fourth and Fifth Years

Academic	Periods	Non-academic	Periods
R.E.	2		
English	4	Integrated humanities	8
History	2		
Geography	2		
Physics	3	Integrated environmental studies	11
Chemistry	3		
Biology	3		
Mathematics	4	Maths. (Accounts, Insurance, etc.)	4
Art	2	Art and Craft	2
Music	2	Music	2
Domestic science 3/Woodwork 3		Homecraft studies	10
French	4	Technical studies	10
Latin 3/German 3/Technical drawing	3	Commercial studies	10
P.E.	3	P.E	3

N.B. The two lines would not be mutually exclusive. Pupils could take, for example, R.E., English and History from one line and do the environmental studies from the other.

APPENDIX IV

Charted Basic Movement Patterns Relating to a Variety of Comprehensive School Situations

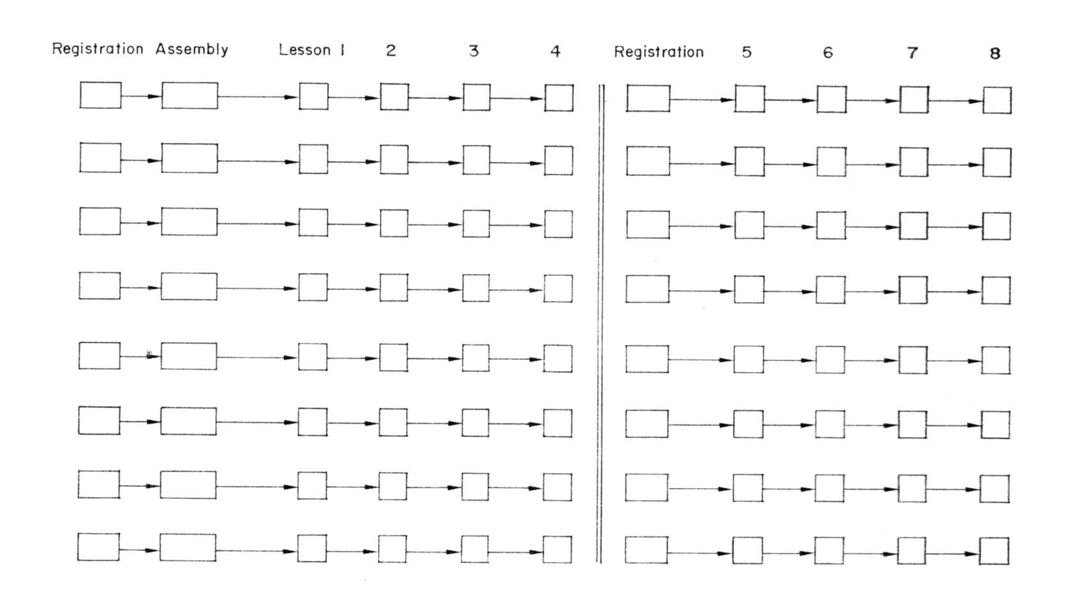

FIG. 1. Year system: streamed forms: basic movement pattern. (See p. 134.)

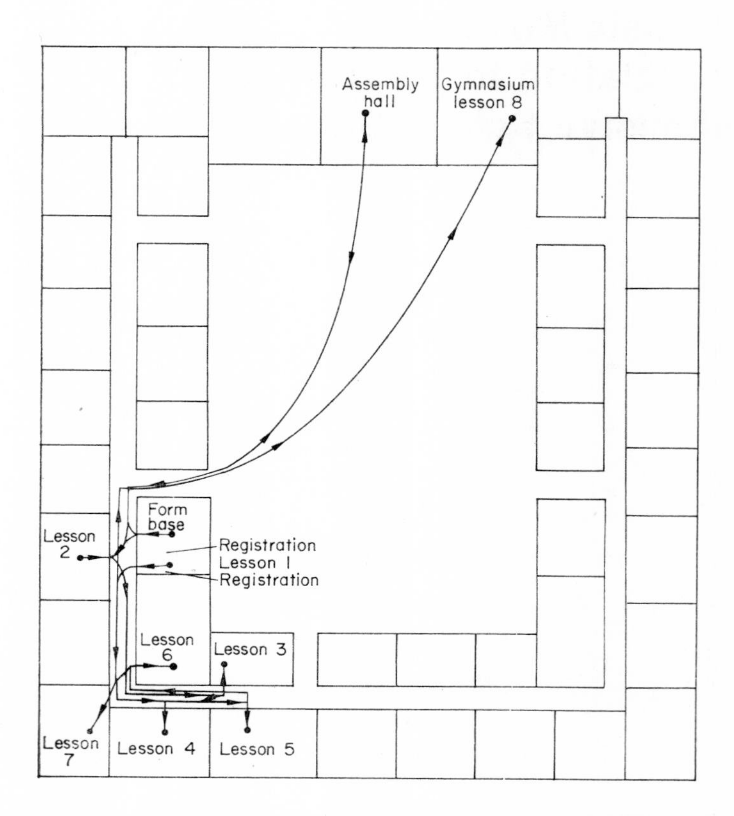

Fig. 2. Movement pattern of year system related to building layout: movement of one class throughout the day if the year is confined to one area of the school. (See p. 134.)

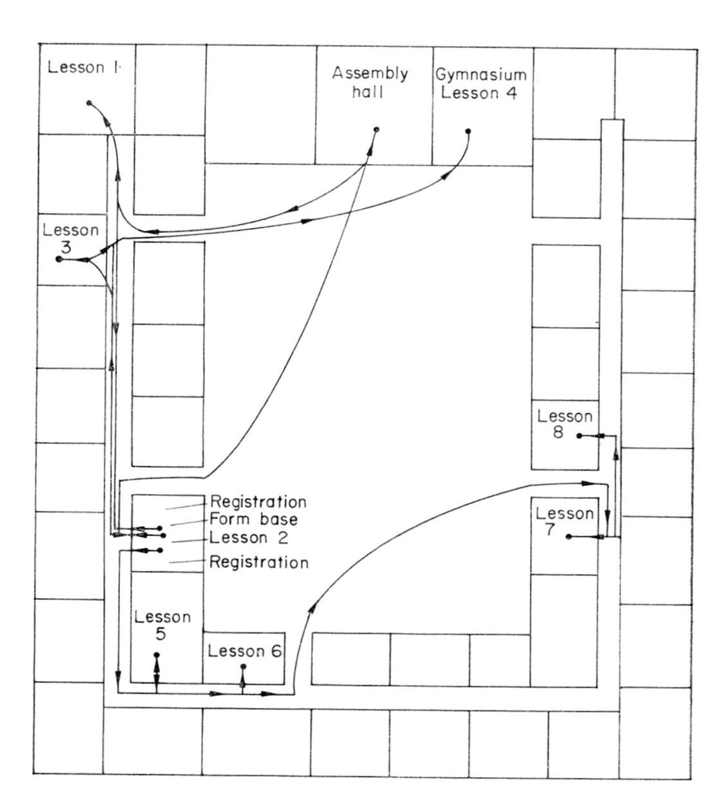

FIG. 3. Movement pattern of year system related to building layout: movement of one class throughout the day, if the year moves over the whole area of the school. (See p. 134.)

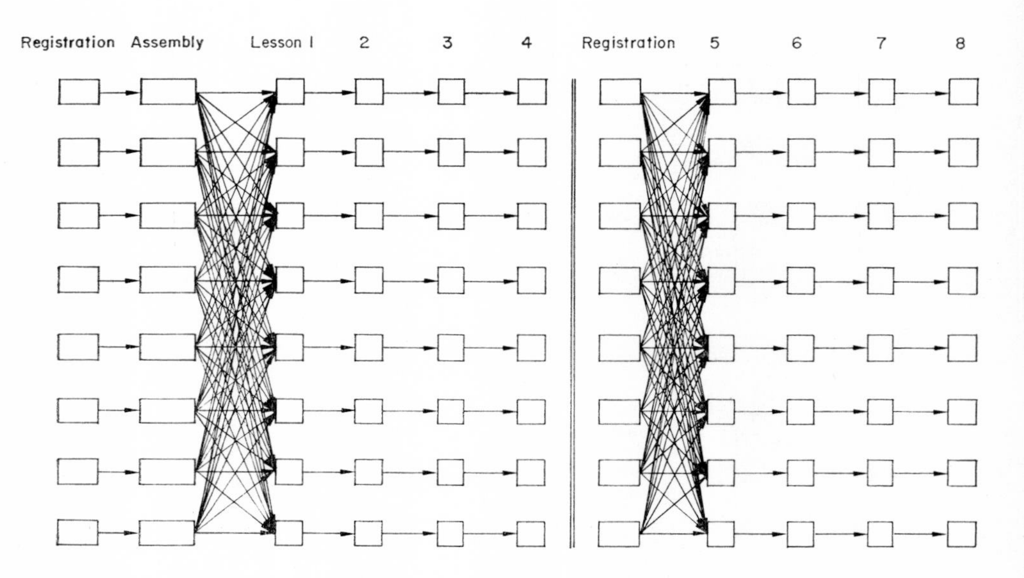

FIG. 4. Year system for teaching combined with mixed ability tutor group system for social purposes: basic movement pattern. Hence referred to as "the combined system". (See p. 135.)

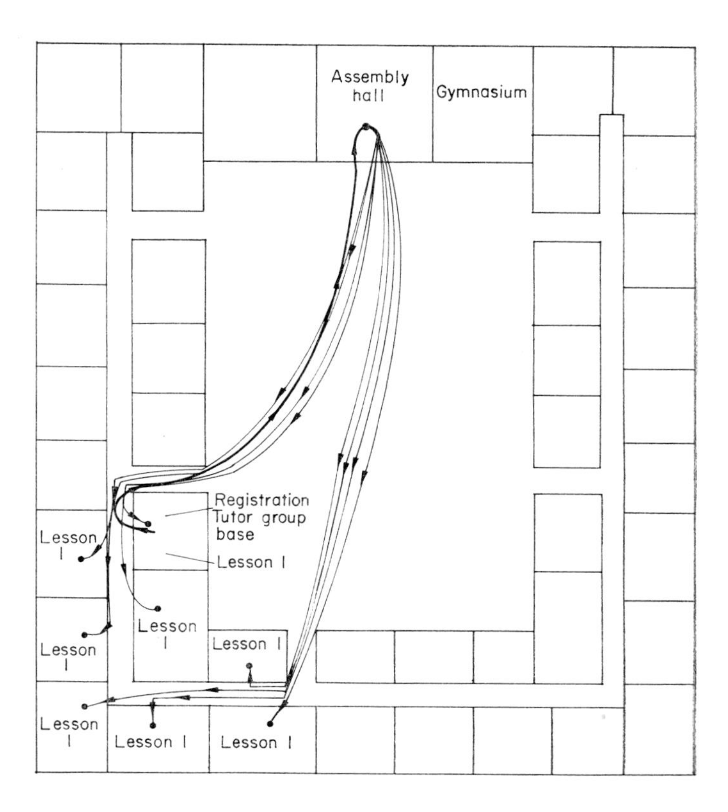

FIG. 5. Movement pattern of the combined system (streamer teaching groups with unstreamer tutor groups) related to building layout: movement of one tutor group (group base > assembly > first lesson) if confined to one area of the school. (See p. 135.)

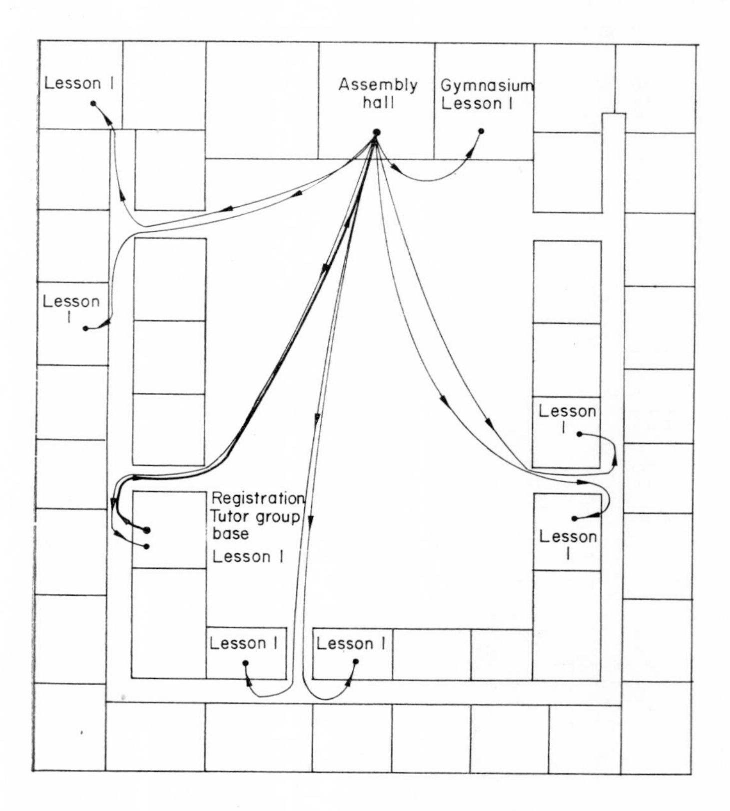

FIG. 6. Movement pattern of the combined system related to building layout: movement of one tutor group (group base > assembly > first lesson) if moving over the whole area of the school. (See p. 135.)

(a) Year system: Unstreamed Teaching and Social Groups. Figs. 1, 2 and 3. (See also p. 135.)

(b) Junior/Middle/Upper School System: Streamed Forms. Figs. 1, 8 and 6. (See also p. 135.)

(c) Junior/Middle/Upper School System: Streamed Teaching Groups and Unstreamed Tutor Groups. Figs. 4, 9, 8, 6 and 3. (See also p. 135.)

(d) Junior/Middle/Upper School System: Unstreamed Teaching and Social Groups. Figs. 1, 2 and 3. (See also p. 135.)

FIG. 7. Movement patterns. The movement pattern for each system can be traced by following the figures in the order prescribed.

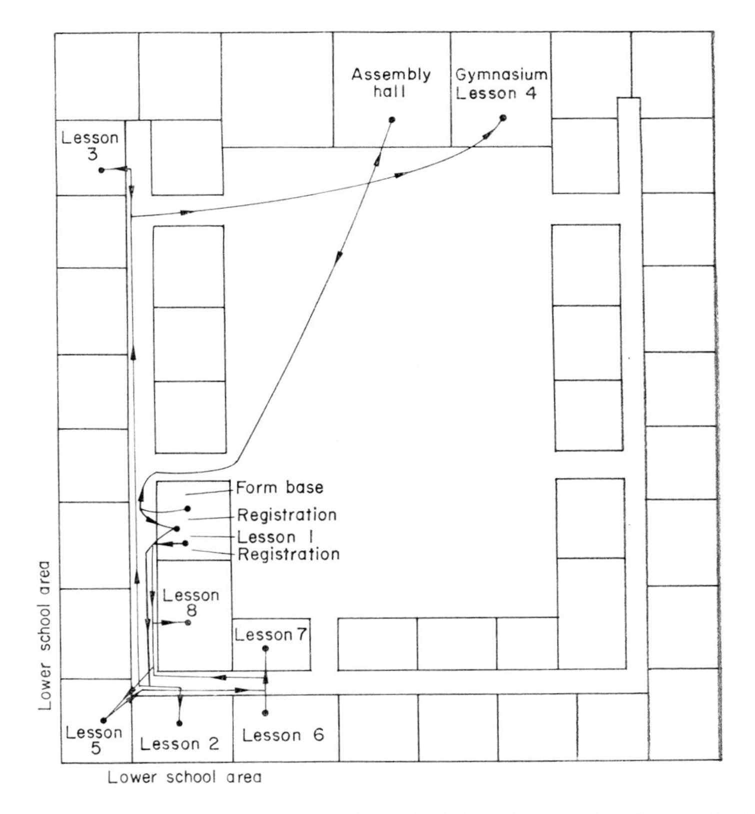

FIG. 8. Movement pattern of lower school (in junior/middle/upper school system) related to building layout: movement of one form throughout the day if confined to one area of the school.

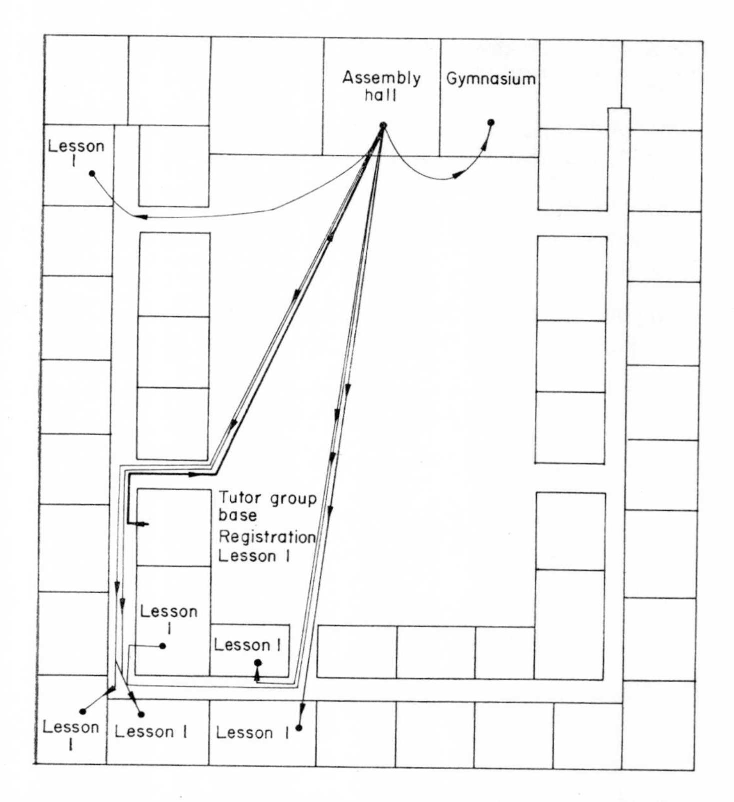

FIG. 9. Movement pattern of lower school (in junior/middle/upper school system) related to building layout: movement of one tutor group (group base > assembly > first lesson) if confined to one area of the school. (See p. 135.)

(a) House System: Streamed Teaching Groups and Unstreamed Tutor Groups. Figs. 4, 5, 6 and 11. (See also pp. 135–6.)

(b) House System: Unstreamed Teaching and Social Groups. Figs. 1, 2, 3 and 11. (See also pp. 136–7.)

FIG. 10. Movement patterns.

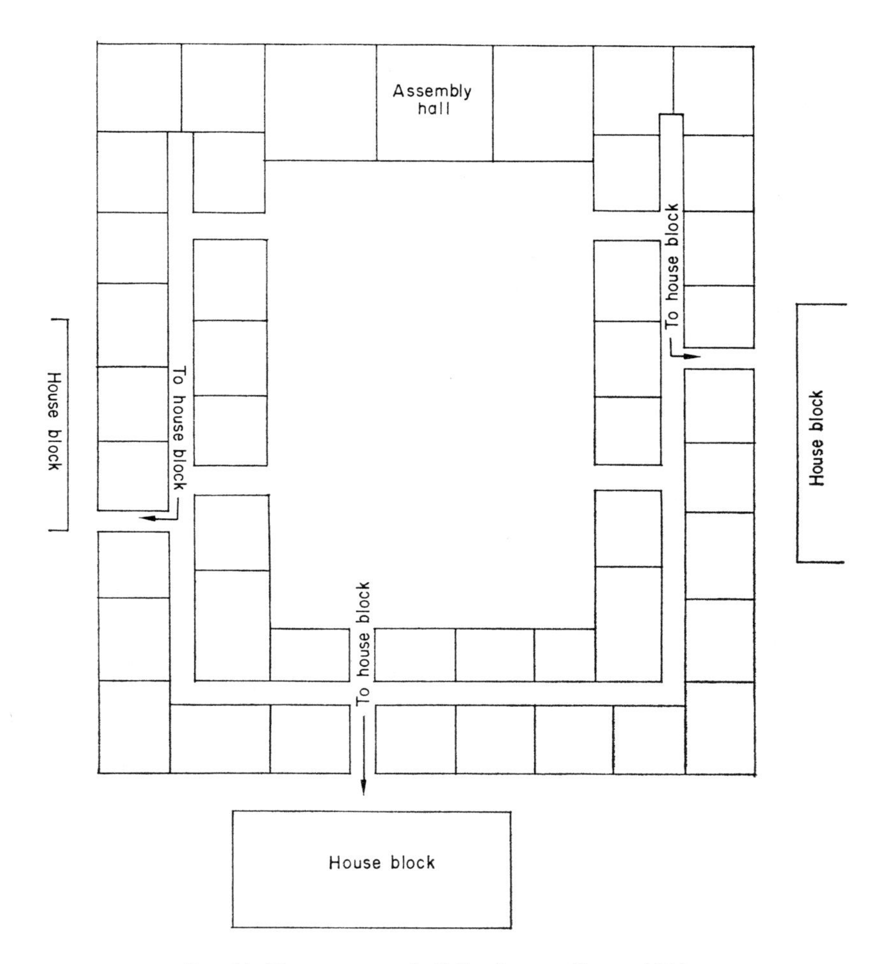

FIG. 11. House system: building layout. (See p. 136.)

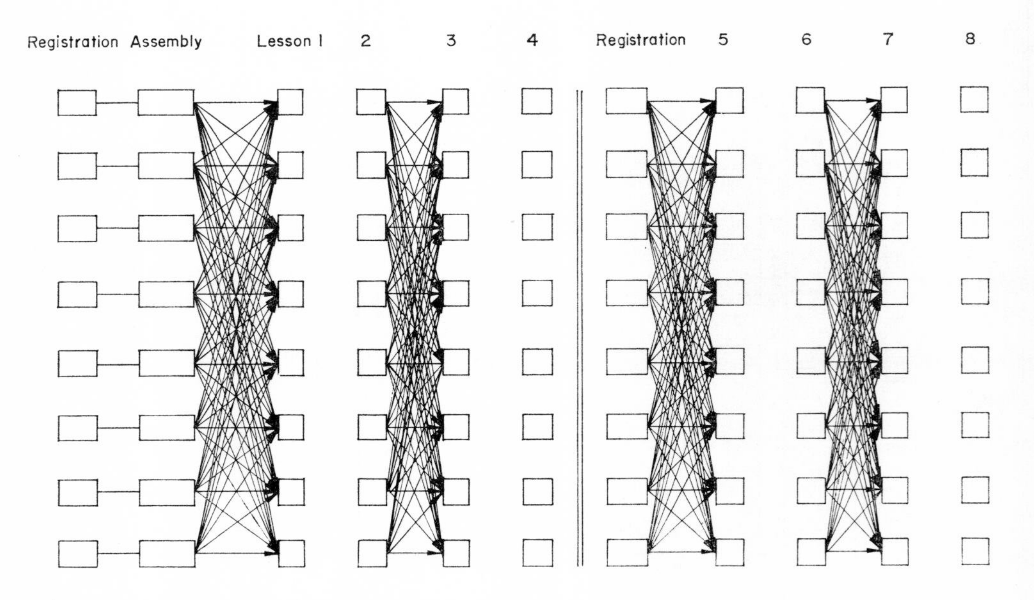

FIG. 12. Fourth, fifth and sixth years: basic movement pattern of sets and options groups, when double periods are used. (See p. 140.)

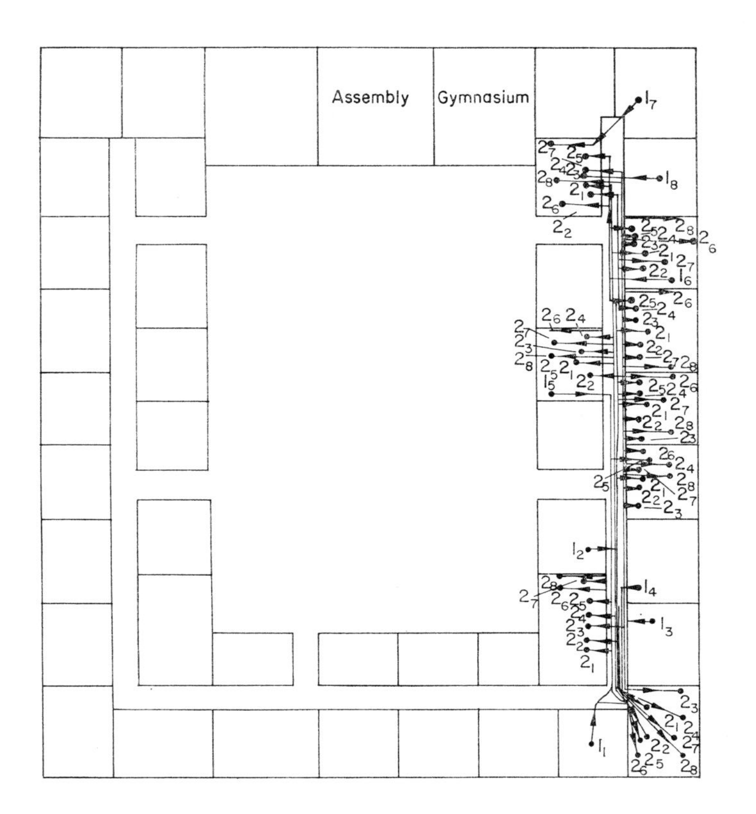

FIG. 13. Movement pattern related to building layout: movement of fourth/fifth year if confined to one area of the school (See p. 140.).

1_1, 1_2, 1_3, 1_4, etc. Different groups of a year at their first lesson.
2_1, 2_2, 2_3, 2_4, etc. Different groups of a year at their second lesson.

N.B. The groups at the first lesson will not be identical with those at the second. The directional arrows illustrate the movement from first to second lesson.

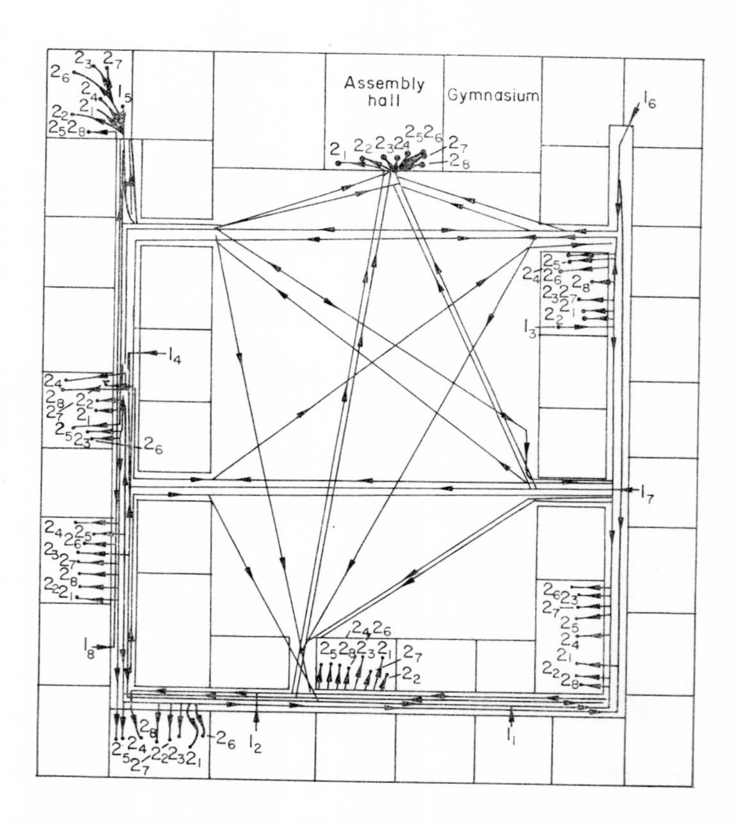

FIG. 14. Movement pattern related to building layout: movement of fourth/fifth year if moving over whole area of school. (See p. 140.)

See key to Fig. 13.

Index